D0840830

Unrepentant, Self-Affirming, Practicing

Unrepentant, Self-Affirming, Practicing

Lesbian/Bisexual/Gay People within Organized Religion

Gary David Comstock

CONTINUUM · NEW YORK

1996

The Continuum Publishing Company
370 Lexington Avenue, New York, NY 10017

Printed in the United States of America

Library of Congress Cataloging-in-Publication Data

Comstock, Gary David, 1945–
Unrepentant, self-affirming, practicing : lesbian/bisexual/gay people within organized religion / Gary David Comstock.
p. cm.
Includes bibliographical references and index.
ISBN 0-8264-0881-8
1. Homosexuality—Religious aspects. 2. Bisexuality—Religious aspects. 3. Gay men—United States—Religious life. 4. Gay men—Canada—Religious life. 5. Lesbians—United States—Religious life. 6. Lesbians—Canada—Religious life. 7. Bisexuals—United States—Religious life. 8. Bisexuals—Canada—Religious life. I. Title
BL65.H64C65 1996
200'.8'664–dc20 95–49440
CIP

Contents

List of Tables

Acknowledgments

I want to name and thank those who contributed directly to my study of lesbian/bisexual/gay people within organized religion.

I am grateful to several people at Wesleyan University — Rhonda Kissinger for transcribing interviews; Janet Morgan for supervising the computer programming; Heather Rhoads for designing and directing data analysis; and Yvonne Martinez, Valerie Smith Matteson, Cashman Kerr Prince, and Martin Reames for data entry.

I appreciate the willingness of gay people affiliated with the United Methodist Church and the United Church of Christ to complete my questionnaire and the additional interest of those respondents who volunteered for follow-up interviews. I wish that I could have interviewed all who volunteered. I am grateful for the time and personal accounts given to me by the twenty people I selected. Over one-half of them asked that their names be used with their comments. The comments of the others are reported anonymously.

George F. Hodgdon (Affirmation: United Methodists for Lesbian, Gay and Bisexual Concerns) and Jan Griesinger (United Church Coalition for Lesbian/Gay Concerns) were patient, thorough, and efficient in helping me distribute my questionnaires. They also provided me with back issues of their organizations' newsletters, as did the following people and organizations: James D. Anderson (Presbyterians for Lesbian & Gay Concerns), William H. Carey (National Gay Pentecostal Alliance), Rob Gregson (Office of Lesbian, Bisexual and Gay Concerns, Unitarian Universalist Association), Bruce Grimes (Friends for Lesbian and Gay Concerns), Randle Rick Mixon (American Baptists Concerned), Sandip Roy (Trikone: Gay & Lesbian South Asians), Jim Sauder (Brethren/Mennonite Council for Lesbian and Gay Concerns), and William H. Wahler (World Congress of Gay and Lesbian Jewish Organizations).

I am also grateful for the work of the many researchers whom I acknowledge and discuss in the following chapters. Without their work this book would not have the breadth, detail, and depth to be a study of gay people within the many manifestations of organized religions in our society.

I gratefully acknowledge Patricia Broughton's permission to reproduce her poem "Standing Witness" as it appeared in the summer 1989 issue of *Open Hands*.

My lover/partner, Ted, has been the constant and most significant source of support, critical evaluation, encouragement, and love in this and my previous work.

Preface

Unrepentant, Self-Affirming, Practicing

The policies of religious bodies concerning homosexuality have been challenged and often altered in recent years because studies in medicine, biology, and psychology are finding that sexual orientation is most often constitutional rather than chosen or conditioned.[1] In grudging recognition of these findings, many religious leaders now say that while "homosexual behavior" is sinful, "homosexuality itself" is not.[2] The sin is not the "predisposition" to homosexuality but expressing and acting on it. Church policies typically counsel or require reorientation, abstinence, or discretion for homosexually oriented people, especially for clergy and candidates for ordination. Such terms as "unrepentant," "self-affirming," and "practicing" have been written into the formal positions of some religious bodies to describe the kind of homosexually oriented person who is not accepted. To be accepted one must be self-reproaching, self-denying, and celibate. One is not to declare frankly and openly love for or sexual intimacy with a person of one's own gender.[3]

These prescriptions have created a dilemma for many gay people who have been encouraged by the gay liberation and civil rights movements from the 1970s to the present to be more visible and assertive throughout society. Leonard Patterson, for example, wrote about his experiences at Ebenezer Baptist Church after he moved to Atlanta in the 1970s. Because he enjoyed the services, the singing of the choirs, and the preaching of the Reverend Martin Luther King Sr., he eventually joined and became active in the church. He felt that he was "in a unique position at Ebenezer to help the image of 'the homosexual' in America since this church represents liberation and stands as an oasis for the downtrodden" in the tradition of Martin Luther King Jr. He also met the man who became his lover and partner, and he too joined the church. Together they were successful in reorganizing the church's youth group and in expanding its size and activities. Leonard also became immersed in other aspects of church life at Ebenezer, such as the children's ministry, prison ministry, shut-in ministry, and young adult fellowship.[4]

Leonard found that their acceptance in the church was contingent "on being discreet about our relationship," but he "felt that in order for the myths about gay relationships to be dispelled and for them to be seen as healthy alternatives, we would have to invite church groups to our home." However, those invitations, coupled with Reverend King Sr.'s retirement, brought abrupt changes in attitude toward them. The new pastor told Leonard that leading a double life, even marrying and having a male lover on the side, would have made him acceptable and "more 'respectable.'"[5]

Because Leonard decided not to follow the new pastor's advice, he said his life was made miserable. On Sundays he was attacked from the pulpit; he was insulted at meetings; and, as time passed, he had to resign his offices in the church. His participation in the many activities at Ebenezer "had once been a joy, and now it was a nightmare." What had been for him "the mecca of Black liberation," the home of "the prophet of non-violence and social change," the church "where all oppressed persons should feel compassion," was "just another political and social club where, if you played the right games, you inherit the power and prestige of an elite group." This experience left both Leonard and his partner with a "strong distrust for organized religion."[6]

However, the kind of tolerance, acceptance, and leadership that the Reverend Kings advocated has prevailed in some religious bodies to foster welcoming environments for gay people.[7] The United Church of Canada, for example, has called on the church to repent of its persecution of homosexual persons and maintains that "there is no reason in principle why mature, self-accepting homosexuals, anymore than mature, self-accepting heterosexuals, should not be ordained." The Union of American Hebrew Congregations also urges its member congregations "to achieve the fuller acceptance of gay and lesbian Jews" by welcoming them "as singles, couples, and families."[8] And in 1994, the Progressive National Baptist Convention, the denomination cofounded by Reverend King Jr., adopted a policy statement recognizing the "God-given and moral right to be protected against discrimination due to sexual orientation" and claiming that "God's love includes everybody, welcomes anybody, denies no one."[9]

Religious bodies most often choose to engage in abstract discussions about homosexuality and to prohibit homosexual behavior rather than to examine the actual lives of lesbians, bisexuals, and gay men and to take seriously the many dimensions of their lives. In my work, I turn to and examine the experience of lesbian/bisexual/gay people in their churches and synagogues—where they belong, what they do, what they believe, how they feel, and what they think about their religious communities. I prefer to use the term "lesbian/bisexual/gay people," but for the sake of simplicity I shall most often use the term "gay people." When it is necessary to distinguish between the experiences of the different groups among these people, I shall use the separate terms "lesbians," "bisexuals," and "gay men."

Lesbian/Bisexual/Gay People within Organized Religion

My research on the experiences of lesbian/bisexual/gay people as they have dealt with the policies and practices of organized religion will be organized into seven chapters.

Chapter 1 offers a historical overview and presentation of the positions and actions taken by a full range of religious bodies. The discussion summarizes the colonial origins and legacy of much current church policy but focuses primarily on developments in North America after World War II.

Chapter 2 discusses various sources and methods for studying the experiences of lesbian/bisexual/gay people in organized religion and then describes the empirical studies that have been conducted, including my own national survey of two religious bodies. Taken together, these studies cover the following religious bodies and traditions: the Roman Catholic Church; traditional Native American religion; Islam; different organizations within Judaism; various denominations within the traditional black church, such as the African Methodist Episcopal Church and Jehovah's Witnesses; the Universal Fellowship of the Metropolitan Community Church and other independent gay Christian organizations; the Unitarian Universalist Association; mainline Protestant denominations, such as the United Church of Christ, United Methodist Church, Presbyterian Church (U.S.A.), Southern Baptist Convention, and American Baptist Churches in the U.S.A.; the Mennonite Church and Church of the Brethren; the Religious Society of Friends; and the Church of Jesus Christ of Latter-day Saints (Mormon).

The findings from these studies are then presented, organized, and analyzed in five chapters (chapters 3 through 7) that address the religious affiliations, lay participation, clerical positions, beliefs and faith communities, and feelings and thinking of gay people within organized religion.

Chapter 3 is titled "Belonging, Leaving, Switching, and Shopping" and examines religious upbringing and backgrounds, current religious affiliations, switching in and out of different religious bodies, leaving established religious bodies to join independent gay alternatives, and finding new opportunities within established religious bodies.

Chapter 4 is titled "Service, Participation, Leadership, and Advocacy" and documents the religious service and participation of gay laity, the obstacles and encouragement they have encountered, their leadership roles and responsibilities, and the advocacy role they have assumed to advance their acceptance and recognition within religious bodies.

Chapter 5 is titled "Seminary, Ordination, Ministry, and Employment" and traces the experiences of gay people as they have prepared to become clergy, have been ordained or refused ordination, have gained or been rejected from clerical and other church-related positions, and have engaged in various forms of ministry.

Chapter 6 is titled "Belief, Theology, Support, and Community" and examines the beliefs and theologies of gay people and how they have found and formed the communities in which to express and exercise them.

Chapter 7 is titled "Evaluations, Feelings, Reasons, and Challenges" and presents gay people's personal feelings about and evaluations of the religious bodies with which they are affiliated. Finally, their reasons for remaining within these religious bodies and the challenges they see facing them are discussed.

Before going to chapter 1, I shall provide some background information about "organized religion" in North America.

Organized Religion in North America

The five major faiths or religions in the world are Judaism, Christianity, Islam, Buddhism, and Hinduism. Within the United States, 86 percent of the population identifies as Christian; more than 2 percent identifies as Jewish; and slightly more than one percent identifies as Islamic, Buddhist, and Hindu. One-half percent is involved in "other" religions; and 8 percent of the population identifies with no organized religion.[10]

Christians usually identify as Roman Catholic or Protestant.[11] Approximately one-quarter of all Americans are Catholic;[12] and about 60 percent are Protestant.[13]

Because Jews, Catholics, and Protestants have different terms for the national or international bodies into which they are organized (movements, rites, and denominations, respectively), for the sake of simplicity I shall use "religious body" as a common term for each of them. I shall also use the common term "congregation" when referring to the local synagogues, parishes, or churches that comprise these larger religious bodies. If the context of the discussions in the following chapters requires the more specific term (movement, rite, denomination, synagogue, parish, church), I shall use it. "Organized religion" is the common and overarching term that I shall use for the religious bodies and member congregations into which Judaism and Christianity are organized.

Islam, Buddhism, and Hinduism also have regional and national organizations in North America. But because their organizational structures are much more decentralized and their adherents much fewer than for Judaism and Christianity, I shall refer to the faith itself (Islam, Buddhism, and Hinduism), and not to the national organizations within each, as a "religious body."[14]

Appendix A lists the sixty-five largest Jewish and Christian religious bodies in the United States, according to the number of adherents in each; it also includes the number of adherents to Islam, Buddhism, and Islam.

Organized religion in Canada will also be discussed in the following chapters, but much less extensively. Appendix A also lists the forty-eight largest Jewish and Christian religious bodies in Canada. Reliable statistics for Islam, Buddhism, and Hinduism are not available.

The religious bodies listed in these tables represent the most visible and dominant manifestation of organized religion in North America. Most of the religious bodies referred to and discussed in the following chapters are listed in Appendix A.

Chapter One

Historical Overview

Colonial Origins and Heritage

Disapproval and prohibition of sexual relations between people of the same gender in the United States can be traced to its colonial links with organized religion.[1] The passage from the Book of Leviticus that prescribes death for "a man who lies with a man as with a woman" was adopted into legislation and enforced by the colonies of Massachusetts, New Hampshire, New York, New Jersey, Pennsylvania, and Connecticut.[2] Although capital punishment for such "crimes" was repealed after the Revolutionary War, this religious influence continues to be found in the wording of some legal proscriptions against homosexual behavior today;[3] and judges, lawmakers, and law enforcement officials continue to support their antihomosexual decisions and actions with references to the Bible and Christian tradition.[4] As recently as 1986, in its decision to uphold the constitutionality of Georgia's sodomy statute, the United States Supreme Court stated in its majority opinion that "proscriptions against [homosexual] conduct have ancient roots" and in a concurring opinion that "condemnation of these practices is firmly rooted in Judeo-Christian moral and ethical standards."[5]

But not since the theocracy of Puritan New England has organized religion engaged so actively in the prohibition of same-gender sexuality as it does today. Until recently, homosexuality was not a topic for open discussion within religious bodies. For example, during the formation of the Church of Jesus Christ of Latter-day Saints (Mormon) in the first half of the nineteenth century, sex between men or between women was addressed only rarely in speeches, diaries, ecclesiastical court transcripts, and other contemporary records. Founder Joseph Smith made no recorded statements on the subject, and it does not figure prominently in the pronouncements of subsequent Mormon leaders until after the middle of the twentieth century.[6]

Disapproval of same-gender sexuality within various religious bodies typically was made clear by the glorification of heterosexual marriage and childbearing, rather than by the formal recognition of and direct attack on homosexual behavior. The infrequent discovery or apprehension of "deviants" did provide the opportunity to condemn the "sin" and reaffirm the heterosexual norm. Horatio Alger himself, a minister at the Unitarian Church in Brewster, Massachusetts, was dismissed in 1866 for such "gross immorality." Unlike most others whose careers were subsequently ruined by such exposure, Alger moved away and gained fame as a major ideologue of the American dream. Typically though, same-gender sexuality and same-gender-oriented people were invisible and ignored—in the words of the committee that dismissed Alger, they were "too revolting to think of."[7]

In 1929 in New York, even when Reverend Adam Clayton Powell denounced from the pulpit and in the press what he saw as the widespread presence of homosexual parishioners and clergy in Harlem's churches, many congregations seemed willing to accept them as long as they were discreet. Rumors directed at particular pastors did not prevent churches from hiring them; and support for Powell's campaign did not solidify within the black church.[8]

Although programmatic efforts to prohibit homosexuality do not stand out in the history of American religion, there is one exception: the suppression of the *berdache* tradition among Native American tribes. In traditional Native American cultures, the *berdache* is an androgynous or effeminate male with important religious and economic roles. *Berdaches* mix the behavior, dress, and social roles of men and women and are known for their spiritual, intellectual, and artistic contributions to their communities. Beginning in the late nineteenth century, federal government agents incarcerated *berdaches,* cut off their hair, forced them to wear men's clothing, prohibited many of their ceremonies, and made them do manual labor not associated with their tribal role. Christian missionaries, however, would play the major role in condemning and effectively discrediting the *berdache's* role among Native Americans. Anthropologist Walter Williams gathered these remarks about the 1920s and 1930s from John One Grass, a Lakota medicine man:

> When the people began to be influenced by the missions and the boarding schools, a lot of them forgot the traditional ways and the traditional medicine. Then they began to look down on the *winkte* [or *berdache*] and lose respect. The missionaries and the government agents said *winktes* were no good, and tried to get them to change their ways. Some did, and put on men's clothing. But others, rather than change, went out and hanged themselves. I remember the sad stories that were told about this.

Only among the most traditional and oldest Native Americans would the *berdache* still be considered a sacred person. With the conversion of most Native Americans to Christianity, this once important position came to be looked on with hostility and ridicule. Few people took up the *berdache* role, and they did so secretively. As one reported: "Indians don't want to be mocked anymore by the outside white world, it has happened so many times. So, we keep it secret about *winkte*."[9]

Within Native American culture, the *berdache* had been relegated to the same position and status as homosexual clergymen in the dominant culture. And most of the latter, as recalled by Robert Wood, a gay clergyman who was seventy-one years old in 1994, "lived blighted lives of self-repression, unrequited love, suspicion, or outright persecution (when visibility created scandal) because of their sexuality."[10] World War II and its aftermath, however, would alter the visibility of homosexual persons and the response of organized religion and society to them.

Post–World War II Changes

The War and Subsequent Significant Events

Historian John D'Emilio credits World War II with having "created something of a nationwide coming out experience" for many homosexuals, not by encouraging same-gender sexuality, "but by shifting its location and changing its context." By releasing many young, single men and women from familiar homes and neighborhoods and placing them in gender-segregated environments, mobilization for the war provided the opportunity for homosexuals to meet one another. After the war, many chose not to return to their hometowns but to remain in the cities through which they had been processed for wartime assignments and demobilization. The neighborhoods they established in these cities — Los Angeles, San Francisco, Seattle, Atlanta, New Orleans, New York, and Boston — subsequently attracted other homosexuals from throughout the country and would emerge as the major centers of the lesbian/bisexual/gay population.[11]

Three events following the war altered the customary silence on homosexuality and the invisibility of homosexuals: the publication in 1948 and 1953 of the Kinsey reports on male and female sexual behavior; the federal government's persecution of homosexuals under Senator Joseph McCarthy's House Un-American Activities Committee from 1950 to 1955; and the issuing of *The Wolfenden Report* by the British Parliament in 1957. Alfred Kinsey found that "persons with homosexual histories are to be found in every age group, in every social level, in every conceivable occupation, in cities and on farms, and in the most remote areas of the country." The scientific objectivity of the Kinsey reports and their immediate and lasting popularity as best-selling books made them a serious and influential factor in normalizing the subject of homosexuality. McCarthy's attacks initially fueled active disapproval of homosexuality, but the discrediting of his committee's unfair tactics eventually brought into question society's treatment of homosexuals. *The Wolfenden Report* influenced the completion in 1962 of the American Law Institute's model penal code to eliminate sodomy statutes; and both paved the way for the decriminalization of private, consensual, adult homosexual relations in many states.[12]

Pressure from the Church of England was responsible for the preparation of the *The Wolfenden Report* and its being issued as an official document by the British Parliament. During the twenty-five years following the war, organized religion in the United States, with occasional influences from Great Britain, would also respond with increasing attention to the growing discussion of homosexuality, to the greater visibility of homosexuals, to discrimination and laws against them, and to its own treatment of them. A summary of various responses follows.

Breakthrough Publications

Numerous events in publishing signaled the new involvement of organized religion in the discussion of homosexuality.

In his 1943 book, *On Being a Real Person,* the founding minister of the Riverside Church in New York, Reverend Harry Emerson Fosdick, was the first church leader to call attention to the poor training of clergy to deal with homosexuality. Representing an educational movement that had begun in the 1920s to equip pastors with clinical counseling skills, Fosdick suggested that clergy should be as prepared to help with the concerns of homosexuals as they were with other human problems. Although he spoke of homosexuality as a "disease" or "dangerous tendency," he departed from condemning it as a sin and said it was a "tendency" that could be "denied overt expression and redirected so as to eventuate in some of the best work done on earth by men for boys, or by women for girls." On the other hand, in a 1948 issue of *Christianity and Crisis,* Henry Van Dusen, the president of Union Theological Seminary in New York, reacted in panic to Kinsey's findings as evidence of "degradation in American morality approximating the worst decadence of the Roman era." His heated rejection of homosexuality and Fosdick's acceptance of and pastoral concern for homosexuals represented the two major approaches with which organized religion would subsequently struggle.[13]

The most noteworthy, groundbreaking publication, however, came in 1955 in Britain with Derrick Sherwin Bailey's *Homosexuality and the Western Christian Tradition.* It was the first scholarly work to challenge traditional interpretations of allegedly antihomosexual biblical passages and to examine the European church's historical persecution of homosexuals. It would become a foundational work for subsequent scholarship and for discussions within religious bodies about homosexuality.[14]

In 1960, Reverend Robert W. Wood of the United Church of Christ published *Christ and the Homosexual,* "the first book to openly declare one need not be heterosexual to be Christian" and "the first written [about homosexuality by a homosexual] with the author's real name and church affiliation."[15] Other publications proposing greater tolerance and support would follow throughout the 1960s.

In 1963, the Friends Home Service Committee of London issued *Towards a Quaker View of Sex,* a report that urged the church "to come of age" and to take "a fresh look at homosexuality." In 1966, in *Toward a New Understanding of the Homosexual,* Methodist minister H. Kimball-Jones recommended, without endorsing homosexuality, that the church should recognize the validity of mature homosexual relationships and encourage fidelity within them. In 1967, Anglican theologian Norman Pittenger argued for the full acceptance of homosexuals by the church in his book *Time for Consent: A Christian Approach to Homosexuality;* and the United Church of Christ and the United Presbyterian Church both brought out the same special issue on the civil rights of homosexuals in their respective social justice periodicals, *Social Action* and *Social Progress.* In 1968, *Christian Century* magazine favored proposals to reform sodomy laws and to end employment discrimination and police abuse of homosexuals, but continued to doubt the moral desirability of homosexuality.[16]

In 1969 Pilgrim Press published *The Same-Sex: An Appraisal of Homosexuality,* the first book to gather and present views by homosexuals themselves. Also in 1969, in the first Reform statement on homosexuality and Judaism, Solomon Freehof upheld the traditional view of homosexual behavior as sinful;[17] and Spencer W. Kimball, an elder in the Church of Jesus Christ of Latter-day Saints, published *The Miracle of Forgiveness,* which would subsequently dominate Mormon policy on homosexuality as "an ugly sin." In the following year, his book was condensed into a nine-page church manual called *Hope for Transgressors.*[18]

In 1970, three Roman Catholic scholars published different positions on homosexuality: in a Catholic clerical journal, Jesuit theologian John J. McNeill argued for the acceptance of monogamous homosexual relationships as a lesser evil than promiscuity; in *Sex: The Radical View of a Catholic Theologian,* Michael Valente argued for a theology that would recognize homosexuality as natural and good; and in *Toward a New Catholic Morality,* John Milhaven maintained that homosexual behavior was "wrong and unChristian."[19]

In the following year, in an article for a Catholic academic journal, ethicist Charles Curran offered a position between total condemnation and total acceptance, and Westminster Press anthologized a variety of positions in *Is Gay Good? Ethics, Theology, and Homosexuality.* In 1972, Ralph Blair, a theologically conservative homosexual, would add to the growing number of theological perspectives. In his privately published pamphlet *An Evangelical Look at Homosexuality,* he argued that Christian evangelism and homosexuality are not contradictory.[20]

In addition to the growing debate among Christians and among Jews, an increasing number of anthropological studies were published throughout the 1950s and 1960s that found homosexuals regarded favorably, if not as sacred, in other cultures. Margaret Mead's *Male and Female: A Study of the Sexes in a Changing World* in 1949 and Clellan Ford and Frank Beach's *Patterns of Sexual Behavior* in 1951 were turning points for gaining a cross-cultural perspective on homosexuality. Studies of the Native American *berdache* were published in several academic journals;[21] and the respect and religious significance afforded this role by many tribes gained public attention in the 1971 major motion picture *Little Big Man* and in the popular 1972 book *Lame Deer, Seeker of Visions.*[22]

Gay Churches, Homophile Organizations, and Religious Leaders

In addition to publications about homosexuality and religion, some innovations, organizational changes, and reforms were developing. In Atlanta, for example, a young minister in the independent Catholic movement organized what was probably the first church for homosexuals. Services were held for the first time in a gay bar on Christmas Eve in 1946 for eighty-five people. They named themselves the Eucharistic Catholic Church and were the forerunner for the formation of other kinds of openly gay churches.[23]

Homophile organizations were also founded outside of organized religion but with links to it. The Mattachine Society, a male homosexual emancipation group, was started in 1948 with the help of a Unitarian minister; and its first national convention took place at the First Universalist Church in Los Angeles in 1953. Of eight women who founded another group called the Daughters of Bilitis in 1955, two would become founding members of the Council on Religion and the Homosexual (CRH) in 1964 in San Francisco.[24]

The CRH's origins lay in the efforts of Reverend A. Cecil Williams and Reverend Ted McIlvena of Glide Memorial Methodist Church in San Francisco to begin a ministry in 1962 to "castoffs," including homosexuals, in the city's Tenderloin area. McIlvena also organized a four-day consultation between homosexual activists and sixteen Protestant ministers from several denominations and cities. Afterward, the CRH was formed in San Francisco to promote continuing dialogue between the church and homosexuals.

One event sponsored by the CRH was a turning point for the homophile movement. At the council's New Year's Eve dance for the homosexual community, the police harassed, intimidated, and arrested without cause many of those attending. The liberal ministers insisted on fighting the charges and exposing abuse by the police. For once, the judge, jury, and news media took the side of the homosexuals because, as historian John D'Emilio notes, "the ministers provided a legitimacy to the charges of police harassment that the word of a homosexual lacked." The long-standing complaints of homosexuals were finally believed; police practices in bars actually changed; and the CRH felt encouraged to fight on for the freedom of homosexuals.[25]

The CRH would establish chapters in other cities and for ten years serve as the main organization for educating clergy about homosexuals and meeting with the leaders and decision-making bodies of various denominations, including the United Church of Christ, the Episcopal Church, the Lutheran Church in America, and the Methodist Church. D'Emilio claims that the CRH "provided the spark that ignited debate on homosexuality" within the churches. It was "able to take advantage of the theological ferment and social activism that infected American religion in the 1960s in order to press for reconsideration of Christian attitudes toward same-sex eroticism."[26]

In 1971, the First National Conference on Religion and the Homosexual was held at the Interchurch Center in New York. With seventy participants from eleven denominations, it was the most broadly based conference ever convened to discuss homosexuality and religion and was covered by the mainstream news media, including the *New York Times, Washington Post, Time,* and *Ladies Home Journal.*[27]

Actions by Religious Leaders and Discussion by Religious Bodies

Positions on homosexuality began to be taken more frequently and with greater disagreement among religious leaders and within religious bodies.

In 1957, the archbishop of Westminster of the Roman Catholic Church, Great Britain, issued a statement saying, "Catholics are free to make up their own minds" about whether criminalizing or decriminalizing private acts of homosexuality between consenting adults "harms the common good"; but in the United States in 1965, the archdiocese of New York successfully lobbied the New York state legislature not to repeal its sodomy law.[28]

In 1959, the Church of Jesus Christ of Latter-day Saints assigned elders Kimball and Mark E. Petersen to be in charge of sexual cases for the church. The recommendations that they developed for the counseling and dismissal of homosexuals were practiced by the church for the next decade. Counseling consisted of pressure to change and the opportunity to "repent" before excommunication was imposed.[29]

The National Council of Churches (NCC), an umbrella organization for Christian denominations, first discussed homosexuality in 1961 at its North American Conference on Church and Family. In 1966, it sponsored a seminar, "The Church and Homosexuals," for thirty-six participants but did not inform the news media or issue a follow-up report.[30]

In 1962, the Anglican bishop of Woolwich, Great Britain, appealed for reform of "our utterly mediaeval treatment of homosexuals."[31] In 1965, the Episcopal Diocese of New York went on record as being in favor of repealing sodomy laws; in a speech at Duke University in 1966, Episcopal bishop James Pike argued for repeal of all laws against sexual behavior between consenting adults; and in 1967, the Diocesan Council of the Episcopal Church in California urged an end to entrapment and police harassment in gay bars. Also in 1967, Episcopal priests from the Northeast held a symposium and urged that homosexuality be considered morally neutral and that homosexual relationships be judged by the same standards as heterosexual relationships.[32]

In 1965, the National Federation of Temple Sisterhoods passed a resolution opposing discrimination against homosexuals. It was not implemented because the Union of American Hebrew Congregations failed to present, let alone discuss or vote on, the matching resolution prepared for its 1965 convention.[33]

In 1968, in Los Angeles, Reverend Troy Perry, a defrocked Pentecostal minister, founded the first predominantly homosexual Christian denomination. It was called the Universal Fellowship of Metropolitan Community Churches and would establish its churches in all major cities within a few years.[34]

Post-Stonewall Debates and Activism

Groundbreaking Actions by Religious Bodies

In June of 1969, the Stonewall Rebellion in New York City prompted the beginning of the gay liberation movement. The visibility of lesbians and gay men was dramatically increased and transformed as they formed their own organizations and spoke out for and demanded recognition by major institutions, including religious ones.[35] Religious bodies were forced to face the issue of homosexuality not only because it was so openly discussed in society but because lesbians and gay men were actively working within those bodies to become more visible and gain acceptance. Groundbreaking actions by four religious bodies would bring the issue into sharper focus for other religious bodies.

In 1970, the Lutheran Church of America and the Unitarian Universalist Association became the first denominations to adopt formal statements opposing discrimination against homosexuals and encouraging education about homosexuality within their churches.[36] In 1972, the United Church of Christ became the first denomination to ordain an openly gay candidate for ministry, Reverend William Johnson.[37] In the same year, a gay synagogue, Beth Chayim Chadashim, was founded in Los Angeles and applied for membership in the Union of American Hebrew Congregations.[38]

These events demonstrated that the issue of homosexuality was not simply a topic for abstract discussion by religious bodies but involved people in their midst who wanted to be recognized and accepted.[39]

A Primary and Continuing Issue

After 1972, the discussion of homosexuality moved from what had been the province of a few religious scholars, leaders, and religious bodies to major debate and voting in most bodies. Within five years no fewer than fourteen religious bodies would make public statements — most to support civil rights for homosexuals while maintaining that homosexuality was incompatible with their own traditional teachings.[40]

These first actions, however, did not close down or conclude debate but set it in motion and provided the framework for its continuation. No social issue would gain the attention of religious bodies more often and dramatically than homosexuality and abortion.[41] Few bodies have not addressed homosexuality; and for most it would be a returning topic at their general meetings. For example, in a survey of delegates prior to its 1992 General Conference, the United Methodist Church found that homosexuality was the most frequently cited issue facing the denomination: "Clearly, the United Methodist Church and the entire Christian community continues to struggle with the issue of homosexuality and the appropriate role of the church in influencing societal and denominational policy on this issue."[42] Some religious bodies have conducted studies of sexuality; many have engaged in lengthy and recurring debates; and most have taken positions that range from acceptance and welcome to condemnation and expulsion of self-affirming, practicing gay people.[43]

Division and Unity

Although many religious leaders worry and complain that the issue divides and threatens unity,[44] Harlan Penn of the Presbyterian Church (U.S.A.) observes that these are "unjustified and hysterical fears." He explains that turning away from gay issues does not satisfy those who have threatened to leave because they "are generally unhappy about a long series of developments in our denomination, ranging from ordination of women to affirmative action to representation of racial ethnic groups in governing bodies." He says that adopting gay-positive stances and programs has not resulted in loss of membership for local Presbyterian congregations. A small number of people usually leave for another congregation, but a larger number join because of the newly stated inclusiveness.[45]

Similar observations have been made in other denominations: Mark Bowman, coordinator of the Reconciling Congregation Program, monitors local United Methodist churches that have voted to declare publicly their acceptance and support of lesbians and gay men. He observes that, in spite of the general declining memberships of mainline Protestant denominations, these local congregations typically increase in size after taking such a stand.[46] In Massachusetts, after the Wellesley Congregational Church publicly declared itself pro-gay, its pastor, Reverend William B. Abernethy, reported: "Some gay men and lesbians appear to be worshipping here more often and feeling more at home as they do. The few dissenters who have left have not had a major negative impact on the congregation's spirit, program, or subsequent financial pledge drive."[47] This pattern seems to hold at the national level also. When the United Church of Canada voted after years of debate to welcome and ordain lesbian/bisexual/gay people, less than 1 percent of its membership and churches left.[48]

Furthermore, studies have shown repeatedly that recent growth rates of religious bodies are determined by birthrates within those bodies and by their concentration within regions whose general population is growing or declining, and not by their positions and debates on homosexuality. Research reveals (1) that emphasizing social justice and rejecting exclusivity do not cause denominational decline; (2) that being open to change and serving the needs of persons outside the local congregation, rather than just the needs of current members, are necessary for congregations that want to grow; and (3) that congregations with liberal members are not less likely to grow than those with more conservative members.[49]

The issue of homosexuality has not provoked massive departures from religious bodies; rather, it has provoked more discussion within those bodies and greater insistence about remaining *within* them. Both sides of the debate have been inclined to dig in and stay; and many people have come to change or to understand more clearly their traditions and beliefs though the issue of homosexuality.[50]

Relevance, Excitement, and Influence

Rather than dividing and weakening religious bodies, the issue of homosexuality seems to have enlivened organized religion and given it relevance within the larger society. In her keynote address to Presbyterians for Lesbian and Gay Concerns at the 1991 General Assembly of the Presbyterian Church (U.S.A.), Roman Catholic lesbian theologian Mary Hunt remarked on the fevered attention and publicity given to religious bodies when dealing with homosexuality:

> Little did I know when I agreed to speak that things would be this hot. It has been a heady week for religion. It does not get much better than this: all the major newspapers covering your story, "Nightline" featuring the Presbyterian report on sexuality as if it were as important as the invasion of a small Third World country, the Reverend Elizabeth Carl ordained as an Episcopal priest in Washington as an out and about lesbian, and President Bush bawling his eyes out at the assembly of the Southern Baptist Convention recalling the decision to unleash troops to bomb Iraq back to a pre-industrial state.
>
> The President, commenting on the ordination of Ms. Carl, said: "Perhaps I'm a little old-fashioned but I'm not ready for that."[51]

In 1992, when Pullen Memorial Baptist Church in Raleigh, North Carolina, announced its vote to endorse same-gender holy unions, one member recalls that after Sunday service "television cameras were already set up at our door to record members' responses. The story was front page next morning. It quickly spread, to our astonishment, across the country and even to Germany and Australia."[52] Controversies over homosexuality at the meetings of religious bodies; the latest acts of removing, hiring, or ordaining gay clergy; and decisions by local congregations to include or exclude gay people have been given time and space consistently by the news media.[53]

No current issue has provided organized religion with a greater opportunity to be heard and influential; and religious denominations and their leaders have not been silent in their opposition and support when gay rights legislation has been considered by city councils, state legislatures, and federal agencies.[54] For example: in 1985, the Salvation Army and the Roman Catholic Archdiocese of New York pursued and won legal exception from an executive order that required unbiased hiring by those contracting with the city to provide services;[55] whereas in 1991,

Reverend Amos Brown, the pastor of Third Baptist Church in San Francisco, and several other African-American religious leaders were among the more outspoken supporters of California's gay rights bill.[56]

General Support for Civil Rights

In the early 1990s, a broad-based "Christian religious right" — made up of many local and statewide organizations, independent churches, the National Association of Evangelicals, Pat Robertson's Christian Coalition, individuals from many denominations, and often supported by the Roman Catholic hierarchy and conservative black pastors — convinced voters in several municipalities to outlaw gay rights legislation.[57] The leaders of this movement advocated a codification of antihomosexual laws not unlike that of colonial New England. Some even discussed, and others called for, the reinstitution of capital punishment for homosexual behavior.[58]

A survey of the general population, however, does not show majority opposition to gay rights among those within any religious tradition — except Eastern Orthodox, to which the smallest percentage of the general population belongs. Among these various religious traditions, opposition ranges from a low of 11 percent to a high of 54 percent, with an average of 31 percent of the general religious population opposed to gay rights (see table 1).[59]

Also, nearly one-third of the major religious bodies have formally endorsed some form of civil rights for gay people. And in 1994, some politicians sympathetic to the Christian Coalition began to advise softening its opposition to homosexuality.[60]

Secular versus Religious Reform

Religious bodies tend to be more generous, supportive, and liberal about employment and housing rights in the secular sphere than they are when considering their own practices, traditions, teachings, and rules.[61] For example, in 1977, two years after passing a resolution calling for full civil rights for homosexuals, the Union of American Hebrew Congregations voted to delete from that resolution the "call for nondiscrimination within Jewish communal and Reform organizations."[62] Also, in 1977, a survey of delegates to the General Synod of the United Church of Christ showed that 78 percent favored laws guaranteeing civil rights for gay people, but only 40 percent were in favor of ordaining them.[63] Indeed, the most heated debates and deeply felt controversies have occurred when religious bodies have tried to decide under what conditions gay people may participate within them.

TABLE 1
Percentages of General Population within Various Religious Traditions and Percentages of Those within Religious Traditions Opposed to Gay Civil Rights (N=4001)

Religious tradition	% of population	% anti gay rights
Evangelical Protestant	26	48
Roman Catholic	23	24
Secular	20	24
Mainline Protestant	17	27
Black Protestant	8	31
Jewish	2	11
Conservative Nontraditional	2	38
Non-Judeo, Non-Christian	1	14
Liberal Nontraditional	1	13
Orthodox	<1	54
All	100	31

Source: Lyman A. Kellstedt et al., "Religious Traditions and Religious Commitments in the USA" (paper prepared for the Twenty-Second International Conference of the International Society for the Sociology of Religion, Budapest, 19–23 July 1993), 6–7.

Positions Taken by Religious Bodies

The positions that religious bodies have discussed, examined, and/or taken can be categorized as follows.[64]

1. *Rejecting:* Relying on a particular interpretation of selected biblical passages, this view says that homosexual acts and the homosexual condition/orientation are sinful and prohibited by God. If homosexual people do not acknowledge, renounce, and change their sinfulness, they should be expelled from the religious body. The Southern Baptist Convention, for example, condemns homosexuality as an abomination in the eyes of God, urges its local churches "not to afford the practice of homosexuality any degree of approval," and expelled two of its churches for blessing same-sex unions and licensing a gay candidate for ministry. The Greek Orthodox Church, Lutheran Church–Missouri Synod, National Association of Evangelicals, Roman Catholic Church, and Orthodox Judaism have taken similar positions.

2. *Semirejecting:* Emphasizing the biological, especially genital, differences between women and men, this view rejects homosexual acts but not homosexual people. Homosexual people should reorient to heterosexuality or lead a life of complete sexual abstinence. The Presbyterian Church (U.S.A.), for example, prohibits its presbyteries from asking candidates about their sexual orientation but also prohibits the ordination of an openly lesbian or gay candidate. Celibate candidates may be ordained. The United Methodist Church, American Baptist Churches in the U.S.A., Disciples of Christ, and Conservative Judaism have taken similar positions.

3. *Semiaccepting:* Relying on the primacy of the female and male union for producing children and making families, this view sees homosexual orientation as an acceptable, but inferior, way of living. Those who cannot attain the ideal of heterosexual marriage may enter a permanent, monogamous homosexual relationship as the only way to find a measure of sexual/affectional humanization. The Central Conference of American Rabbis (Reform Judaism), for example, has resolved that all rabbis, regardless of sexual orientation, should "be accorded the opportunity to fulfill the sacred vocation which they have chosen" but warns that "publicly acknowledging one's homosexuality...can have grave professional consequences." Concerning same-sex unions, it "affirms that heterosexuality is the only appropriate Jewish choice for fulfilling one's covenantal obligations."

4. *Accepting:* Relying on a tradition and biblical theme of equality and freedom in personal relationships, this view sees homosexual people as part of the divine plan of creation and homosexuality as natural and as good as heterosexuality. Full participation, including ordination and same-sex unions or marriages, is encouraged. The Unitarian Universalist Association, for example, not only ordains openly gay candidates but has an affirmative action program to place them in local parishes. The Unitarian Universalist Association, Reconstructionist Judaism, and numerous regional meetings of the Religious Society of Friends are the only religious bodies to approve officially of same-sex unions. The United Church of Canada, United Church of Christ, and Moravian Church have taken accepting positions.

Indecision and Certainty

While most religious bodies fit into one or the other of these categories, others are uncertain about and in the process of finding and articulating their positions and practice.[65]

The Episcopal Church in the United States, for example, originally disallowed the ordination of noncelibate homosexual candidates; but in 1989, when faced with the subsequent and controversial ordination of an openly gay man by one of its bishops, the House of Bishops resolved that the issue of gay clergy is "presently beyond our ken." The bishops then called for further discussion, even while admitting that "dialogue is not going to produce consensus," and voted simply to "affirm and support" another bishop's statement disapproving of the ordination. Five years later, the 1994 General Convention passed a resolution guaranteeing nondiscrimination in the ordination process.[66]

The Church of Jesus Christ of Latter-day Saints has also shifted its approach to and treatment of gay people. In 1973, in its first public statement on the matter, the church condemned both homosexual feelings and behavior as "inherently sinful" and implemented aggressive measures "to change the 'mistaken' sexual 'choice' of those with homosexual feelings." Security police at Mormon-run Brigham Young University pursued homosexual students and reported them to school administrators. Vigorous corrective therapy and counseling stressed prayer and fasting, mind control, avoidance of certain behaviors and associates, and electric-shock and vomiting-aversion therapies. A former Mormon missionary, Robert I. McQueen, in his position as managing editor of the national gay magazine *The Advocate,* criticized church policy on gays and was excommunicated. But the reported lack of success with the various therapies, the first public questioning of church policy by individuals, and the formation of a national support group for gay Mormons had the effect of prompting wider discussion and recognition of homosexuality. In the 1980s, articles in Mormon-oriented periodicals by scholars and clinicians continued to question the validity and effect of church policy. Church leaders wanted to hold to a strict standard but acknowledged that they "do not really understand these problems." Veering from the church's previous condemnation of both orientation and behavior, church elder Boyd Packer said in 1990, "What one is may deserve unlimited tolerance, what one does only a measured amount." The *Bishop's Handbook* was subsequently revised to emphasize celibacy and not cure or conversion. Church policy softened a little, and excommunication is no longer encouraged.[67]

A 1986 self-study committee for the Lutheran Church in America mirrored the indecision, confusion, and dilemma of other religious bodies when it found that "this church can neither condemn, nor ignore, nor praise and affirm homosexuality."[68] But a survey of Christian denominations in 1984 showed that three-quarters had been certain enough to take official positions. Of the surveyed denominations, 80 percent condemned homosexuality; 70 percent required homosexuals to change their behavior; 53 percent assumed some responsibility to help their homosexual members; and 31 percent supported some form of civil rights for homosexuals.[69]

Non-Judeo-Christian religious bodies have also taken a range of positions: Buddhist institutions within North America seem neither to marginalize their lay homosexual constituents, impede their full participation, require their abstinence, nor deny them ordination; and the Dalai Lama has publicly expressed acceptance of same-gender relationships.[70] The growing Islamic presence in the United States, on the other hand, is generally expected to support the social forces that are intolerant on issues of sexuality and that disapprove of homosexuality.[71] The Islamic Information and News Network, for example, urges Muslims to condemn homosexuality and to deny homosexuals human rights; but a few gay Muslims have found tolerance within particular mosques.[72] Native Americans who practice traditional rather than Western religions often tolerate and respect sexual and gender-role diversity. Within a few Native communities and organizations, leaders have encouraged lesbians and gay men to take on important ceremonial and spiritual roles.[73]

Excluding and Silencing

When most religious bodies have taken positions that disapprove of and condemn homosexuality, they have done so by ignoring, silencing, and obstructing the voices of gay people.[74] At national meetings during deliberations on gay issues, gay people usually have not been invited or allowed to speak. At the 1992 General Assembly of the Presbyterian Church (U.S.A.), the presiding officer or "Stated Clerk" successfully blocked floor discussion on gay-related matters and got them voted down or referred to committee. A spokesperson for the gay organization said, "It was a very friendly assembly, because the Stated Clerk would not let us talk."[75] The 1992 General Conference of the United Methodist Church denied the spokesperson for the gay organization an opportunity to speak during the plenary discussion on the report that had been commissioned by the denomination to direct its policy on homosexuality.[76] Gay spokesman Morris Floyd observed that "society and church discount our lives by acting as if we did not exist — even when we are the subject of the story!"[77]

Ironically, the debates about homosexuality usually exclude the voices of lesbians and gay men; and those writing the studies of homosexuality consult biblical scholars, theologians, and church members about their thoughts and feelings about gay people but do not survey and examine the experiences of lesbians and gay men themselves. The 1984 survey of denominational positions, mentioned earlier, concludes that religious bodies do not deal with "homosexual persons present in their company as a people-to-people situation." They "ignore personal histories in actual time and place within their own ranks" and focus instead on "traditions, procedures, and authorities."[78]

Efforts to Change Official Policy and Practice

Members' Views of Policy and Positions

Although a religious body's position may not reflect the views of all its members, surveys of members from various religious bodies have found general agreement with those positions. The following list runs from the religious groupings whose members were most accepting of homosexuality to those least accepting: Unitarians, Jews,[79] Christian Scientists, Episcopalians, members of the United Church of Christ, Presbyterians, Lutherans, black Northern Baptists, Methodists, Northern Baptists, Disciples of Christ, black Methodists, Mormons, members of the Reformed Church, black Southern Baptists, Southern Baptists, Nazarenes, Seventh-Day Adventists, evangelicals and fundamentalists, members of the Church of Christ, Pentecostals, members of Holiness churches, members of the Church of God, Jehovah's Witnesses, and members of the Assemblies of God.[80]

Members of reputedly liberal religious bodies were more likely to accept homosexuality than were members of conservative, evangelical, and fundamentalist denominations, but there were notable exceptions. Catholics, for example, tend to be more liberal than the position taken by the Vatican.[81] Also, a survey of members of the gay-positive Unitarian Universalist Association in 1988 showed a mix of negative views that range from some outright hostility to a large group of respondents who found it difficult to approve of openly gay minsters.[82] And in 1991, the *Los Angeles Times* conducted a survey of 1,237 adults that showed 62 percent opposing the exclusion of lesbians and gay men from ordination. Such opposition was found "to be broad-based, shared by majorities of Roman Catholics, non-Catholic Christians, Jews and people who identify with no religion." Even many biblical fundamentalists said they would allow ordination. One man who believed in a literal interpretation of the Bible said, "They probably didn't have the information in Bible days that we appear to have today. I think it's an inherited thing, not something that homosexuals choose voluntarily. Predicated on that, I feel they should be included." A woman who is a Jehovah's Witness echoed his sentiment: "According to the Bible, homosexuality is wrong, but I listen to talk shows and know some gay people who say they were like this since childhood. Gays are people too and could do a good job."[83]

Organizing within and in Response to Religious Bodies

Disagreement with and defiance of policy by members have fostered alternative programs and organizations within some religious bodies. These include conservative efforts to oppose change and liberal efforts to encourage it. Within the United Church of Christ, for example, the Biblical Witness Fellowship has lobbied persistently, but unsuccessfully, to prevent the development of the denomination's increasingly pro-gay position. Efforts to help gay people, on the other hand, have developed support groups, educational and advocacy programs, and independent gay congregations.

Support

Gay members have formed support groups and caucuses within or outside of most nationally recognized religious bodies, regardless of the positions taken by them. These organizations represent Hindus, Buddhists, and Muslims, as well as Jewish, Catholic, and Protestant bodies. The groups' activities, their recognition by established religious bodies, and the conditions under which they meet vary. For example, the Unitarian Universalist Association funds its Office of Lesbian and Gay Concerns; the Vatican, fearing growing acceptance of homosexuality, has banned Dignity, the organization of gay Roman Catholics, from meeting on church property; the American Baptist Churches in the U.S.A. voted not to recognize the establishment of gay caucuses by its members; and the Presbyterian Church (U.S.A.) rescinded an earlier official recognition of its gay organization. Most of these gay groups are independent of and not funded or formally endorsed by their respective religious bodies.[84]

The importance of these organizations for gay people within various religious bodies is captured by the comments of Ina Mae Murri, a leader in the Mormon group, Affirmation:

> We fill a need for many members of the church. Why? Because gay and lesbian members approach the church troubled and anxious and in search of compassion and understanding. Instead, we find a refusal to listen to our feelings at all levels.... We find tunnel vision, people refusing to look beyond "sinful" behavior to see the tremendous loss of uncounted souls who would be active, contributing members if allowed to be ourselves and not forced to hide a most important facet of our personal lives....
>
> So in recent years the only place to turn to has been Affirmation. We are a self-help support and social group. We do not try or intend to take the place of the church. In the past eight years we have been a lifeline for thousands seeking understanding and caring from others like themselves. I pray for the day when Affirmation is not needed, when we have an understanding of the plan of salvation that could include a recognition of our love, and when

> we have better trained church officials and members to help us sort through the pieces of the puzzles of our lives.[85]

In Los Angeles, a Muslim man looked forward to the formation of Salaam, a new group in Los Angeles, because it "will offer me a safe place to begin my own interpretation of Islam on the issue of homosexuality."[86]

Education and Advocacy

In addition to providing support networks for gay church members, organizations work to educate non-gay members and to influence church policy and practice. One type of program developed by eight of the gay groups is a grassroots movement of encouraging and helping local churches to declare independently of the larger denomination that they officially welcome gay people. Such churches are generally referred to as "welcoming" and are variously called Open and Affirming, Supportive, Reconciling, or "More Light" Congregations within different denominations. These programs have provided some local congregations with a way to protest the anti-gay laws of the bodies to which they belong. Only the two most pro-gay denominations, the United Church of Christ and the Unitarian Universalist Association, endorse and support the welcoming congregation movement on the local level.[87]

A counterprogram, called Transforming Congregations, within the United Methodist Church seeks to welcome homosexual members who want and are willing to change their sexual behavior and orientation. This effort is part of a larger ex-gay Christian movement of several independent organizations, such as Exodus International, Regeneration, Day One, Desert Stream, Liberation in Jesus Christ, and Homosexuals Anonymous, with programs to "cure" homosexuals from "sinful" same-sex attraction.[88]

Independent Congregations

Groups of gay people have also independently formed their own local churches, synagogues, Zen centers, and sanghas;[89] and a few of these have been accepted as members within mainstream religious bodies.[90] For example, in 1989 the Zen Center in San Francisco recognized the development of the Gay Buddhist Club into the Hartford Street Zen Center (or One Mountain Temple) by certifying its gay abbot as an authentic teacher and living representative of Buddha's lineage.[91] Also, the Union of American Hebrew Congregations has accepted at least four gay synagogues into its membership. These synagogues joined together to organize the First International Conference of Gay and Lesbian Jews in 1976 and by 1980 formed the World Congress of Gay and Lesbian Jewish Organizations.[92] As noted earlier, in the late 1960s the Universal Fellowship of Metropolitan Community Churches (MCC) was founded as a denomination independently of any established religious body and has continued to expand and develop a ministry to and by gay people.[93] However, even though the MCC met all qualifications for membership in the National Council of Churches, its application and admission have been denied twice — in 1983 and 1992.[94]

Gay American Indians (GAI) was founded by Randy Burns and Barbara Cameron in 1975 in San Francisco. Originally a support group for urban gay Indians, GAI soon enlarged its activities to cultivate and update the *berdache* tradition within the general Indian community. After some initial resistance, community leaders began to recognize, welcome, and encourage GAI's participation in the community's ceremonies and programs. Within ten years, GAI grew to six hundred members nationwide and published an anthology of work by gay American Indians. In the late 1980s in Minneapolis, gay Indians gathered under the umbrella name "Two Spirited People" and spawned the formation of other groups in San Diego, Toronto, and New York City.[95]

Summary

The informal and nearly unspoken disapproval of homosexuality within organized religion prior to World War II rested on a legacy of antihomosexual legislation and persecution in colonial times and was marked by infrequent campaigns against "sexual deviants."

Social changes brought on by World War II and by developments in the social sciences, government, and law generated unprecedented attention to and discussion of homosexuality in America. The introduction and expansion of religious scholarship and published writing about homosexuality, the formation of homophile organizations with the support of some religious leaders, and efforts by religious leaders and religious bodies influenced public policy and discussion.

The Stonewall Rebellion of 1969 and the emergence of the gay liberation movement in the 1970s inspired greater activism by gay people within religious bodies. The progressive measures initiated by some bodies and the heightened debate and controversies embroiling others fostered greater social attention and awareness within organized religion. Uncertainty and indecision have characterized the deliberations of many religious bodies, but most have taken definitive formal positions.

In response to the lack of acceptance by religious bodies, gay people have formed organizations to support one another, to educate others, to advocate for change, and to gather independently of religious bodies that reject them.

The debates, studies, and positions taken by most religious bodies reflect their desire both to control and to distance themselves from those who are most affected. Religious bodies have passed laws and taken positions that directly affect gay people, but they have not consulted gay people or involved them in the decision-making process. A 1983 plan to address homosexuality in the Archdiocese of San Francisco did, however, break new ground by insisting that along with church teachings the experiences of gay people must be considered; but a follow-up practice of such inclusion was not developed, nor has a comprehensive, systematic study of such experience within any denomination been conducted.[96]

The task of gaining a full understanding of gay people within organized religion has yet to be completed. A proposed "Social Statement on the Church and Human Sexuality" prepared for the Evangelical Lutheran Church in America in 1993 simply, but poignantly, provides a guideline for the task: "This is not an abstract issue but an embodied human reality in our midst."[97]

Chapter Two

Methodology and Studies

This chapter discusses approaches to the study of lesbian/bisexual/gay people within organized religion. The section on methodology reviews the approaches that established religious bodies have taken and then advocates a shift from their study of homosexuality as an abstract category of sexual behavior to the study of the experiences, social interactions, and involvement of gay people within religious bodies. Support for this shift is found in recent theology, social theory, and social science. Next, experiential writing by gay people in organized religion is identified and reviewed, and a systematic observation and analysis of experiences are then pursued by investigating the empirical studies of gay people in religion. Finally, the scope and purpose of my own research to deepen, expand, and complete a comprehensive study of gay people within organized religion are described and discussed.

Methodology: Ways of Knowing

Homosexuality or Lesbian/Bisexual/Gay People?

In 1988, the United Methodist Church directed a committee to "study homosexuality as a subject for theological and ethical analysis"; to draw on the work of biblical scholars, theologians, ethicists, and scientists; and to "seek the best biological, psychological, and sociological information and opinion." The committee was not directed to solicit information from the denomination's gay constituency; nor did the denomination's customary categories for the inclusiveness of committee membership — gender, racial/ethnic groups, clergy and laity, and geography — provide a formal means for the inclusion of gay people. The committee did, however, meet with "several hundred persons," many of whom "identified themselves as gay, lesbian, ex-gay, ex-lesbian, parent and relative, friend, church official, pastor, church member"; and it recognized "their testimony [as] an indispensable background for consideration of homosexuality as a biblical/theological and scientific question." But information gathered from lesbians and gay men makes up a very small part (less than 3 percent) of the final report.[1]

Two other studies of human sexuality, not only of homosexuality, by the Evangelical Lutheran Church in America and by the Presbyterian Church (U.S.A.), also relied on the work of scholars and experts and made an effort as well to "listen to the voices" of clergy and laypeople. Selected anecdotes were used to preface and illustrate various discussions, but those from lesbians and gay men (one-half page of the fifty-page Lutheran report and one page of the one-hundred-page Presbyterian report) informed neither the substance of the reports nor the basis from which conclusions were drawn.[2]

Claiming that this kind of "anecdotal material" and "personal testimony" cannot settle by themselves the kinds of issues the committees were asked to address, each of the Methodist, Lutheran, and Presbyterian study committees shaped and presented its research within a theoretical framework that was compatible with the denomination's religious tradition. For the Methodists this framework was theological, and they attempted to consider homosexuality within an understanding of "God's love." The framework for the Presbyterians was relational psychology, and homosexuality was affirmed within a social ethic of gender equality. The Lutherans' framework was the Bible, and the report sought to validate homosexuality through the biblical commandment "to love one's neighbor." All three reports did seriously address gay issues and did make positive recommendations for the inclusion of lesbians and gay men within their respective denominations (even though none has been accepted, and two have been rejected, by the legislative bodies that commissioned the studies); but none provided in-depth information about the lives of lesbians and gay men within those religious bodies.[3]

What Is Not Known?

The United Methodist committee's report was perhaps most useful for recognizing what remains unknown, what needs to be studied, and how it should be studied. Realizing that "the church's access to knowledge is not limited to scientific studies" and that "insights can be gained through the church's experience with gay and lesbian persons in its midst," the report posed a series of questions that it left unanswered but that apparently were important for this denomination's theological and pastoral concerns: "Do homosexuals manifest the 'fruit of the Spirit'? Is their faith mature and growing? Do they behave in unselfish, caring ways? Do they serve gladly and creatively? Do they practice self-discipline?"[4]

For a gay person these questions may seem naive and their answers obvious (one knows that they would never be asked of heterosexuals as a specific group of people); and they signal the limited and superficial understanding that religious bodies have of gay people. To its credit, the report owned up to its own limitation:

> The fact that homosexuality has been so generally stigmatized within the church makes it more difficult to answer such questions, for we often do not know who the gays and lesbians are! ... We have been struck by the numbers of reported instances in which this or that local church ... has suddenly discovered that some highly treasured member or leader has been gay or lesbian all along.[5]

After more than twenty years of discussion, debate, and studies, many religious bodies do not know who gay people are, what they do, how they feel and think, and why they stay within those groups. Research, therefore, must begin with and move from this recognition of what is not known. The Methodist's committee report is helpful for posing the research problem and identifying the area in which research needs to be done.

Experiences of Lesbian/Bisexual/Gay People

My approach privileges the experience of gay people even more than suggested by the Methodist report, for it begins not with that report's observation that "insights can be gained through the church's experience with gay and lesbian persons in its midst" but with gay people's experience with the church. My work shifts the topic and method of research — from the topic of "homosexuality" to "the lives of gay people"; from biblical, theological, and psychological understandings and interpretations of homosexuality to understandings that rest on empirical studies of gay experience; from the church's view of gay people to gay people's view of the church.

I am not the first to call for the recognition and study of gay experience within religious bodies. For example, in response to the Vatican's claim that "homosexual activity is not a complementary union, able to transmit life; and so it thwarts the call to a life of that form of self-giving which the Gospel says is the essence of Christian living," theologian Xavier John Seubert has said that the "life-giving" relationships of gay people have not been taken seriously:

> Until the leadership in the church is more willing to come face to face with Christian homosexuals and listen to the depths of their experience in order to search with them for the paths that will lead to understanding and dialogue in promoting their welfare, we will not get beyond an essentialism that has little to do with the real lives of gay men and lesbian women, and even less to do with their welfare.[6]

My shift away from officials, authorities, and experts with positions on homosexuality to lesbians and gay men as the subject matter and sources of knowledges is also not without support in contemporary theology, social theory, social movements, social ethics, and science.

Interest and Objectivity

Since the 1970 publication in the United States of Brazilian educator Paulo Freire's *Pedagogy of the Oppressed,* efforts to recognize, value, and learn from those who are socially marginalized or powerless have gained a measure of credibility and practice in the church and academy. Freire argued that the "epistemological advantage" for understanding and solving social problems rests with those who experience and suffer from those problems, rather than with experts trained in the social and political sciences who study them.[7] His thesis became the basis for organized movements by the poor in Latin America and by people of color, women, and gay people in North America. The needs, plans, and hopes of these groups came to be expressed in various forms of "liberation theologies."[8] Although these "theologies from below" have not replaced the hierarchical structures and "theology from above" of most religious institutions, they have nudged several religious bodies into listening to, welcoming, and acting on behalf of the socially less powerful, as with the ordination of women and the development of programs to end racism, sexism, hunger, and homelessness.[9] Organized religion's relationship with its gay people, however, has not been informed and shaped by a willingness to learn about and from them. Instead, organized religion continues to view them from above and to keep them at a distance from the policy-making that affects them.

According to Christian ethicist Beverly Harrison, the major opposition to studies based on the "epistemological advantage of the disadvantaged" is "that they lack 'objectivity,' that their proponents are caught up in advocacy and cannot make reasoned judgments like more 'dispassionate' people." She points out, however, that such criticism obscures the differences between "liberationist" and "idealist" views of knowledge. The liberationist "assumes that everyone has an 'interest' focused toward and invested in some configuration of social relations" and that to be objective is to "own these loyalties and commitments rather than profess to stand above them." The idealist assumes that objectivity is achieved by a particular method of inquiry from a detached location, such as in academic or religious institutions, without examining the "specific allegiances and investments in society" of those institutions. The liberationist perspective claims what idealist epistemologies fail to acknowledge — that "every method of human inquiry is rooted in social interest," that "knowledge is a form of power, with moral implications for how we use it," and that one should be "accountable to those affected by the power of knowledge."[10]

Because positions of power within religious institutions are for the most part held by and assigned to men who identify as heterosexual and because the heterosexually formed family is the valued and acceptable constitutive unit, it is not surprising that the various studies of and positions on homosexuality are based on idealist and detached views of gay people by non-gay people. Such studies preserve the control, structure, and organization of religious institutions by denying, forgetting, and rendering invisible those closest to and most directly affected by the issue. Religious institutions have studied and taken positions on homosexuality without examining their own limits, interests, and biases and without regard for the impact that those studies and positions would have on the people directly affected by them. Such "detached" objectivity has been achieved from above at the expense of those below.

Embodied Objectivity

My decision to privilege the experiences and perspectives of gay people is also supported by recent feminist scientific theory. Science historian Donna Haraway, for example, distinguishes between "embodied" and "disembodied" objectivity. Embodied objectivity, which she advocates, is based on "situated knowledges" — that is, what we know from our experiences within our particular social situations. Disembodied objectivity is based on "transcendent knowledge" — that is, what we know by being indifferent to and by distancing ourselves from what we study. Haraway is suspicious of the latter approach because it is "an illusion" or "false vision promising transcendence of all limits." By pretending not to be personally interested, we do not have to take responsibility for whom or what we study. Situated knowledge is admittedly only a partial perspective, but one that promises objectivity and clarity not by viewing from a distance but by "connection." Situated knowledges become objective when they are joined and one learns "how to see faithfully from another's point of view."[11] Haraway writes:

> The only way to find a larger vision is to be somewhere in particular. The science question in feminism is about objectivity as positioned rationality. Its images are not about the products of escape and transcendence of limits, i.e., the view from above, but the joining of partial views and halting voices into a collective subject position that promises a vision of the means of ongoing finite embodiment, of living within limits and contradictions, i.e., of views from somewhere.[12]

Haraway concedes that a serious danger in diminishing the value of disembodied or transcendent knowledge is romanticizing the situated knowledges of the less powerful. Therefore, the test for embodied objectivity must be the relentless, expansive, and endless joining of knowledges from various situations, and none is "exempt from critical re-examination, decoding, deconstruction, and interpretation." Haraway does, however, claim that the socially powerful are more likely to ignore knowledge that would threaten to change how and what they control, whereas the subjugated would seem to promise knowledge that could transform the world. The subjugated have the potential and advantage to spark inquiry that may unsettle preconceptions and familiar approaches.[13]

Situated Knowledges

On their own, gay people certainly have utilized their "situated knowledges" to write about their experiences in organized religion. Several books by openly gay clergy who have been removed from or denied access to positions within their denominations have been published by mainstream and gay publishers. These include personal stories by Troy Perry, a former Pentecostal minister who founded the Universal Fellowship of Metropolitan Community Churches; Carter Heyward, who was among the first group of women ordained as priests within the Episcopal Church; Chris Glaser, a Presbyterian who unsuccessfully challenged his denomination's law against ordaining lesbians and gay men; John McNeill, a gay Roman Catholic priest who was silenced by the Vatican and expelled from the Society of Jesus; Rose Mary Denman, a United Methodist minister who lost her ministerial status in an ecclesiastical trial; Antonio Feliz, a Mormon bishop who came out of the closet; James Ferry, whose license to exercise his duties as a priest of the Anglican Church of Canada was withdrawn; and Mel White, a former speechwriter for leaders of the Christian Right and currently dean of the gay Cathedral of Hope in Dallas.[14]

Anthologies of autobiographical writings by gay Roman Catholics, Jews, and Native Americans have also been published. Descriptions of some of these follow.

In *A Faith of One's Own: Explorations by Catholic Lesbians,* editor Barbara Zanotti identified "both negative and positive features" that many Catholic lesbians "have come to experience" in exploring "the complexities of our dual identity":

> Among the negative consequences recorded here are public hatred, job loss, silencing, invisibility, psychological labelling and the

> loss of family and friends. Developing the survival skills needed to stand outside does, however, offer surprising positive results: from the outside looking in we are able to see the oppressive structure of patriarchy with considerable clarity and... are free to create ourselves.[15]

So, too, the more than fifty essays in *Lesbian Nuns: Breaking the Silence,* edited by Rosemary Curb and Nancy Manahan, charted similar paths of experiences that led to the contributors' eventual rejection of the Catholic Church as a legitimate religious institution.[16]

Although many lesbian and gay Jews have chosen either to exile themselves from the Jewish community or to remain by staying in the closet, Christie Balka and Andy Rose, the editors of *Twice Blessed: On Being Lesbian or Gay and Jewish,* see the essays in their volume pointing to a third alternative, that "of affirming both our Jewish and our lesbian and gay identities" and "living our lives based on the wisdom of two cultures." They add, however, that the contributors take "personal and professional risks by writing here."[17]

In the preface to *Living the Spirit: A Gay American Indian Anthology,* Randy Burns writes, "This book is not just *about* gay American Indians, it is *by* gay Indians." United in their effort to continue and change their traditional responsibility and spiritual role as "special people" within their communities, more than twenty writers describe both reservation and urban experiences and speak of "our pain, but also our joy, our love, and our sexuality."[18]

Inspired by the example of their gay son and nephew, two Mormon brothers, Ron and Wayne Schow, and a social worker, Marybeth Raynes, compiled *Peculiar People: Mormons and Same-Sex Orientation.*[19] An essay written by the gay man's father poignantly summarizes the experience of gay people in the Church of Jesus Christ of Latter-day Saints and mirrors that of those within other religious bodies:

> Consider the psychological burden borne by Mormon homosexuals in particular. From their youth the seeds of low self-esteem are planted. From both adults and peers they hear the deprecating epithets, the scornful aspersions, the biased misinformation about gays which cause them to feel contemptible. They struggle to understand their difference in an environment which demands conformity. They hide their feelings from the world, even from loved ones, and hate themselves for this deception. They discover that there are laws against homosexual intimacy. They read books confirming their fear that they are flawed or mentally ill. And when they desperately need to turn to the church for comfort and assurance, it proclaims its condemnation by counseling them to deny

> their own nature. Ironically, the more orthodox the individual, the more he believes he is wicked and the more he suffers from this institutional repudiation of his identity. His "tainted" sexuality seems to him the central fact of his existence and colors all facets of his life. How compatible is such a mental state with the self-love essential for spiritual progress?[20]

This anthology begins with personal stories by gay Mormons, which are followed by personal accounts by family members and friends and the findings of social scientists and theologians.

Another anthology, *Bi Any Other Name: Bisexual People Speak Out,* published in 1991 and edited by Loraine Hutchins and Lani Kaahumanu, contains a section titled "Spirituality: Healing the Spirits." Individual stories were written about moving from a Catholic upbringing to Wiccan Goddess-worship, reappropriating one's Jewish background, moving from a Jewish-Catholic background to Buddhism, and creating new sacred rituals and spiritual guidelines.[21]

The writers in Rakesh Ratti's anthology, *A Lotus of Another Color: An Unfolding of the South Asian Gay and Lesbian Experience,* share the cultural heritage of the Indian subcontinent. Five discuss the influence of Hinduism or Islam on their lives. Although positive views of same-sex eroticism are identified within the religious traditions, Ratti observes that the "common thread that connects all of the personal experiences contained within these pages" is "the sense of isolation that we felt when we first realized that we were gay or lesbian."[22]

Experiential pieces have also appeared from time to time in liberal religious periodicals, such as *Lilith, Sojourners, U.S. Catholic, National Catholic Reporter, Christianity and Crisis, Sh'ma, Tikkun,* and *Moment;* in gay periodicals, such as the *Advocate;* and even in some conservative magazines, such as *The New Republic.*[23] *Open Hands* is a quarterly magazine of the Reconciling Congregation Program, the network of United Methodist local churches that publicly welcome gay people. Each issue has been organized under a particular theme, such as youth, aging, holy unions, AIDS, racial minorities, bisexuality, families, and campus ministry. It has also provided information about the experiences of gay people in denominations other than its own. *Second Stone,* "a national ecumenical Christian newsjournal with specific outreach to sexual orientation minorities," has presented interviews, feature articles, book reviews, commentary, a listing of resources, and a calendar of events. The newsletters of the caucuses and groups formed by gay people within different religious bodies have also featured personal accounts and correspondence on a regular basis.[24]

Individual, Extraordinary, Unconnected Stories

Within the above-mentioned formats of autobiographical books, anthologies, periodicals, and newsletters, gay people have written about experiences that have included remaining silently within various religious bodies, reforming religious institutions from within, breaking one's silence and being silenced, and leaving familiar settings to form alternative places, meetings, and groupings. Gay scholar-activist Robert Goss observed that what the writers of these various testimonies have in common "is the deep conflicts that they have experienced and continue to experience with institutional" religion. As "one who has struggled with this conflict for nearly two decades," Goss summarizes these experiences as "discrimination, exclusion, condemnation, terrorism, and violence."[25]

But these published narratives do not represent the full range of gay experience within organized religion for two main reasons. First, most are about and by clergy and laypeople who are active and publicly open about their sexual orientation. The experiences of those members who are less active or more closeted tend not to be revealed. Second, defeats and negative experiences dominate the literature. Successes and positive experiences, as few as they may be, are not as likely to be written about and given notice. Also, the various kinds of experiences have not been systematically examined and analyzed. The "critical re-examination, decoding, deconstruction, and interpretation" that Haraway says are necessary for making the "connections" between experiences have not been attempted. Although the autobiographical, anecdotal accounts offer valuable insights into gay experience in organized religion, "the joining of partial views and halting voices into a collective subject position" has not occurred.[26] The newsletters of the many gay religious groups are the most likely source of the more ordinary, less newsworthy experiences that would add to and complete the more dramatic stories found in books and magazines, but a systematic screening and study of them have not as yet been done.

Because social science has developed tools for systematic inquiry, observation, and study, a review of empirical studies of gay people in religion may provide a counterpart to the lack of overview, inclusion, integration, and analysis of varied experiences by the assorted autobiographical and anecdotal literature reviewed above.

Empirical Studies

Few attempts have been made to collect and analyze systematically data from a cross section of gay people within organized religion. Studies about homosexuality and religion in the social sciences, like those by religious bodies, have most often been concerned with the attitudes of non-gay people.[27] However, twenty-six recent empirical studies of gay people in various forms of organized religion have been conducted (hereafter referred to as the "religion-focused" studies); and another ten studies of gay people have some findings related to organized religion (hereafter referred to as the "religion-related" studies). With both limitations and strengths, these studies offer a resource for beginning to connect, examine, and interpret gay experiences within organized religion. Information about the date, geography, and purpose of each study; the researchers' names; the size and makeup of the samples; the data-gathering methods used; and the kind of data collected are discussed below and provided in table 2 for the religion-focused studies and in table 3 for the religion-related studies. My own study is also included in table 2, but it will not be discussed until later in this chapter. The actual data and findings from these studies will be presented in subsequent chapters.

Twenty-Six Religion-Focused Studies

The researchers for the religion-focused studies sampled different groups of gay people, used different data-gathering techniques, and pursued different lines of inquiry.

In 1994, Michael Dickens surveyed gay and bisexual men of African descent for his master's thesis at Wesleyan University. He distributed a questionnaire through the Connecticut chapter of the gay organization Men of All Colors Together (MACT) and at a meeting of the local African-American Gay Men's Support Group. His study of the effect of societal racism and homophobia upon his twenty-three subjects focused on their religious affiliation and the role of the black church. His sample was predominantly college-educated, middle- and upper-middle-class, and upper-income.[28]

In 1994, Odette Lockwood-Stewart, a campus minister, reported information that she had gathered from Christian students on sixty college campuses "from all theological and political perspectives, from all orientations, and from all regions of the United States." In the context of workshops and other student settings, she asked students "to describe their experiences, perceptions, and questions" about homosexuality and the church. She presented her findings in a special issue entitled *Campus Ministry with Sexual Minorities* published by *Open Hands* magazine.[29]

In 1992 at the Sixth National Conference on Undergraduate Research, Alissa Nelyn Steelman presented her research on the various kinds of relationships that gay people have established with the organized Christian church. Drawing from interviews with gay community

TABLE 2

Summary of Twenty-Seven Studies of Lesbian, Bisexual, and Gay People in Organized Religion

Researcher(s)	Date	Sample					Methodology		
		Size	Geographical area	Clergy/Lay	Women/Men	Religious bodies	Inquiry/Instrument	Distribution/Access	Data
Dickens	1994	23	Connecticut	lay	men	the black church (various denominations, such as African Methodist Episcopal)	questionnaire	support group and mailing list of organization for gay men of color	quantitative
Lockwood-Stewart	1994	60 campuses	United States	lay	women/men	Christian	workshops	national speaker and leader of workshops on campus ministry	qualitative
Comstock	1993	488	United States	clergy/lay	women/men	United Methodist Church United Church of Christ	questionnaire interviews	mailing lists of denominational gay caucuses	quantitative qualitative
Primiano	1993	5	Philadelphia	lay	women	Dignity (Roman Catholic)	participant observation interviews	worship services, meetings, social events	qualitative
Blincoe	1993	2	New York City	traditionalist	woman/man	traditional Native American	interview	American Indian Community House (NYC) staff and officer	qualitative
Steelman	1992	203	California	lay	women/men	Christian other	questionnaire interviews	gay organizations	qualitative
Foster	1992	35	Toronto	lay	men	Roman Catholic Church	questionnaire	gay Catholic groups and friendship networks	quantitative
Sears	1991	36	South Carolina	lay	women/men	Southern Baptist African Methodist Episcopal Jehovah's Witnesses fundamentalist, other	interview questionnaires	community organizations, friendship networks, newspaper ads, gay-owned businesses	qualitative quantitative
O'Brien	1991	264	United States	clergy/lay	women/men	Roman Catholic Church	questionnaires	chapter meetings of gay Catholic organization	quantitative
McFadden	1991	12	United States	clergy/lay	women/men	Church of the Brethren	interviews	networking as executive in AIDS ministry and parish ministry programs	qualitative
Schow and Raynes	1991	17	Utah and Idaho	lay	women/men	Church of Jesus Christ of Latter-day Saints	counseling interviews	professional counseling practice	qualitative
Carney and Davies	1991	10	North America	clergy	women	United Church of Canada United Methodist Church Episcopal Church Roman Catholic Church United Church of Christ	questionnaire	professional and friendship networks	qualitative
Thumma	1991	7	Atlanta	lay	men	gay Evangelical parachurch	interviews participant observation	meetings, newsletters, correspondence, literature	qualitative

Researcher(s)	Date	Sample					Methodology		
		Size	Geographical area	Clergy/Lay	Women/Men	Religious bodies	Inquiry/Instrument	Distribution/Access	Data
Franks, Templer, Cappelletty, Kauffman	1990–1991	115	San Francisco Bay area	lay	men	Catholic, Jewish, Protestant, other, none	questionnaire	AIDS self-help organizations and support groups	quantitative
Sipe	1990	200	United States	clergy	men	Roman Catholic Church	counseling interviews	workshops and counseling sessions	qualitative quantitative
Alexander	1989	5	United States	lay	men	Church of Jesus Christ of Latter-day Saints	correspondence	local and national meetings of gay Mormon organization	qualitative
Wolf	1989	101	United States	clergy	men	Roman Catholic Church	questionnaire	friendship networks	quantitative qualitative
Fischer	1989	11	San Francisco Bay area	clergy	women/men	Unitarian Universalist Presbyterian Church (USA) United Church of Christ	interviews	friendship and professional networks	qualitative
Miller	1989	6	United States	clergy/lay	women/men	United Methodist Church Roman Catholic Church Presbyterian Church (USA) Faith Temple	interviews participant observation	travel, word of mouth, gay organizations, friendship networks	qualitative
Unitarian Universalist Association	1989	330	North America	clergy/lay	women/men	Unitarian Universalist	questionnaire	denominational periodical	quantitative
Reh	1989	115	United States	clergy/lay	women/men	Presbyterian Church (USA)	questionnaire	national conference	quantitative qualitative
Stout	1987		Utah	lay	women/men	Church of Jesus Christ of Latter-day Saints	counseling interviews	professional counseling practice	qualitative (quantitative)
Williams	1986	71	21 tribes	traditionalist	women/men	traditional Native American	interviews participant observation	travel, word of mouth, gay organization, friendship network	qualitative
Murphy	1986		Ohio	clergy (religious)	women	Roman Catholic	counseling workshops	professional counseling practice	qualitative
Rabinowitz	1983	4	New York City	lay	men	Reform gay outreach synagogue	interviews participant observation	member of synagogue and Talmud class	qualitative
Wagner	1981	50	United States	clergy	men	Roman Catholic Church	interviews	friendship networks	qualitative quantitative
Bauer	1976	150	Denver	clergy/lay	women/men	Metropolitan Community Church	participant observation	employed as church's director of education	qualitative

TABLE 3

Summary of Ten Studies of Lesbian, Bisexual, and Gay People with Attention to Religious Factors

Researcher(s)	Date	Sample					Methodology		
		Size	Geographical area	Clergy/Lay	Women/Men	Religious bodies	Inquiry/Instrument	Distribution/Access	Data
Laumann, Gagnon, Michael, and Michaels	1994	3,432	United States	lay	women/men	Protestant, Catholic, Jewish, other	questionnaire interviews	area probability sampling National Opinion Research Center	quantitative
Weinberg, Williams, and Pryor	1994	682	San Francisco Bay area	lay	women/men	Protestant, Catholic, Jewish, other	participant observation interviews questionnaire	sexuality support, education, and information organizations; sex/social clubs	quantitative qualitative
Remafedi, Resnick, Blum, and Harris	1992	34,706	Minnesota	lay (adolescents)	women/men	general	questionnaire	classroom settings with approval by parents and University of Minnesota Institutional Review Board	quantitative
Partners Task Force	1990	1,749	United States	lay	women/men	Protestant, Catholic, Jewish, other	questionnaire	gay press, gay churches, gay community organizations	quantitative
Schneider, Farberow, and Kruks	1989	108	Los Angeles area	lay	men	Protestant, Catholic, Jewish, other, none	questionnaire	gay college organizations, rap groups at gay community center	quantitative
Jay and Young	1977	5,400	United States and Canada	lay	women/men	Protestant, Catholic, Jewish, other	questionnaire	gay organizations, periodicals, radio shows, social clubs, and areas	quantitative qualitative
Greenberg	1973	86	United States	lay	men	Protestant, Catholic, Jewish, other	questionnaire	homophile organizations	quantitative
Bell and Weinberg	1970	979	San Francisco Bay area	lay	men	Protestant, Catholic, Jewish	questionnaire	public news media; gay organizations, mailing lists, baths and bars; personal contacts; public places	quantitative
Weinberg and Williams	1969	1,057	San Francisco Bay & New York City areas, United States	lay	women/men	Protestant, Catholic, Jewish	questionnaire	gay organizations, mailing lists, and bars	quantitative
Kinsey, Pomeroy, and Martin	1948 1953	5,300 5,940	United States	lay	men women	Protestant, Catholic, Jewish	questionnaire interviews	community & professional groups, organizations, institutions, networks, lectures, and individuals	quantitative

leaders and 203 survey respondents in California, she reported that the "survey was extremely informal and individual responses were completely subjective."[30]

In 1992, as a student in sociology at the University of Toronto, Paul Foster surveyed Catholic gay men in Toronto to find out why they remain within the institutional church. Targeting men between the ages of twenty-five and forty-five, he distributed seventy questionnaires and received thirty-five responses. Foster admitted that because he had to rely on two local gay Catholic support groups and his own friendship network, his sample did not represent all gay Catholics: "The population I wanted to make statements about is a hidden group because of the current policies of the Church towards gays."[31]

Another study of Catholics was conducted by Thomas O'Brien and published in 1991 in the *Journal of Homosexuality.* Questionnaires were distributed through various Dignity chapters and return-mailed to him. His geographically diverse and anonymous sample of 264 lesbians and gay men is likely to be more representative than those acquired through the face-to-face distribution and collection used by Foster; but O'Brien acknowledged that a gay organization is a limited population and not apt to yield "a true indication of general gay/lesbian Catholic consensus." He also surveyed a comparable population of generally straight Catholics, the young adult prayer and Bible study group in his local parish, to serve as a control group for his study.[32]

In 1991 Ralph McFadden's report about gay clergy and laity in the Church of the Brethren was published in the journal *Brethren Life and Thought.* McFadden conducted interviews and listened to stories as part of his work as an executive in the denomination's parish ministry and AIDS ministry programs. From approximately twelve interviews, he identified major themes or viewpoints that represent "the feelings" of gay people who are connected with but remain doubtful about the institutional church.[33]

Within the previously mentioned anthology *Peculiar People: Mormons and Same-Sex Orientation,* published in 1991, there are three studies of gay people with backgrounds and experience in the Church of Jesus Christ of Latter-day Saints (Mormon). In "Difficult Choices for Adolescents and Adults," therapists Ron Schow and Marybeth Raynes present a profile of seventeen clients with various familial situations, interpersonal relationships, and problems with the church. In "Sin and Sexuality: Psychobiology and the Development of Homosexuality," psychiatrist R. Jan Stout offers observations from twenty-four years of counseling gay Mormons. A third study, "Suicidal Behavior in Gay and Lesbian Mormons," was conducted by Christopher J. Alexander, a leader of Affirmation, the national organization of gay Mormons. He solicited and received "a handful of written narratives" from male participants at local and national gatherings from the mid- to late 1980s.[34]

In *Redefining Sexual Ethics,* another anthology published in 1991, Deborah Carney and Susan Davies reported their study of lesbian and bisexual women involved professionally in North American churches. They contacted fifty-five women and received ten responses from women in the United Church of Christ, the United Church of Canada, the United Methodist Church, the Episcopal Church, and the Roman Catholic Church. Carney and Davis acknowledged that the "distribution of the questionnaire was spotty, precisely because no one knows who many of the women are or where they are working," and "we heard of many women who were unable to return the questionnaires because such a simple, anonymous action would be too dangerous to their continued work."[35]

In a 1990–91 issue of *Omega: Journal of Death and Dying,* Kent Franks, Donald Templer, Gordon Cappelletty, and Inge Kauffman published their study, "Exploration of Death Anxiety as a Function of Religious Variables in Gay Men with and without AIDS." A total of 115 men between the ages of nineteen and fifty-eight were recruited through AIDS self-help organizations and support groups in the San Francisco Bay Area. With provisions for anonymous return, a questionnaire asked respondents about their current religious belief and observance, identification with childhood religion, and the effect of organized religion on their lives.[36]

Richard Sipe's 1990 book, *A Secret World: Sexuality and the Search for Celibacy,* is a study of sexuality and celibacy among heterosexual and homosexual Catholic priests based on interviews with and reports by fifteen hundred people from 1960 to 1985. One-third were priests who were in some form of psychotherapy; another third were priests who shared information at meetings and in workshops; and the other third were "their lovers, sexual partners, victims, or otherwise direct observers of" their behavior. In a chapter on homosexuality involving approximately two hundred subjects, Sipe discusses the reported frequency, increase, and variety of homosexual behaviors and the personal, social, and ecclesial conditions under which they occurred.[37]

James G. Wolf's 1989 sociological study, *Gay Priests,* focuses "on the emotional component of sexuality as it affects the lives of" gay men of the Roman Catholic clergy. He received 101 responses by distributing nationwide a questionnaire among friendship networks of gay priests. Because his sample was "a self-selected group," he maintains that his results were not representative and that his study was "mainly exploratory" rather than definitive or conclusive.[38]

In 1989, Clare Fischer reported her study of lesbian and gay religious leaders and their values and attitudes concerning family, church, and community. Conceding that her study was not scientific methodologically, that the sample was limited, and that its subjects were not chosen randomly, Fischer reported interviews with five women and six men in the San Francisco Bay Area affiliated with the United Church of Christ, the Unitarian Universalist Association, the Presbyterian Church, and the United Methodist Church. Fischer's study was part of a special issue of the *Journal of Homosexuality* that was subsequently published in book form under the title *Homosexuality and Religion.*[39]

Neil Miller's 1989 book, *In Search of Gay America: Women and Men in a Time of Change,* was the result of his travels and interviews with lesbians and gay men in medium-sized cities, small towns, and rural areas. Part of his research focused on gay leaders in organized religion. After discussing Rose Mary Denman's trial in Dover, New Hampshire, and the excommunication of a priest by the Catholic Church in St. Cloud, Minnesota, he turns to Louisville and the local Presbyterian church that defied denominational policy by ordaining a gay elder and by hiring a gay seminarian as its student minister. Miller finishes with James Tinney, founder of the black, gay, evangelical Faith Temple in Washington, D.C., and one of his parishioners, a former member of Sun Myung Moon's Unification Church.[40]

In 1989, Lawrence Reh surveyed the participants at a national conference organized to advance the participation of gay people in local congregations of the Presbyterian Church (U.S.A.). The 115 respondents were equally divided between women and men and came from eleven states and forty-five local churches. Over one-half identified as lesbian or gay and one-third as non-gay. His questionnaire focused on the readiness of respondents to oppose the denomination's prohibition of openly gay ordination. Findings were published in *More Light Update,* the newsletter of Presbyterians for Lesbian and Gay Concerns.[41]

From 1987 to 1988, the Unitarian Universalist Association conducted a survey "to collect some basic information about how UUs feel about the inclusion of gay and lesbian (and bisexual) persons" in the denomination. Of the 2,362 respondents, 2,012 were heterosexual, 119 were gay men, 100 were lesbians, and 111 were bisexuals. The reported findings are almost exclusively about the heterosexuals' responses. A brief section of the final report presents how lesbian, gay, and bisexual respondents evaluate the policy and practice of the denomination.[42]

From 1986 to 1987, Leonard Primiano conducted fieldwork at the meetings and worship services of the Philadelphia chapter of Dignity. He found that the women of Dignity "had a unique personal perspective on Catholicism and on Dignity"; and their perspective became the focus of a study that was published in a 1993 issue of the journal *New York Folklore.* Having noticed a distinctive lack of female presence and members at the chapter's functions, he sought to discover through interviews and participant observation how and why "this most marginalized of religious groups [did] itself marginalize the community of homosexual Catholic women."[43]

In a 1986 issue of *Women and Therapy,* Sheila Murphy published her research on counseling lesbian members of Catholic religious orders. Her observations and recommendations were based on her work as a professor and psychologist who conducted a private practice with women religious and led workshops for women religious on sexuality and celibacy.[44]

Walter Williams's 1986 anthropological study, *The Spirit and the Flesh: Sexual Diversity in American Indian Culture,* involved seventy-one gay or *berdache* informants from twenty-one tribes. Included in his findings is information about their religious role and spiritual contributions in reservation and urban settings. A companion for this study is Deborah Blincoe's interview with a lesbian and a gay man at the American Indian Community House in New York. It was published in the same issue of *New York Folklore* as Primiano's study of Dignity and added an East Coast and women's perspective to the more Western and male orientation of Williams's study.[45]

In 1986, James Sears interviewed thirty-six lesbians and gay men between the ages of eighteen and twenty-eight in South Carolina. Published in 1991 as *Growing Up Gay in the South: Race, Gender, and Journeys of the Spirit,* his research examined the influence of white churches (Southern Baptist and fundamentalist) and black churches (African Methodist and Jehovah's Witness) on the lives of young gay people.[46]

From 1984 to 1985, Scott Thumma studied a small, gay evangelical group, or "parachurch," in Atlanta by means of participant observation at meetings, personal interviews, and a review of its newsletter and correspondence. An average of eight people attended biweekly meetings, and the newsletter was mailed to four hundred people. Formed to help people reconcile their gayness with their evangelical Christian identity, the group attracted gay white men who had been raised in the rural South or Midwest in such conservative evangelical denominations as the Southern Baptist Convention, the Lutheran Church–Missouri Synod, the Church of Christ, and the Assemblies of God. Thumma's study was published in 1991 in the journal *Sociological Analysis.*[47]

In 1983, Henry Rabinowitz's article on Congregation Beth Simchat Torah, the gay-outreach synagogue in New York City, was part of a symposium entitled "Homosexuals and Homosexuality" in the American Jewish Congress's publication, *Judaism: A Quarterly Journal of Jewish Life and Thought.* To illustrate the role played by the synagogue in the lives of its members, Rabinowitz interviewed four members of his Talmud class. From Conservative, Hasidic, and Orthodox backgrounds and currently employed as computer programmers, businessmen, and executives, the four men described how they became involved in the synagogue, what their degree of involvement was, and how conflicts between their sexual and religious identities were resolved.[48]

Richard Wagner's doctoral dissertation, "Gay Catholic Priests: A Study of Cognitive and Affective Dissonance," was published in 1981. Relying on friendship networks to construct his sample, he selected and interviewed fifty priests. His subjects discussed mandatory celibacy, reasons for joining the priesthood, involvement in the gay community, the church's and gay community's attitudes toward sexuality, disclosing sexual orientation to other priests, and experiences of discrimination from other priests.[49]

In 1976, Paul F. Bauer's participant-observation study of Denver's Metropolitan Community Church was published in the journal *Pastoral Psychology.* Bauer, a heterosexual professor of education and psychology, worked for ten months as the church's director of Christian education and based his study on over one hundred hours of observation. The church was founded in 1971 and had grown from 16 to 150 official members by the time of Bauer's study.[50]

Ten Religion-Related Studies

Ten other studies, while not focusing on organized religion, do provide some information about its influence on gay people and homosexuality (See table 3).

The groundbreaking studies of human sexual behavior by Alfred Kinsey, Wardell Pomeroy, Clyde Martin, and Paul Gebhard documented and compared the incidence of homosexuality among Jewish, Catholic, and Protestant subjects and among those who were religiously active and inactive. Their data were taken from interviews conducted with 5940 white women and 5300 white men from 1938 to 1947 throughout the United States.[51]

In the mid- to late 1960s, Martin Weinberg and Colin Williams surveyed 1,057 male homosexuals in the United States, with a concentration in the areas in and around New York City and San Francisco. Among the findings in their published study, *Male Homosexuals: Their Problems and Adaptations,* was information about "the relationship between the homosexual's religious background and the way he experiences and manages his homosexuality" and about "conflict between religiosity and sexuality."[52]

In 1970, Alan Bell and Martin Weinberg conducted a study of 979 homosexual women and men in the San Francisco Bay Area. Published as *Homosexualities: A Study of Diversity among Men and Women,* it included findings on religiosity, regularity of attendance at formal religious functions, and the effect of sexual orientation on religious feelings. This study was significant for the gender and racial balance of its sample.[53]

Jerrold Greenberg's study of eighty-six young male homosexuals was published in a 1973 issue of the *Journal of the American College Health Association.* Respondents were solicited through homophile organizations, and questionnaires were returned anonymously by mail from such diverse geographical locations as California, Nebraska, New York, and Oregon. Along with data about sexual behavior, family background, employment, and recreational activities, information about religious affiliation, belief, and attendance was gathered from his sample of predominantly white college students.[54]

In the mid-1970s, Karla Jay and Allen Young conducted a study of the sexual experiences and lifestyles of lesbians and gay men throughout the United States and Canada. With samples of 1,000 women and 4,400 men, their book, *The Gay Report,* included a statistical comparison of the religious backgrounds of respondents with their current religious affiliations and provided some personal comments about the influence of religion on their sexuality.[55]

In a 1989 issue of *Suicide and Life-Threatening Behavior,* Stephen Schneider, Norman Farberow, and Gabriel Kruks published the results from their study of suicidal behavior in adolescent and young-adult gay men. They received 108 responses to their questionnaire from gay men in Los Angeles who belonged to gay college organizations or attended rap groups at the gay community center. Included in their report were findings about the religious affiliations of suicidal and nonsuicidal respondents.[56]

In 1990, the Partners Task Force for Gay and Lesbian Couples published the findings from its national survey. In addition to listing the religious affiliations of its 1,749 respondents, the report included information about the role of clergy and religious bodies in supporting lesbian and gay couples and the frequency with which couples have symbolized their commitment with a religious ceremony.[57]

In 1992, four researchers, Gary Remafedi, Michael Resnick, Robert Blum, and Linda Harris, published their study of sexual orientation in adolescents in the medical journal *Pediatrics.* With a representative sample of 34,706 junior and senior high school students in Minnesota, they explored patterns of sexual attraction, fantasies, and behaviors and included the influence of religiosity on these patterns.[58]

In 1994, Martin Weinberg, Colin Williams, and Douglas Pryor's study, *Dual Attraction: Understanding Bisexuality,* was published. Their sample of 305 bisexuals, 280 homosexuals, and 190 heterosexuals was drawn from several sexuality support and education organizations in the San Francisco Bay Area in the 1980s. Among the findings that were presented and compared are the religious backgrounds and current religiosity of those within each sexual identity grouping.[59]

Also in 1994, Edward Laumann, John Gagnon, Robert Michael, and Stuart Michaels's study, *The Social Organization of Sexuality: Sexual Practices in the United States,* was published. They used area probability sampling to select and interview 3,432 women and men throughout the United States. Among the data collected is information about the religious affiliation and attendance of those who engage in same-sex practices and identify as homosexual or bisexual.[60]

Strengths and Weaknesses of the Thirty-Six Studies

As a whole, the thirty-six studies offer both strengths and weaknesses for understanding the experiences of gay people within organized religion. As the above discussion and tables 2 and 3 show, they do cover a wide range of religious bodies, many geographical areas, and approximately fifty years. Women and men, clergy and laity, and different age and racial groups were studied; various methods of inquiry, such as questionnaires, interviews, and participant observation, were used to gather data that are both quantitative and qualitative; and the researchers were both gay and non-gay. However, none of the studies provides a comprehensive view of gay experiences within any single religious body, with the possible exception of the Roman Catholic Church and traditional Native American spirituality. The strengths and weaknesses of the studies will be discussed in terms of the size and makeup of their samples and the kinds of data gathered.

Sample Sizes

Seven of the religion-focused studies concentrated on Roman Catholics, and some of these studies have the largest samples. Williams's study of Native American gay men was comprehensive because of the number of informants involved from different tribes and locations. The samples of other religion-focused studies that targeted specific religious bodies were small. Of these the Unitarian study has the largest sample but presented very limited information about its respondents. Bauer's study of the Metropolitan Community Church in Denver involved participant observation of a congregation of 150 but did not solicit information from all members. Because the samples for the three Mormon studies were small and/or from clinical populations, their findings could not be considered representative of gay experience in that church. Since the samples for twelve of the twenty-six religion-focused studies each included only two to thirty-six subjects and together represented more than twenty religious bodies, no one body was considered in detail.

Of all thirty-six studies, eight of the religion-related studies have the largest samples and also include comparable heterosexual components, but they look at broad religious traditions (Protestant, Catholic, Jewish) rather than at specific religious bodies within them.

Makeup of Samples

Researchers' methods for accessing subjects influenced the makeup of their samples. Making contacts with subjects or distributing questionnaires via friendship networks and at meetings of gay people yielded highly self-selected, "ideal," or "opportunistic" samples: that is, not a cross section of the gay population but those who identify somewhat openly and want to provide information. Because gay people vary in their degree of visibility, they do not comprise a population that can be sampled representatively.[61] In some cases, measures were taken to protect anonymity and encourage a wider response, such as providing for anonymous return-mailing of questionnaires (for example, the studies by O'Brien; Wolf; Greenberg; and Franks, Templer, Cappelletty, and Kauffman). With the exception of the Unitarian survey, none of the religion-focused studies provided a means to make contact or to distribute and collect questionnaires in a way that allowed subjects complete anonymity. Because the Unitarians' questionnaire was printed and made available in its denomination-wide, rather than its gay, publication, that study probably reached and represents the broadest cross section of gay people within a religious body.

Kinds of Data

Researchers' methods for questioning subjects determined the kinds of information that was collected. Using questionnaires provided the opportunity to collect data that could be quantified, although open-ended questions were also included by some to gather anecdotal information (for example, Wolf; Reh; Weinberg, Williams, and Pryor; and Jay and Young). Interviews and participant observation yielded anecdotal data, but the large number of interviews conduced by some researchers provided for quantification of responses (for example, Sipe; Wagner; Weinberg, Williams, and Pryor; and Kinsey, Pomeroy, and Martin). The twenty-six religion-focused studies have produced data that were mostly anecdotal. The ten religion-related studies produced mostly quantitative data, and their statistical analyses were more sophisticated than those of the other studies.

My Own Study

This section describes my own research, which consisted of three parts: separate surveys of gay people within the United Methodist Church and the United Church of Christ; follow-up interviews with ten respondents from each survey; and the screening of the newsletters from eleven gay religious organizations. My surveys and interviews are combined, reported, and summarized as one study (see table 2). After describing my surveys below, I shall discuss my screening of newsletters (see also table D.1 in Appendix D).

Filling in the Gaps

My research was guided by my desire to make up for gaps in current knowledge and to reproduce and extend the strengths of the reviewed studies. I wanted to maintain and extend their collectively wide geographic diversity, and in addition I sought a large sample that would represent laity as well as clergy, women and men equally, and bisexuals. Because the Roman Catholic Church, Native American tradition, independent gay religious bodies, and Church of Jesus Christ of Latter-day Saints (Mormon) either had been studied somewhat comprehensively or had received the individual attention of several studies, I sought to make up for the lack of focused, in-depth information about specific mainline Protestant denominations. I wanted the thrust of my study to be quantitative, to push further toward accessing an anonymous cross section of gay people within specific religious bodies, to be followed up with anecdotal input, and to provide for comparison of data about gay experience in different religious bodies.

Two Different Protestant Denominations

From 1991 to 1993, I collected data from gay people within the United Church of Christ (UCC) and the United Methodist Church (UMC). I chose these two denominations because of their differences.

The UCC is small, with a membership of 1.6 million. Its governing structure is bottom-up. Local congregations are autonomous decision-making bodies. Decisions made on the national level recommend, but do not mandate, local practice. The UCC's national policy is to ordain and welcome gay people; but local churches have responded variously to this policy. Its gay organization, called the United Church Coalition for Lesbian/Gay Concerns (UCCL/GC), has a mailing list of eight hundred and is officially recognized by the denomination.[62]

The UMC is large. With a membership of nine million, it is the second largest Protestant denomination in the United States. Its governing structure is episcopal[63] and top-down. The top decision-making body prohibits the ordination and appointment of "self-avowed, practicing homosexuals," states that "we do not condone the practice of homosexuality and consider this practice incompatible with Christian teaching," and bans the denomination's funding of any group that "promotes the acceptance of homosexuality." The UMC's gay group, called Affirmation: United Methodists for Lesbian and Gay Concerns, has a mailing list of 294 and is not officially recognized by the denomination.[64]

Distribution of Questionnaire

I distributed my questionnaire through the gay organization of each denomination. My research project was announced in the newsletter of each organization, and a questionnaire was subsequently sent to each person on the two mailing lists.[65] The questionnaire had been pilot-tested on and changed according to suggestions by the ten national council members of UCCL/GC and the nineteen national council members of Affirmation.[66]

At this point in the history of gay people, using the mailing lists of these kinds of organizations is the most effective way to approximate a representative sample of gay people within religious bodies. One need not join or participate in the organization to be on the mailing list; and gay people have come to expect and rely on their organizations to maintain the confidentiality of mailing lists and to package mailings discreetly. Gay people who are less able or willing to be visible and active within organizations are often on and reachable through these mailing lists. To encourage response I provided each questionnaire with a postage-paid envelope, return-addressed to me.

The UCC mailing consisted of 800 questionnaires, and 289 were returned, for a return-rate of 36 percent. The UMC mailing consisted of 294 questionnaires, and 199 were returned, for a return-rate of 68 percent. One-third of each sample volunteered for follow-up interviews.

Collecting Quantitative Data

My seventeen-page questionnaire consisted of yes/no, multiple-choice, and short-answer questions and was designed for both clergy and laypeople. Questions to clergy asked about experiences in seminary training, in preparing for ordination, and in seeking and maintaining employment. Questions to laypeople asked about participation and leadership on all denominational levels, membership on committees and boards, and lay ministry within and outside the denomination. Inquiries were directed to both clergy and laypeople concerning disclosure of sexual orientation and reactions to it. Respondents were also asked to evaluate their denomination's practice concerning gay issues and to describe their feelings about belonging to the denomination and their reasons for continued affiliation with the denomination.

Survey Sample

The demographics of the UCC and UMC samples, with the exception of gender (UCC women, 49 percent; UMC women, 29 percent), were very similar. Slightly over one-third of the respondents were in their thirties, one-third in their forties, and 15 percent each in their twenties and fifties-plus. Ninety percent identified as lesbian or gay and 10 percent as bisexual. One-quarter were employed as clergy; one-quarter were social workers, therapists, nurses, administrators of nonprofit organizations, or teachers; nearly 20 percent held blue-collar and other working-class positions; 15 percent were doctors, lawyers, professors, engineers, or business executives; and 15 percent were in middle-class service positions, such as sales. Ninety percent had received bachelor's degrees; two-thirds held master's degrees; and 15 percent had doctorates.

For each of the UCC and UMC survey samples, responses were received from thirty-six states, plus the District of Columbia. Highest response rates were from New York and California, and these rates were probably influenced by the estimated high concentration of the general gay population in New York City, San Francisco, and Los Angeles. Other response rates from states and regions reflect the distribution of the general non-gay memberships of each denomination.[67]

Interview Sample

One-hundred-one UCC survey respondents and sixty-two UMC survey respondents indicated that they were interested in participating in a follow-up interview. I contacted prospective interviewees first by letter and then by telephone to discuss and schedule a later phone interview. I selected ten people from each denomination with a balance among men and women, lay and clergy, and various occupations, ages, and geographical areas.[68] Interviews lasted from forty-five minutes to one hour, were taped with the interviewee's permission, and were then transcribed and sent to each person for changes and approval.[69] (See "Profiles of Twenty Respondents" in Appendix C.)

Collecting Qualitative Data

In my selection of interviewees I tried to choose those who might be more likely to provide in-depth information about controversial issues.

For example, I chose some respondents who had indicated on the questionnaire that they had performed a same-sex union/wedding or had had one performed for them. I chose clergy who indicated that they were engaged in ministry as openly gay people, clergy with positions in which they do not or cannot disclose, and clergy who had been dismissed because of their sexual orientation. I chose laypeople with membership in restrictive local churches, as well as those whose congregations had decided to welcome officially gay people (Reconciling Congregations [RCs] in the UMC, and Open and Affirming [ONA] churches in the UCC). I was also interested in those who indicated having worked on programs to educate non-gay people.

In addition, the follow-up interviews provided me with the opportunity to compensate for what my quantitative data could not do or did not show. For example, because only one respondent in each of the UCC and UMC survey samples identified as African-American, and one as Hispanic in the UCC survey sample, the particular experiences of people of color could not be quantitatively described. But I could and did weigh the number of interviews and kind of inquiries to include and favor these respondents and their experiences.

In general, the qualitative data from the interviews allowed for the narrative depth and detail missing in or suggested by the quantitative findings. They provided a different kind of information that informed or challenged the numbers and allowed me to pursue the surveys' underrepresented respondents and unanswered questions. The quantitative data from the surveys signaled targets, topics, and directions for more in-depth probing in the interviews.

Screening Newsletters

Because I wanted to include and learn about the variety of gay experiences within organized religion, I also screened the newsletters of eleven gay religious organizations for a five-year period, 1988–93 (see table D.1 in Appendix D). These regularly issued periodicals contain correspondence, features, narratives, and news about the activities of the organizations' members.

Three of the newsletters — *Waves* of the UCCL/GC, *Affirmation* of Affirmation UMC, and *Open Hands* of the Reconciling Church Program (also UMC) — provided additional information about my surveyed groups; but in an effort to provide a wider treatment of and focus on religious bodies not included or sufficiently represented in the empirical studies that have been conducted, I selected and screened eight additional newsletters.

The *Voice of the Turtle,* by American Baptists Concerned for Lesbian, Gay and Bisexual People, and *More Light Update,* by Presbyterians for

Lesbian and Gay Concerns, are newsletters of gay people affiliated with two other mainline Protestant denominations. The American Baptist Churches in the U.S.A. is a bit smaller than the UCC; and the Presbyterian Church (U.S.A.) is almost twice as large. Both denominations have restrictive policies and laws concerning gay members.

Dialogue is published by the Brethren/Mennonite Council for Lesbian and Gay Concerns and represents people from the Mennonite Church, the Church of the Brethren, and related denominations, including the Amish. These churches share an Anabaptist tradition known for social reform, pacifism, and strict separation of church and state, and together are considerably smaller than the UCC.

Two other newsletters, *Interweave World* (formerly *UULGC World*), published by Unitarian Universalists for Lesbian, Gay and Bisexual Concerns, and *FLGC Newsletter,* published by Friends for Lesbian and Gay Concerns, include experiences within yet other small denominations, but ones that are progressive on gay issues and not necessarily Christian.

World Congress Digest is the newsletter of the World Congress of Gay and Lesbian Jewish Organizations, which represents fifty organizations from twenty-one states in the United States and from eleven other countries. Some of the member organizations are affiliated with the Federation of Reconstructionist Congregations or the Reform movement's Union of American Hebrew Congregations.

The Apostolic Voice is the newsletter of the National Gay Pentecostal Alliance. This independent gay denomination was founded in 1980 and had established seven small churches in five states by 1993.

Trikone: Gay and Lesbian South Asians is the name of a newsletter sponsored by an organization of the same name, both headquartered in San Jose, California. Although the organization is not specifically religious, the newsletter is the only resource that provides ongoing and regular accounts by gay people who are practicing Hindus and Muslims or from Hindu and Muslim backgrounds.

Conclusion

In the following chapters I shall attempt to engage objectively in a discussion and analysis of lesbian/bisexual/gay people in organized religion. I seek an "embodied," rather than a "disembodied," objectivity, which means that I will not try to rise above and transcend the experiences of gay people but will try to engage them directly in a search for connections, differences, and complications. I do not pretend to be personally uninterested in this discussion and its outcome. The original motivation for beginning this work was my own question of why I remain within organized religion and endure the uncertainty, anxiety, and hostility that seem so frequent as to be normative — and I belong to the UCC, a reputedly liberal and pro-gay denomination! The test of objectivity for me will be to take the experiences of other gay people as seriously as my own, not to reduce or enhance the picture by avoiding or elevating those experiences that are more or less attractive, and to be responsible for finding the many, and possibly conflicting, truths about many experiences.

I have decided not to focus on the already published autobiographical books and anthologies by gay people because they are familiar, well-known, and widely read and also because they do not represent a cross section of experiences. They can be relied on as signposts to dig further and uncover more, but they provide neither a common base nor a critical analysis of experiences. I will instead focus on the findings from the empirical studies because (1) they have attempted to reach, measure, and describe a greater, more diverse, and more representative universe of experiences; and (2) they have used the tools of social science to begin the task of critically examining and analyzing those experiences. I join my own research to those studies to advance the work of understanding the experiences of gay people within organized religion.

The combined sources of information — thirty-six empirical studies, plus my own surveys, interviews, and screening of newsletters — provide for the observation and examination of gay people within a range of religious bodies, traditions, and organizations. These include the Roman Catholic Church; traditional Native American religion; Islam; different organizations within Judaism; various denominations within the traditional black church, such as the African Methodist Episcopal Church and Jehovah's Witnesses; the Metropolitan Community Church and other independent gay Christian organizations; the Unitarian Universalist Association; mainline Protestant denominations, such as the United Church of Christ, United Methodist Church, Presbyterian Church (U.S.A.), Southern Baptist Convention, and American Baptist Churches in the U.S.A.; the Mennonite Church and Church of the Brethren; the Religious Society of Friends; and the Church of Jesus Christ of Latter-day Saints (Mormon). The studies also provide for some insights into the United Church of Canada, the Episcopal Church, the Evangelical Lutheran Church of America, and Buddhism and Hinduism.

Chapter Three

Belonging, Switching, Leaving, and Shopping

This chapter presents and discusses empirical data about the membership and affiliation of lesbian/bisexual/gay people within organized religion. Religious affiliations are discussed under such broad categories as Protestant, Catholic, and Jewish early in the chapter and then in terms of specific religious bodies and activities within those broad categories as the chapter progresses.

Religious Upbringing and Backgrounds

In 1948 when Alfred Kinsey, Wardell Pomeroy, and Clyde Martin published their findings on sexual behavior in the human male, they admitted that they "were totally unprepared" to find the high incidence of homosexuality revealed by their research. They were surprised not only by the frequency but by its consistency and similarity throughout the United States — in large cities, small towns, or rural areas; in colleges, church schools, state universities, or private institutions; in one region or another.[1]

Of the social factors that did seem to influence the rates of reported homosexual activity, educational levels and class were significant and religious groupings (Jewish, Catholic, or Protestant) were not. But within the particular religious groups themselves, homosexual activity was reported less frequently among persons who were most observant and more frequently among those who were not. The differences were not large but lay constantly in that direction. The same pattern was found for marital and nonmarital heterosexual activity.[2]

The findings from Kinsey's subsequent study of women published in 1953 conformed to those about men with this difference: adherence to religious restraints initially delayed women more than men from engaging in masturbation, premarital sex, and homosexuality, but once they had begun such activities, women were much less affected than men by their religious backgrounds.[3]

From a time that predates the study of recognizable gay populations, Kinsey and his cohorts provided a number of findings about homosexual activity and organized religion: (1) People who had homosexual interests and acted on them were everywhere. They were not more or less likely to originate from Southern Baptist, Mormon, Unitarian, Jewish, or Catholic backgrounds. (2) Adherence to religious teachings influenced the frequency of homosexual activity as much as it influenced heterosexual activity — not a great deal. Other social factors, such as class and level of education, were more influential. (3) Although women seemed to be more influenced by organized religion, they were more likely than men to forgo restrictive teachings once they engaged in homosexual activity.

TABLE 4

Percentages of Non-gay and Gay Populations from Various Religious Backgrounds, as Found and Reported by Various Studies

	Roof & McKinney	Weinberg & Williams	Jay & Young	Weinberg, Williams & Pryor		
Background	General or Non-gay	Gay Men (N=1,057)	Lesbians & Gay Men (N=5,086)	Bisexual (N=205)	Homosexual (N=274)	Heterosexual (N=185)
Protestant	57%	53%	54%	34%	43%	45%
Catholic	28%	29%	30%	20%	25%	20%
Jewish	2%	9%	7%	24%	17%	20%
other/none	13%	10%	9%	21%	15%	15%

Sources: Wade Clark Roof and William McKinney, *American Mainline Religion: Its Changing Shape and Future* (New Brunswick, N.J.: Rutgers University Press, 1987), 16. (N is not given in the study. The respondents in Roof and McKinney's study may include lesbian, bisexual, and gay members, but I choose to use the term "non-gay" in my discussion for the sake of establishing terms that will clarify comparison. The study does not attempt to report data by sexual orientation of respondents.) Martin S. Weinberg and Colin J. Williams, *Male Homosexuals: Their Problems and Adaptations* (New York: Oxford University Press, 1974), 95, 248. Karla Jay and Allen Young, *The Gay Report: Lesbians and Gay Men Speak Out about Sexual Experiences and Lifestyles* (New York: Summit Books, 1977, 1979), 810–11. Martin S. Weinberg, Colin J. Williams, and Douglas W. Pryor, *Dual Attraction: Understanding Bisexuality* (New York: Oxford University Press, 1994), 365. I have calculated percentages from the data in the latter two books.

In the 1960s Martin Weinberg and Colin Williams were the first to identify and study homosexual populations within certain urban populations, and their findings showed that the religious upbringings and backgrounds of gay men mirrored those of the general or non-gay population (table 4). A comprehensive, nationwide study of lesbians and gay men by Karla Jay and Allen Young in the 1970s provided further evidence of similarity with the non-gay population (table 4). In both studies, the only noticeable deviation was the consistently larger percentage of Jewish respondents among lesbians and gay men.[4] Another study by Weinberg, Williams, and Douglas Pryor in San Francisco in the 1980s also found similarity among bisexuals, homosexuals, and heterosexuals, but bisexuals did report Jewish and nonmainstream religious backgrounds slightly more often and Protestant backgrounds less often than homosexuals and heterosexuals (table 4). The data from these three different studies showed that gay people do originate within the full-range of religious backgrounds without disproportionate concentration in any of them.[5]

Religious Backgrounds and Relating to Homosexuality

Weinberg and Williams also found no general relationship between religious backgrounds and the manner in which respondents related to the homosexual world. Those from conservative religious traditions were not more or less likely to have psychological problems. The ones who took their religious backgrounds very seriously did report being more depressed, unstable, worried about exposure, and socially awkward with other homosexuals than those who had dismissed or were more casual about their backgrounds. Generally, though, it was found that religiously observant homosexuals showed greater anxiety and guilt after their first homosexual experience but then went on to reinterpret their religious traditions as not being at odds with homosexuality. Only the most devout were not able to neutralize the conflict between their religious background and their sexuality.[6]

In James Sears's study of young gay people in the South, one subject recalled going to talk with a well-known Southern Baptist minister during his high school years because he was feeling extremely confused about his homosexuality and bothered by the antihomosexuality of people in the church. The minister said "that whatever he said in the room would be very different from what he preached in church. 'I have to take a different stand when I am in the pulpit but in here I'm not like that.' " The young man appreciated his honesty and the nonjudgmental advice he offered: "When I told him that I didn't believe in all of that [anti-gay stuff], he wasn't offended. He was just there for me. He said, 'Get close to the Lord, find you a good lover, and be happy.' " This young man has since become interested in Eastern religions but bears no hard feelings toward his Southern Baptist parents and former friends. "Some people can't help the way they feel. When I hear some redneck calling somebody 'faggot,' it doesn't provoke feelings of anger inside me.

I feel pity. This boy is only mimicking what he has been taught as the Gospel Truth."[7]

Others have not been as successful in separating themselves from the anti-gay influence of their religious upbringings. A Jehovah's Witness in Sears's study spoke about his church's reaction to his effeminate behavior: "By the time I was nine or ten I started to get a lot of flak from the church. I would be going from door to door with an elder in our Congregation.... He would say, 'Why are you walking like that? Why do you talk like that? Do you have any idea how these people are looking at you? You're degrading God's name.'" His minister told him that he was "a disgrace" and he should change the "swish" in his walk and the whine in his voice. These comments, of course, were "very confusing" for this young man and caused him to feel "an intense amount of self-hatred."[8]

He developed several coping strategies. He became more active in the church by devoting hours of private time to prayer and Bible reading as well as proselytizing in the field. "If I prayed all the time and stayed active in the church, maybe somehow I could appease God in some kind of way and He wouldn't be so angry at me." He also adopted masculine mannerisms. "It was an effort, but something I did. I would make myself walk a certain way. I would make my voice sound a certain way. I would make myself sit a certain way." And as a result, his parents, ministers, and fellow church members treated him with more respect.[9]

After graduating from high school, he married a woman whom he knew he did not love, moved to another town, and joined another congregation of Jehovah's Witnesses. He soon became homosexually active and told his wife, who told the church committee. "The elders started coming down heavy on me.... I was frightened; I was drained. I was so weak emotionally and mentally. Deep down I didn't want them to excommunicate me. I felt I wouldn't have anything to live for. See, I was told from day one that without the church you're nothing; you're as good as dead." After being expelled from the church for leaving his wife, he said, "I got really heavy into drugs and alcohol and was whoring around. I couldn't hold a job because I was an alcoholic and drug addict." A period of drifting and living off others ended when he formed a relationship with another gay man. He found employment and stopped doing drugs but had not yet come to terms with the church: "My name is still on the church's record. I have written a letter to tell them that I want to be disassociated from them. I'm planning on mailing it this week. I've been putting it off for a month.... Even though I have decided to separate myself from the church, there is still a lot of religion ingrained in me."[10]

Other Responses to Religious Background

Jay and Young gathered these anecdotes to illustrate various reactions to and accommodations with religious backgrounds and upbringing:

> My religious upbringing (Catholic) squashed my sexuality. I learned that I could be a madonna or a whore, a wife and mother (in that order, of course) or a sinner. No middle ground. No allowance for variation. I hate the Catholic hierarchy—how I ever escaped I don't really know.

> I am a practicing Catholic whose sexual orientation doesn't get in the way. I worked this all out years ago, and though the Pope would have a stroke, it gets me by. I think I'm pretty well adjusted in all phases of my life. Let me be blunt: sucking a cock Saturday night and going to Communion Sunday morning doesn't seem out of line for me. Maybe I'm fooling myself, but I honestly believe that God won't mind.

> I'm Jewish, and was brought up with Judaism as a heritage and not a dogma, so it has not had a formidable effect on sexuality.

> The Jewish religion (and I've had twenty-five years of it) treats women like shit. And when you confront an Orthodox person with this second-class treatment, the men *and* women will tell you that the woman has a very honored place — in the home, under the management of a husband.

> My religion was very helpful in enabling me to accept myself as I was and to accept others with differences.... The Christianity I was raised in was one of love.

> I am very religious. I believe in the message of Jesus and am a conservative not unlike Anita Bryant except I feel Jesus' atonement was for *all,* including gays!! The influence extends to how I live my life and sex life. That is why I hardly ever trick. And feel I shouldn't, really. Jesus didn't die to give us a sex smorgasbord.[11]

In *Trikone,* the newsletter for gay and lesbian South Asians, a Hindu man and a Muslim man reported the following:

> I was a monk in the Ramakrishna order, and the monks were very supportive in my coming out process. That I cherish that association with the Ramakrishna order is nothing at all to deny.[12]

> My upbringing was culturally very Muslim but not particularly religious. Growing up, I resented Islam because of the sexism and double standards I saw in it, which are present in almost all religions like Christianity. Recently, I've come to realize that a lot of

> the bad parts are really other people's interpretations. Islam has a bad reputation especially in the West. I now culturally identify myself much more as Muslim and have become proud of my heritage. I have found a lot of good secular values in Islam.[13]

These expressions of homosexuals' need to counter, reinterpret, credit, dismiss, or adhere to the teachings and practice of their religious backgrounds lead to the following discussion about the continuing observance of those traditions.

Observing Religious Backgrounds

Religious observance can be discussed in terms of attendance at religious services and in terms of religiosity or devotion to formal religion.

Attendance

In their 1970 study, Alan Bell and Martin Weinberg compared the attendance and religiosity of homosexuals and heterosexuals in San Francisco. They found that a greater percentage of homosexual than heterosexual respondents (69 percent and 55 percent, respectively) had not attended formal religious functions in the three months prior to the study. Higher rates of nonattendance for homosexuals than for heterosexuals were reported among women (74 percent, homosexual; 55 percent, heterosexual), men (67 percent; 56 percent), blacks (59 percent; 43 percent), and whites (71 percent; 59 percent).[14]

Twenty years later, Edward Laumann, John Gagnon, Robert Michael, and Stuart Michaels's study of sexual practices in the United States also found that homosexual identity and activity were related to nonattendance. Those in the adult population who attended religious services least frequently were more likely to identify as homosexual or bisexual (2.2 percent, women; 4.7 percent, men) than those who attended most frequently (0.3 percent, women; 1.5 percent, men).[15]

Other studies have found that demographic and social factors were associated with nonattendance among gay people. According to Bell and Weinberg's study, whites were nonattenders more often than blacks (71 percent and 59 percent, respectively) and women more often than men (74 percent and 67 percent, respectively). Of all racial and gender subgroupings, white homosexual women reported not attending with the greatest frequency (75 percent).[16] Jerrold Greenberg's study of college-age gay men reported the highest rate of nonattendance (79 percent).[17] Kent Franks, Donald Templer, Gordon Cappelletty, and Inge Kauffman's study of gay men with and without AIDS found that those without AIDS were more often nonattenders than gay men with AIDS (63 percent, non-AIDS; 47 percent, AIDS).[18]

Religiosity

In their 1970 study in San Francisco, Bell and Weinberg found that homosexual respondents claimed to be "not at all religious" more frequently than heterosexuals (48 percent and 36 percent, respectively). Higher rates for homosexuals held among women (49 percent, homosexual; 26 percent, heterosexual), men (48 percent; 41 percent), blacks (29 percent; 16 percent), and whites (52 percent; 41 percent).

In the study conducted by Weinberg, Williams, and Pryor in San Francisco in the 1980s, the findings about religiosity showed greater similarity among gay and non-gay respondents than did the 1970 findings by Bell and Weinberg.[19] For example, in the later study, 78 percent of heterosexual and homosexual respondents and 79 percent of bisexual respondents reported being "not at all or a little religious." Nearly identical percentages across these groups held also for reports of moderate, strong, and very strong religiosity.[20] The apparent shift to greater similarity may have been due to social changes or to the selection of the heterosexual sample from sexuality organizations rather than from the general population as in the earlier study. Gary Remafedi, Michael Resnick, Robert Blum, and Linda Harris's findings about adolescents in the late 1980s in Minnesota, however, did conform more to the earlier study—but for males, not females. These researchers found that 59 percent of homosexual boys and 23 percent of bisexual boys, compared to 17 percent of heterosexual boys, considered themselves to be "not at all religious."[21]

The AIDS epidemic may also have affected the degree of religiosity among gay men. Franks, Templer, Cappelletty, and Kauffman's study of gay men during the AIDS epidemic in San Francisco shows significant differences with gay men in Weinberg, Williams, and Pryor's study before AIDS in San Francisco. For example, 78 percent of pre-epidemic respondents, compared to 18 percent of postepidemic respondents reported little or no religiosity; and 12 percent of pre-epidemic compared to 36 percent of post-epidemic respondents, reported strong religiosity. Although religiosity appears to have increased after the epidemic, Franks and his cohorts did not find much greater religiosity among those with or without AIDS (strongly religious: 31 percent, non-AIDS; 39 percent, AIDS).[22]

Summary

The percentages of gay and non-gay people from each religious background are similar, but over time gay people become less observant of those backgrounds than the non-gay population. Social changes, such as increased acceptance of gay people and the AIDS epidemic in some geographical areas, may have influenced and increased gay people's degree of observance. A comparison of religious backgrounds with current religious affiliations may offer important insights into their experiences within organized religion.

Current Religious Affiliations

The shift of gay people away from their religious backgrounds suggested by the above findings is confirmed when their backgrounds are compared with their current affiliations (see table 5). Jay and Young's study reported significant movement away from the mainstream faiths and toward other, personal, and no religious affiliation, and "none" (47 percent) replaced "Protestant" (54 percent) as the most popular religious affiliation.[23]

TABLE 5
Comparison of Religious Upbringing with Current Religious Affiliations of Lesbians and Gay Men

Religion	Upbringing (N=5086)	Current (N=4625)
Protestant	54%	21%
Catholic	30%	12%
Jewish	7%	3%
other	4%	17%
none	5%	47%

Source: Karla Jay and Allen Young, *The Gay Report: Lesbians and Gay Men Speak Out about Sexual Experiences and Lifestyles* (New York: Summit Books, 1979). I have calculated percentages from the data in this book.

From her interviews with and survey of gay people in California, Alissa Nelyn Steelman identified five categories of responses to organized Christianity that substantiate and elaborate on the pattern found by Jay and Young. The categories were: (1) "Status Quo," those who did not want to leave or be singled out in their congregations or who said their congregations accepted their open homosexuality; (2) "Inner Denominational," those who formed support groups within their religious bodies to counter and change exclusive policies and practices; (3) "Extra Denominational," those who left or were asked to leave mainline churches and then joined or formed gay churches; (4) "Spiritually Inclined," those who left or never joined the church because of negative experiences but who participated in personal or group approaches to non-Christian spirituality; and (5) "Non Spiritual or Religious," those who had had too many anti-gay experiences and/or felt too much animosity toward the church to want any religious/spiritual affiliation or to change what was seen as a hopelessly oppressive institution.[24]

Rates of departure from various religious backgrounds were also found to be associated with such demographic and social factors as gender, race, and AIDS. Jay and Young, for example, found consistently and significantly higher rates of departure for lesbians than for gay men (81 percent, women; 61 percent, men).[25] These gender-related findings were the opposite of what has been found in the non-gay population.[26] Whereas a greater percentage of lesbians than gay men ended up as nonaffiliated (51 percent, lesbians; 46 percent, gay men), in the non-gay population men are more often nonaffiliated than women (5 percent, women; 10 percent, men).[27] And whereas a greater percentage of lesbians than gay men have become affiliated with alternative and personal forms of religion (26 percent, lesbian; 12 percent, gay men), the gender ratio within the non-gay population for "other" religions has a slight male bias.[28]

Michael Dickens's study of gay and bisexual men of African descent also documented a major dropping away from the historically black Protestant denominations, such as Baptist, African Methodist Episcopal, and Pentecostal (55 percent, past; 12 percent, current), and an overwhelming swing to current nonaffiliation (52 percent). The Metropolitan Community Church (MCC) was the most frequently reported current affiliation (16 percent). Twelve percent of the respondents had also shifted to such traditionally white liberal Protestant denominations as Episcopalian, Presbyterian, and the Religious Society of Friends.[29]

In his study of the Native American *berdache,* Walter Williams found a growing number of gay Indians forgoing their Christianized upbringings and turning to traditional Native spirituality. This shift was aided by two factors in the 1970s: (1) a return to Native traditions by Indians in general, which was inspired by the activism of the American Indian Movement (AIM); and (2) the migration of young gay Indians to urban centers and their exposure to the gay liberation movement. As Ronnie Loud Hawk related to Williams, "In the last few years, respect for *winkte* [or *berdache*] has increased, more than it had been, as more people return to respect for the traditions. Some mixed-blood Indians condemn 'queers,' but the traditional people stick up for them." Michael One Feather added:

> My grandparents accept my being gay, and we have a really good relationship. My grandmother got over her Christian prejudices, and like others has returned more to the traditional Indian way of looking at it. She told me that one male out of every generation in our family is a *winkte* and she had to accept it. She explained that in the old days people let them live and did not ridicule or bother them. There was the Indian belief that if anyone treated them badly then something bad would happen to them.... It helps me to know of the *winkte* tradition.

The Indian and gay movements have given those who identify as gay or lesbian the confidence to participate visibly within the Native community. Randy Burns, one of the founders of Gay American Indians (GAI) in San Francisco, says, "In the Indian community, we are trying to realign ourselves with the trampled traditions of our people.... Sometimes we are booed or jeered, but it doesn't last long." Now he says that the elders even come to them "asking us to be part of their ceremony."[30]

Of the various subgroups within the gay population, only among gay men with AIDS was a noticeable return to or staying with, rather than departure from, religious backgrounds observed, especially in the form of a return to Catholicism (29 percent, AIDS; 14 percent, non-AIDS) and a move away from "other" affiliations (22 percent, AIDS; 44 percent, non-AIDS). Other data also showed that two-thirds of gay men with AIDS compared to one-third of gay men without AIDS reported that their current religion is the same as that of their childhood (62 percent, AIDS; 31 percent, non-AIDS); conversely, two-thirds of gay men without AIDS compared to one-third of gay men with AIDS reported adhering to a belief system not associated with organized religion (37 percent, AIDS; 64 percent, non-AIDS).[31]

Perhaps the most compelling evidence of gay people's shifting away their religious backgrounds is the consistency with which various studies have reported their current religious affiliations. Differing noticeably from their religious backgrounds, the current religious affiliations of gay people in various geographical areas at various times over twenty years have remained consistently low with regard to Protestantism and Catholicism, high with regard to Judaism, and very high with regard to "other" and "no" affiliation (see table 6).

This dramatic shift from religious backgrounds by gay people is made even more apparent when their current religious affiliations are compared with those of the non-gay population. National surveys of the gay and non-gay populations in 1990 showed that in addition to reporting Protestant (28 percent, gay; 60 percent, non-gay) and Catholic (17 percent, gay; 26 percent, non-gay) affiliations less often, gay people more often than the non-gay population reported Jewish affiliation (9 percent,

TABLE 6

Comparison of Current Religious Affiliations of Gay Samples from Five Studies

Current Affiliation	Bell & Weinberg [San Francisco, 1970] Gay (N=977)	Greenberg [National, 1973] Gay Men (N=86)	Jay & Young [National, 1977] Gay (N=4,625)	Franks et al. [San Francisco, 1990] Gay Men (N=115)	Partners [National, 1990] Gay (N=1,749)	Kosmin & Lachman [National, 1990] Non-gay (N=113,723)
Protestant	28%	27%	28%	31%	28%	60%
Catholic	14%	17%	17%	21%	17%	26%
Jewish	2%	5%	9%	6%	9%	2%
other/none	56%	51%	46%	42%	46%	12%

Sources: Alan P. Bell and Martin S. Weinberg, *Homosexualities: A Study of Diversity among Men and Women* (New York: Simon and Schuster, 1978), 280; Jerrold Greenberg, "A Study of Male Homosexuals (Predominantly College Students)," *Journal of the American College Health Association* 22 (1973): 58; Karla Jay and Allen Young, *The Gay Report: Lesbians and Gay Men Speak Out about Sexual Experiences and Lifestyles* (New York: Summit Books, 1979), 810–11; Kent Franks et al., "Exploration of Death Anxiety as a Function of Religious Variables in Gay Men with and without AIDS," *Omega: Journal of Death and Dying* 22 (1990–91): 46; Partners Task Force for Gay and Lesbian Couples, *Partners' National Survey of Lesbian and Gay Couples,* special issue of *Partners: Newsletter for Gay and Lesbian Couples,* May/June 1990, 3; Barry A. Kosmin and Seymour P. Lachman, *One Nation under God: Religion in American Society* (New York: Harmony Books, 1993), 15–17. Percentages calculated from data in above books.

gay; 2 percent, non-gay) and nonaffiliation or affiliation with alternatives to the dominant faith traditions (46 percent, gay; 12 percent, non-gay) (see table 6). Non-gay people would appear to have adhered to their religious background much more often than gay people.

Switching

But movement away from and among various religious backgrounds has been on the rise among the non-gay population, also. Since the 1960s, "switching" from one religious body to another has become more frequent among Americans. Jews and African-American Protestants, followed closely by Catholics, are the least likely to switch. Among the other groups, conservative Protestants are least likely to switch, followed, in order, by moderate Protestants, liberal Protestants, people with no religious preference, Unitarians, and evangelicals/fundamentalists. Liberal denominations, such as the Unitarian Universalist Association and the United Church of Christ, often benefit from switching because they are seen as attractive alternatives, especially by members from moderate and conservative denominations. Conservative denominations have been able to hold their own and attract some members out of moderate denominations. Moderate Protestant denominations, on the other hand, such as the United Methodist Church, Evangelical Lutheran Church of America, and Presbyterian Church (U.S.A.), have lost disproportionately from switching because the general movement has been in the conservative and liberal directions.[32]

Switching In and Out—UCC and UMC

Information from my survey of gay people within the United Church of Christ (UCC) and the United Methodist Church (UMC) revealed switching patterns that both conform to and deviate from those of the non-gay population.

Switching In—UCC

The UCC respondents in my survey have switched into the denomination at a rate considerably higher than that of non-gay people (53 percent, gay; 39 percent, non-gay). Nearly one-half of gay switchers (45 percent) reported having done so because of the UCC's national record of support for gay people, and over one-third (38 percent) switched in because a local UCC church welcomed them as gay persons. Most switched from mainline moderate Protestant denominations — Methodist, Presbyterian, Baptist, Lutheran—and from Catholicism.

One man who joined the UCC as an adult had this to say when I interviewed him: "I was raised in the Evangelical Covenant Church. It was a more conservative denomination than the UCC. I grew up and went to church and Sunday school and made my confirmation—the whole shebang. Then when I went to college I came out relatively quickly, met my partner relatively quickly, and left the church behind relatively quickly. For the first twelve years that my partner and I lived together the church was not an issue or an item at all." I asked when and how it became an issue. "In 1985 I started attending a congregation in Evanston. I can't even remember how I got there. I went on Easter just as lots of people get the impulse to go to church on Easter, although I remember saying that I felt that I would go for at least two weeks after Easter. I just stayed and I liked it. It was a very affirming place, and the minister was UCC. It was a nondenominational congregation attached to the chapel at Northwestern University." I asked: "Do you see yourself as having made the right decision, that the UCC was the right denomination for you?" He replied: "I knew that the General Synod[33] had said that it was OK to ordain gays and lesbians. So I thought, 'OK, that's good.' It wasn't as if I tried all the Methodist and Episcopal churches and did a lot of comparison. It was more that my gut feeling was that no matter what happened on the local level, you could always fall back on the people at the top, even if they don't have the power to tell the local churches what to do."

John Lardin, another UCC member I interviewed, was attracted to a local UCC congregation because it had welcomed him as a gay man. "Actually two friends of mine, one sang in the choir and the other was the organist, and for about three years they kept saying, 'You really ought to come to church sometime.' They knew I had been really active in the Catholic Church when I was growing up and that I had been church shopping for a number of years, bouncing around here and there, just trying different places out, never really comfortable anywhere. So they finally convinced me after about three years of saying, 'Try us.' I didn't know much about Protestant churches and didn't know anything about the UCC. So I said, 'Fine,' and I got hooked immediately." I asked what hooked him. "With that particular congregation it was the Friendship Time, the time we have after church, a refreshment and social hour kind of thing. I never have been and I won't be closeted and closed about my sexual orientation to people; and some folks knew before I ever got there that I was coming and they knew my story. It was almost as if people made a special effort to welcome me and made me feel welcome so that I'd want to come back. I finally became a member about six months afterward and ended up really getting myself into it. Within a year of being there I ended up being chair of two different committees and then was elected to the church council. I ended up jumping in with both feet when it came to the UCC and didn't have any apprehension about doing that or didn't question whether I should or not."

Switching Out—UCC

Nearly one-quarter (22 percent) of the UCC respondents in my survey also reported having left and later returned to the denomination; and for over half of them (53 percent), this temporary departure was related to their sexual orientation.

I also asked respondents which denomination they would belong to if they were not now a member of the UCC, and most reported "none/unsure" (41 percent), followed by the Unitarian Universalist Association (25 percent), the MCC (11 percent), the Religious Society of Friends (Quaker) (11 percent), the Episcopal Church (8 percent), and other (4 percent). Several of the people I interviewed explained their reluctance to consider leaving the UCC. Charlotte Stacey said, "Circumstances led me to the UCC, being hired as an organist and choir director. I didn't even know what UCC was before that. I didn't even know what General Synod was. My whole life, including my whole coming out process, is a lot of coincidences and part of that has led me to be as active and known as I am in the local church and wider denomination. If for some reason something terrible happened in my church and we were kicked out — which would just never happen — I'd go to another UCC church because that's what I am. If I was suddenly asked through my company to move to some town where there wasn't a UCC church, I'd join a local church that would be a Protestant church, and it would be toward the left. I would not be joining a Southern Baptist church. There's no way I could feel comfortable in a church that's right of center. But that's the same way I would feel about being a member of certain UCC churches. I know I wouldn't join them. I mean Biblical Witness [a fundamentalist interest group in the UCC] is not my bag, and if that was the kind of UCC church that was in my town and they offered me fifty thousand dollars to be an organist and choir director, I wouldn't take it."

Countering the reluctance to leave, however, was the one-sixth of UCC respondents (13 percent) who said they currently had a religious affiliation outside of the denomination that was more important to them. This percentage was greater than that found in studies of non-gay church attenders who have outside affiliations (8 percent).[34] Most of outside gay affiliation was reported as occurring in interfaith organizations (24 percent), the MCC (21 percent), the Unitarian Universalist Association (21 percent), the Episcopal Church (9 percent), or in Buddhist, Catholic, or Quaker activities (6 percent each).

Mark Ehrke grew up in a small town in Minnesota where his family belonged to a church from the more conservative, evangelical side of the UCC tradition. After moving to Minneapolis and becoming active in a liberal UCC church, he found himself drifting away and looking for excuses to leave. "I think initially why I thought I left was that I really didn't feel welcome as a gay person. But once I had spent some time away, it became a bigger thing. I remember vividly one of my first experiences with Quakers after getting involved with the Gay Quaker group here in the Twin Cities. It was a yearly meeting, a regional gathering of Quakers in this area. It was held at a camp. We were sitting around the campfire talking; and I remember for the first time in my life saying, 'I'm not sure I'm Christian.' My church, my upbringing, never gave me the permission or space to say that or to ask that question. And being able to say that and the response that it got were very healing. A lot of people were saying, 'Well, I'm not sure if I am either,' and other people were saying, 'I am, but there's lots of room in the Quakers for people who aren't,' and other people said, 'I'm not, and that's fine.' That's one of the things I have appreciated about Quakers; it's about finding your own truth. And as liberal as the UCC is, the emphasis is really less on finding your *own* truth; in the Friends there's a lot of room for exploring where exactly it is that you are. I have found from my experience with religious groups that I feel sort of hypocritical being part of any sort of Christian church. And this is a conversation I have had with many people."

Responses from gay people in the UCC confirmed and magnified a national pattern of switching toward more liberal denominations. Most of those who had switched in came from conservative and moderate anti-gay denominations and had sought out the more liberal, pro-gay record and practices of the UCC. Respondents who were considering switching out of the UCC would seek an even more accepting, liberal setting; and those who currently participated in non-UCC religious activities did so for the most part in such settings.

Switching In—UMC

Membership and joining patterns for UMC gay respondents were different both from non-gay UMC members and from gay UCC respondents. For example, UMC respondents were somewhat less likely than the UMC non-gay membership (32 percent, gay; 37 percent, general) and much less likely than their UCC counterparts (32 percent, UMC; 53 percent, UCC) to have switched in from another denomination.

Unlike gay UCC switchers, UMC respondents, of course, did not report a pro-gay denominational policy as a reason for switching in; and a welcoming, pro-gay local church was reported less often as a reason as well (26 percent, UMC; 38 percent, UCC).

UMC respondents who switched in came for the most part from other moderate Protestant denominations—Presbyterian, Baptist, and Lutheran—and from Catholicism.

When I interviewed Katie Sanetra, she was attending a small urban United Methodist church in the Capitol Hill district of Seattle. She described it as "a radical church" because it officially welcomed lesbians and gay men; it had ongoing programs to feed and clothe street people; and many of its members were active in social issues in the larger community. She said the membership was about two-thirds women, one-half lesbian and gay, mostly middle-class, and about one-quarter lower-class.

She had recently moved to the city. "What I did was move from Everett down to Seattle where I can walk to the church that I've been attending for the last four or five years. Before that, for four years, I drove forty miles round-trip to go to this church." I asked if her move to Seattle had anything to do with the church. She responded: "Yes. It makes it closer for me to be with the community here. It had to do with that and also the fact—in spite of being in what you might call a high-crime area—I feel safer down here, because there's a large gay and lesbian population here."

Katie was not raised as Methodist. "My grandparents were Mormons, so Mormonism was sort of a main thread through my upbringing. My mother didn't like Mormonism, so I went to a Mennonite Bible school, and I was baptized First Christian. But then my mother quit that church because the preacher had said that only First Christians could go to heaven and she didn't believe that. Then during high school I mostly went to a Congregational church. Through it all for some reason I always felt like God is a very present thing in my life. Jesus, too."

"How did you find the Capitol Hill Church?" I asked. She said: "It happened when I was going to school down here in Seattle. One of the women that I met in school wanted to be a Lutheran minister. I hadn't been to church for a very long time, and she started me thinking about different things, because we would often talk about gays and lesbians. She would take me to her church, which I found very stifling. It was horrible. They just sort of sat there and got up and down, and I didn't feel there was any humanity in it. It was a repressive church. The only lesbian-positive one that I knew about was the Metropolitan Community Church, so I started going to MCC in Seattle. At that time they had their services in the Capitol Hill Methodist Church building. Capitol Hill had rented it to them for the first ten years or more of their life. I met two women there, and then when the MCC got another minister and he seemed to be telling us the same thing that the mainline church does and nothing new—nothing that I hadn't ever heard before—I said I wanted something else. So I quit going there and started going to the Capitol Hill UMC church. I've been there since."

Katie had never formally joined the church because she does not believe in the exclusive divinity of Jesus Christ, a requirement for membership. But she was active, supported, and participated in the life of the church, including leading parts of the worship services. She said she appreciated the strong female presence in the church, studied feminist theology, and would like to have had the church be more open to exploring different avenues rather than simply a Bible/Christ approach. "When we have our passing of the peace, it's sort of pandemonium because everybody is up hugging and saying, 'Hi,' and new people coming in find it somewhat off-putting if they can't relate to the intimacy expressed, and I think that's a strong point and a problem. The church is mostly feminine, and I think that has to do with why we have this high level of intimacy. I think a lot of men, mainly straight men, feel threatened by this level of intimacy, because they just can't sit there and shake a hand; well, they can, but to see all these women going around hugging each other and some of the men too, they find it very threatening."

She said that although some people were uncomfortable "with our odd little flavor," the oddness was what attracted her. Without it she said she would have to leave. When I asked why she even wanted to attend a Christian church, she said, "I see church as a very supportive community. I go to church because—and it's only this specific church—of the community. If they changed the community to where I cannot speak or feel that I cannot speak or feel that I am not listened to, then I would not go any longer. I would have to find something else."

Switching Out—UMC

When asked which denomination they would join if they were to leave the UMC, most respondents said "none/unsure" (35 percent), followed by the UCC and Episcopal Church (19 percent each), the MCC (15 percent), and the Unitarian Universalist Association (12 percent).

Randy Miller had this to say about his reluctance to disaffiliate from the UMC: "At one point I saw my vocational role as being in the church. Then, having come out and struggled through the General Conference,[35] the church became far less important emotionally. The church is still fairly important, but in a different way. I see it as the arena where you debate, discuss, argue, and do battle, rather than a base of emotional support." After the General Conference voted to maintain its negative gay policy, Randy withdrew from his national staff position and other involvements. I asked if distancing himself for awhile from the church was necessary to get the strength to come back to it. He said: "I think so. Even though I wasn't driven out in the way that many closeted gay people are driven out, I felt like I was exiled." I asked if he ever thought of becoming a non-Methodist. "No, I don't. I tried in my period of exile. I went to MCC mostly for social connections, but I'm too staunchly United Methodist. It wasn't the liturgy and the hymns. I'm pretty flexible about that. But I want some United Methodist connection around me. I owe this sort of debt to my local church. I think they did a lot of parenting of me when I was in junior high and high school, and in return I did a lot of growing up in the church and working in the church. So, it's in my blood. I just don't know where I would go. Episcopalians are too different for me. It's hard to explain, but it's for a lot of reasons that I feel connected to the tradition of liturgy and even to the struggle of the United Methodists."

One-quarter (26 percent) of the UMC respondents, however, did report having current religious involvements outside of the denomination that were more important to them than the UMC. Most of these were involved with the MCC (31 percent), the Episcopal Church (19 percent), and interfaith, Unitarian, or UCC activities (8 percent each). This pattern of outside involvement differed from that of non-gay UMC members, of whom only 10 percent participated regularly in outside religious activities; and the most frequently reported were in Presbyterian, Baptist, Roman Catholic, Assemblies of God, and other Protestant churches.[36]

The UMC respondents were also more likely than their UCC counterparts to have another religious affiliation that was more important than their own denomination (26 percent, UMC; 16 percent, UCC); and they were less unsure about leaving (35 percent, UMC; 40 percent, UCC). The UCC respondents with outside affiliations were drawn to the theological latitude of interfaith organizations, while UMC respondents were primarily attracted to the theologically conservative, pro-gay MCC. Also, a slightly greater percentage of UMC respondents than UCC respondents at one time temporarily left their denomination (27 percent, UMC; 22 percent, UCC). Compared to the percentage of the non-gay Protestant population that had ever left and returned to their denominations (22 percent),[37] that of UCC gay respondents (22 percent) was the same, while that of UMC gay respondents was somewhat higher (27 percent). The reason for leaving was more frequently related to sexual orientation for UMC than for UCC respondents (77 percent, UMC; 53 percent, UCC).

Influences on Switching

Gay Policies

Because of the anti-gay UMC policy and the pro-gay UCC policy, some differences in responses from the two sets of respondents were expected. For example, the greater percentage of UCC respondents switching in suggests that gay people are more likely to be attracted to a denomination that welcomes them; and the higher percentage of UMC respondents reporting ever having left, and having done so because of their sexual orientation, suggests that gay people are more likely to leave a denomination that does not welcome them.

The greater shifting away from less friendly, more rejecting religious settings was also documented by Jay and Young among the full range of religious bodies. For example, among Protestant denominations the rates of departure of gay people increased from those that are liberal to those that are moderate and conservative (48 percent, 63 percent, 77 percent, respectively). In Judaism, rates of departure were higher in the Orthodox than non-Orthodox movements (82 percent and 61 percent, respectively). The only religious bodies to show gains were the Unitarian Universalist Association and the Religious Society of Friends (63 percent and 29 percent, respectively); and a remarkable shift to Buddhism, alternative religions, personal spirituality, agnosticism, and atheism was evident (well over 100 percent). Religious bodies that are theologically and socially conservative (and most often anti-gay) were not less likely to be among the ones in which gay people are born and raised, but they were certainly more likely to lose them or drive them out.[38]

In addition to being influenced by the gay policies of religious bodies, the switching patterns of gay people were associated with these demographic variables—sexual identity, gender, and age.

Sexual Identity

Among UMC and UCC respondents, those who identified as bisexual were less likely to have switched into the denominations than respondents who identified as lesbian or gay (8 percent vs. 34 percent, UMC; 45 percent vs. 53 percent, UCC). Bisexuals appeared to be a more stable, less mobile population within these religious bodies. Because bisexuals have received less attention than lesbians and gay men in research generally, there are insufficient resources for comparing and discussing these findings in more detail. I shall, however, continue to introduce the findings from my survey about the bisexual respondents. I would only suggest here that the lesser frequency of switching by bisexuals may be related to the more recent development of a bisexual movement within the gay community, that is, a movement that would encourage their more visible participation within society's institutions.[39]

Gender

Jay and Young's study showed that among the few religious bodies in which the membership of gay people has grown, the rate for women was less than for men (for example, Religious Society of Friends, 18 percent for lesbians and 38 percent for gay men) or represented a small loss (e.g., Unitarian Universalist, –7 percent for lesbians and +100 percent for gay men). Lesbians' gains were noticeable and their rates greater than gay men only as regards alternative and personal religions.[40]

Women were more likely than men to switch to alternative and personal religious practices rather than to other mainstream religious bodies, but even among mainstream bodies women were more often switchers than were men. For example, in my survey a greater percentage of female than male respondents had switched into the UMC and UCC (53 percent, women; 39 percent, men). Women more often than men had also temporarily left the denominations at one time or another (28 percent, women; 21 percent, men). The exception to the heightened switching patterns of women was the greater frequency with which the male respondents reported maintaining along with their UMC or UCC affiliation an outside affiliation that was more important to them (15 percent, women; 23 percent, men). Among the non-gay population also, men reported switching their religious affiliations less often than women (never switched: 70 percent, women; 73 percent, men).[41]

Age

Research on organized religion in America has found that age, in addition to gender, is a major predictor of switching patterns. Within the non-gay population, 64 percent of those switching into liberal Protestant denominations, such as the UCC, are over forty-five years of age, while 50 percent of those switching into moderate Protestant denominations, such as the UMC, are of that age.[42] Gay switching patterns, however, differed from those non-gay norms. The greatest percentage of those switching into both denominations in my survey were in their thirties. Also, when compared with their respective non-gay denominational memberships, the UMC and UCC samples in my survey showed a gay membership that is more evenly distributed among the various age groups, not weighted to the over-fifty group, and concentrated in the thirty-to-forty-year-old group.[43]

Outcome of Switching among Non-gay and Gay Populations

The reported switching patterns of gay people mirror only vaguely those of the non-gay population. Although there is a general drift away from established religious bodies, gay people report switching from them much more often than non-gays (4 percent, non-gay; 65 percent, gay), and this switching has not resulted in the kinds of small gains that some liberal or conservative Protestant denominations have reported as regards non-gays. Non-gay people have also shifted at a much higher rate to nonaffiliation (156 percent, non-gay; 614 percent, gay).

When specific Protestant denominations and other religious bodies are rank-ordered and compared by the number of non-gay and gay adherents, gay people show less affiliation with the mainline Baptist, Methodist, Lutheran, and Presbyterian denominations and greater affiliation with the more socially liberal, and somewhat more gay-positive, Episcopal Church; with various forms of alternative and Eastern religions; and with the gay-oriented MCC (see table 7). As Michael Dickens found in his study of gay and bisexual men of African descent, an "overwhelming majority" were currently not active in any organized religion or were members of the MCC. He concluded that "these men have either completely turned away from the church out of lack of acceptance, or have joined a church which ministers directly to them as gay or bisexual men."[44] Leaving organized religion has proven to be the best option for many gay people.

TABLE 7
Rank Order of Current Religious Affiliation by Number of Non-gay and Gay People

non-gay (N=113,723)	gay (N=4,625)
Catholic	Catholic
Baptist	Episcopal
Methodist	other
Lutheran	Jewish
Presbyterian	MCC
Jewish	Eastern
Pentecostal	Baptist
Episcopal	Methodist
Mormon	Lutheran
other	Goddess

Sources: Barry A. Kosmin and Seymour P. Lachman, *One Nation under God: Religion in Contemporary American Society* (New York: Harmony, 1993); Karla Jay and Allen Young, *The Gay Report: Lesbians and Gay Men Speak Out about Sexual Experiences and Lifestyles* (New York: Summit Books, 1979).

Leaving Established Religious Bodies

When the pastor of her local church announced support for the antigay policies of the Presbyterian Church (U.S.A.), Tracy Archibald felt compelled to respond: "I can no longer remain a member of this church in good conscience. If I maintain my own privacy (which I have), then I am 'acceptable' and allowed to be a part of the church family; if I state honestly who I am — a gay woman, a gay Christian — then I apparently am part of a movement which you find 'outrageous' and 'unacceptable.' "[45] Jan Stout, a psychiatrist who counsels lesbian and gay Mormons, echoed and captured the situation succinctly: "To remain active, loyal, guilt-free, and accepted in the Mormon Church, homosexuals must do two things — remain celibate and abstain from engaging in eroticism with a member of one's own sex. This is *the* moral choice with which they are faced." From twenty-four years of clinical experience, Stout observed that because of the impossibility of this dilemma imposed on them by the church, "the majority of Mormon homosexuals eventually drift away from their faith, live tenuously in the closet, or react with angry disillusionment."[46] As Christopher Alexander also found in his study of suicide among gay Mormons, some find their way out of the pain of their religious upbringing and into a life of independence and wholeness with differing degrees of success: "Some of the respondents who are still alive continue to struggle with fleeting thoughts of suicide. Others have overcome their impulses and are living well-adjusted lives. One person wrote: 'I am honest, hardworking, loving, happy, and gay. My family loves me. I am living life for me. I have never thought of suicide since that time. I have also never been back to church.' "[47]

Jean Burgess described coming to terms with her sexuality and leaving the Mormon church as a process that enabled her to grow spiritually rather than to be defeated and discarded. She did not become aware of her homosexual feelings until she was thirty years old. At the time she was the mother of four children and the wife of a Mormon bishop. Before this time she was a dedicated church member; her life revolved around church activities; and she supported her husband's work. After meeting another Mormon woman who was struggling with her own homosexuality, she said she "embarked on a struggle of my own which was intense enough to cause me eight consecutive sleepless days and nights as I began confronting feelings hidden for many long years." She met with a counselor at Latter-Day Saints Social Services and "felt strongly impressed to go off completely alone to read the Book of Mormon from cover to cover and to think and pray." Her husband supported her decision to spend a weekend alone to reflect on her faith. A journal entry about the weekend reads:

> I wasn't sure what would be the result but felt that it would prove helpful in facing some of the decisions that are mine. It did. I read the Book of Mormon from start to finish in just under two days.... I learned a lot from it and had some very meaningful prayers, the most meaningful of which was the prayers I said before I ever started reading. I poured my heart out to my Heavenly Father. I expressed a great sadness to him for all of the pain that I have caused others (most particularly [my husband]) by not being true to my feelings, even though I was not aware of it at the time.
>
> I also told him my feelings about my sexuality and about the church; that right now I am feeling very homosexual and that it is hard for me to conceive of being any other way. I told him that I felt that I would need to accept and be at peace with my homosexuality.... I went on to pray to him that if his will for me included me not expressing my homosexual feelings and changing my sexual orientation, I was willing to do that as well. I completely trusted him to give me the answers I was seeking.

The answers that she received were not the ones she expected. She left the weekend "with a completely different understanding of the scriptures and knew that the church would never again meet my needs in the way it had in the past." She also knew "that my Heavenly Father loved me as I was and not only wanted me to accept my sexuality as part of his creation but to rejoice in it as well."[48]

Afterward, she requested that her name be removed from church records. Because she had not yet been sexually involved with another woman, there were no grounds for excommunication, but she said that "for integrity's sake I felt I had to formalize my separation from the church before acting on my sexuality." Although there have been times when she has been sad about having left the church and her marriage, she felt that "because I arrived at my decision through what I believe was a spiritual process, I have never had the need to question the 'rightness' of the choices I have made concerning my sexuality." She noted that "ironically, as my self-awareness concerning my sexuality increased so did my spiritual awareness." At the end of her story, Jean was working as a social worker and living with the woman whose problems had originally prompted her own process of exploration. She was also sharing joint custody of her children with her former husband, who had remarried.[49]

Although gay people have left their respective religious bodies in vast numbers, many have done so only after serious consideration, much patience, and regret. After the UMC's 1992 General Conference, Bob Jenkins expressed in a letter to his local church why staying for him was no longer acceptable. Twenty years earlier, when the UMC first took its stand against homosexuality, he had "felt as though I had been cut to the heart by the very church which I loved and served." He decided to stay in the denomination because it had a strong record on so many other social justice issues, and he thought that justice for lesbians and gay men would become one of those issues: "Surely one day I would be accepted fully and unconditionally by my own religious denomination. Unfortunately, that day has not come, and I can no longer wait." By proclaiming once again in 1992 that "homosexuality is incompatible with Christian teaching," the UMC had deflated his willingness to remain in it. He said he had "grown weary of being criticized for something that is part of my divinely created being," and, after fifty-eight years as a devoted Methodist, he would no longer commit to an institution that "relegates me to second-class citizenry." He begged the members of his local church to remember that others, "who could likely be your mothers and fathers, your brothers and sisters, your children and grandchildren, your friends and associates," live under this kind of oppression, but "normally, they just fade out of the life of the church without ever expressing their deep loss at not being fully accepted."[50]

Creating Independent, Alternative Religious Bodies

The Variety of Alternative Religious Bodies

After his travels throughout the United States to interview gay people from all walks of life, Neil Miller concluded that "in view of the hostility of most mainstream religious institutions toward homosexuality, it is not surprising that large numbers of gays and lesbians have ventured into the spiritual wilderness to establish their own churches and synagogues, even their own denominations." He observed further that "most often, these have been along traditional lines."[51] Lesbians and gay men have often replicated the religious bodies they have left, rather than creating new forms of religious expression.

In his study of an MCC congregation in Denver, Paul Bauer found that many members had been asked to leave mainstream churches because of their homosexuality or had left on their own after listening silently to repeated condemnations of homosexuality. The MCC countered that rejection by offering a supportive community and a conservative theology. This urban gay congregation undid Christian prescriptions against homosexuals by appropriating and emphasizing a positive message for gay people from other parts of the Christian tradition and Bible. Bauer writes: "The work and love of Jesus Christ in dealing with all types of people is the foundation for their own repentance and acceptance. Through accepting Jesus Christ, each MCC member's efforts to solve his problems become part of a solution to a community problem." Members felt both accepted by God and supported by their fellow worshipers. They believed that Jesus would listen to the requests of the gay community, just as he listens to all of humanity.[52]

Scott Thumma also found that rejection by a religious tradition and then reconciliation with, not repudiation of, it were central to the formation of a gay, evangelical "parachurch" organization in Atlanta known as Good News. Thumma reported that almost all members said they had felt or experienced rejection from a church congregation because of their homosexuality. Most came to the organization "in the midst of an identity crisis" and "expressed a strong desire to resolve the felt tension between being a conservative Christian and having homosexual feelings."[53]

Good News helped members to become reconciled to their gayness but still to retain their conservative, evangelical religious identity. Permission to question doctrines, to reinterpret scripture, and to alter beliefs was cast in terms of accepting "God's will for us to be gay and Christian." The new identity was strengthened and maintained by faulting conservative denominations for not accepting gays in the Christian fellowship and by creating an elitist group identity: that is, "We're the real Evangelicals because we know and follow God's will."[54]

Good News also infused many of the morals of the conservative evangelical lifestyle into the gay lifestyle, such as requiring that sexual activity be guided by biblical principles of committed relationships, not by "wanton desires." The organization guaranteed potential members that it adhered to the statement of faith of the National Association of Evangelicals; and its own statement of faith read: "The members of Good News profess their individual and corporate faith in the basic Biblical Truths of the full authority of Scripture, a personal commitment to Jesus Christ as Savior and Lord, and the urgency of Sharing the Gospel message in both word and deed." Parts of the conservative evangelical tradition were emphasized or adapted to accommodate a gay identity, while the basic premises were claimed and affirmed. Gay identity, too, as it has been developed within the secular gay community, was criticized for being overly sexual and was refigured as responsible and committed affection. Members of Good News came to accept themselves as gay Christians without giving up their evangelical identity. The affect of this reconciliation for many was verbalized by one member: "I cannot express the spiritual release of standing clean before the Lord."[55]

When Neil Miller interviewed Reverend James Tinney, the founder of the black, gay, evangelical Faith Temple in Washington, D.C., he asked why it was important for black gay people to have their own church. Tinney said there were two reasons: "On the one hand, black gays couldn't be open in black churches; on the other, they didn't feel comfortable in the Washington area's largely white MCC churches." It was not that other gay churches were racist but that black gay people needed to belong to something that was culturally familiar and specific to their backgrounds. Because many had spent their childhoods in Baptist and Pentecostal churches, "when [they] come to our church, they feel at home. It is a lot like the churches they grew up in."[56]

Tinney admitted that he was slow to realize the importance of focusing on the culture and theology of the black Pentecostal tradition. At first he experimented with some of the new developments in liberal Protestantism, such as nonsexist language; and the church was seen by some as a political rallying point for the black gay community. When it moved away from a political, liberal, activist approach to religion and began to stress "personal salvation" instead, Tinney claimed that it found its roots and identity.[57]

One of the parishioners of Faith Temple, a former member of Sun Myung Moon's Unification Church, agreed with Tinney. Isaiah Poole told Miller that he had "grown up surrounded by religion," and by joining the Unification Church, "I saw myself as part of a movement that would change the world, that was God's active plan to change things."

When he was with the "Moonies," he did not see himself as gay, but after some time began to see himself as two distinct people — "One the loyal Unification church member and the other was the guy out cruising the bars and bookstores." He told Miller that he heard Moon refer to homosexuality only once, when he said homosexuals "should be hit on the head with a baseball bat." After he met and fell in love with a man, he sat down in prayer, put the matter in God's hands, left the Unification Church, and moved in with the man. When Faith Temple was founded, he and his lover were among its first members.

Isaiah said that in the beginning, Faith Temple had "a protest edge to it. Half of it was to worship and the other half was to show off your sexuality and to show that we could be Christians and gay too." But then attention was turned to a serious study of the Bible, and he and a core group of continuing members gained a new but familiar viewpoint: "We were ready to do business with the Lord," he said. "Sexuality and race takes care of itself after that."[58]

This pattern of departing from, refocusing on, criticizing, refining, and reclaiming one's tradition has been repeated by other gay individuals and organizations. In 1980, after failing "in their search for a church where they could worship freely," William Carey and Judy Schwarz founded the National Gay Pentecostal Alliance (NGPA). Until 1983, gay non-Pentecostals, who had no churches of their own in which to worship, were welcomed by NGPA. By 1984, however, its leaders "experienced a revelation of the meaning of holiness, and began to teach it and to stand firm for Apostolic truth." Churches and people belonging to NGPA then had to subscribe to and teach that particular truth. As with other efforts to establish separate churches that have been discussed above, the NGPA leaders also criticized the religious bodies that had rejected them and asserted their own "truer" Pentecostal credentials. Reproaching the United Pentecostal Church for being "bound by the spirit of judgment" rather than by "a spirit of brotherly love," they also asserted that "the only people who recognize the spirit of judgment, and who know what it's doing, happen to be Gay."[59]

Example of a Traditional Alternative

Independent gay churches and synagogues have tried to be "as real as" or "better than" and not a diluted version of mainstream religious bodies. Their attraction for many gay people is in providing what has been denied, not in offering something new. And as studies have shown, for many gay people they do provide a return to and involvement with organized religion that had not otherwise been possible. This point was illustrated in Henry Rabinowitz's interviews with the men in his Talmud class at the gay synagogue, Congregation Beth Simchat Torah, in New

York City. Each had a different story about his background, how his introduction to the gay synagogue occurred, and what his involvement with it was.[60]

Rafram, for example, had studied Talmud since childhood. He grew up in a poor Jewish neighborhood. His parents were from a long line of Hasidim. He attended and was ordained by the most prestigious Orthodox yeshivah in the United States. He said: "If it had been acceptable to remain single in the yeshivah, I would have stayed, but the social pressure to marry was too tough for me.... Everyone I knew was getting married and I had fewer friends. I felt guilty, apart, limited, and lonely, and knew that I had to get away from the Orthodox world."[61] He saw a psychiatrist who advised him to date women. He tried without success. On his thirtieth birthday, he thought about suicide and did not know what to do until he read an article in the *New York Times* by Merle Miller, who talked positively about his own homosexuality. Rafram then decided to come out into the gay world.

Occasionally he attended a gay church group — "not for the religious aspect but because I liked the people" — where he met and became lovers with one of the active members. During this time, he said, "I was not observant [of Judaism], except for Shabbos, which I usually spent at home with my parents." When the Episcopal priest, in whose church the gay group met, sought to form a group to meet the needs of the Jews who attended, Rafram did not think the idea would work and did not want to give up spending Shabbos with his parents. The gay synagogue started without him.[62]

Later, after he read that it had formed, he gave his parents an excuse for not joining them on one Shabbos and visited the gay synagogue. He said: "It was so nontraditional at that time, it was a culture shock. I didn't put on a *yarmulke* [skullcap] and I didn't *daven* [pray]. I went a few more times; the group was eager for leadership. The first time I led services I was sweating; I still had my phobia of public observance. But as soon as the service began, I felt completely at ease, and the phobia disappeared completely, never to return."[63] Rafram continued to lead the *shul* (synagogue) for several years.

Ahai's route to the synagogue followed a somewhat different path. In college he had planned to become a rabbi. He was president of his Hillel chapter and studied independently with an Orthodox rabbi. He was also struggling with his sexual desires for men, which seemed to him to be "directly in conflict with Jewish life and my expectations of marriage, family, and being a rabbi." He could not ignore those desires and realized that "the gay aspect of my personality was a natural part of me." He went on to say: "Since I felt my gay identity and my Jewish identity to be antithetical, I stopped all my involvement in Jewish life; I simply did a flip-flop. Before then I had been practicing Judaism and avoiding my sexuality; afterwards I began to practice my sexuality and to avoid my Jewish life. The choice seemed automatic at the time; I was only nineteen and I tended to see things in black and white. I had no one to talk to about such choices."[64] Subsequently, he cut off ties with his Jewish friends and associated with a "non-Jewish gay crowd" that he met in bars and gay organizations.

He saw an advertisement for Congregation Beth Simchat Torah in 1974, was intrigued, but hesitated to attend because he "was afraid that it would be a mockery of a synagogue, that they wouldn't take the services seriously." When he did attend he "was pleasantly surprised to find that the synagogue was not a farce but a group . . . committed to Jewish life." He said he became involved very quickly because "I had a good Jewish education and my talents were needed." His responsibilities in services compelled him to resume his Jewish studies. The Talmud class was formed, and it "reawakened the interest in Talmud that had begun in my college days."[65]

Both men shared the similarities of coming from observant families, having studied Judaism as children, having fallen away from Jewish observance while coming out in the gay world, and then finding Congregation Beth Simchat Torah as a way to return to Jewish observance, study, and community. But Rabinowitz pointed out that this pattern may be changing because the gay synagogue is now available for people to turn to when, not after, they come out: "They need not feel they must leave the Jewish world in order to fulfill their sexuality. The synagogue and its members encourage newcomers to explore and retain both their sexual identity and their Jewish identity."[66]

Signs of some change and welcome have occurred within mainstream Judaism as well. At the 1990 General Assembly of the Council of Jewish Federations, three different sessions were devoted to addressing the concerns of lesbian and gay Jews—one on their spiritual needs, another on coming out, and a third on Jewish communal and family responses to AIDS.[67]

Finding New Opportunities within Established Religious Bodies

Because independent gay churches and synagogues have been established and because some mainstream religious bodies have undergone reforms to be more accepting, gay people who want to be active within organized religion have more choices than they once did. Many have negotiated within mainstream bodies to find more acceptance and have achieved varying degrees of success in different congregations and at different times. Roy Dahl recently wrote that "my most profound experiences of acceptance or rejection have happened within the Mennonite Church community."[68]

Describing the worst time as the "pain of isolation" and the best time as "the power of love," Roy put the negative experiences into three categories. The first category was "an accumulation of every insensitive, uninformed, or judgmental remark about homosexuality which I have heard from church people." The second category was "specific incidents," such as the time when a Mennonite pastor said he would be "very hesitant" to serve him Communion. The third category was "what the church did not do." For Roy this latter category was the most damaging because he said he had "felt no freedom to deal with the discovery of my sexuality in the context of the church community" and, therefore, had gone "through most of the process in solitude."[69]

For him positive experiences were "fewer in number but their impact was greater." A high point was when he shared his personal story about being gay with his congregation, and while not expecting rejection, he "was not prepared for the overwhelming expression of love, solidarity, acceptance, and encouragement." The response, which was "immediate, spontaneous, and caring," showed him "what Christian community could and should be" and gave him "hope for the future of all people in the Mennonite Church."[70]

Roy also made a claim that is shared by other gay people who have tried to find a place within established religious bodies. He said that "[my] congregation is by far the biggest factor for my being part of the Mennonite community today," and he added that official positions by the larger denomination of which the congregation is a part "will not alter their unconditional love and concern." Even in religious bodies that have taken the most anti-gay positions, gay people have been able to find local congregations that are pro-gay.[71]

That local congregations can resist and neutralize somewhat denominational policy was shown further by findings from my survey. Similar percentages of UMC and UCC respondents reported that they were completely open about their sexual orientation within their local congregations (43 percent, UMC; 48 percent, UCC) or open to some people within the congregation (46 percent, UMC; 44 percent, UCC).[72] If the UCC's pro-gay national policy contributed to a greater degree of "outness" by UCC respondents, the difference is not statistically impressive.

Other factors, such as gender, sexual identity, geography, and age, also seemed to be associated with rates of outness. Within both samples, women were less likely than men to be out in their local congregations (40 percent women and 45 percent men, UMC; 43 percent women and 54 percent men, UCC); bisexuals were less likely to be out than those who identified as lesbians or gay men (31 percent bisexuals and 44 percent lesbian/gay, UMC; 15 percent bisexual and 53 percent lesbian/

gay, UCC); and geographically, outness was reported least often by respondents in New England and the Lower Midwest (0 percent and 14 percent, UMC; 37 percent and 21 percent, UCC) and most often by those on the West Coast (71 percent, UMC; 67 percent, UCC). Among age groups in the UMC, respondents in their twenties were out most often, and those in their thirties were out least often (48 percent, twenties; 40 percent, thirties); in the UCC, respondents in their thirties and forties were out most often, and those over fifty were out least often (53 percent, thirties and forties; 33 percent, fifties plus).

But what appeared to affect outness most directly for both UMC and UCC respondents was the practice of the local church, as illustrated by my finding that of those belonging to "welcoming" congregations, at least three-quarters reported being out (84 percent, UMC; 75 percent, UCC), compared to about one-quarter of those who did not belong to welcoming congregations (29 percent, UMC; 28 percent, UCC) (see table 8). Certainly, gay respondents were out much more often in welcoming than in nonwelcoming congregations; but even in nonwelcoming congregations, more than one-quarter of UMC and UCC respondents were out, and in welcoming congregations as many as 15 percent of UMC respondents and one-quarter of UCC respondents were not out (100 percent minus 84 percent out, UMC; 100 percent minus 75 percent out, UCC; not in table).

TABLE 8

Percentages of UMC and UCC Respondents Who Reported Being "Out" in "Welcoming" and "Nonwelcoming" Congregations

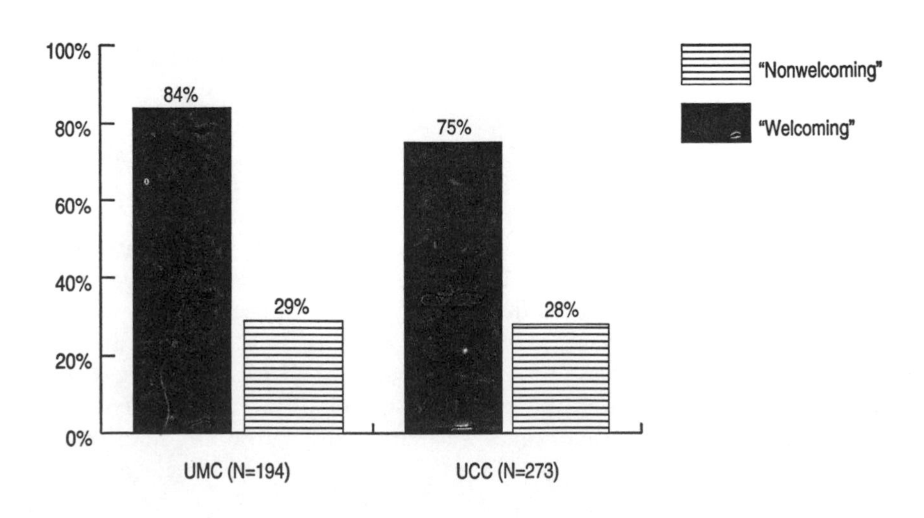

These findings do not mean that opportunities in the UMC are the same or better than in the UCC. After all, a greater percentage of the UCC than UMC respondents reported belonging to welcoming congregations (26 percent, UMC; 40 percent, UCC), probably because nationwide a greater percentage of UCC than UMC local churches have declared themselves welcoming (0.2 percent, UMC; 2 percent, UCC). Also, the number of these welcoming congregations has increased at a higher rate in the UCC than in the UMC (388 percent, UMC; 448 percent, UCC). But the rate of increase for welcoming congregations in the UMC has been high, too, and is evidence that a pro-gay movement has taken hold and is progressing within a reputedly anti-gay denomination.[73]

In 1993, one year after the UMC General Conference voted to retain its anti-gay policy, Affirmation reported "many cracks forming in the institutional edifice as people circumvent rules they can neither support nor overturn." The organization claimed that more pastors are conducting same-sex unions; boards of ministry and bishops are appointing people they know to be gay; and "local churches *are* inviting lesbians, gay men and bisexual persons into the full life and ministry of their congregations."[74]

In his study of the Presbyterian Church (U.S.A.), Lawrence Reh also found regular acceptance of and participation by gay people in some local congregations. In spite of their denomination's anti-gay policy, over 90 percent of his respondents said they personally knew gay people in their local congregations; over 80 percent said they knew of gay clergy who were open about their sexual orientation; and 60 percent said they knew gay deacons and elders in their home churches.[75]

Local congregations that have recognized and accepted their gay members have in turn attracted others to join them.

"Shopping" for Congregations within Religious Bodies

In my interviews with both UMC and UCC respondents, I found that people often "shop" within the denomination for particular local congregations that will welcome them as gay people. Mary Gaddis, for example, reported that she is a member of one UMC congregation but attends another because it is her partner's home church "and the folks are good folks." She said, "They include Judy and me and recognize us as a couple. This is a church that she has been a member of all of her life. When she gets invited someplace, I'm invited because they recognize that we are a couple."

I interviewed one UMC clergyman who was employed as a clerical worker in a UMC-affiliated institution. He could not be open to the larger denomination without losing his ordained status, but he was a member of a local UMC congregation where he was out as a gay man. He said that he felt "absolutely" and "unconditionally" welcome in this congregation because the people there have "made premeditated decisions to be open and welcoming. They know for someone like me that there is a certain risk in being open to them, and they help maintain that security as a safe place for me to worship and to be who I am. They welcome us as a couple even though my partner is not as involved in the congregation as I am. They respond to single and coupled gay people who come to the congregation as they would to any other new member and almost a little more so. It's like they spot them and make sure they introduce folks to regulars — other gay folks who have been involved in the congregation — as a way of saying, 'This is OK, here are some other folks like yourself.' When it comes to introducing new gay members to the congregation, they're introduced as a couple who, for example, met in college. They pay attention to the particular details of people's lives, rather than acting as if they're just two single men. There are little things like that, and they make a difference. They go out of their way to do that sort of thing."

I asked what else they have done to welcome gay people. "Whenever and wherever the congregation goes about their business of saying what the congregation does and is like, they include that we're a Reconciling Congregation, so that when a new pastor is being assigned, she or he fits within the parameters of what we're looking for. The congregation is saying, 'One of our ministries is to this community'; and so, the person coming into the congregation knows that this is going to have to be part of his or her ministry or there is going to be a conflict there. It's really hard to say, but it's almost without exception that this community has come together knowing this is part of the agenda for everyone. They've worked through personal ignorance and fears and learned how to talk. So, there's just not any lines drawn the way they are normally in a regular congregation, where gay/lesbian folks are not included as a part of the discussion. There's intentionality about it."

I asked: "Is this because it is a traditionally liberal congregation or has this congregation done some things that required major changes for its own image and way of doing of things?" The clergyman responded: "Part of it was going through in a very systematic, determined way the conversation about how to become a Reconciling Congregation. They did that discussion very carefully, very thoroughly, so that every part of the congregation was included in the discussion. And they came out of it overcoming their ignorance and realizing that this issue touched a lot more of their lives than folks might normally assume — people who had gay children and had never talked about that before, members of the congregation who had remained closeted and never talked about it before, and someone whose ex-husband was gay and she was still friends with him and never had a place to talk about that before. So, they moved as a community to a place where there was resolve around this issue at a comfort level; and now it's just sort of assumed. On a typical Sunday morning somewhere between 8 and 10 percent of the congregation are openly gay and lesbian folks who are there. People know them as gay or lesbian, but it's just like knowing heterosexual people. It's not a big deal."

I asked: "When you say they went through the Reconciling Congregation process very thoroughly, how did they know what to do, what was their process?" He responded: "I'd say they made space for everyone to talk about it, to feel safe to have fears or anxieties about it. They took their time, and they talked about it on every level. Like the parenting group, folks with grade-school-age kids, they talked about it — 'What does this mean for us in raising kids?' The adult education group talked about it, the spiritual life groups and fellowship groups talked about it, even the Administrative board talked about it. Each asked, 'What does this mean for us in the work we do?' All these different groups asked, 'How does this affect our life in church?' They had various gay/lesbian groups come in and talk to the congregation. They talked about the issues of where the larger church stands. They were in dialogue with the district superintendent, and the bishop knew they were going through this process. It's not something they hid or tried to slide by with. It was very intentional. It wasn't something the administrative board passed and then everyone else just went along with it."

The shopping for local congregations that people have done often goes beyond finding a gay-friendly setting and means looking for a congregation that will satisfy other interests and needs. For example, Peter Ilgenfritz and his partner shifted from one UCC congregation to another, and both were welcoming congregations. "We had looked a long while for a church in our first year here in Chicago, and we stumbled on one. In a lot of ways it was a very good church, an Open and Affirming congregation; about 10 to 15 percent of the congregation is gay. It was a real good mix of people. What we found missing though in that church was that all the emphasis was on social action and social outreach; and the church really neglected pastoral care of the membership. In getting to know some people there, we found a lot of people felt alienated and hurt by that, and we had felt a little bit of that ourselves. So we sought out a new church to go to, one in which we could be comfortable and worship as a couple, one with a good balance of both the social gospel as well as some pastoral care. We've only been at the new one for about two months; and it's been a good place so far." "So your shift really wasn't about gay issues?" I asked. He said: "No, it wasn't. It was more around, maybe just the style of the ministry."

A UMC woman I interviewed was also in the process of moving to another local congregation for reasons related to more than her being a lesbian. "It has to do with classism mostly, classism and racism. I really want to be in an integrated congregation. The new congregation has become a Reconciling Congregation, but the issue of classism is what's most compelling for my transferring. The church where my membership is currently is a large, downtown steeple church. Most of the people who go there are white, upper-middle-class. There are few people of color who attend that church, but they too are very upper-middle-class, highly educated people. The church that I intend to belong to is small and in an integrated neighborhood, predominantly black but other racial minorities live there as well, and it also has difference in theological perspectives."

I then asked: "Do you think there is something to the church you're moving to, its being integrated and non-upper-class, that makes it more receptive to gay people?" She responded: "I think there is a correlation in that they are more receptive to minorities and the social justice struggle than a church where most people have not had to struggle." I asked how open she could be in either of the churches. "I choose to be quite open wherever I am right now. Interestingly enough, one remains closeted unless you choose to come out to every person you meet, because the assumption is always that you are heterosexual. So when someone sees a woman, a professional woman my age, they assume that I am either divorced or single, that I live by myself, and that I have a friend at best. When we joined the large church, I met with the pastor and told him that we wanted to join and that we were a lesbian couple, and he was very supportive. But from the word go there was a problem, things like their taking pictures of new members and not wanting so-called nonrelated family people together in a photograph. And they introduced new people by their last names, so if your name is Betty and Joseph Smith, you're automatically introduced as a couple, but if your last names are different, you cannot get introduced as a couple at all. We discovered that since we are not married, there is no way to put us in the computer as a couple; so, we get two of everything. The other thing is just the nonrecognition, like unless we came out to everybody individually, the assumption is that we are not a couple. So if the people we came out to were working on a dinner and we both bought tickets, we would be seated together; but there was always the possibility that unless we asked specifically to be seated together, we wouldn't be. It's just ongoing, just how the church is designed to foster relationships as heterosexual couples and families and not recognize same-gender couples."

"Do you not see those problems happening in the new church?" I asked. She said: "It's a much smaller church; so it's easier somehow to deal with that. Most of that other fluff simply doesn't exist in a smaller church. And also because it's more like a family itself, the word gets around very quickly about people. Probably in the few months that we've been going there people know that we are 'a couple.' And the pastor supports and encourages it."

When I interviewed B. J. Stiles, he and his partner were also looking at and considering more than one UMC congregation. "I've lived in Washington for twenty-four years and for the first five or six years was a married ordained clergy on special appointment.[6] My family and I were very active in a congregation. We helped with education, were on the board, raised funds, etc. I then became inactive for approximately ten years, mostly I think for professional reasons of travel. Following my divorce, I started attending church irregularly. Then my partner and I sort of auditioned a couple of congregations, and we have been regular visitors. Neither of us is yet a member of this congregation. We're regular visitors but not involved in the day-to-day life of the congregation. We attend church on Sunday morning, and we attend some special events. Neither of us is active in any of the committees of the church."

I asked: "Can you say something about what you were looking for and what you found?" He replied: "I think in the auditioning we were looking for a church whose liturgy, theology, and congregation we felt comfortable with. We were not expecting to become very, very active. So we wanted a congregation, first, that was nonjudgmental, nonhomophobic, and diverse, and, secondly, in which the liturgy and the content of the service was nonsexist, inclusive, literate, and contemporary."

"What did you find?" I asked. He responded: "I found a lot that was boring, traditional — not blatantly offensive, certainly not in the explicit homophobic sense, but a lot of congregational life that was very dull. At least visually, most congregations were not inclusive. Most congregations were predominantly middle-aged and seemingly middle-class, married, and straight. Going to church seemed more like going to a political or social organization. The more middle-class and bland the more unsatisfactory it was, because there seemed to be neither a conviction nor a culture that was built on the strength of theological diversity. Then we found the church we now attend. It has extraordinary diversity visually in the congregation, extraordinary culture and style in the service itself, a blend of very informal activities with not high church, but a very ritualized, liturgy."

I said: "Can you give me an example of something that has impressed you there?" He replied: "One of the earliest things that truly startled both of us on the second or third service we attended was the introduction of a group, sitting very close to the pulpit in the center section of the sanctuary, of fourteen or fifteen adolescent black males and a white middle-class heterosexual couple. This was the prison group that the church was working with, and the man and woman were their sponsors. These are kids who had been arrested and jailed overnight and were candidates for reform school. And the church had formed this juvenile-detention program, had become the parole organization working with these kids, and was providing the kids with literally a buddy system to help on literacy and job training. And as we watched that group — the entire group came back six months later to acknowledge the baptism of a child of one of the guys in the group — we were struck that it's the kind of thing you sometimes read about in church newsletters that a congregation is doing, but you don't often see. I know about street ministries that some organizations do in which people from the congregation go someplace else; but it really shocked me and pleasantly surprised me to see the liturgical life of the congregation committed to bringing this part of the secular community inside, just not within the church walls, but inside the church's sociology."

First-Class Citizenry in Some Religious Bodies

That gay people can stay and shop within mainstream religious bodies to find not only a gay-friendly setting but one that meets other needs and interests signals perhaps a shift from a more restrictive past as well as an opening up of options not directly related to sexual orientation. Some gay people have had the chance not only to be open about their sexuality but to experience and become involved in a range of religious activities. The shopping patterns and interests of gay people do not seem much different from those that researchers have documented about the "baby boomer" population in general: "They are apt to 'shop' with a consumer mentality for both a congregation and denomination that meets their personal, ideological, and family needs. There is considerable fluidity, of people switching denominations and selecting congregations because of an exciting worship leader, good music, social action program, shared concerns, self-help recovery groups, religious education programs, even a large and convenient parking lot."[77] The confidence and assertiveness with which some gay people select and participate in religious activities would suggest they have moved beyond the status of second-class citizens in some arenas of organized religion.

In the late 1980s in Washington, D.C., the Unitarian Universalist Association established a new urban congregation "to make inroads into communities traditionally under-represented" within the denomination. The minister initially tried to attract African-Americans, but George Adams, a gay member of the congregation, also saw an opportunity to develop a connection with the gay community. He placed an announcement in the local gay newspaper inviting people to attend. The congregation soon had an active membership of forty people that is about one-half people of color and one-third openly gay and lesbian.[78]

Conclusion

Data from many studies reveal significant differences between the religious affiliations of non-gay and gay people. Although they come as often from the same religious backgrounds as non-gay people, gay people are statistically less observant and loyal to those backgrounds. Furthermore, the tendency among the general population in North America to nonaffiliate and to switch affiliations is noticeably greater among gay people. The profile of religious bodies with which gay people most often affiliate is unlike that for non-gay people. Unlike non-gay people, for example, gay people are not attracted to the established conservative, evangelical, and Pentecostal religious bodies; and non-gay people are not drawn nearly as often as gay people to the Episcopal Church, the Metropolitan Community Church, and Eastern and other nonmainstream religions. Many gay people not only have left the established religions that reject or do not welcome them but have created and been drawn to independent, alternative religious bodies that meet their needs. But others have been able to shop for and find welcoming congregations even within the most hostile denominations. Within certain local churches and on various denominational levels, they have become active as gay people. The next chapter moves away from issues of membership and affiliation to the participation, leadership, and contributions of lesbian/bisexual/gay people within religious bodies.

Chapter Four

Service, Participation, Leadership, and Advocacy

A Tradition of Spirituality: Connection and Service

Major religions have long recognized that in addition to observing their own particular forms of worship and governance, they have a social responsibility to advocate for, share with, and care for the needy.[1] In much traditional Native American practice, however, religious observance is not distinct and separate from service to the community. Community service is religion, not simply a by-product or extension of it. One's religious role and ceremonial participation are defined and shaped by one's contributions to the community. A religious or spiritual person is a helping person.[2] The recent experiences of gay American Indians have illustrated their spiritual role as special helpers and provide a basis from which to examine the participation of non-Indian gay people both within the walls of their churches and synagogues with their fellow members as well as within the wider community for others in need.

The organization called Gay American Indians (GAI) was originally formed by gay Indians in San Francisco to deal with the "double oppression" they experienced in cities and on reservations — homophobia from Indians and non-Indians as well as racism from gays and non-gays. Barbara Cameron, one of the founders, said that "we were first and foremost a group for each other" that focused on getting job and housing referrals and providing social opportunities and support for new arrivals to the city. They also felt a sense of responsibility to teenage gay Indians on reservations, many of whom committed suicide when they found no approval or support for their sexual/affectional feelings.[3]

The degree to which the families of these teenagers were assimilated or traditionalist often determined how they treated their gay children. For example, in his study of sexual diversity in American Indian culture, Walter Williams reported that "a westernized father found out that his teenage son was in a relationship with another adolescent boy. He severely beat the boy, and then ordered the tribal police to put the son in jail." Unlike "the abuse heaped on many young homosexual Indians by their Christianized parents," younger gay Indians who come out to traditionalist families "will sometimes have an elderly relative who takes them aside and tells them about the *berdache*."[4]

Because the leaders of GAI were quick to realize that gay people were more often tolerated by Indians who respected, rather than rejected, their Native traditions, the organization expanded its role from meeting the immediate needs of gay Indians and initiated a history project to study their past. They found that people similar to themselves had lived openly in over 135 North American tribes. They had had important responsibilities and made special contributions to their communities as artists, providers, and healers. Women hunters and warriors provided food for their families, defended their tribes, and some became shamans and medicine people. Male *berdaches* specialized in arts and crafts and filled important social and religious roles. Members of GAI did not claim that lifestyles within the current gay community matched the cross-gendered social roles practiced in the Indian past, but they did see themselves as appropriating that tradition.[5]

What GAI and other gay Indians have chosen to emphasize from the tradition is the "spiritual" role of the ancestral *berdache*. As articulated by Paula Gunn Allen, this spirituality is based on an understanding of one's connection with one's ancestors, other people, one's community, and the world:

> When I was small, my mother often told me that animals, insects, and plants are to be treated with the kind of respect one customarily accords to high-status adults. "Life is a circle, and everything has its place in it," she would say. That's how I met the sacred hoop, which has been an integral part of my life.
>
> There is a spirit that pervades everything....
>
> This spirit, this power of intelligence, ... appears on the plains, in the forests, in the great canyons, on the mesas, beneath the stars. To her we owe our very breath, and to her our prayers are sent blown on pollen, on corn meal, planted into the earth on feather-sticks, spit unto the water, burned and sent to her on the wind....
>
> She is also the spirit that informs right balance, right harmony, and these in turn order all relationships in conformity with her law.[6]

The spiritual or connectional role of the ancestral *berdache* had three major characteristics that gay Indians have adopted and developed: (1) making "special" contributions to the community; (2) helping other people; and (3) serving as "go-betweens."[7]

A Special, Helping People

A forty-six-year-old man interviewed in 1982 by Williams exemplified the above characteristics: Terry Calling Eagle lived on a Lakota reservation. He was responsible for preparing people for such sacred ceremonies as sweats, smoking the sacred pipe, and vision quests; and he led the prayers and blessed the central pole for the Sun Dance. Williams reported that Terry was also continuously involved in helping people with practical matters, such as visiting the sick and driving them to the doctor, helping them sell their beadwork, conveying messages for people without telephones, and keeping a supply of blankets and staples to give to people in need. Terry said, "If I practice the *winkte* [or *berdache*] role seriously, then people will respect me. I've worked as a nurse, and a cook in an old age home. I cook for funerals and wakes too. People bring their children to me for special *winkte* names, and give me gifts." He had also participated in the occupation of Wounded Knee by the American Indian Movement in 1973. Williams was struck by how "different from the average man" Terry was because "he defines his existence around his helping role and his intense spirituality."[8]

In the Maritime Provinces, Williams also interviewed a Micmac *geenumu gesallagee* (or *berdache*) who was devoted to serving his community. Joseph Sandpiper said that there were other prominent Micmac leaders like himself. Williams reports that within the community it was known and accepted that they were sexually active with men. "They wear men's clothes, but will often wear a woman's sash as symbol of their status." After serving two terms as the chief of his reservation, Joseph began a college course in public administration to gain additional skills that would help him as a "Go-Between for his people, mediating with the outside world."[9]

In urban settings, too, gay Indians saw themselves sharing with the *berdache* of the past the traits of helping people, serving the community, and contributing their special skills. But their efforts to become a visible part of the Indian community were not well received at first. For instance, GAI was not allowed to post its flyers at the local American Indian Center; it was told to remove its booth from an American Indian Day celebration; some non-gay Indians expressed open hostility; and even the traditional elders hesitated to be vocally supportive. But in time, the Indian community came to see that the gay community in San Francisco had political power and that GAI was a respected organization within that community. Also, GAI altered its approach and reached out to the Indian community in different ways.[10]

Erna Pahe, vice-chair of San Francisco's Board of Urban Indian Health and a former president of GAI, said that becoming aware of and committed to other programs and problems in the Indian community was a significant move for the organization. Members of GAI became involved in the work of all of the agencies in the Indian community, even though they might never utilize their programs themselves. Erna said, "When their funds are being cut and what they really need is a whole bunch of Indians to go over there at city hall and speak up, they'll say, 'If you want people to come out, call GAI.' " Also, after GAI's influence in the gay community resulted in the appointment of its members to government positions, non-gay Indian leaders sought its help in gaining access to local politicians. Whereas the ancestral *berdache* had been relied on as a "go-between" to ameliorate relationships between men and women, today's gay Indians expanded that role to advocate and negotiate for the Indian community with the outside world—to be "the go-betweens between the Indian community and the governmental agencies."[11]

Overcoming Barriers to Participation

Gay Indians readily admitted that many problems remain. For example, reports of anti-gay discrimination and violence on reservations are frequent; major Native American civil rights groups have failed to support gay rights; and a 1994 poll on eleven Canadian reservations found that 80 percent of the respondents were opposed to homosexuality, a disapproval rate higher than that of the non-Indian population.[12] But gay Indians have accomplished much in the way of gaining a respected position within some Indian communities. For example, in New York a gay Indian group called WeWah/BarCheeAmpe formed in the late 1980s and soon became fully integrated into the city's American Indian Community House (AICH). Curtis Harris was both a member of WeWah and on staff at AICH; and Leota Lone Dog, another WeWah member, was on the AICH board of directors. Curtis said that "because of the incredible leadership here at the Community House, which is primarily heterosexual," WeWah has been completely supported. "We've never had an attack, no one's criticized us." WeWah was active both in the gay community and in the Native community. One year the group was honored to serve as grand marshal for New York's Gay Pride Parade. Its members were also on various councils within the Indian community and were often asked to represent AICH at outside non-gay functions. Leota said that the line between WeWah and AICH was "very blurred" because "we're just as much a part of the Circle" as the gallery, theater, social services, day care, and other programs and groups. "We're all working towards one goal. It's not a separate goal. The main impetus is that we maintain our identities as Indian people."[13]

The willingness and eagerness of some Indian communities to recognize and value the contributions of their gay people have been prompted and sustained by some decisive actions by non-gay Indian leaders. Salyoqah Channey, for example, is a respected elder, grandmother, and spiritual leader who has publicly expressed appreciation for GAI's work and joined its board of directors. "I think they're being very, very helpful because they're enlightening non-Indians to our needs. They're doing a real civic duty. They're trying very hard to help our people and that's why I'm involved." Randy Burns, a cofounder of GAI, has said that "when you have elders coming to us, asking us to be part of their ceremony, that's spiritual, that's cultural, that's Indian." For many gay Indians, the foundation is being built for what Leota Lone Dog says is the important work not only of going back to the traditions but of creating new traditions in order to survive in today's world. "Even our ceremonies are revised in order to adapt to the people who are taking part in them now."[14] As Paula Gunn Allen writes: "The purpose of a ceremony is to integrate: to fuse the individual with his or her fellows, the community of people with that of the other kingdoms, and this larger communal group with the worlds beyond this one."[15] Williams observes that nowadays, especially among traditionalists and their communities, gay Indians are criticized not for their sexual behavior but if they are not fulfilling their spiritual role for the community. Many Indians seem to realize the importance of their participation and contributions.[16]

Pervasive and Diverse Participation

Within their respective communities, gay American Indians have reclaimed and staked out a spiritual role that is defined both by participation and leadership in religious ceremonies and by serving the diverse needs of their people. These qualities of involvement, leadership, and service are not unlike those demonstrated by non-Indian gay people in other religious bodies throughout North America. Writing in 1981 about the black Pentecostal tradition with its characteristic drama and emotional forms of expression, Reverend James Tinney said:

> Pentecostalism is the "earthly heaven" for sissies (and closeted homosexuals) of all types. Estimates of the percentage of Pentecostal members who are gay run as high as 70 percent. Who can know for sure? Certainly, there is no quarrel about the fact that obviously gay, flamboyant and queenly males and masculine-type females exist in abounding numbers in Pentecostal churches.... If our churches were to instantly get rid of the homosexuals in them, they would cease to remain "Pentecostalist." For the gospel choirs and musicians (the mainstay and pivot of our "liturgy") would certainly disappear.[17]

And in an anonymous monograph published in 1978, a homosexual Mormon wrote:

> We belong to your priesthood quorum, we teach your Sunday school class, we pass the sacrament to you each Sunday, we attend your primary classes, your faculty meetings, your family reunions, and your youth conferences. We sell you your groceries, we keep your books, we police your streets, and we teach your children in school. We preside over your wards and even your stakes. We are your sons, your brothers, your grandsons, and who knows but by some riddle of nature, we would be you.[18]

Jan Stout, a past president of the Utah Psychiatric Association and assistant professor of psychiatry at the University of Utah School of Medicine, said that from twenty four years of counseling gay Mormons, "I can attest to this diversity."[19]

Service within Religious Bodies and within the Wider Community

Findings from my survey of gay people in the United Methodist Church (UMC) and United Church of Christ (UCC) provided further evidence of such active and extensive participation. When asked if they had ever been involved in what they consider to be service or ministry[20] within their denominations, over three-quarters of lay respondents said yes (77 percent, UMC/UCC; 82 percent, UMC; 74 percent, UCC). These ministries most often involved teaching Sunday school and leading worship. Choir, music, and art activities, working with youth groups, and involvement in various community projects were next, followed by mission and outreach programs, visiting the infirm, and gay task forces. Participation was mostly on a volunteer rather than for-pay basis (71 percent, volunteer; 27 percent, paid and volunteer; 2 percent, paid).

When asked if they had ever been involved in what they considered to be ministry outside of their denominations, again over three-quarters of UMC and UCC respondents, lay and clergy, said yes (76 percent). These ministries within the wider community most often involved various forms of counseling and AIDS-related services. Food and housing programs, gay and lesbian projects, and general community services were next, followed by interfaith activities, various kinds of advocacy, programs for battered women, and youth projects. And here too participation was mostly volunteer (64 percent, volunteer; 29 percent, paid and volunteer; 7 percent, paid).

These kinds of extradenominational ministries have also been reported by gay people in other religious bodies. For example, Beverly

Brubaker and Joann Jones, members of the Brethren/Mennonite Council for Lesbian and Gay Concerns, operate two foster care homes for the mentally retarded and coparent eleven children.[21] And during the 1980s in northern California, Reverend Jane Adams Spahr of the Presbyterian Church (U.S.A.) pioneered a ministry to gay youth in area high schools that won the recognition and respect of the secular community.[22] For some, this kind of involvement is their full-time employment.

Examples of Service within the Wider Community

Mary Gaddis, a UMC laywoman, spoke to me about founding an independent business with some initial assistance from the denomination. "About 1985 or maybe a little earlier, I started a nonprofit organization called Women Empowering Women, which teaches women construction skills to help them get jobs in the construction industry or be able to do their own home repair stuff. I'm a steam fitter. I'm the first female steam fitter in my union, and there are about two thousand men. So I started this nonprofit, for-survival organization which got its original funding from the Women's Division of the United Methodist Church. Right now, for the last year, Women Empowering Women has been working with another organization, Trades Women Inc., that does support stuff for women in the trade. What we're hoping to do is to open our own training support center in the San Francisco Bay Area. To give you one idea of how we're doing, we've had a budget of around $30–40,000 a year and we're looking at going to a $750,000-a-year budget. So we're just exploding. That's where a ton of my energy has been going."

I asked if this project and work are like church for her. "Definitely. It's just a whole different way of doing ministry. It's magic. There is a house that we're finishing, completely rehabbing, that is going to be used as transitional housing for homeless families, which is exciting enough in itself; but more exciting than that is we've had probably a half-dozen homeless women working on the house. They are working on the house as peers of women who have incomes probably of fifty thousand dollars a year. There is no place that those kinds of women can be peers except in something like this. It's exactly about doing God's work.

"What I've also been doing in the last three years is teaching a class called Women in Skilled Trades. It's to get women into the trades. I teach it five days a week, and I teach some other women's stuff on Saturday. So that brings me to the seventh day of the week, and I need to breathe. I could be going to church, but I often choose to sit at home on my butt, or rework the handouts for the classes to make them better for those women, or hang out with my nephews. There is a whole life that needs to be lived. And time is really probably one of the crucial elements.

"The time that I'm putting into Women Empowering Women now, five to ten years ago I was doing that in the church and specifically around gay and lesbian issues, and before that I was youth counselor and that kind of stuff. So essentially what I've done is simply shifted where my energy goes."

B. J. Stiles, a UMC clergyman whom I interviewed, saw his current position as president of the National Leadership Coalition on AIDS as "a 180-degree turn" from a previous forty years of being "intensely involved in denominational strategies and politics." Although no longer appointed or employed by the UMC, B. J. still saw himself as involved in ministry. "It's really a shift in foci for my ministry and my calling. I would seldom use the term 'ministry' overtly or publicly at work, but I really feel that what I am currently doing is very much an extension of and consistent with my original views about what it means to be an ordained clergy. It's absolutely consistent with my pastoral approach throughout my life. And I feel in the AIDS institution that I'm working in I have far more relevance and effectiveness than had I remained in the institutional church. I'm able to accomplish things quickly, and I'm very much a pragmatic person. My friends and my board of directors understand that I am ordained and that I have a continuing and formal relationship to my church. But I don't perform my job as a clergy, and I don't seek to make that part of my professional experience always explicit."

I asked: "Can you say something about how you moved into this job and became involved with it?" He responded: "At the point in my life when I finally began to accept my own sexuality, when I was willing to accept that I am homosexual, not heterosexual, several fairly radical decisions emerged. I divorced; I 'came out' within a year and a half of being divorced; I changed my employment base; and I ceased being an employee of any institution and spent two years of my life self-employed as a freelance writer and as a consultant. All of this occurred in 1981, 1982, and 1983, which paralleled the emergence of AIDS. Therefore, the AIDS epidemic became the crucible or a vortex in which I was working out my own life choices, and I couldn't make a decision about my homosexuality without coming to terms with the devastating effect of AIDS on the predominantly gay and bisexual community. I needed to learn about that not only to protect my health but to recognize that I was choosing to be gay and to come out of the closet at a time when potentially there was nothing but devastation occurring for gay men. So the AIDS crisis has provided both personal and professional channels in which to redirect my energy and to utilize my training."

When I asked B. J. to describe the effect of his work and the organization, he said that "many of us literally have run an underground railroad using our church connections in which, to use one example, a good friend would call me from St. Luke's Hospital in New York City and say, 'B. J., I'm down the hall from Fred Smith. Fred's parents have been here visiting him, they're leaving tomorrow to go back to Webster Grove, Missouri, and they're devastated. They've just come to New York, they've found out that their son is gay, he's dying of AIDS, they're crestfallen. They have to go home, and they have nobody to talk to. Do you know anybody in Webster Grove?' And I'll say, 'No, I don't know anybody in Webster Grove, but I know somebody in St. Louis.' He'll say, 'Here's their name and phone number. Get the person in St. Louis to initiate some contact with these people. They need somebody to talk to.' That networking is a mixture of the AIDS world, the gay world, the gay and lesbian underground; and those of us with traditional religious institutional training and connections sort of put up a satellite and suddenly you've got all these foundlings. But if the satellite weren't there, then the foundlings can't find one another without some intermediary. There's not a single place in the country where I go to make a speech or be a resource person on the AIDS epidemic in which somebody is not going to come up to me after the presentation and want to talk. At least a third of the time what they need to talk about is their feeling of being silenced or paralyzed or vulnerable if they make more public whatever is their involvement with homosexuality and with AIDS."

B. J. said that many non-gay people approach him during his numerous talks throughout the country, so I asked how they used him as a resource, what do they want from him? "They want my story. They want my history. They want to know, 'How did you get where you are? And how did you manage at the point in your life when you were fearful or confused or vulnerable? How did you manage to deal with that and become the person you appear to be?' That line of questioning isn't gay versus straight, but most of the people who are interested in those questions have some relationship to homosexuality. They are a parent or a sibling or a dear friend of a gay person. And they are troubled because their family member or their friend is in difficulty or confused or whatever. I get it from people who are trying to help themselves or trying to help someone else. Out of the stories of thousands of people who are in the closet, I realize the extraordinary burden imposed by being in the closet, whether you are gay or straight. And I encounter, especially in my professional work, an enormous number of examples of the 'closetedness' of older Americans who can't and won't talk about the fact that their son or their grandson is affected by AIDS. And they are particularly hesitant to talk about that with their minister or in their congregation." B. J. said he continues to be affected by the number of "very ordinary mainstream older American men and women," many in their sixties and seventies, who are "painfully affected by the AIDS epidemic and have nobody to talk to."

"Are you into this kind of involvement for a long time into the future?" I asked. He said: "I can't imagine, given the nature of the AIDS epidemic, that I will do anything further during my lifetime that wouldn't have an AIDS component. Given that I'm fifty-nine, I have to recognize that by age sixty-five I am likely to retire. And I also think it's wise for this organization, since I am the founding president and in my fifth year, to look for what the organization needs in the next two to three years. That means a rotation or a successor to me. There is no phenomenon of burn out for me in terms of doing AIDS work, but there is a question of there being additional needs in the AIDS epidemic that because of my age and my experience I could make a contribution to, if I did something other than what I'm doing. What I'm now doing can be done quite effectively by a number of other people, and there are ways in which maybe the future of the organization may be enhanced by a person with a different background. Our primary focus is on AIDS as a workplace issue. Most of our members are Fortune 500 corporations; and since I do not have an M.B.A. nor have I ever worked for a corporation, there's a logical argument that the next director of this organization ought to be a businessman or woman with fifteen or twenty years in the corporate arena."

Obstacles and Encouragement

Obstacles to Full Recognition and Participation

That gay people participate extensively within their religious bodies and serve the needs of people in their wider communities is apparent. But as reported with the experiences of gay Indians, their participation and service are often unrecognized and rejected. Reverend Tinney, for example, added to his positive appraisal of the warm and celebratory Pentecostal environment that "there was a sense, of course, in which the 'holiness or hell' judgment was continually applied to homosexuals," and it was "painful, as a result."[23] And the need for the Mormon man to write and publish his story anonymously is itself telling. From counseling gay Mormons, Jan Stout drew this summary of their conflicts, problems, and resolutions, which has parallels and similarities with the experiences of other gay people who try to remain and participate as members of religious bodies:

> Some men struggle for years to change their sexual orientation or to experience an inkling of heterosexual interest. Beyond traditional psychotherapy, scripture reading, and church counseling,

> some have sat for hours viewing pictures of naked men while receiving painful electric shocks for negative behavioral conditioning. Some claim a cure, which many view with skepticism. Others resignedly accept their situation, while still others become bitter, disillusioned, and nihilistic. Some claim they have found love, comfort, and self-acceptance in their homosexuality. The spectre of excommunication looms over all who refuse to change their views. The most tragic cases seek the ultimate goal of suicide. A minority choose to lead abstinent, celibate, or morally neutral lives.[24]

Knowing that the religious bodies with which they are affiliated disapprove of and discriminate against them, and yet desiring to be active members, many gay people negotiate, accept, and/or protest conditional participation within them.

For example, one gay Presbyterian wrote to his local church to explain why he had not become a member, even though he had been attending and actively involved for eight years. He said that he took his relationship with the church very seriously. "I have tried to contribute to the life of this congregation by tithing, singing in the choir, teaching Sunday School, being a member of the Christian Education and Local Mission Divisions, and the Peace Task Force." His reason for not taking on formal membership stemmed from the decision of the General Assembly of the Presbyterian Church (U.S.A.) to forbid local churches from ordaining "self-affirming, practicing homosexual persons" to the office of elder. In the Presbyterian Church, elders are laypeople whose responsibilities include visiting and caring for people and informing the pastor of those who need special attention. Although he was not seeking to be an elder himself, he felt that this was a central role that should be open to gay people, and he would not join the church "as a second-class member," as one who was not allowed to participate as fully as other members.[25]

Another mainstream Protestant denomination, the Evangelical Lutheran Church of America, prohibits the ordination of openly gay and lesbian people but upholds their right to be members, just as it does for other "sinners" who seek spiritual guidance. But controversies over gay membership still erupt in local churches. In 1993 at Messiah Lutheran Church in Virginia Beach, Virginia, the president of the church council quit when it accepted a gay couple for membership. The council and pastor had the support of the district bishop, who delivered the sermon at the ceremony welcoming the couple as members. After the service, the congregation held a closed-door meeting in which homosexuality was discussed as both a sin and a gift from God.[26]

Other controversies have not been handled so evenly, as Loreen Fox-Shipley and her partner discovered after fifteen years of active membership at the First Mennonite Church in Phoenix. Three other members had been involved in political activity to block a gay rights ordinance that was subsequently passed by the city. They then directed their anger and efforts to "cleansing" the church of participation by homosexuals and managed to influence the congregation. Loreen wrote that "for a time, we were allowed to attend services as tolerated guests. When the degree of hostility and its personal nature became evident to me, I resigned my position as deacon." Six months later a congregational meeting was called with homosexuality as the only agenda item. For Loreen and her partner "it was an evening of anger, bitterness, grief, and tears. Bert and I were compared to prostitutes and whores. About two-thirds of the members saw us as sinners. Half voted for us to stay, but only under certain conditions." Now Loreen and Bert "know that their place in this congregation is not reconcilable" and have found "peace, rest and safety" outside of it.[27]

Finding Fuller Participation in Alternative Religious Bodies

Such controversies and rejections in established religious bodies have led many gay people to seek, find, and create alternatives in which they may participate more fully. Tim Tyner explained that he was attracted to the local chapter of Affirmation (United Methodists for Lesbian and Gay Concerns) because "an unwritten policy of our local congregation was that gays could not serve on committees or in any visible position except in the choir." At Affirmation, on the other hand, he enjoyed, planned, and was part of inspirational worship services, Bible study, educational programs, AIDS ministry, and outreach to retirement centers.[28]

In Paul Bauer's study of the Denver congregation of the Metropolitan Community Church (MCC), he observed a very welcoming and tolerant attitude toward visitors and members. Even those who saw MCC as "a sexual hunting ground" and could be differentiated from those with "a sincere religious interest are not frowned upon by the official members. The attitude is that 'They are here, as opposed to a gay bar, and are listening to the word of 'God.' " The ones who attended initially for social or sexual reasons often became full-fledged members, and "as with most new converts to a new organization, they work in the church with a zeal often embarrassing to long-term members." Bauer observed one such person who "worked in the church office doing typing, filing, answering the phone, etc., to the point of physical exhaustion." Out of concern for further physical harm, his doctor finally had to limit his work to three days a week. He was also elected to a seat on the governing body of the church.[29]

In Henry Rabinowitz's study of members of a gay synagogue, one of his subjects recalled attending hesitantly for the first time, but then being "pleasantly surprised by how much I liked the women and men who were gathered there." And shortly they began to ask for his help with services because he was one of the few with a Jewish education. His involvement in the gay synagogue, which was not near his residence, subsequently provided him with the confidence and curiosity to visit other synagogues in his own neighborhood — "something I just wouldn't have done a few years ago." Although he was sharing his life with another man, he *davened* (prayed) in a nearby synagogue in which he was seen as an available bachelor. He kept his personal life hidden and politely refused the constant attempts to introduce him to available women. To minimize matchmaking efforts he went to a synagogue in which people were not very friendly and did not ask questions. His alternative involvement at the gay synagogue, on the other hand, let him be part of a community without hiding his personal life.[30]

But not all gay people who have participated in these alternatives to established religious institutions have found them satisfying. Some alternative forms of religious organization perpetuate restrictive practices of the established bodies. In his fieldwork in the Philadelphia chapter of Dignity, the organization of gay and lesbian Catholics, Leonard Primiano discovered "a distinctive lack of female presence at the group's liturgies." Of 250 people at a Sunday Mass, about ten would be women. Many lesbian Catholics found the services "unappealing, uncomfortable, offensive, even repulsive." The problem lay not in specific words or actions against women by the chapter but "with the pervasive atmosphere of Dignity itself." Not only was attendance predominantly male, but in adherence to the institutional church, women were not allowed to be the central celebrants of the Mass. Primiano concluded that "Dignity was an organization that questioned the stances of the Church's male hierarchy on issues of sexual morality but it wished to remain in some way aligned with the institution that hierarchy administered," that is, with the exclusively male order of priests. One man said that "we bend over backwards to use the right language and to get women involved," and "they are probably overrepresented proportionally on committees and boards just because we are desperate to get as many involved as we can." He claimed not to know what else they could possibly do to involve women. However, neither he nor the others would consider violating the rule of male celebrant. Primiano observed that for them "such action would defeat the whole purpose of Dignity's existence," which is not to replace the Catholic Church but to remain officially Catholic.[31]

Finding Encouragement to Participate within Established Religious Bodies

Rather than driving gay people away to seek and create alternatives, other established religious bodies have made changes to welcome and encourage their participation. In January 1992 the following statement was made public by the Cornwall Monthly Meeting of the Religious Society of Friends in New York:

> When people seek membership in Cornwall Monthly Meeting, we do not judge them by the outward ways in which the world divides people, but rather we accept them according to the presence of the spirit which unites us all.
>
> Likewise, when Friends are led to declare marriage or life partnerships these are not scrutinized according to worldly distinctions, but are celebrated as revelations of the Spirit.
>
> Cornwall Monthly Meeting wishes to affirm that gay and lesbian members, attenders, and visitors are entitled to and will be given the same care and consideration from the meeting as heterosexual members, attenders, and visitors.[32]

There have been many other efforts by established churches to encourage gay participation: at a special Sunday ceremony in June 1990, the Lakeshore Avenue Baptist Church in Oakland commissioned members of its congregation to march in San Francisco's annual Lesbian and Gay Freedom Day Parade.[33] In 1992, after Coloradans voted to nullify and prevent gay rights legislation, four UCC churches ran an ad in the *Denver Post* that read: "In these painful days after the Amendment 2 vote, we speak our Christian convictions to you. We love you as our neighbors. We welcome you into our churches. We join with you in the continuing struggle for justice." And in 1993, First Congregational Church in Memphis publicly and financially came to the support of two lesbian members who lost custody of their children and sought to appeal the court's decision.[34]

Measuring and Quantifying Problems and Advantages

Because the respondents from my survey reported how often they have encountered both problems and advantages in belonging to and participating in their local churches, my findings should help to provide a quantitative picture of the positive and negative treatment of gay people within organized religion.

As shown in table 9, few of the respondents in my survey reported ever having had their membership withdrawn or denied by a local church because of their sexual orientation (2 percent, UMC; 3 percent,

UCC). But because the rejection and removal of membership in general are unheard of in either denomination, these low rates are significant.[35] More noticeable is the frequency of having had their membership become an issue of controversy. Nearly one-quarter of UMC respondents and nearly one-fifth of UCC respondents (24 percent, UMC; 17 percent, UCC) reported that because of their sexual orientation their membership had been publicly contested within local churches. And nearly one-quarter of UMC respondents and over one-tenth of UCC respondents (24 percent, UMC; 11 percent, UCC) had at some time not been allowed to participate fully in the life of a local church because of their sexual orientation. When these various kinds of problems (membership denied, membership contested, and participation limited) are taken together, over one-third of UMC respondents and nearly one-fifth of UCC respondents (35 percent, UMC; 18 percent, UCC) reported having encountered obstacles in a local church.

As also shown in table 9, over one-third of both UMC and UCC respondents (39 percent, UMC; 36 percent, UCC) have had either their membership welcomed or their participation encouraged at a local church because of their sexual orientation. The benefits of being gay would seem to outweigh the problems. One respondent even added to his questionnaire that he had been encouraged "ad nauseam" to participate as an openly gay man in his congregation. Although his experience may be the exception, it does show that some congregations take very seriously a responsibility to be welcoming and affirming of gay people.

Effect of Denominational and Local Policies and Practices

The greater percentage of UMC than UCC respondents who reported problems (35 percent, UMC; 18 percent, UCC) may be due to the UMC's official anti-gay policy.

A survey conducted by the UMC showed that over two-thirds of both the delegates to the 1988 General Conference (or quadrennial meeting) as well as a representative sample of local church members agreed with denominational positions that homosexuality is incompatible with Christian teaching, that it is a sin to be a practicing homosexual, that openly declared or practicing homosexuals should not be ordained, and that the denomination should ban the use of church funds by any group promoting the acceptance of homosexuality. More than one-half also agreed that the UMC should condemn the practice of homosexual behavior, but close to 90 percent thought the denomination should minister to homosexuals without condemning them (that is, condemn the behavior, not the person, and counsel celibacy). Over three-quarters of the delegates and two-thirds of nondelegates said that practicing homosexuals should be accepted into the membership of the UMC. This

TABLE 9
Percentages of UMC and UCC Respondents Reporting Problems and/or Advantages Because of Their Sexual Orientation in Membership and/or Participation in Local Churches

	UMC (N=188)	UCC (N=279)
membership denied	2%	3%
membership contested	24%	17%
participation limited	24%	11%
any of these problems	35%	18%
membership welcomed	30%	31%
participation encouraged	33%	32%
any of these advantages	39%	36%

rate of acceptance leaves, of course, a substantial one-quarter to one-third opposed to such members, which may explain the problems with membership and participation reported in local churches by my UMC respondents. But the high rate of acceptance of homosexual members by delegates and members may also explain why my gay UMC respondents reported being welcomed and encouraged to participate with more frequency than being rejected and limited.[36]

In the UCC, on the other hand, from 1973 to the present on the national level, the General Synod (or biennial meeting) and Executive Council have passed a series of resolutions recommending the increased inclusion and participation of gay people within the denomination on all levels. These resolutions recommend: (1) ordaining and providing equal employment opportunities for gay clergy; (2) studying human sexuality in greater depth; (3) identifying and opposing institutionalized homophobia within the denomination; (4) addressing the pastoral needs of gay people and their families; (5) providing education about AIDS and assisting people with AIDS; (6) welcoming the participation and ministry of gay people in local churches; and (7) opposing state sodomy laws and advocating civil rights for gay people.[37] They have not been passed without facing organized opposition, especially from a recognized special interest group within the UCC calling itself the Biblical Witness Fellowship. At the 1993 General Synod, for example, this group tried unsuccessfully to pass a resolution to "lead gay, lesbian and bisexual persons away from their sin." A pro-gay stance has prevailed on the national level.[38] This favorable record is borne out, albeit less enthusiastically, by the opinions of those in what might be described as a typical UCC congregation. The parishioners of Bethany Congregational UCC, located in the predominantly white community of East Rockaway, New York, on the south shore of suburban Long Island, did not fall precisely into a liberal or conservative camp on most social issues. When asked about homosexuality, 40 percent said it should be accepted openly; 37 percent said it should be quietly tolerated; and 23 percent did not accept it or were uncertain.[39]

Demographic Factors Related to Membership and Participation

In addition to the influence of denominational and local policies and practices on respondents, such demographic variables as their gender, sexual identity, age, and geographical region, as well as whether they switched into or were raised in the denomination, were associated with different membership and participation experiences.

Gender

On average, UMC women reported problems with membership and participation a bit more often than men (36 percent, women; 34 percent, men), but they also reported having been welcomed and encouraged more often (43 percent, women; 37 percent, men). Among UCC respondents, men reported problems more often than women (15 percent, women; 21 percent, men), but they also reported having been welcomed and encouraged more often (34 percent, women; 38 percent, men). Not only does one gender within each denomination report having both more problems and more advantages than the other gender, but the prevailing gender is not the same for both denominations. The differences between women and men in each denomination, however, are consistently small (less than 10 percent).

Sexual Identity

In the UMC and UCC, bisexual respondents reported problems (8 percent, bisexual; 14 percent, lesbian/gay) and advantages (17 percent, bisexual; 33 percent, lesbian/gay) less often than lesbians and gay men.[40] In both denominations, membership and participation for bisexuals may have been both rewarded and penalized less frequently because they are less visible within their local congregations. As shown in the previous chapter, bisexuals were out less often than those who identified as lesbians or gay men.

Age

When membership and participation are considered according to the various age groups of UMC respondents, those fifty-and-over reported problems least often (13 percent compared to range of 15 percent to 21 percent, other ages), and those in their forties reported advantages most often (42 percent compared to range of 25 percent to 36 percent, other ages). For UCC respondents, however, those in their twenties reported problems least frequently (5 percent compared to range of 9 percent to 14 percent, other ages) and advantages most frequently (49 percent compared to range of 14 percent to 36 percent, other ages). Compared with the UMC, the UCC seems to have provided a friendlier environment for young gay people and a less friendly place for older gay people.

Geographical Regions

The findings about geographical regions and membership and participation were similar for UMC and UCC respondents.

The UMC respondents in the South reported problems more often (28 percent compared to range of 9 percent to 15 percent, other regions) and West Coast respondents reported advantages more often (52 percent compared to range of 0 percent to 41 percent, other regions) than those from other regions.

Although my survey did not provide enough UCC respondents from the South to make up a distinct statistical category, respondents within a combined regional grouping of the South, Southwest, and West reported problems more often (18 percent compared to range of 7 percent to 13 percent, other regions) and advantages less often (16 percent compared to range of 17 percent to 53 percent, other regions) than respondents from other regions. West Coast respondents, like their UMC counterparts, reported advantages more often than respondents from other regions (53 percent compared to range of 16 percent to 42 percent, other regions).

Not unrelated are findings from the earlier-mentioned survey conducted by the UMC of its 1988 General Conference delegates and local church members: respondents from the South showed the highest levels of conservatism; respondents from the West Coast showed the lowest levels of conservatism; and liberal/conservative feeling and geographical area of respondents played the major role in shaping their opinions about homosexuality.[41] This documented three-part association of conservative ideology, the South, and anti-gay treatment in the UMC leads to another observation: because over one-half (52 percent) of UMC local churches are located in the South, the passage of anti-gay legislation by the General Conference is not surprising. In the UCC, on the other hand, only 13 percent of its local churches are located in the South.[42]

Raised in versus Switched In

In the UMC, respondents raised in the denomination reported problems as often as those who had switched in (16 percent, raised; 17 percent, switched). In the UCC, respondents raised in the denomination reported problems more often than those who had switched in (13 percent, raised; 9 percent, switched). In both the UMC and the UCC, switchers reported advantages more often than those who had been raised in the denominations (27 percent raised, 42 percent switched, for UMC; 27 percent raised, 37 percent switched, for UCC).[43]

As noted in the previous chapter, a greater percentage of UCC respondents than UMC respondents had switched into their denominations and did so for gay-related reasons. The above findings about membership and participation reinforce the notion that, as with switchers in general, gay switchers are motivated to find comfortable and supportive religious settings and have found them in both the UMC and UCC, but with greater frequency and success in the latter. Respondents who were raised in their current denominations have encountered problems more than or as often as switchers, perhaps because they have been in them longer, have decided to confront or endure the obstacles in their home churches, and/or have been less able or less inclined to seek more favorable settings.

Summary

When membership and participation were examined in relation to demographic variables, the most noticeable differences between UMC and UCC respondents had to do with gender and age. Problems and advantages were reported more often by women than men in the UMC and by men more often than women in the UCC, but by small margins in both. Older people in the UMC and younger people in the UCC reported problems less often and advantages more often. Otherwise, findings for UMC and UCC respondents tended to be similar and to show: (1) that bisexuals experienced problems and advantages more frequently than lesbians and gay men; (2) that the South was a more problematic region and the West Coast a more advantageous one for gay membership and participation; and (3) that gay people who switched in have experienced fewer problems and enjoyed being welcomed and encouraged to participate more often than those who were born or raised in the UMC and UCC.

The quality of membership and participation can be more completely understood by examining the specific roles played by gay people, the positions they have held, and the responsibilities they have assumed within religious bodies.

Leadership and Responsibilities

Gay and Non-gay Members

Over four-fifths of both UMC and UCC respondents in my survey had served on boards and committees in local churches (85 percent, UMC; 83 percent, UCC); and over one-half of them had served as the chair of boards and committees (58 percent, UMC; 51 percent, UCC) (see table 10). For UCC respondents, the boards and committees on which they had served had most often been responsible for executive governance (55 percent), education (28 percent), and finance (20 percent); and UMC respondents had most often been involved with executive governance (58 percent), social issues (32 percent), and education (19 percent) (not shown in table).

Surveys conducted by the national offices of each denomination allow for some comparisons of non-gay members with my survey respondents (see table 11). For example, 65 percent of UCC non-gay members, compared to 83 percent of my gay respondents, had participated on boards and committees; and the same percentage (51 percent) had held office in them.[44] In the UMC, 67 percent of non-gay members, compared to 85 percent of my gay respondents, had served on boards and committees, but a greater percentage of non-gay members had served as chair (78 percent, non-gay; 58 percent, gay; not in table).[45] Thomas O'Brien's use of a heterosexual control group in his study of gay Catholics produced similar findings: 70 percent of the non-gay Catholics, compared to 90 percent of the gay respondents, had been active in local church committees and groups.[46] The comparison of findings from these various studies suggests that gay people willingly and even disproportionately shoulder the responsibility for the operations and programs of their local churches.

Leadership on Various Denominational Levels

Respondents in my survey were also asked to report their participation on boards and committees on other than the local level of their denominations. Although the organization and structure of many religious bodies is similar, each uses different names for its various structural levels. So that comparisons between the UMC and UCC can be made

TABLE 10
Percentages of UMC and UCC Respondents Who Have Served on, Chaired, and Been "Out" on Boards and Committees at Various Denominational Levels

	UMC (N=194)	UCC (N=277)
local level	85%	83%
as chair	58%	51%
"out" during	40%	50%
district level	40%	36%
as chair	40%	50%
"out" during	21%	31%
province level	49%	40%
as chair	39%	42%
"out" during	22%	39%
national level	8%	18%
as chair	25%	23%
"out" during	25%	42%

simply, I have established and shall use these common terms for their denominational levels—local, district, province, national.

Table 10 shows that among UMC and UCC respondents, the percentages for participation on boards and committees on the four levels, as well as the percentages for chairing boards and committees at these levels, were similar. The 2 to 10 percent differences on the various levels show more frequent participation for UMC respondents than for UCC respondents on all but the national level, and higher rates of chairing are split between UMC and UCC respondents (local and national, UMC; district and province, UCC).[47]

Diane Darling spoke of her participation at the province level as the moderator of the UCC Northern California Conference. She had just completed her one-year term of office when we spoke, and I asked her to recall how the earlier nominating and selection procedure for the position went. She said that for the most part "it went real smoothly," but "there was some resistance." The question of whether or not the conference would declare itself as Open and Affirming (ONA)[48] was also on the agenda, so "there were a number of folks from some of the dissenting churches who were really at that meeting to let their views be heard about ONA. Usually the recommendation of the nominating com-

TABLE 11

Participation on Local Church Boards and Committees by Non-gay and Gay Members in the UMC, UCC, and Catholic Church

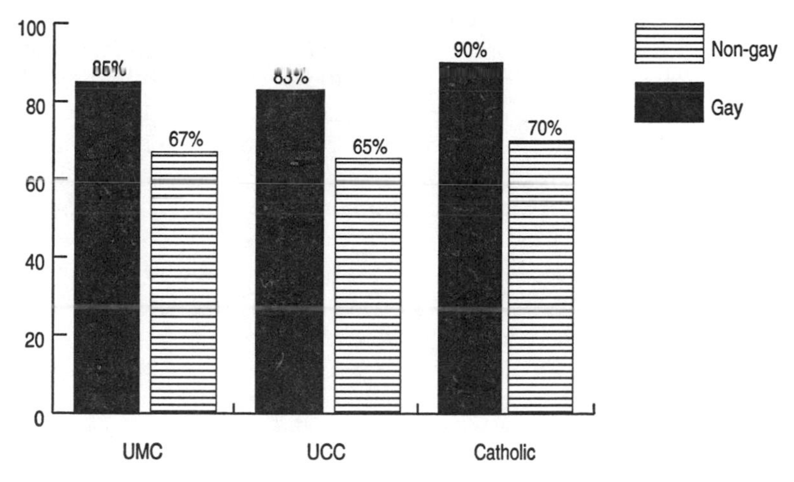

Sources: The table combines information from my own study with that from the following works: Timothy J. Gilbride, Mearle L. Griffith, and C. David Lundquist, *The Survey of United Methodist Opinion: A Research Tool for Informed Decision Making* (Dayton: Office of Research, General Council on Ministries, United Methodist Church, 1990); Wade Clark Roof and William McKinney, *American Mainline Religion: Its Changing Shape and Future* (New Brunswick, N.J.: Rutgers University Press, 1987); Thomas O'Brien, "A Survey of Gay/Lesbian Catholics concerning Attitudes toward Sexual Orientation and Religious Beliefs," *Journal of Homosexuality* 21 (1991).

mission goes through without any question. You never get 'no' votes; people usually feel that it's great that someone wants to serve on the conference. But after my nomination, someone said, 'Let's make it by acclamation,' and they said, 'OK'; but some people dissented and later in the meeting called for a voice vote. Then there were these 'no' votes, maybe twenty-five. It was just a little vocal minority, but people were kind of stunned. I saw them looking at each other like wondering why would anybody vote 'no.' Then later the pastor from one of the dissenting churches made a speech about how awful it is that this conference is going ONA, that he can't believe an open lesbian has just been elected to the highest office in the conference and how horrible can you get?"

Diane said the experience was not personally devastating because "it was like they weren't talking about me, but about something in their imagination about who I am or what I represent to them. It had nothing to do with me. And my stronger feeling I think was that it's good to get this kind of talk out in the open. It's important for us to realize that it is still there in our denomination. What was painful about it is that most of those against were members of either the African-American or Armenian congregations. That division, that we fight each other, was most painful. It was hard to see ethnic and racial minority church folks as the vocal ones about gay men and lesbians not belonging, that they shouldn't be affirmed. The outspoken pastor went home and pulled his church out of the conference, but he soon left that church himself. So they are gone, but at some point may come back. Since then there have been a couple of other churches that really got upset about the ONA vote and threatened to leave, or there was discussion about their withholding financial support. But nothing else crummy has come of it; they've simmered down. It became very clear with this particular group who were vocal at our meeting that diversity is one thing, but fundamental differences about what the word of God means and is to us and what the Bible is and what it means to be a Christian are another. I don't know if there's any more glue left to hold us together in one conference. I think what we're seeing a lot of is that this stuff is going to come to a head, this is the battleground topic."

Her term in office, however, was uneventful but much appreciated by the conference. "It's just like any year for any moderator I guess. It's been a pain-in-the-butt year for the conference. We're having the problems of recession in California. It's just killing local churches and the conference budget. So we've been dealing with a lot of that. I just did my job as moderator and my pastoring in the local church. It's been an exhausting year, and I was so glad it was over. All of the work is behind the scenes except for four days when suddenly you're a leader at the annual meeting. And there I got wild acclamations for my role. I got a wonderful response for my leadership. Whatever it is that I did, it was just the right time for me to be moderator for the conference's life. People said it was good that I was the one there leading it this past weekend. I got lots of affirmation. When the meeting was over, I thanked the conference ministers and the ministers thanked me and gave me a little gift. There was a standing ovation, and then I thanked all the people, thanked the planning committee, and thanked my partner, Elaine. I said, 'This conference and this place is really holy ground for us, this is where we first met and where we first thought we might be falling in love, and you are our family in many senses of the word. You're the people we consider home and family. The church has brought us together. The church is so much a part of our lives that I thank you for all that you've been for us, and I thank Elaine for supporting me when I do this.' It was good just to be able to say that. On one of the evaluation forms there was a comment that said, 'How wonderful to see the visible love and commitment between Diane and Elaine; that's a good thing for all of us no matter what our sexual orientation is.' It was nice, it was important to affirm that, how important this church is for us and they are for us."

Full Participation and Full "Outness"

Table 10 also shows that the percentages of respondents who had served openly as gay people on boards and committees were consistently greater for UCC respondents than for UMC respondents on all levels. The 10 percent difference between UMC and UCC respondents on the local level increases to a 17 percent difference on the national level. When compared to the UCC's similar rates of "outness" on the local and national levels (50 percent, local; 42 percent, national), the UMC's noticeable decrease of "outness" from local to national (40 percent, local; 25 percent, national) may be seen as a result of increasing proximity to the level responsible for making and enforcing anti-gay policy.

In my interview with UCC laywoman Charlotte Stacey, the extent of participation by gay people as well as the complexity of coming out in that participation were given depth and detail. "I'm the organist and choir director in my church. So in a sense I'm a part-time paid employee. Presently, I also happen to be the moderator of my church. In the past I have been chairperson of the Finance Board and chairperson of Christian Education. I've always taken a very active part in the church. I would say my partner is the same way. And I would say for the most part we've been well received with a few minor exceptions. How do we explain this? We have never stood on the mountaintops and said to everybody, 'By the way, we're lesbians.' However, because of my activity in the Connecticut conference's Committee on Homosexuality—when I first became involved with it five years ago, I knew I was going to be a speaker or facilitator at some of the local churches—I did go to my diaconate and came out to them. Diaconates change every year or so, and from that point on I would say of the 110 members that come to the church on an active basis probably 80 or 90 of them know by now. Specifically, it has never been a public issue, but we've been threatened by its becoming one. There is at least one person in my church who has been actively trying to do anything he can to get us out of the church."

I asked what form his efforts take. "Gossip, threats, literally blackmail at one point. The former minister of the church and I used to lead the youth groups for about seven years; and at one point he wanted to take a break, so I said I'd take the senior group. At that point this other guy just thought the roof was going to come off if I, this lesbian person, was going to be in charge of these kids, like, 'My God, think of what's going to happen!' And supposedly this person went to the minister and said, 'If you put Charlotte in charge of this, I'm going to go to the newspapers.' The minister got back to me about this and ended up telling him, 'Go ahead,' and the guy didn't do anything. A couple of times he threatened again, like, 'Over my dead body will she become the moderator of the church.'

"In fact, anytime this person caused any waves, it always backfired. He always tried as soon as a new minister came in to talk to him about homosexuals; and the new minister would say, 'What's the big deal?' and showed again that, 'You're not going to get support from me on this; and if you're going to make waves, we'll just bring it to a church meeting.'

"Marge and I have no doubts in our minds that if someone ever decided to call a church meeting and called this to an issue, there may be some people who would be uncomfortable, but in no way would we not get a large majority of support. My concern is they don't still understand the issue, because their support is more for Marge and Charlotte who they don't see as being like 'those other people,' whoever those other people are."

Charlotte says that this concern informs what she says and does when she goes to other churches for the conference's Committee on Homosexuality. "One of the exercises I do when we go out to churches is to start off by putting up a piece of newsprint and saying, 'Let's write down all the words that come to mind when you think of a lesbian or a gay person.' I intentionally let them come out with all the negative words; and just about every single church I go to always comes out with a lot of them. After letting them come up with their negative words, I turn around and say, 'How many of you know somebody who is gay or a lesbian?' Lately, the numbers are getting larger and larger as time goes on, and so I say, 'OK, give me words to describe them, words you associate with those people,' and immediately the words are all positive. And that's the beginning of our discussion of Homosexuality 101, as I call it. There still always seems to be a reverting back to the stereotype in their mind when they're thinking about the unknown person versus the one that they know. That's an ongoing struggle."

But these sessions were often personally challenging and even threatening. Charlotte remembered one incident at a church close to her own town. "When I went out there at that time I hadn't been very open, not at all in my town and not really in my own church for that matter. In the process of their going around and introducing themselves, I found out one of the gentlemen lived right down the street from me in my town, where I was on the Board of Education. All of a sudden I realized I could say something about being a lesbian and it could get back into the town and become more of an issue than I was ready for. I felt very vulnerable. But just because I was a member of the Committee on Homosexuality didn't mean that I was gay, because we do have members who aren't. So I didn't come out at that moment. I just handled it as one of the committee's members, saying, 'We're part of the conference's Office on Church Life and Leadership, and we're concerned about social issues.' I was very third-person oriented in my comments, but people listened and responded. The interesting part is that to finish up the evening, I went around the room and asked them what they could tell me about gay and lesbian people. This particular guy — the one who lived down the street from me — said he always could tell when someone is gay or a lesbian. It struck me as, 'Oh great, this guy knows, he thinks he knows, or he does know.' Well, because there was such a change in attitude by the end of the evening from everyone and especially from him, like his eyes had been opened, I played a little game. I said, 'By the way, I never told anybody here whether I was a lesbian or if I'm straight. I'd like to go around the room, and you tell me what I am.' Half of them said, 'I don't know,' and 'We don't care.' Some of them said, 'Well, maybe you are, maybe you're not.' When it got to him, he looked at me and he said, 'I don't know.' Everybody laughed and said, 'Come on, John, you said you could always tell.' We finished that exercise, and I went on to another question and he looked at me and said, 'Wait a minute. Aren't you going to tell me?' And I looked at him and proceeded to tell him about the fear I had when I first started. I said, 'I was afraid to let you know. You're in my town, you know I'm on the Board of Education. What if I was and what if you told others?' And he looked at me and said, 'I'd never do that'; and I said, 'I know you wouldn't, so I can tell you that I'm a lesbian.' It was just a moment, a trust moment, a moment in which I let this person know. I realized there had been this two-hour period in which a real change had occurred in people just from being able to talk to somebody, to ask questions and brainstorm together."

When I asked Charlotte if she planned to do one of the Committee on Homosexuality's sessions in her own local church, she said, "Someday it will happen," and added, "I'm not militant, I'm more understanding in realizing that people move slowly. Everybody comes into this issue with their own paradigm from all different sources and information, and I think everybody needs to grow. As long as everybody can keep an open mind, they're going to change. And there has already been a lot of changing in our church and a lot of acceptance and a lot of questioning and a lot of open minds."

When Charlotte was chairperson of the search committee for a new minister for her local church, the committee as a whole decided that they wanted to make sure that the issue of homosexuality was brought up so that they would get a gay-positive minister. Charlotte explained, "It was ironic how that came out, because I didn't initially come out to the search committee, although I knew at least half of them knew." The suggestion to ask candidates how they felt about homosexuality came after a mock interview with a neighboring minister. The committee was practicing how to ask questions about handling conflict, and the minister said, "Well, if you want to talk about how I've handled conflict in the past, how would you like it if you're in your church one week and a couple comes up to you and says, 'My daughter is a lesbian, and I want our church to become Open and Affirming.' How do you feel about that?" Charlotte told me that she was shocked, but "half the committee all leaned forward and said, 'Tell us more about what happened,' like forget about search committee business, 'We want to know what happened to your church when that issue got brought up.' " She went on to say: "After he left, some of the members stayed together in the kitchen, and I came in and they looked at me and said, 'We've got to bring this issue up.' I looked at them and said, 'You're right,' which meant to me I had to come out to the committee the next week. So when I did come out to the committee they all looked at me and said, 'We know. Yes, and after last week's meeting, we know this could somewhere along the way become a controversial issue in our church. So let's find out how a prospective minister would hear and talk about it.' But I didn't initiate this; so I felt good about that. It was my friends who did it. They felt it was important enough to say, 'If we're going to get a minister in this church, he ought to be Open and Affirming, so we know that's the direction our church will be heading.' "

Demographic Variables

Participation on boards and committees by UMC and UCC gay respondents can be discussed and analyzed further according to their gender, sexual identity, age, and geographical region, as well as by whether they switched into or were raised in the denomination.

Gender

In the UMC and UCC, similar percentages of women and men reported participation on boards and committees, chairing of boards and committee, and being out during their participation and/or chairing (UMC women/men participation 47/45 percent, chair 37/43 percent, out 29/26 percent; UCC women/men participation 42/47 percent, chair 39/44 percent, out 38/42 percent).[49] The most noticeable differences were more frequent chairing by UMC men and more frequent outness of UCC men.

Sexual Identity

UMC and UCC bisexuals reported participating on and chairing boards and committees more often, but being out in their participation less often, than lesbians and gay men (UMC bisexual/lesgay participation 50/45 percent, chair 51/40 percent, out 15/29 percent; UCC bisexual/lesgay participation 56/35 percent, chair 49/41 percent, out 17/46 percent).[50]

Randy Miller, one of the UMC laymen I interviewed, described events at the UMC's General Conference that may help to show why bisexuals hesitate to be out more often in the church. The group, Affirmation: United Methodists for Lesbian and Gay Concerns, had recently decided to add "bisexual" to their name, literature, and proposals. Randy said, "I didn't expect the vehemence, but I did expect that we would get grief from people about bisexuality at General Conference. Not the vehemence. They just don't believe a person can be bisexual. I really thought that we got a lot of bigoted statements from people who should know better and not only people from the Southeast. They just said some very prejudiced things about bisexuality that really threw me for a loop. At the same time I never imagined that for some people, i.e., the conservative evangelicals of the church, that somehow bisexuality is a far greater sin than being gay. So at General Conference it was heralded as one of the signs of our degeneracy, like one of the leaders of the conservative evangelicals stood up and said, 'See, at the last General Conference they were just gays and lesbians, and at this General Conference they've added bisexuals to their list.' We then had liberals coming up to us and saying, 'Please, drop the word "bisexual" in anything that you do. It's causing the Study Committee's "Report on Homosexuality" to be in jeopardy.' So it's definitely muddied the waters. I didn't realize when we took a stand on bisexuality that it would actually end up a risky thing to do. But we're not backing down on it."[51]

Even in such liberal and pro-gay religious bodies as the Unitarian Universalist Association, bisexuality has not been met with the same degree of acceptance as has homosexuality. At its 1989 General Assembly, a proposal to establish a Welcoming Congregation Program met serious opposition in the form of an amendment to delete "bisexual" from its wording. Jay Deacon, the director of the denomination's Office of Lesbian and Gay Concerns, observed: "Seems they thought 'bisexual' equals promiscuous. The 'bi-' must mean twice as much sex! Or with twice as many people. Or that a bisexual is always having sexual relationships with both sexes and can't engage in a committed relationship." The amendment, though, was defeated by a two-thirds vote.[52]

On the local level in the UMC some efforts have been made to welcome bisexuals. The Reconciling Task Force at Wheadon United Methodist Church in Evanston, Illinois, for example, listened to a request for inclusion from one of its bisexual members, then initiated wider discussion with more members, developed an educational program, and proposed that the church "intentionally name and include bisexuals in our life together" and "be aware of the various issues around bisexuality." The entire process took six months, at the end of which the Administrative Council passed the proposal and changed the wording in the church's public statement about being a Reconciling Congregation.[53]

Age

Older respondents generally have had more time and opportunities to belong to committees and to be elected to office. For both UMC and UCC respondents, the percentage of those who had participated on and chaired boards and committees increased with each older age group, but the percentage of those who were "out" during participation was greater among the younger age groups (41 percent) than among older groups (25 percent).

Geographical Region

By geographical regions, UMC and UCC respondents from the West Coast were out in their participation on boards and committees more often than respondents from others regions (47 percent compared to an average of 23 percent for other regions, UMC; 52 percent compared to an average of 39 percent for other regions). In the UCC, participation was similar across regions (range of 40 percent to 47 percent); but in the UMC, participation was reported most often by respondents in the Lower Midwest (67 percent compared to average of 45 percent for other regions).[54]

Raised in versus Switched In

As with older respondents, those who were raised in the UMC or UCC had had more time and opportunity to participate and hold office than have those who had switched into the denominations. In the UMC and UCC, respondents raised in the denomination more often than switchers reported participating (51 percent raised, 35 percent switched, UMC; 50 percent raised, 39 percent switched, UCC) and chairing (41 percent raised, 40 percent switched, UMC; 47 percent raised, 34 percent switched, UCC). Switchers, however, in both the UMC and UCC reported being out in their participation more often than those raised in the denominations (26 percent raised, 30 percent switched for UMC; 36 percent raised, 46 percent switched for UCC).[55]

Summary

The findings from my survey would suggest that gay people perform the duties, assume the leadership roles, and take on the responsibilities for the ongoing programs, administration, and maintenance of the religious bodies to which they belong. Their involvement would appear even to exceed that of non-gay members.

My findings also showed that restrictive policy has not prevented gay people from participating in leadership positions, since UMC respondents participated on and chaired boards and committees more often than UCC respondents. However, higher rates of participation and chairing were not associated with higher rates of outness. The UMC respondents reported being out less often than the UCC respondents in their participation. Bisexuals participated more often than lesbian/gay-identified respondents but were out less often. The same was true for older respondents compared to younger ones. The regions with respondents who participated most often were not the regions with respondents who were out most often in their participation. And respondents raised in their denominations participated on and chaired boards and committees more often than switchers, but switchers were out more often in their participation.

This association of higher rates of leadership with lower rates of outness would suggest that identifying openly as lesbian, bisexual, or gay may have reduced opportunities for participation in established leadership roles and positions. Many gay people affiliated with mainstream religious bodies, therefore, have forgone this kind of institutionally sanctioned participation and leadership and instead channeled their efforts into activism and advocacy for change within their respective bodies. Their participation as activists and advocates will be discussed next.

Advocacy

Demonstrations and Protests

A well-documented form of participation by openly identified gay people has been to protest and demonstrate against the anti-gay policies and practices of their religious bodies. This kind of activity has happened at all levels. On the local level, for example, in 1993 twenty-nine gay people demonstrated during Mass at St. James Cathedral in Brooklyn. They were protesting what they considered to be the hypocrisy of the bishop's pastoral letter on homosexuality. In it the bishop condemned discrimination and violence against homosexuals but also opposed laws that would "legitimize homosexual activity" and wrote that homosexuality was "ordered toward an intrinsic moral evil." The demonstrators sat in the pews and wore T-shirts with slogans denouncing anti-gay violence and the portrayal of their sexuality as evil. When the bishop began his homily, they stood two-by-two in silence. When he finished, they held aloft enlarged photographs of victims of bias-related crimes. The largest was of Brendan Fay, a gay member of this parish who had been stabbed a week earlier. The protestors then slowly walked out together.[56]

Also, on the local level, gay people have joined with others to defend congregations from anti-Semitic attacks. In Eugene, Oregon, before Passover, Temple Beth Israel was fired upon with semiautomatic weapons after a city newspaper featured a human interest story about members of the Jewish community, including a lesbian. A local gay rights group joined with a number of other community organizations to stand vigil outside the synagogue during the observance of the Passover holiday.[57]

On the national level, various kinds of demonstrations have taken place. The actions of gay Jews have been international in scope. In 1979 eleven gay and lesbian Jewish groups donated money to the Jewish National Fund to develop the Lahav Woodland in Israel as a living memorial to "the countless homosexual men and women who gave of themselves to build and defend the land of Israel." A standard dedicatory ceremony was to be held with the placing of a plaque acknowledging their contribution. The ceremony was canceled at the last minute, and a blank plaque was installed. Thirteen years later, the plaque was inscribed when the World Congress of Gay and Lesbian Jewish Organizations gained the backing of the Union of American Hebrew Congregations and the American Jewish Congress to pressure the fund to complete the customary procedure for recognizing large donations.[58]

More recently, in the spring of 1994 at the Yad Vashem Holocaust Memorial in Jerusalem, 150 gay people from twelve countries gathered to memorialize the tens of thousands of homosexuals who were killed in Nazi death camps. Nineteen rabbis had placed an ad in the *Jerusalem Post* saying the ceremony would be an "abomination"; officials at the monument refused to approve the observance; and twelve Orthodox Jews disrupted the ceremony by shouting, "No More Gays!" "Homos! May God save you!" and "Don't touch me! You are full of shit and AIDS!"[59]

A few religious bodies have not stood in the way of full participation by their gay members but have actually decided on the national level to join with them in demonstrating against discrimination and for civil rights in the secular arena. For example, the president and trustees of the Unitarian Universalist Association decided to reschedule a board meeting so that they could march in the 1993 March on Washington for Lesbian, Gay, and Bisexual Rights.[60]

At National Meetings

Generally, though, the most frequent and recurring demonstrations by gay people within organized religion have occurred at the national meetings of their respective religious bodies and have been staged to protest decisions to maintain anti-gay policies and the exclusion of gay people from the discussion leading up to those decisions. When I asked Randy Miller to say something about the UMC's General Conference of 1992, he said: "I warned people. I was like Cassandra. I was predicting and no one would listen to me. I just thought there was a clear pattern. I had worked in electoral politics, so I can sort of count votes before they're cast. I said without some intervention of the Holy Spirit — and I don't think she's showed up for a long while at General Conferences — this is how the votes are going to come down; so we should prepare ourselves and not hope. But you really can't tell people not to hope, especially when it has to do with including them. It was sort of not devastating but somewhat devastating. Not as devastating as the last time. I was in a very different emotional place in my life now. The church plays a much lesser role. I'm not financially dependent on the church. The ecclesiology that I live out of had changed. It was still sort of devastating to have folks vote not to have a speaker from Affirmation or a gay/lesbian person speak and then to vote down in a very mean sort of way the best part of the Study Committee Report, which meant overturning the part about homosexuality. It was not an enlightened discussion. It was the lowest-common-denominator-type of argument that regurgitated all the old prejudice and bias like, 'I was raped by a man when I was twelve years old,' and 'Homosexuality is a disease and a sickness that is unknown in our country in Africa.' It was this kind of a discussion, despite all the high talk beforehand that we were going to discuss theology and ethics. It was people regurgitating homophobia at a very low level. And it was very painful. They sang 'Standing on the Promises,' and I wish I could say I used to love that hymn before they sang it, but I hated it before they sang it, and I hate it even more now."

He went on to explain that after a difficult vote "they usually try to do something to recognize or bring the delegation or conference into order or whatever, and whoever the organist was just started playing 'Standing on the Promises.' And, of course, the conservatives leapt on that with great joy and started singing 'Standing on the Promises,' as if they had just saved the church. Probably some of the liberals just sang it because it's a way of showing unity for the church. It was the whole General Conference. It was just very ill-done, and I think that makes it hurt even more."

I asked: "What did Affirmation do after that?" He replied: "We sang 'We Shall Overcome.' I wasn't going to do it because I don't like using it that way; but I did because I wanted to support other people who felt we needed to make some kind of statement. And I had participated earlier in the day in the disruption of the General Conference by holding up a thirty-foot banner, 'The Stones Will Cry Out,' to protest the fact that General Conference had not had an openly gay or lesbian person address that body for the past sixteen years; so I had done my response. I felt that we had made the best statement there that we could; but then we did sing 'We Shall Overcome.' Some of the delegates did join in, but most of the delegates had left by then. And we've sung at so many General Conferences, you begin to question its effect."

I asked: "Was your personal feeling or response to leave the whole thing or to dig in?" He responded: "No, my response was to leave; and I started walking out because I was disgusted that every four years we go through this. But then other people started singing, so I came back because I'm sort of a caretaker. Then I did a TV interview right after that. And, lo and behold, I sort of fell apart in the TV interview, which just shows me again that I was more affected by this than I wanted to be. Even being a part of a Reconciling Congregation and knowing the General Conference has absolutely no connection to my home church—most people there don't even know about General Conference, they don't want to know — still it was very painful. I just thought about what kind of impact this will have on the people who really are in the middle of the road, in the conservative churches."[61]

At the 1990 General Assembly of the Presbyterian Church (U.S.A.), a major item on the agenda was the work of its Special Committee on Human Sexuality, with majority and minority reports. A consensus document did not bode well for gay people; and efforts to mitigate its negative impact were voted down by margins of 65 to 35 percent. At the conclusion of debate, Michael Purintun recalled that the "moderator called for a moment of personal privilege and talked to the Assembly about pain. He told them that the decisions made by the Assembly were helpful for some, but had crushed the hopes of others. He then explained that a group of people had asked for permission to demonstrate in silence before the Assembly" and invited them to come forward. Nine people carrying a large wooden cross then led a procession up the aisle of the assembly floor. "Many of them were crying, the room was totally still." Michael went on to describe his own participation in these words:

> I turned to the woman seated next to me and asked, "Are you going to walk?" "I'll stay here with you, or walk with you if you wish. I want to be with you!" I gulped, "I think I'd like to walk." As we were rising, I noticed quite a number of people were joining the procession, the press of the crowd was great. Many people were weeping quietly. As I was standing there I looked over to see

> my mother standing with tears streaming down her cheeks. She reached her hand out to me and said, "May I walk with you?" By this time all I could do was nod and take her hand. As we walked together, I wondered if my dad would be embarrassed, or upset. Then I looked forward to see him standing in a line waiting to join the procession. I walked forward with my parents down that long aisle feeling more blessed than I have ever felt.

The cross was held aloft at the front of the hall, and the five hundred or more marchers went to either side of it. Four people then pounded large nails into the cross; and the only sound in the hall was the hammering of the nails. Someone then began to sing the Holly Near song "We Are a Gentle, Angry People." The others joined in singing as they slowly exited the hall.[62]

The first demonstration against the denomination called the American Baptist Churches in the U.S.A. occurred at its biennial meeting in 1993. In 1992 the General Board had passed a resolution calling "the practice of homosexuality incompatible with Christian teaching" and would not allow the gay group, American Baptists Concerned, to have its usual booth in the exhibition hall. The group responded by holding prayer meetings and hymn singing outside the convention center and leafleting delegates as they entered. The General Board subsequently passed a "resolution calling for dialogue on issues of human sexuality."[63]

Group Recognition and Booth Space

Ever since the 1970s when gay people began forming their own organizations within religious bodies, the refusal both to recognize them as "official" groups and to let them have booth space at annual meetings has been an ongoing point of contention and protest. In 1991, for example, within the Friends United Meeting (FUM) a plan to restrict the meeting times and places of "unofficial Quaker groups" at an upcoming triennial session was challenged by Friends for Lesbian and Gay Concerns and then changed by the FUM's Planning Committee to accommodate the group.[64] Protests by groups in other religious bodies have not been as successful. Beverly Brubaker, for example, wrote that gay Brethren and Mennonites "need to be much more aggressive (ooh, are Brethren allowed to use that ugly word?!) and demanding." She proposed that instead of staying in the separate room, removed from the real exhibition space, that they are given at the annual conference, "we should take a table, some chairs, and our literature, and nonviolently go into the exhibit area and just set up. We should do this every year until we are given the space that we have a *right* to have. We have tried for years to be quiet and cooperative. And I do not believe that we will be given our space unless we demand it."[65]

A more recent issue, but one that has engaged many religious bodies intensely and gained the attention of the news media, has been same-sex unions[66] (also referred to as holy unions, covenant services, commitment ceremonies, weddings, and marriages).[67]

Same-Sex Unions

Some religious bodies, such as the Reconstructionist Rabbinical Association, Unitarian Universalist Association, and various meetings of the Religious Society of Friends, approve of and perform same-sex unions.[68] Other bodies, such as the Presbyterian Church (U.S.A.) and Episcopal Church, have left approval up to local clergy and districts; but the issue remains highly contested and under recurring review within them.[69]

In 1992 at All Saints Church in Pasadena — the largest Episcopal church west of the Mississippi — Reverend George Rivas blessed the union of two gay men at a ceremony witnessed by five hundred guests. Afterward, he said that because "homosexuality is such a divisive issue, I'm sure there is a great deal of distress" over the ceremony, "but the people who were there, who know these men, knew this was appropriate and good."[70] In an open letter to her Unitarian church in Minneapolis, Kit Ketchum wrote: "I am immensely proud when I say to a new acquaintance or an old friend, 'Helene and I were married three years ago, in church.' The legal and financial boundaries are still standing, but your support, in allowing gay marriages, is a wondrous beacon of hope and progress."[71] In 1992, after a Jewish newspaper in San Diego printed the announcement and photo of a union between two lesbians, it received four times the usual amount of mail. Some canceled their subscriptions, while others appreciated having the discussion opened for them. The editors replied, "They are part of our Jewish community and, as such, were entitled to have news about their commitment ceremony published."[72]

The ways in which same-sex unions have been recognized vary greatly according to such factors as the personal preferences of couples and the traditional practices of religious bodies. A member of the Church of the Brethren, for example, said that "in good Anabaptist tradition" he and his partner did not "feel the need for a public ceremony." Once, a visiting preacher at his church — "an aged, wise, well-known, and highly respected churchwoman" — asked others and then him about his relationship and ended the conversation by saying "God bless you." For this man "that pronouncement has remained as much of a church wedding as we have ever had or ever needed."[73]

Recognition of Unions Signals Full Participation

For many gay people being able to have their relationships formally recognized and blessed by their religious bodies is the most significant indicator of whether they are accepted and welcome to participate fully and equally within those communities.

Over one-half of both UMC and UCC respondents in my survey said that the recognition/performance of same-sex unions by their denominations "is very important" (58 percent, UMC; 55 percent, UCC); one-third said it "is important" (33 percent, UMC; 35 percent, UCC); and only one-tenth said it "is not important" (9 percent, UMC; 11 percent, UCC).

Having Same-Sex Unions Performed

About one-tenth of both UMC and UCC respondents had asked pastors to perform same-sex unions (11 percent, UMC; 15 percent, UCC) and had had unions performed (7 percent, UMC; 9 percent, UCC). These had occurred a bit more frequently in the UCC, but both UMC and UCC respondents had received the pastor's support almost all the time (95 percent, UMC; 98 percent, UCC) and the congregation's support about three-quarters of the time (75 percent, UMC; 67 percent, UCC).

When I asked Randy Miller what he thought about same-sex unions and the impact they have had on organized religions, he said, "I think they're great. Personally, I don't know that I would go through a holy union although I was present and celebrated with people at one in Washington; and it was a very powerful event. Not only was the service powerful, but there was a whole uproar and furor about whether this should happen in the United Methodist Church. It was another one of those issues that pushed good liberals to decide what they are going to do about this, 'Do we like gay and lesbians enough to celebrate their holy unions?' In the case where I was involved, they decided to go ahead and be supportive of holy union. I think that unless they're stamped out by legislation, they will have a positive benefit in the church."[74]

I said: "What is it that makes non-gay people move to where they can accept, recognize, or celebrate holy unions?" He responded: "I think they finally get the idea about the experience of love or whatever you want to call it between two gay or lesbian people; and they make the connection that this in some ways is no different than a wedding. I mean they have trepidations, but they eventually see that this is not so radical to them, that two people want to be a part of each other and want to make a commitment to each other." Randy maintained that such occasions, though difficult for some, have "helped to move us beyond simple ignorance to a new level of social tolerance and understanding."

I also interviewed a UCC laywoman whose commitment ceremony had been performed by her pastor. Selena Blackwell said that her partner had been the one to bring up the idea. "When Dody first mentioned it, I was convinced after my divorce from my husband that I was never going to go through that again. She kind of mentioned it and then I think she more or less forgot about it. But it kind of stuck with me and so I was talking to my pastor and I was saying how Dody had mentioned this and I wasn't sure how I felt. He's the one who convinced me that I ought to do it." I asked what his reason was. "He said that it was real important to make a public statement about this type of commitment, to have the support, to get the support, to make a public declaration in a way. He felt that it was his role as a pastor to help celebrate things God brings together, and he felt that this was one of them."

Originally they were going to have the ceremony performed in a UCC church in the nearby town from which Dody had recently moved. But Selena said the minister she asked there "got real cold feet. First, she didn't want to do it in the sanctuary; she wanted to do it in one of the rooms they use for receptions. I didn't particularly like that idea. First, actually, she wanted to do it in our house. Dody basically said that she'd been a longtime member there for decades, had been one of the biggest contributors to the church, and she felt that this was her church. Since the minister wouldn't have a problem marrying some stranger off the street, Dody felt she deserved equal treatment. Then this minister went to their board of deacons to get permission (which isn't done for regular weddings), and again Dody said this should be like marrying anybody. But the minister felt like this was different. Basically it was just her homophobia and fear. So my pastor agreed, not just agreed, but he had always said, 'If you want me to do it, I would be happy to.'"

"Who came to the ceremony?" I asked. Selena replied: "There were some members of my church. Those family members who were in the area came—like Dody's son, who happened to be home from Germany; her daughter and son-in-law came; my kids and ex-husband came. In fact he helped out at the reception. He's been very supportive and been a friend. There were some, not a large number of, friends from Dody's former church, my friends from various committees that I work on, and some members of the United Church Coalition for Lesbian/Gay Concerns came. I think we had about fifty couples."

As with the weddings of other members, this ceremony took place in the church's sanctuary. No objections were raised by members of the congregation. And the people who attended were impressed and moved. "There were a lot of straight people there, and because this was different in their realm of experience, they were thinking more about the service than they would at your average wedding. We just got a lot of positive feedback on how thoughtful and spiritual, how very meaningful, the service was. A number of people said it really helped them with their own personal struggle with homophobia."

Selena said that the ceremony "challenged some of the stereotypes that people were dealing with. Here was a mainline church with a straight white minister performing a service. It was interesting for some also because it wasn't an ONA church. And yet this very meaningful service affirming the commitment of two women was happening in it. Dody and I also worked really hard developing the service so that it was meaningful to each of us but so that it also had a very spiritual dimension, that the hymns we sang talked about the realm of God being inclusive."

For Selena the only negative part of the experience was that it ended up being the hottest day of the year. "It was a hundred degrees that day, and everybody was sweating. I was just glad it wasn't raining, so people could go out on the patio. That was the only thing that I really regretted. I guess the other thing is that I wish I had had it videotaped."

I asked if she had any advice for others who might be thinking about having a same-sex union ceremony. "I don't know. Just your standard marriage-type stuff, but also that when you do it make sure you are aware of the issues, the particular issues facing gay couples. Because it's not legally sanctioned, you don't get the usual kind of spousal protection; so you need to get advice on how to protect yourself legally." I asked: "You mean for doing wills and that kind of thing?" She said: "For doing wills, prenuptials, whatever, if you're into that sort of thing. Just things like giving each other the power of attorney, living wills, making sure that the family knows that this is something you're doing and that whether the family agrees with it or not they are to respect the other partner for making decisions about your life. For instance, my parents totally don't want anyone to know about our union, but I don't really care as long as my kids know, my ex-husband knows, and Dody's family all know. But I can see how some couples could do this and end up with problems and regrets later on. You need to get all your ducks in a row about being gay; the state doesn't do it for you."[75]

I asked her: "Do you think that having done the ceremony made you take care of those things that gay couples otherwise don't attend to?" She responded: "Yes. Having the ceremony for me solidifies this relationship. We were together a couple of years, so it's hard to say what would have developed if we hadn't had the ceremony. For me it was an act that was pretty profound. I tend to have to wake up and pay attention. It was like getting hit over the head with the realization about needing to protect the relationship because of the absence of legal and state protection."[76]

I asked for her opinion about the qualifications of non-gay clergy to perform these ceremonies, if she thought someone who has not had the experience of being gay can respond to the needs of those who are. "I think so, if they're honest with themselves—and I think Rich was particularly honest with himself. He told us that theologically he knew what was right. He had his own personal fear a lot of times that he had to work through, but there was no reason not to do it. Plus, I had been working on Rich ever since he was called to the church. I was testing him out to see if he was going to be severely homophobic, and if he was, I was going to leave because I wasn't going to have my issues dealt with as problems all the time."

"Did he ever present any problems that you had to struggle with when you were planning the service?" I asked. Selena replied: "Not really. He was helpful. In a lot of ways though we had to be in a position to help him too. He did some pastoral counseling with us, like he does with all the couples getting married, and he in general would not have been very helpful to a young gay couple who had not had the experience of marriage. Like I'd been married thirteen to fourteen years; Dody had been married thirty something years; so we knew about marriage. I had done a lot of reading; I had my own personal experiences as a gay person; and I knew a lot of gay people—he didn't have any of that. In the process we would just generally start talking. He was kind; he was as helpful as he could be at the time, but I think like any pastor he needed to—and did—expand his vision a little bit more than the standard stuff one gets out of seminary training."

I asked if he acknowledged that he was learning from Selena. "Yes, all the time. Even now he says how much in doing that ceremony, working through that ceremony, really helped him." "Does he say specifically how or just kind of generally?" I asked. "Mostly generally," she said, "but the most specific thing he said is that it made him act according to his theological beliefs."

Ongoing Problems, Restrictions, and Punishment

But clergy and congregations across all religious bodies continue to struggle with the issue of same-sex unions.[77] Kit Ketchum pointed out that even among Unitarian Universalists, "Many congregations or clergy are 'just not comfortable enough' to actually perform gay marriages."[78] Among Southern Baptists, pastor Mahan Siler and his congregation in Raleigh stood against denominational policy to bless the commitment between a gay member and his partner.[79] Among ministers in the Evangelical Lutheran Church in America, gay weddings have been conducted in some regions quite regularly in violation of the denomination's official position.[80]

As a result of controversies over same-sex unions in various UMC local churches, bishops have taken different positions and given different advice for the churches in their districts. Randy Miller pointed out that same-sex unions are "not legal, but they're not illegal either, meaning that there is nothing in the UMC's Book of Discipline addressing holy union"; so some bishops have said "that no clergy could be involved in performing holy unions" in their districts, while another, like "the bishop here in the California Pacific Conference, accepts holy union and has offered to help write liturgy for holy unions." Because unions are not covered explicitly by the UMC's anti-gay policy, bishops have been able to advance their own positions.

Some UMC leaders, after hearing that same-sex unions were being performed in their districts, have issued restrictive regulations and punished the clergy who officiated.[81] Tim Tennant-Jayne has described the effect his ceremony had in his district. He and his partner had talked about clergy whom they might ask to lead their service, and "there was a woman, a lesbian, who was attending one of the churches I was at who was on Honorable Location [a nonparish assignment] from her conference. She was somebody that my lover really liked; and so we asked her if she would do the service, and she was agreeable to it. We talked briefly about having a pastor who was on Regular Appointment do the service. However, we chose this woman not to avoid any complications, but simply because she was who we liked."

Aware that the ceremony had occurred, the bishop subsequently made a statement that she did not want same-sex unions performed in UMC buildings or by UMC clergy in her district. Later on, the woman who performed the ceremony for Tim and his partner chose to tell the bishop that she was not a "practicing homosexual" and would be celibate, so that she could be appointed to serve a parish. The bishop appointed her but not before the cabinet, the bishop's advisers, questioned her extensively about the ceremony she had performed. Tim said, "My friend got a lot of flak for it. They asked her why she did it; and part of her response was that when she had been in an earlier parish, people would ask her to bless their pets and their boats, so why shouldn't she be asked to bless a relationship between two people? I guess the cabinet got kind of sheepish looking and thought, 'That makes sense.' They were very clear about the outcome, though; they made her promise that she would not do a union service while she was under appointment."

Planning and Designing Unions

In its national survey, Partners Task Force for Gay and Lesbian Couples found that 16 percent of the responding couples had symbolized their commitment to their relationships with religious ceremonies.[82] As revealed in recent books about same-sex unions, most ceremonies have occurred in nonchurch and nonsynagogue settings and have been designed by the couples themselves.[83] But couples often seek to have ordained clergy officiate. After describing the details of planning and arranging their own ceremony, one lesbian couple said: "We even had an ordained United Methodist minister. This was very powerful and significant for us. It felt right. We joked with our pastor because joining a lesbian couple was her first official act since her ordination a short time before. What a way to begin her ministry in the United Methodist Church!"[84]

Tim Tennant-Jayne, a UMC clergyman himself, had performed four commitment ceremonies, all in nonchurch settings. "I think that generally that's been the couple's decision. They did it where they felt comfortable. One did it at a friend's home. Another one did it in their own home. I've done two in bars, because that's where the people had met. It's not even so much that they go through the hassle of finding out which churches will say yes and who will say no; it's just knowing that most churches are uncomfortable. People don't even ask."

I asked if he thought there is something to be said for creating ceremonies out of the particular experience of gay people, of doing them in homes, natural settings, parks, bars, and places with which there is a personally meaningful connection, as opposed to copying the way that ceremonies are done for heterosexual couples. "Yes, because when I have done the ceremonies each time, I have worn my white alb with stole and looked the priestly role. The first one I did, we had a dozen people show up at this bar. Every man there — it was all men — were all in black leather, and here I am in white alb. It was like, 'Who stands out in this crowd?' However, God came into that setting and was present for that union. God comes into the bars or the condos or whatever. With the regular heterosexual wedding, I think it's real easy to say, 'We go to God for the blessing, and then we go to the bars for the fun.' There's a separation there. And I can say that also having done regular weddings, having been married myself to a woman, the mainstream culture is very much saying, 'OK, you do the wedding, you get that over with, you pay a priest or minister to be there, then you go for the good stuff, the flowers that you want to decorate with or the bridal dress to show off, the spread of food, the dance, whatever.' I think because we ended up having to integrate both settings — we had the ceremony in the bar and faced the dance floor and then turned around for the food — there's a connection made there that is not easily broken. You don't go to a separate building; you party right there where the ceremony happened."

At the time of our interview Tim did not have a parish assignment and was employed as a stained-glass worker. As an openly gay clergyman who had encountered employment difficulties within the UMC and who had continued to identify and be active as a clergyperson within the gay community, his comments provide for a shift and transition from this chapter's examination of the predominantly lay participation of gay people within organized religion to a focus on their ordination and employment within various religious bodies.

Chapter Five

Seminary, Ordination, Ministry, and Employment

Overview of Employment Opportunities and Job Security

In his interviews with gay people throughout Middle America, Neil Miller talked with three clergypeople[1] who had been punished by their religious bodies because of their sexual orientation. The first was Rose Mary Denman, a United Methodist (UMC) minister whose bishop began formal proceedings to void her ordination after she wrote about being gay in a gay newspaper. She was tried by an ecclesiastical court in New Hampshire and suspended from performing ministerial duties. The second was Bill Dorn, a Roman Catholic priest who had been dismissed from his post at the Newman Center at St. Cloud State University in Minnesota after he wrote an article criticizing the Catholic Church's position on homosexuality. A few weeks after his dismissal he announced he was gay, and his bishop then defrocked him. Two years later the church excommunicated him. The third clergy interviewed by Miller was James Tinney, an ordained Pentecostal minister who was about to serve his first church when he told his wife about his homosexuality. She told their pastor, who then performed an exorcism on Tinney that he said did not work. Years later in Washington, D.C., Tinney held a citywide gay revival and founded the black, gay Pentecostal Faith Temple. On the eve of the revival the bishop of the Washington diocese of the Church of God in Christ publicly excommunicated him.[2]

The diversity of gender, race, geography, and religious bodies represented in these events is reinforced in other stories reported in the newsletters of gay religious organizations.[3] The following are a number of examples.

When Bet Hannon, the pastor of the Friends church in West Branch, Iowa, planned to move into the parsonage with her lover, many members were upset. Made up of rural and small-town people with views ranging from liberal to evangelical and conservative, the congregation weathered the controversy and voted to maintain and support her.

However, the Iowa Yearly Meeting subsequently met and terminated her contract.[4]

At Bethany Presbyterian Church in Sacramento, a parishioner found out and told others that pastor Scott Anderson was gay. Scott explained to the congregation that he would resign and not fight to stay for three reasons: (1) he did not want to subject himself to the "scorn," "derision," and "enormous backlash" that would ensue because of the "pervasive homophobia in our denomination"; (2) the controversy would split and probably destroy the congregation; and (3) his official removal "would simply be a matter of time" because of the denomination's national position that "self-affirming, practicing homosexuals cannot be ministers."[5]

Ross Merkel, the pastor of St. Paul's Lutheran Church in Oakland, was removed from his position and from ordained status after coming out to his congregation during a service celebrating his fifteen years as an ordained minister. The congregation voted to keep him, but his bishop said that the removal was "necessary since, as an openly 'practicing homosexual,' he is not in compliance" with the guidelines for clergy of the Evangelical Lutheran Church of America.[6]

Mark Crosby received a Doctorate of Ministry in pastoral counseling from Andover Newton Theological Seminary and was the director of a psychiatric day care program in Waltham, Massachusetts, when the Committee on Chaplaincy and Pastoral Counselors of the American Baptist Churches in the U.S.A. refused to endorse him because he is an openly gay man. The committee later also withdrew its endorsement of Susan Vanderburgh in Phoenix after she came out as a lesbian. Such denominational endorsement is required for membership in the nation's major accrediting body for pastoral counselors.[7]

There are also stories of success. For example, in 1992 at University Baptist Church in Minneapolis, Nadean Bishop became the first openly gay minister to be hired by a local congregation within the American Baptist Churches in the U.S.A.[8] Also, Reconstructionist and Reform Judaism, the United Church of Christ (UCC), the Unitarian Universalist Association (UUA), and the American Friends Service Committee have developed equal opportunity programs to help place gay clergy and lay employees.[9] But because these religious bodies are the most liberal and with the exception of Reform Judaism not among the largest, their efforts are not widely representative of organized religion. Even within them, regional bodies and agencies often oppose such programs;[10] and in local congregations, search committees usually refuse to consider openly gay candidates, members have great difficulty in accepting or voting for those who do get nominated by search committees, and administrative boards fire closeted clergy who come out after being hired.[11]

Sexual Behavior

Because most religious bodies have taken positions forbidding the ordination and hiring of openly gay people and because polls show that most people support those positions, employment opportunities and job security for gay clergy are uncommon.[12] The opposition to gay clergy seems to rest on perceptions about their sexual behavior, although gay clergy themselves—like their heterosexual counterparts—rarely if ever describe, discuss, or promote their sexual practices.

Susan Vanderburgh, for example, came to the attention of officials in her denomination because of an article she wrote for the newsletter of the American Baptist gay organization. In it she discussed coming out as a lesbian in terms of being from an evangelical background, believing in a theology of building inclusive community, finding a basis for her ministry in the biblical account of Christ's ministry to outcasts, and thinking that the church needs to repent of dividing and excluding people. She did not speak about her sexual activities, and yet the Ordination Standards Committee withdrew recognition of her ordination "on the basis of her continued unrepentant practice of homosexual behavior."[13]

Sexuality, Relationships, Responsibility

Gay clergy most often want to have their partners, households, families, and friends validated and recognized as a resource for and component of their professional lives. As with non-gay clergy, they want to be able to refer to and rely on their loved ones without hiding and secrecy. They are not any more inclined than non-gay clergy to want to describe their personal sexual lives. In James Wolf's national survey of over one hundred gay Catholic priests, when respondents were asked about sexual activity, they wrote about love, responsibility, and relationships. For example:

> I see love as calling for sexual expression when intimacy grows between two people. I also see sexual expression as healthy and bonding activity which relieves the burden of stress and affirms the lovedness of both people. I also realize that it can cause stress if not integrated into the context of love.

> I have just come out of the closet regarding acceptance of my homosexuality within the last two months. At the present time, I feel sexual activity with others carries no morality with it *per se.* The "morality" involved here is the responsibility to oneself and the other person.

> If in a relationship the two become genitally involved, they must realistically weigh the ramifications of their actions.... I really believe that healthy human love between people is a share in God. I do not, however, see promiscuity or easy sex as having this blessing.[14]

The enthusiasm with which religious bodies focus on the sexual behavior of gay people and deny the affectional and social dimension of their lives reflects a collective fascination fueled more by prurience and imagination than by the expressed interests, concerns, and needs of gay people. Not much is said by gay clergy in organized religion about their sexual behavior, but much is presumed by religious bodies who want to control what they imagine that behavior to be.

Confidential Information

Of all studies about gay clergy, Richard Sipe's research on heterosexual and homosexual Catholic priests provides the most information about private sexual behavior because it was gathered within confidential settings, such as counseling sessions, workshops, and support-group meetings.[15] From his work as a psychotherapist from 1960 to 1985, Sipe identified these various subgroups of homosexual behavior: the "pseudohomosexuality" of those who fear they may be homosexual but cannot resolve that they are or are not by occasional sexual experimentation; the "defensive homosexuality" of those who are afraid of or want to avoid heterosexual propositions; the "regressive homosexuality" of those who develop a mature public work life around friendships and shared duties and a hidden play life of secret sexual encounters in bars or rest rooms regardless or perhaps because of the danger or possibility of damage; the "situational homosexuality" of heterosexually oriented priests for whom a longtime friendship and isolation lead to a sexual exchange between friends; the "obligatory homosexuality" of those who do not want to accept their homosexual orientation and therefore find the celibate, homosocial environment of the priesthood a haven of peaceful and productive work; and the "committed homosexuality" of those whose "sexual attraction, fantasy, emotional and social preference, and their self-identification or awareness are all congruent."[16]

Sipe observed that those within the subgroup of "committed homosexuality" may or may not be celibate. He described the celibate ones as among "the most observant of religious celibates, self-aware and self-restrained, dedicated to their ideals and selfless in their service to others." The relationships of the noncelibate most frequently were long-term, free of guilt, and maintained at a geographical distance with partners who are "appropriate in terms of age, mutual consent, and circumstance." These priests kept their sexual activity "completely split off" from their professional lives and considered it "necessary and inconsequential." It rarely, if ever, came to the attention of civil authorities. Because much of this activity involved "genuine friendship and loyalty, without interfering with the practice of their ministry," it was "experienced as an aid to the priests' lives and vocations."[17]

Sheila Murphy's observations about lesbian Catholic religious were less comprehensive than Sipe's study of gay priests, but they have the similar benefit of having been made in confidential situations. She too found that many of the lesbians "who feel called to ministry...have struggled with and accepted their same-sex orientation, have embraced its value in their lives, and have opted to commit themselves to the Gospel in celibate communal living." She added that they "are not promiscuous, not ruled by 'raging, perverse passions'; they are not emotionally sick, developmentally delayed, or mentally unbalanced."[18]

Sipe also observed that since 1978 another subgroup has emerged within the "committed homosexual" subgroup. These priests ally themselves with gay rights, speak freely in supportive environments about themselves as gay priests, and more often find their support outside the church. Many refuse to lead a double life and "feel it is a part of their vocation to be honest about their sexual orientation and that sexual activity is their God-given right." Most "disregard celibacy as not possible or desirable."[19]

Apparent and Real Information

From his data collected over three decades, Sipe estimated that generally 18 to 22 percent of Catholic clergy are homosexually active or compelled toward homosexual involvements. From 1978 to 1985, the reporting of homosexual behavior by his subjects increased significantly to between 38 and 42 percent.[20] Sipe claimed that this increase is both apparent and real.

There *appears* to be an increase because proportionately more nongay than gay priests have left the church to marry and form relationships. The apparent increased number of gay priests is in fact an adjustment in the proportion of gay to straight priests. Also, the feminist and gay movements have made people aware of what has always been the homosocial organization of clerical life. The all-male, monosexual, hierarchical structure of the church is the same, but people recognize and name it now.[21]

But there is also a *real* increase in the number of gay priests and concrete causes for it. Many priests have accepted the open expression of sexual affection encouraged by the gay liberation movement of the

1970s. This open expression and greater tolerance of homosexuality, coupled with the church's need to recruit more priests and thereby alter standards for admission to seminaries and religious houses, have "increased the appeal of the priesthood to some who openly identify themselves as gay."[22]

The following are among Sipe's estimates of homosexual behaviors among priests:

> About twenty percent of all priests have some homosexual orientation.
>
> About ten percent of all priests are homosexually active.
>
> About half of the priests who describe themselves as homosexual practice celibacy. The same proportion is found for priests who have a heterosexual orientation.
>
> Six percent of all priests have been sexually involved with children or minors. Four percent of those priests (less than one-half percent of the total) have a homosexual orientation.
>
> Four percent of all priests have a secure homosexual orientation and relationships that are guilt-free and constant or sequentially stable.
>
> For three percent of all clergy, homosexual activity is part of a mental health problem which may involve poor impulse control, excessive narcissism, depression, and alcoholism.[23]

Few reports of the latter kinds of problems were found by Wolf or by Richard Wagner in his interviews with fifty gay Catholic priests. Wolf observed that his respondents' "lives are not best described as chronic and silent suffering," and "for the most part, [they] have accepted the fact that they are gay and are thankful for it."[24]

Vow of Celibacy

When Wolf asked his respondents how they dealt with celibacy, 41 percent said they consider their sexual lives as separate from their lives as priests; 25 percent said they have not resolved the issue; 20 percent said they abstain from sex because of personal choice; 4 percent said they abstain because they feel they are forced by church law to do so; and 11 percent provided a variety of other answers. In Wagner's study, thirty of his fifty subjects said they felt no guilt about violating their celibacy vow.[25]

Comparing his data with those from studies of non-gay priests, Wolf found that celibacy was much more problematic for his respondents

(11 percent, non-gay; 63 percent, gay) but so was the loneliness of the priesthood (15 percent, non-gay; 44 percent, gay).[26] Their problems with celibacy, therefore, had more to do with affectional than with sexual needs, that is, with the need to form a loving relationship.[27] As one respondent wrote, "I love the priesthood" and "to leave would be the hardest thing in my life," but "I don't think I can survive as a human without a lover. If Church authorities force the issue with me, I'll leave the priesthood to keep my freedom to be in a loving relationship."[28]

Murphy observed that while both lesbian and nonlesbian religious have to decide whether or not they can personally endorse celibacy, the task was often more complicated for homosexual women because of their own confusion about lesbianism or because of the homophobia of their peers and superiors. Not all approached or solved the problem in the same way: "Some women are comfortably gay and desirous of living celibately. Others will be comfortably gay and unsure of celibacy. Unaware of their sexual orientation, some may try to work out their psychological and sexual identity within the context of a religious life style." Murphy concluded that when women religious do become sexually involved with other women, "it is *as* serious — not *more* serious — than when they become heterosexually involved."[29]

Wolf observed that his respondents, unlike non-gay priests, "have gone beyond a stage of merely questioning the Church's authority in requiring the vow of celibacy to a point where they have managed to compartmentalize their sexual lives from their lives as priests." Only 8 percent felt that their sexuality often interfered with their work as priests. Rather than simply conform to and silently suffer these restrictions, most gay priests have been able to form and protect their relationships.[30]

Professional and Sexual Compatibility

Working on and resolving the difficulties and problems of being homosexual in the priesthood did not seem to have made priests dissatisfied with their role: Wolf found that gay priests were happier with their lives than non-gay priests (85 percent, non-gay; 96 percent, gay) and almost as certain about remaining in the priesthood (89 percent, non-gay; 82 percent, gay). Most gay Catholic priests would appear to be men who "with varying levels of frustration" have found a great deal of fulfillment with their professional responsibilities that was not dramatically different from that of priests in general. For them "homosexuality and dedication to the priesthood are not mutually exclusive."[31]

Many gay clergy were able to accommodate themselves to and find satisfaction in their respective religious bodies because they had acknowledged and developed their sexual/affectional interests before and/or during their seminary training for the profession.

Seminary

Sexual Awareness and Development

Three-quarters of Wolf's respondents reported that they were aware of their homosexuality before they entered seminary; 20 percent said they became aware during their seminary years; and 5 percent said they became aware after seminary.[32] In their study of lesbians and bisexual clergywomen, Deborah Carney and Susan Davies also found that a large majority (80 percent) had been aware of their sexual orientation in seminary.[33] Murphy observed that Catholic women applying to religious life are now more diversified in age and background than previously. "Some have been married, some have lived with lovers, and some arrive with no sexual experience at all." Although "some have thought long and hard about sexuality and relationships and have come to a mature understanding and acceptance of themselves," others are "less settled in themselves" and "may or may not be comfortable... about the place of relationships in their lives."[34]

The findings from these studies by Wolf, Carney and Davies, and Murphy suggest that most gay seminarians begin or complete their training with some awareness of their sexual orientation. But such awareness does not necessarily include feeling confident, comfortable, or open about their sexual identity. One of Wolf's respondents wrote:

> I was afraid of dealing with the issue of my orientation in the seminary because I was afraid I would not be accepted or ordained. I had many friends who were active homosexuals in the seminary process. I would listen to them, their struggles, their failures and successes and would process what all of that could possibly mean in light of my felt homosexual orientation. I simply passed it off as a "phase" I was going through. No luck; the "phase" was causing me to be seriously depressed and also in a homosexual relationship with a married man.[35]

In retrospect, the women in Carney and Davies's study also recognized the importance of honesty, purpose, certainty, and clarity when entering into and engaging in seminary life. They provided the following advice for other women entering seminary: "Know what you really want and why. Know where your integrity line falls and live by it"; "Check out the school and the support afforded there"; "Seek counseling"; "Be prepared for battle and pain and heartache"; "Decide whether to be open or in the closet and then know what your options are from there"; "Be clear about the difficulties of the closet"; and "Maturity is essential. Don't start young."[36]

One of the UMC clergymen I interviewed said, "I started realizing or acting on my sexual orientation when I was a teenager and really came to some strong understandings about it when I was in college, really sort of confirmed my sexual identity in college. But it really wasn't until I got to seminary that it became apparent how the church's stand on those issues was going to affect my relationship to the church career-wise." During his seminary years the UMC General Conference passed its legislation prohibiting gay ordination. "There were still all kinds of possibilities until 1984 when the church said, 'We don't want you.' It was at that point that I realized I was really going to have to reconsider whether I could seek appointment at a local church. And it was at that point that I came out to my family, to my parents, and really started looking beyond the local church. It also affected other people who had to decide whether to keep in the fight or to look in other directions; and it affected, I think, whether a lot of gay/lesbian folks considered going into ordained ministry or not and said, 'It's just not worth the fight.' "

A UCC clergywoman I interviewed recalled that "in terms of my own self-awareness, my own orientation, that came relatively late, that did not come together for me until the last year at seminary. It really scared me in terms of having to decide what I was going to do when I went up for my ordination, because all of the sexual orientation issues came together for me in early fall, and my ordination interview was the following spring."

Encountering Problems

That gay people do encounter problems in seminary settings because of their sexual orientation was shown by findings in my survey of UMC and UCC gay people. About one-quarter (27 percent, UMC; 21 percent, UCC) of those who ever began seminary reported having eventually left, and for over one-half of them (56 percent, UMC; 53 percent, UCC) their reasons for leaving were gay-related.

Personal accounts from other sources describe incidents of coercion and rejection by seminaries. In the late 1970s, for example, because UMC seminaries received denominational funds, they became the focus of denominational legislation that forbade the funding of any group or program to "promote the acceptance of homosexuality." Garrett Theological Seminary dismissed two "self-avowed homosexuals"; Iliff School of Theology refused to admit a candidate for ministry in the Metropolitan Community Church (MCC); and St. Paul School of Theology placed five students on probation for distributing pro-gay literature.[37]

In other denominations, a student at Trinity Lutheran Seminary in Columbus reported that in her senior year the Evangelical Lutheran Church in America issued a "Sexual Conduct Statement" requiring homosexuals to agree to remain celibate in order to become eligible for ordained ministry. As a lesbian in a committed relationship, she saw few options: "I could lie about who I am. I could deny who I am. I could say openly who I am. The first two options meant loss of my self. The third option meant loss of my calling."[38]

A Mennonite woman wrote that her application to the Associated Mennonite Biblical Seminaries in Elkhart, Indiana, was rejected after "I talked with several people at the seminary about what kind of reception I could expect" as an open lesbian in a long-term relationship who "planned to be open about my sexuality." She subsequently enrolled in the UCC-affiliated Chicago Theological Seminary and sought ordination in the UCC.[39]

Murphy observed that many Catholic religious orders for women require psychological testing of candidates as part of the routine admissions procedure in part because of a growing concern about lesbians already in the orders, lesbians seeking admission, and women applicants uncertain about their sexual orientation.[40]

One of the problems reported by my respondents who had attended and graduated from seminary was verbal harassment. About one-third (33 percent, UMC; 39 percent, UCC) said that they had at some time been verbally harassed in seminary because of their sexual orientation. Identified as the harassers most often were other students (84 percent, UMC; 67 percent, UCC), who were then followed by faculty members (39 percent, UMC; 44 percent, UCC), administrators (39 percent, UMC; 46 percent, UCC), staff members (26 percent, UMC; 18 percent, UCC), and field supervisors (19 percent, UMC; 23 percent, UCC).

Carney and Davies also found that their respondents had experienced "much discrimination" in seminary. "Straight students topped the list of discriminators . . . , followed closely by the administration, other lesbian or bisexual women, financial aid officers, and professors." Respondents who had been closeted in seminary told of how some out lesbians were vocal and hostile in accusing them of being afraid and not honest. Out lesbians, on the other hand, reported that the more closeted women avoided them out of fear of "guilt by association" and resented them because they seemed happy and confident. Many of both out and closeted lesbians said they had not sought support from other lesbians because they were afraid of each other. One reported that when an off-campus support group meeting was planned and announced, no one attended because they did not know one another and were afraid that information about the meeting would get back to church and seminary authorities.[41]

Sipe's study also revealed a problem of sexual harassment in seminaries. He claimed to have "scores of reports from priests about affectionate or sexual approaches or responses from teachers or elders during their training." From the stories of more than one hundred subjects who had found these sexual approaches problematic, he identified an institutionalized system of secrecy sustained by denying that a sexual problem existed and by not wanting to bring scandal to the institution. He maintained that "there is no other single element so destructive to sexual responsibility among clergy as the system of secrecy that has both shielded behavior and reinforced denial."[42]

Further evidence of dissatisfaction and problems were the ratings that Wolf's respondents gave to the influence that their seminary training had on their understanding and development of their sexuality. More than one-half (51 percent) rated it negatively, about one-quarter rated it neutrally (26 percent), and about one-quarter rated it positively (23 percent). Also, only one-quarter of Wolf's study, compared to 70 percent of a study of non-gay priests, felt that their seminary training prepared them well for the life of a priest.[43]

Finding Support

But gay people also reported positive seminary experiences. Several women in Carney and Davies's study spoke about "seeking out" and "finding" the helpful, nurturing, supportive people and places within the seminary community.[44] Sipe also noticed that recently activity within some Catholic seminaries was less secretive, especially among students. Some subjects likened the "flaunting of behavior" to that of a gay bar and reported that students commonly called each other by feminine and pet names. Individuals and groups of seminarians were also known by faculty and students to frequent gays bars "as part of their personal recreational program."[45]

Virginia Wolf, a student at United Theological Seminary in the Twin Cities area of Minnesota, wrote that most of the people attending a 1993 national conference for gay seminarians reported that their seminary experiences were "mostly very good." For many, "seminary provides community" in which they could "find and affirm ourselves." Several "came out at seminary" and experienced the "healing and joy of being who we are." For a few, on the other hand, seminary was "simply the darkest of closets," a place in which people struggled "to hang on to a faith which both nourishes and diminishes us." Virginia said that "the extent to which seminarians experience community or closet depends on the denomination, the seminary, and the seminarian." Two-thirds of those attending were members of religious bodies that consider themselves fully welcoming of gay people—the UCC, UUA, and MCC. Only two attendees were from fundamentalist seminaries and denominations, and "they requested that their attendance be kept confidential and never publicly identified themselves as gay."[46]

She went on to report that at the most liberal seminaries, such as UUA-affiliated Meadville/Lombard (Chicago) and Starr King (Berkeley), gay students are out in all their classes, while at other liberal seminaries they are out in most classes. At seminaries that attract large numbers of students and faculty from conservative denominations, gay students are "uncomfortable" about being out in the classroom.[47]

Virginia said that her own seminary was "a good environment for an out lesbian like me." There was a large gay presence of students, faculty, and staff; specific courses on gay issues were offered; and the gay students could effectively negotiate with the school to meet their needs. Although "no student has ever been deliberately rude or hateful to me," she had experienced some "tense moments" when she began mostly "because of the way I responded to other students' apparent discomfort." She wrote:

> We who are sexual minorities often learn to protect ourselves by being defensive and by expecting rejection. We sometimes react aggressively to the pain of what feels like, and may be, yet one more misunderstanding of who we are. We also sometimes go quietly back into our closets to heal. Although either response is understandable and undoubtedly necessary at the time, neither response allows us, or those who differ with us, to grow.

The environment has allowed her to "feel at home" and to "relax and welcome my own and others' discomfort as opportunity for respectful dialogue."[48]

Several of the UMC and UCC clergypeople I interviewed also said that seminary offered them the opportunity to be more open about their sexuality than they had been in previous settings. For others problems occurred not in seminary but as they sought positions and ordination after graduation. One of the priests in James Wolf's study wrote:

> Shortly after ordination, I was 24 at the time, I strongly felt the need for intimacy that was not limited to sexual intimacy but did not exclude it. The seminary experience allowed the development of deep and abiding friendships with my friends who were available around the clock. After ordination, the sense of solitary living totally reversed that experience. Frequent phone calls and weekly dinners helped but did not counteract the experience of loneliness.[49]

As one of Carney and Davies's respondents advised, "Know the great distance between seminary and the local church."[50] For many gay seminarians the distance between the more permissive seminary setting and the more restrictive local church became apparent during their seminary fieldwork.

Fieldwork

Diane Darling, a UCC clergywoman I interviewed, spoke of how her lover was dismissed from a fieldwork position. It was forty-five minutes away from her own church and "much more conservative." Diane recalled: "When she moved out here, we had begun living together, and she was doing an internship there. She was in her last year of seminary. We had decided to do a covenant service to celebrate our relationship. She told them. And then the trouble started. The people who loved her thought, 'Now we have to rethink a lot of things.' Some of them didn't bat an eyelash, but a lot of the church just said, 'No way.' It's the kind of church that some call a patron church, where a handful of people support the budget and can pull strings. A few of the patrons said, 'If she stays, we're pulling out our money'; so in effect there wouldn't have been a job anyway."

Neil Miller interviewed a gay seminarian who had been hired as a student minister by Central Presbyterian Church in Louisville. This young man had originally applied to seminary without telling the admissions committee that he was gay out of fear of being rejected. As a student, though, most people knew he was gay. In classes that discussed social issues such as homosexuality he was very open. He was also socially and politically active in the gay community and had even appeared on TV during a gay pride march. When hired by Central Presbyterian he came out to the minister and "was sure most of the congregation had figured out he was gay." One of his duties was to head up the church's task force on homophobia. After graduation he was planning not to reveal his sexual orientation to search committees, because it would prevent him from being hired and ordained. Miller wrote that this seminarian "was in a curious position.... His sexual orientation was known to his fellow seminarians, to his teachers, and probably to some church officials. Yet to be ordained, he would essentially have to tiptoe back into the closet." The young man said that he did not want to "put myself forward as a scapegoat" but that "sometimes he felt like a traitor to other gay people by being part of a church that discriminated against gays and lesbians." Miller concluded that this young man "seemed to exemplify a new generation of gay clergy—relatively open about being gay, militant at times, hopeful about his future as a gay person in the church," yet "caught up in the contradictions of the church's stance on gay ministers."[51]

Ordination

Ordination typically requires both seminary training as well as the completion of a preparatory process designed by the ordaining religious body. The ceremony or act of ordination itself is preceded by a written and oral examination by a council or committee of the religious body and occurs before or as the ordinand begins her or his first professional placement.

James Wolf reported that close to 90 percent of his respondents were aware of their sexual orientation and that close to 70 percent were sexually active before the time of their ordinations.[52] But because most religious bodies prohibit ordination of gay people, few openly gay individuals were ordained. Seventy percent of Carney and Davies's respondents even thought it more difficult now than in the past to be ordained as openly gay. They said that AIDS, feminism, and the more public discussion of lesbianism have put ordination committees on the alert and that some religious bodies, such as the United Methodist Church, are "more homophobic now than in previous years."[53]

Reluctance to Be Out

Even within pro-gay religious bodies, ordinands are reluctant to be open.[54] Among UCC clergy respondents in my survey, for example, only 9 percent had been ordained as openly gay.[55] And most ordinands-to-be were not confident about being out during their upcoming ordinations. Forty-five percent said they would be out; 10 percent said they would not be out; and 45 percent were unsure.

The UCC clergywoman I interviewed who was coming to terms with her sexual orientation in the last year of seminary discussed one of the meetings with her ordination committee: "Because I wasn't comfortable enough and didn't feel like I could really articulate all of what was involved for me, because I hadn't been living it that long—there was still too much that needed to come together—I decided not to say anything at that point. And in some ways in looking back now—but I'm also much more comfortable with who I am now—I wish that maybe I had done it differently. So I had to deal with some of the old questions a candidate for ordination gets from ministry committees, like, 'If you have a family and you get married and you're in ministry, how will you balance that?' You know, all the sexist crap from some of the folks on the committee, mostly older women, who want to know all of that. I really had to bite my tongue about what I was going to say."

Selective Outness

In lieu of being completely out, many had managed to be out selectivity during the ordination process. Selective outness usually involved confiding in and gaining the trust of certain church officials, committee members, or members of the congregation the ordinand was serving or about to serve. About one-third of both UMC and UCC clergy respondents in my survey (33 percent, UMC; 38 percent, UCC) reported having been selectively out during their ordination process, as did nearly one-third (30 percent) of Carney and Davies's respondents.[56]

This selective, as opposed to complete or full, outness by gay ordinands was not surprising given the increased attention that religious bodies give to homosexuality. Carney and Davies reported that their respondents experienced discriminatory practices "throughout the process of ordination" most often by staff on the district and province levels,[57] "followed closely by placement committees, other lesbian and bisexual women, and gay men."[58] Gay people have reported that pressure comes from many directions — from officials who want to screen out gay candidates, others who want to recognize and support them, and others who want to avoid the issue and not have gay candidates identify openly, but also from gay people who want candidates to be open and still others who want candidates to be closeted and not stir up trouble. Simply remaining silent about one's sexual orientation was not always an option because some committees pointedly asked candidates if they were homosexual.

Negotiating the Ordination Process

When denied ordination because of their sexual orientation, Carney and Davies's respondents reported having taken a variety of alternative steps, such as relying on the assistance of those in powerful positions, appealing "to every church court possible," switching denominations, settling for a nonordained ministerial position, and keeping the issue alive by reapplying for ordination.[59]

"Irregular" ordination was another alternative used in 1990 within the Evangelical Lutheran Church in America. After the ordinations of Ruth Frost, Jeff Johnson, and Phyllis Zillhart were denied because of their "avowed homosexuality," thirty-five Lutheran clergy gathered and acted in place of the bishop to ordain them. The denomination then tried and suspended the local churches that had sponsored and hired the ordinands.[60]

Successful openly gay candidates understand fully how unusual their own ordinations are. When Cheryl Diane Harrell was ordained at the UCC Church of the Covenant in Boston, she wrote to her friends, "Ordination is a deeply personal act, and yet, a public event as well." Recognizing that many cannot be open without losing their jobs, she said, "I am open, because they cannot be open. I am open because gay men and lesbians should not have to choose between their livelihood and being known by others."[61]

Gay candidates for ordination have to be watchful at each step of the process. As shown by the percentages of my UCC respondents who reported problems at each stage of the process, obstacles and difficulty varied along the way. For example, although less than 10 percent reported problems with receiving their local pastor's support, 35 percent reported problems with receiving the recommendation of their district-level's Committee on Ministry to proceed to the ecclesiastical council, but then only 13 percent encountered problems in getting approved by that council (see table 12).

Craig Hoffman, for example, "came out of the closet" when he was a student at Andover Newton Theological School in the Boston area. By this time he had already completed the first four steps of the UCC ordination process. His home church in Pennsylvania had already recommended him to the district, which had taken him "in-care."[62] Knowing that he did not want to continue "without sharing my life-giving journey of accepting and affirming my gayness as a gift of God," he visited his home church to talk about his gayness with the members of the committee whose recommendation he would need for the next step. He said initial reaction from members was "neutral to positive," but the pastor and district staff were pressuring him not to be open. The official meeting to discuss the local church's recommendation was held a month later. Craig wrote that the "tone of the meeting was quite negative, set by those, including the pastor, who were vocal. Others remained silent." When he asked to hear from those who had not spoken, "a few made affirmative comments." Before the meeting, he had requested that a vote not be taken so that members would have "enough time to process their new knowledge of me." Later that same evening, however, he received a telephone call announcing that at the end of the meeting a vote had been taken with eight to one voting against recommending him. Subsequently, Craig transferred his local church membership to the Church of the Covenant in Boston, was taken in-care of the UCC district in that area, went through the entire ordination process again, and was ordained four years after the rejection in Pennsylvania had occurred.[63]

Although each of the stages in the ordination process presented obstacles with varying degrees of frequency for UCC ordinands, the final stage, known as "seeking a call," presented obstacles far in excess of the

TABLE 12

The Rocky Road to Ordained Ministry: Percentages of UCC Ordinands Who Encountered Obstacles at Each Stage of Ordination Process (N=54)

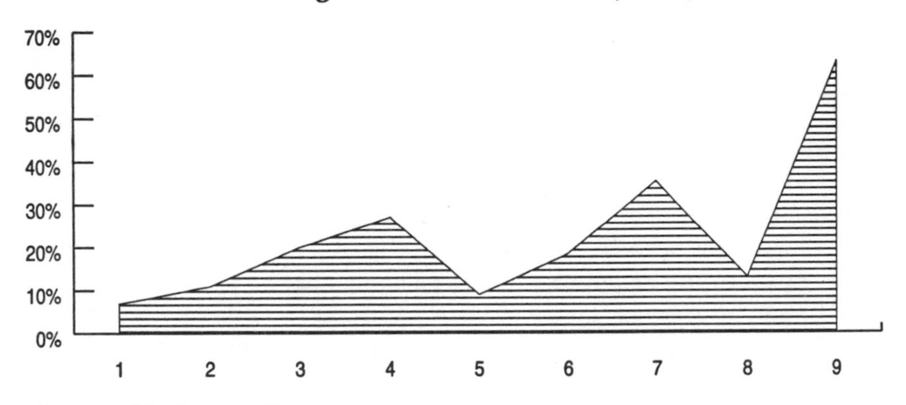

Stages of Ordination Process:

1. Local Pastor and Local Church's Support during In-Care Application
2. Local Church's Recommendation for In-Care Status
3. District's Taking Candidate In-Care
4. District's Support during In-Care Process
5. Local Pastor's Support for Ordination
6. Local Church's Recommendation for Ordination
7. District's Examination and Recommendation for Ordination
8. Ecclesiastical Council and Approval for Ordination
9. Seeking a Call (Obtaining Employment)

others. "Seeking a call" is the term used in most Protestant denominations for getting a job or position as a clergy. In the UCC, a requirement both for becoming and for staying ordained is being "called" to a position that is recognized as "ordained ministry." Nearly two-thirds (63 percent) of my respondents said they had had problems getting such a position.

Coming Out after Ordination

For many gay clergy the process of disclosing and being open about their sexual orientation begins and/or continues after ordination; and disclosing one's sexual orientation or having it discovered by others often causes problems for gay clergy in local churches. Although few were completely open during their ordinations, about one-third of my UMC and UCC respondents (30 percent, UMC; 35 percent, UCC) reported coming out after ordination.[64]

Among gay Catholic priests, about one-third of respondents in Wolf's and in Wagner's studies (29 percent and 36 percent, respectively) had personally disclosed their homosexuality to their superiors. Most of the others said they had not disclosed because they considered church authorities too naive, paranoid, and prejudiced about homosexuality to be of any constructive help and because they feared reprisals, such as loss of current assignments and/or future promotions. All of Wagner's respondents were very concerned about disclosing their homosexuality to fellow priests, too, because they were afraid of losing their respect and of being associated with negative gay stereotypes. Almost all were also concerned about disclosing their profession to secular gay peers, mostly because of the potential for involving the church in a scandalous exposé.[65]

Camouflaging

Gay clergy often are more out at some times than at others and develop various strategies to protect themselves. Mary Gaddis, a UMC laywomen I interviewed, knew a lot of clergy. She said that many have "done a good job of camouflaging; but the other part is you don't have to do it very well. People only see what they want to see. I have a good friend who was a major corporate attorney, a very out gay man, and he decided to go to seminary, and he fully expects to be ordained in the United Methodist Church. I said, 'How do you go back into the closet? I don't understand that concept.' He said it's pretty easy. And I bet he's going to do it. It's because people see what they want to see. Most of the gay and lesbian clergy that I know are incredibly good pastors. They are either great administrators or great preachers or great counselors and for the most part they're a combination of those three. People don't want to lose these wonderful people; so they will be blind to a lot of stuff."

Church officials, for example, often take advantage of certain procedures to protect gay clergy. Within the UMC, "special appointment" or "appointment beyond the local church" is sometimes conferred on gay clergy who cannot find employment or cannot be open as local church pastors.[66] Of the five UMC clergy I interviewed, all had previously served as pastors of local churches, and one had been removed because of her sexual orientation. Four currently had appointments beyond the local church. One of the women's appointment was in campus ministry at a state university. She said, "I have been out to particular individuals along the way, including at one point my district superintendent. When I chose to tell him, he simply said to me he didn't care personally; he just didn't want to know. He didn't want to be in a position to know that information about me or anyone else.

"The other kinds of times when I share information about my sexual orientation with people within the denomination is when I work with young college students, particularly United Methodist students, who are dealing with their own sexuality. At some point they often ask me, particularly when they are young gay men and lesbians; and when they do, I do not deny that I'm lesbian. I don't think I ever have. I just know that sometimes I'm relieved when some people don't ask. But I think that it's real important that I'm open there with them; and that has been helpful, I think, for them to have some models for being a professional within the church and for them to have some sense of their own OKness. So having a relationship with a lesbian within the church lets them have a different sense that they can have their own developing identity.

"I also represent a different kind of relationship with the church and am perhaps freer to be myself, because I've been on 'appointment beyond the local church' for ten years now. So I don't interact with it and the people there on a daily basis. I don't have many ties with the institutional church, even though I'm technically under appointment."

I asked if she found this kind of position more attractive because she is a lesbian. "It is a way to keep one foot in the church. I've tried to figure that out, and I guess in truthfulness I don't know the answer to the question, because I've done the local church number and have loved it and find myself still thinking about maybe doing it again. But I find that it's not worth the grief, if I've got to do it totally closeted. It takes too much energy. It's probably true that it is easier to do it on the fringes of the church."

Emotional Consequences

The terms that gay clergy have used most often to describe living in the closet are "scary," "frustrating," "lonely," and "intolerable," but by far most have discussed the experience as being "extremely painful."[67] One of the UMC clergywoman I interviewed said that having a national policy that allowed clergy to be out would make a big difference psychologically. "It's just painful to run with that incompatible-with-Christian-teaching thing around who I am. I don't care how good I feel about myself; I just get tired of hearing misconceptions about who gay men, lesbians, bisexuals, and other sexual minorities are. It's wearing. It's like a piece of sand in your sock that wears a blister; and it takes energy away from me. It also keeps me from defining my own issues. I think one of the reasons that I am not out is because once a person comes out, that becomes their major issue, and that's not the central issue in my life in terms of what I think I have to contribute to the life of the church, where I want to put my energy; and so it detracts."

Another UMC clergywoman wrote that during her ordination, "I lived in fear of being confronted and having to defend myself." She then said that later, while serving a church and living with her partner, "we both worked hard at taking care of the congregation," but "we also labored to keep our togetherness inconspicuous." She went on to claim that "the fears, stresses, and worries surrounding my life as a lesbian within the church" have taken their "toll on my health and the health of my relationship with my partner. The energy I have expended to censor my life has affected my integrity."[68]

Jeffrey Snyder, a non-gay UMC clergy, told of a fellow pastor who had come out and was developing a gay ministry at the time of the UMC's 1984 General Conference decision. The gay man then "sank into a deep depression," was "hospitalized in a psychiatric ward," and became "deeply closeted" after he went back to serving a local church. Snyder said that the denomination's decision cost the man a great deal: "He pays the cost every day in fear, panic, tension, poor health, and self-rejection. It is costing his parish too. Their pastor isn't free to be himself. He is physically ill much of the time. He is distracted and wonders why God continues to call him to a task that the church says he isn't worthy to perform. The cost is high."[69] This man's experience is not an isolated case; and the costs for others are known to be greater.

In 1988 Phyllis Athey committed suicide. She was a UMC candidate for ordained ministry but had been refused ordination in 1987. A letter issued by the Chicago chapter of Affirmation and the Women's Caucus and the Methodist Federation for Social Action of the Northern Illinois Conference of the UMC read: "Our sister Phyllis is dead. It was the violence of a self-inflicted gunshot wound which technically took her life. In fact, the greater violence was the destructiveness of a church and society which rejected her personhood as 'incompatible' and unacceptable. Death came as much from excluding and fear-filled resolutions, doctrines, and persons as from a bullet." Phyllis had been active at Wheadon United Methodist Church in Evanston, Illinois, and with her partner, Mary Jo Osterman, had founded the Kinheart Women's Center.[70]

Surviving and Gaining

Gay clergy have also demonstrated a history of surviving difficulties, negotiating through obstacles, establishing alternatives, and gaining employment. Ellen Sweetin, for example, spoke about having kept her lesbianism secret for the twelve years that she was a nun and then having recovered from alcoholism when she fully came out of the closet.[71]

Carney and Davies reported that one of their coupled clergywomen reported that "the community knows who we are and how we want to live. We act as family in public, and she's been active in the parish." They were also clear about their priorities if problems should arise: "If it is necessary we will choose each other over the church."[72]

A male pastor who remained closeted wrote that the difficult process of coming to terms personally with his gayness "made me a much better pastor than I ever could have been without it." He said that he learned compassion and tolerance and gained insight into the persecution of other people. "So — though I suffer from the conflicts of being both gay and a pastor — I nevertheless feel complete." He claimed to be "a far healthier and better pastor than when I was denying my gayness." He thought that "the ultimate irony" was that the church would dismiss him for "the very thing that has given my ministry most of its power." He also realized that there may come a time when the closet is no longer healthy, when "my need to take care of myself overcomes my commitment to being a pastor."[73]

Professional Adjustments

As gay clergy become more open, many make professional decisions that alter the course of their ministries and challenge the restrictions of their respective religious bodies.

For example, Diana Vezmar-Bailey, an ordained minister in the Presbyterian Church (U.S.A.), decided in 1989 to "set aside" her ordination. Since being ordained in 1978 she had discovered her bisexuality and begun a process of realizing that "the part of me that is lesbian will no longer be silenced by the church's ruling on ordination of gay men and lesbians." Feeling "deeply sad as well as immensely relieved as I live into this decision," she said, "I celebrate my sexuality, I do not repent it." She went on to explain that "timing is of the utmost importance" in making this kind of decision: "Two years ago, coming out was the farthest thing from my mind," but "it came to a point where ordination was more confining than it was enhancing my life and ministry." She advised others "to pay attention to your own process in this matter" because "not all of us need to be out." She said that one person's decision about coming out does not have more integrity than another's, because "the lack of integrity lies in the church's position on ordination."[74]

Margarita Suárez, a UCC clergywoman I interviewed, had been ordained and hired to serve a local church as an open lesbian. During her pastorate, however, she fell in love with a man. Margarita said that when she came out as a bisexual to denominational officials, "they were extremely concerned that I intended to live with a man without benefit of marriage." She went on: "I did my best to confront the church authorities, explaining the heterosexual privilege associated with marriage and how I did not want to buy into that privilege when lesbian and gay people did not have the same rights and responsibilities." Realizing that she could not win and encouraged by her gay friends "to get married to save my career," Margarita is now a wife, mother of a son, and an openly bisexual clergywoman in the UCC.[75]

For many gay clergy, coming out after ordination means finding employment outside of the formal church or within a more welcoming denomination.[76] Paul Abels, the pastor of Washington Square UMC in New York, for example, publicly acknowledged his homosexuality during 1977 and became "the first openly gay minister with a congregation in a major Christian denomination in America." Critics called for his removal, but his parishioners and colleagues stood by him. The criticism continued and he retired in 1984 when the UMC barred openly lesbian women and gay men from pastoral appointments.[77]

For Gloria Soliz, another UMC clergy, "the pain of [the UMC's 1984] decision became excruciating." She said the stress, cover-up, and lying "caused me to die a little each day," so she took a position as minister of education in a UCC church where she was able to be out. She felt that "it has been a blessing" to be able to provide "professional Christian leadership without having my sexual orientation constantly threatening my ministry."[78]

Ralph McFadden resigned his position as the executive of the Church of Brethren's Parish Ministries Commission and became a chaplain in a hospice program. Although "overwhelming grief accompanied" his departure, he said that in his new position "working with a gay supervisor, counseling a large number of AIDS patients, and developing more insight into myself helped me realize that my 'secret life' in the church was over." He vowed that he would never again be hired in the Church of the Brethren "if I could not be free to identify my sexual orientation if I cared to."[79]

Enduring and Succeeding

Peter Ilgenfritz is a UCC clergyman whose story traces a process of coming out from seminary to employment in the local church. When I interviewed Peter, he told me, "Right after graduating from Yale Divinity School I served as the associate pastor of the First Congregation Church in Ithaca, New York, for two years. Dave and I met at Yale Divinity School (he's a Presbyterian minister), and our relationship began at the end of our second year at Yale. My whole coming out process to myself, to my family, to friends, and professionally really happened in Ithaca. It was during my time there that I came out to myself in a lot of ways and in terms of the church; I did a lot of struggling then. I was not open. I was not telling anybody that I was gay, that was just not an issue in my life when I was looking for that church job. Yet while I was there it became more and more clear that I was preaching my one sermon — everyone has one sermon they always give — that was something about how if there's one place in our society, if there's one place in our lives where we should be free to be ourselves, to know ourselves, to be open before God, it should be in our church community. I was very much talking to the church about the importance of the issues of openness and affirmation, and I realized that for me personally I'd been able to say one thing in the pulpit and have it be such a core, so important to me in my ministry — about people being real, about people being open, about people sharing pain — and yet I myself was not being able to do that in that congregation. I struggled a lot with how to be honest in that congregation and how to remain in the ministry. I struggled and agonized over that a tremendous amount while I was there."

I asked him: "What were some of the things that made and helped you struggle?" He responded: "One thing that was very important was Dave was serving a church as an associate minister in Pennsylvania near Pittsburgh. So our relationship was a commuting one. We'd see each other every couple of weekends; and it became increasingly painful and difficult to live this split life. We realized that our relationship was more important than our jobs. We needed to be together. So part of coming out to others was around saying, 'Hey, this isn't good for us, and we need to be together and to live together and build a life together rather than commuting.' Another part was in just becoming really clear that I couldn't remain and be a minister without being honest, that integrity was so important to how I face issues that I just couldn't do both. I couldn't wear this mask and yet be the minister I wanted to be. So what happened in the end was we both made decisions to resign our church positions."

"So you thought it necessary to leave the position, if you were going to live openly as a gay man?" He said: "Yes, I was going to live openly; and, also, yes, I was going to be able to be faithful. It really came down to a question of how I as a minister felt — or just as a person of faith feels — about the importance of being honest with people, being able to be real and vulnerable, and particularly as a pastor. If I couldn't do that, then I was being hypocritical."

I asked: "But what would have happened if you had said to the Ithaca church that you were going to be open and that you wanted to stay?" Peter replied: "Well, that was what a lot of my struggle was about in that church; and in hindsight I can say what would've happened. I would have gotten thrown out. Looking at that church, it was a very, very conservative group of people, in high, powerful positions. The senior minister would not have stuck up for me; I couldn't assume he would. He so followed the general tenor of that congregation that when some of those people would have threatened to leave or gotten really angry, he would've been swayed by them. To leave was the best choice for me in order to really have some life. To be able to do the most faithful, good thing for myself was to leave."

I asked where he and Dave went. "We moved to Chicago. Dave chose to go to social work school at the University of Chicago, because as a Presbyterian he was unable to remain in the Presbyterian ministry with our relationship being in the open. He graduated last spring with his degree in social work. He's now working as a family counselor. I found a mission program, which was sponsored out here by the American Baptist Church, called the Esther Davis Center, and came on as a volunteer with this group of people that wanted to start an AIDS organization here in Evanston to serve the north suburban area. They needed some leadership behind them, but they couldn't afford to hire a full-time staff person. Although not working in a local church, I felt very affirmed and important as a minister, that this was mission and was involved in some sense with a larger community."

"Were you somewhat relieved to be out of the local church employment arena?" He replied: "No. In ways, yes, being now totally open, I guess as open as I can be in my own work and with my colleagues. People that I work with know that I'm gay. Dave's and my relationship is known to our friends. Our families know we're a couple. That all feels just so important and so necessary. I do miss local church ministry, but I would not seek a church job and be in the closet. I've had my professional profile circulating for the past two years in the UCC, and I'm open in my profile. I have gotten four or five churches that have written me back and said, 'Send us a sermon,' and, 'We're interested in talking more.' And for some of those places, Dave and I have just said we're just not interested in moving there right now, and realized that no, the church is not the be all and end all. There are other factors that get to be important.

"The questions I've been asking myself lately have to do with the difference between what the denomination says and what the denomination does in the world. In spite of what it may want to be, when it comes right down to actual practice it seems to be saying, 'You can't find a church, you can't be a minister, folks that are gay or lesbian can't be in a relationship, you can't be open, you can't do this, you can't do that.' And yet I'm thinking that maybe where I'm at right now is just to do some more struggling with God's sense of call to me — where is God leading me, where does God want me to go with this whole sense of call?"

A few months after the interview Peter wrote to me saying: "I have some exciting new *news* as an addendum. Dave and I are doing a candidating service at St. Paul's UCC in Columbus, Ohio, to be called as copastors of the church. We have the unanimous support of the search committee going into the final process—and we are *hopeful!*" After the visit, however, Peter and Dave sent the following letter to friends:

> We expected the weekend to be one of the best experiences of our lives; instead, it was by far one of the very worst.
>
> We went into a divided, angry church for our open house on Saturday and for our worship service on Sunday—not at all what we had expected from our conversations with the search committee. It seems the search committee had not done any work that they needed to have done to prepare the congregation for our candidacy and rally support. Some horrible things were said to us on Saturday and no one on the committee said anything at the time. We did our worship service Sunday to a stone-faced angry congregation — certainly the hardest service we have ever had to do before. The rules were changed, so we never did appear before the congregational meeting to be presented formally and to answer questions. Instead, the chair of the search committee held a written vote without discussion. We received only 30 of 72 votes in our favor.
>
> Probably the biggest hurt of the weekend was that we never felt welcomed by anyone and instead were made to feel that we were tramps that had come in through the back door.

But Peter and Dave persisted in their search to find a position; and in 1994 they were hired by the twelve-thousand-member University Congregational Church in Seattle to share one position as associate pastors. Although they were not supported by 24 percent of voting members, the decision to hire was historically significant as the first time that a gay couple was hired as copastors by a mainline church.[80]

Ordained Ministry

As in most Christian denominations, the functions of ordained ministry in the UCC are to preach and teach the Bible, to administer the sacraments and rites of the church, and to exercise pastoral care and leadership. Local churches offer positions in which these functions are regularly performed, but "calls" to other positions are also recognized as "ministry requiring ordination." These other kinds of "calls" are as campus ministers and college or university chaplains; hospital, prison, military, and other institutional chaplains; teachers and administrators in seminaries; staff in denominational agencies; missionaries; staff in ecumenical agencies and organizations; pastoral counselors in church-related counseling centers; staff and executives in church-related health and human service institutions; pastoral counselors in secular institutions; and advocates or community organizers for social change.[81]

Although the percentage of Americans involved in organized religions other than Judaism and Christianity is small, Buddhist organizations do have a noticeable presence in some metropolitan areas and have formal processes for training their leaders, which have included gay people. In the late 1980s, for example, William Dorsey became certified as a Zen priest by the senior disciple of San Francisco's Zen Center. Dorsey's work will be described later.[82]

Kinds of Ministry and Rates of Employment

Of the ordained respondents in my survey, over 80 percent (81 percent, UMC; 82 percent, UCC) had at some time served as a pastor or associate pastor in a local church. Currently, one-third of ordained UMC respondents and less than one-half of ordained UCC respondents (33 percent, UMC; 43 percent, UCC) were serving as local pastors; and about one-third of UMC respondents and one-quarter of UCC respondents (31 percent, UMC; 24 percent, UCC) were employed in other forms of ordained ministry (counseling; social work; chaplaincy; seminary staffing, teaching, and administration; and AIDS education, services, and advocacy). Currently, therefore, about two-thirds of ordained respondents (64 percent, UMC; 67 percent, UCC) were employed either as local pastors or in other forms of ministry requiring ordination.

In addition to reporting slightly higher rates of employment as local pastors, UCC respondents also more often than UMC respondents reported being out in those positions (18 percent and 24 percent ever out, UMC/UCC; 9 percent and 23 percent currently out, UMC/UCC). These data, along with the higher percentage of UMC than UCC clergy currently employed in ministries other than local pastoring, suggest that the local congregation is less available to gay clergy within the more anti-gay UMC. But within the UCC, too, there is evidence of gay clergy having not only less access than non-gay clergy to positions as local pastors but less access to other forms of ministry as well.

A comparison of my gay UCC ordained respondents with a sample of non-gay UCC ordained clergy, for example, showed larger percentages of non-gay clergy currently holding positions as local pastors (48 percent, non-gay; 43 percent, gay) or in the other forms of ordained ministry (35 percent, non-gay; 24 percent, gay) and a larger percentage of gay clergy currently having settled for or moved to positions that do not require ordained standing (17 percent, non-gay; 33 percent, gay).[83]

Tim Tennant-Jayne, a UMC clergyman I interviewed, spoke of an informal interdenominational support group that he attended. "I counted one time and I think about a third of the people there were actively working in a parish in some form or maybe as chaplains. And yet at least half, maybe two-thirds, were not in a church-related job, and yet they still identified themselves as clergy. The Roman Catholics use a phrase, 'Thou art ordained a priest forever'; and even though the United Methodists don't, I think there is still that sense that holds through the denominations." I asked what kind of work these people were doing. "One is in computer work; one is doing some kind of counseling work. It's kind of anything that would pay the bills." "But they still saw themselves as clergy?" I asked. He replied: "Yes. There was a part of them that still identified with being clergy. They could hope for the joy of getting up on a Sunday morning and leading services, of being that community person that people depended on."

Examples of Ordained Ministry

Clare Fischer concluded from her study that "perhaps no one generalization is more important than this: Lesbian and gay religious leaders are not single-issue believers or activists." Far from being concerned solely with gay issues, each of her subjects talked about being "engaged in education and ministerial efforts that foster a vision of an egalitarian and socially just order, a perspective that is expansive and energetic."[84] One of the UCC clergywomen I interviewed shared this view: "What I see happening more consistently are folks willing to take more risks across the board. Not necessarily just in terms of the gay and lesbian issues, but whether it be advocacy for the poor or peace and justice issues or whatever. And it seems almost to me as an afterthought — like, 'Oh, and by the way I happen to be part of the gay and lesbian community.'" Findings show that gay clergy are involved in ministries as diverse, ordinary, and special as those of non-gay clergy, but many have to shape their ministries around or away from the restrictions imposed on them by their religious bodies.

One of the UMC clergymen I interviewed was on "special appointment" as an administrative assistant at a UMC seminary. He was also active in Affirmation, the UMC gay organization, and considered much of his ministry to occur through and in it. "I've been involved in various ways — ten years serving as an officer at times and leading worship upon occasion; and I have led over the last several years the Affirmation Bible study here in D.C. The Bible study group is cosponsored by Affirmation and one of the churches in the District. It's just been a wonderful experience. It's the first opportunity for me to lead an all-gay/lesbian group in scriptural study; and for almost everyone in the group it's the first opportunity they've had to discuss the Bible and theology and matters of faith, their own personal faith experience in a totally uncloseted situation. So they can really say what they feel and how the Bible affects their lives and reflect on the scripture and how it really impacts their experience. Usually we just don't have that opportunity in the wider church. So it's a very valuable and strengthening experience, because you've got this community that comes together around scripture and prayer, and yet is able to laugh and joke and be campy about it too."

Other gay clergy by choice or necessity have developed ministries oriented to gay people outside of mainline denominational frameworks, as the following examples show. Eighty percent of the priests in Wagner's study were ministerially active in the gay community.[85] Paul Bauer's study of the Metropolitan Community Church in Denver documented Reverend David Carnes's successful efforts to establish a congregation of 16 and increase its membership to 150 within a few years.[86] The National Gay Pentecostal Alliance has developed a process for educating, licensing, and assigning ministers to serve its churches and to establish new ones.[87] In 1992, Congregation Beth Simchat Torah, the 1,100-member gay synagogue in New York, hired its first rabbi, Sharon Kleinbaum, after twenty-years of relying on lay leadership.[88] In 1989, Zen priest William Dorsey (or Issan) became the abbot of the Hartford Street Zen Center in San Francisco's gay Castro neighborhood and soon enlarged its operations to include a hospice for people with AIDS. In addition to his usual practice of Zen meditation, classes, and lectures, he formed a network of gay, medical, and Buddhist volunteers to provide continuous attendant care for hospice residents.[89]

On the other hand, many gay clergy serve within mainstream religious bodies. When I interviewed Margarita Suárez, for example, she was serving as the pastor of an inner-city UCC church comprised of a "mixture of working-class/low-income neighborhood people and middle-class, socially committed, upwardly mobile people." Margarita told me that she was hired because "I had experience in the inner city, because they are a committed congregation on social justice issues, because the church is in the middle of an Hispanic community, even though the church is Anglo; they wanted someone who was bilingual. The second half of the demography has a high percentage of gay and lesbian people." She said, "This is a church that is a struggling church, and it will continue to be a struggling church, partly because we are not located in an area of high growth. We are located in what traditionally was a more conservative side of Milwaukee and what has always been sort of the immigrant community. The church originally began with the German immigrant community; and as they became more upwardly mobile and moved away, the church didn't necessarily, until recently, really work at trying to incorporate the current community into its population." Margarita and several members had been "working for the last year on trying to develop an ecumenical HIV-AIDS ministry with Hispanic women and children." She said, "We also run a food pantry; we run a food co-op program; we have different educational activities that come into the community and use our space; we house gay/lesbian organizations."

Another UCC pastor I interviewed also served an inner-city church, but one with a congregation that was mostly older people, many of whom had moved out of the neighborhood but continued to attend the church. During his first year, he said that "not a lot really happened because they had just been through three ministers in about four years. So there was a lot of stuff that had fallen between the cracks and a lot of wounds that needed to be healed. People who hadn't been paid attention to needed some attention. There was all this healing and internal work to do. In terms of programs and long-range planning not a lot was done."

"What do they like about you? Why did they hire you?" I asked. He said: "Actually there was a split in hiring me. Some people really didn't think it was a great idea. Obviously there was a majority in my favor. I think they liked my preaching and worship style, and that has worked out very well in the first year. They have a sense they can trust me to lead them or help them lead themselves. We have an older congregation, and I tend to relate well to older people. I've had a lot of experience at it. I think they feel comfortable with me. The people that aren't my big fans have figured out that I am gay; and it's an issue with them, but they don't know how to raise it. But I know if anything happened, they would be the first to lead the (I don't want to say attack, but), the sort of 'We-told-you-this-would-happen' or 'We-suspected-this-all-along' type thing."

I asked: "How do you feel about all this now? Is the arrangement you have with them satisfactory for you in terms of being out?" He answered: "Actually no, but I'm trying to figure out how to resolve that. We had one incident in the fall. I had been approached by the AIDS Pastoral Network here in Chicago. They came to us looking for a space to hold grief support meetings. I brought the request to the church council. I didn't think it was going to be a problem. As I look back I'm not sure whether I was naive or just trying to avoid the possible problems. It was just another building request. But it was put off to the next meeting so members could be surveyed. In the meantime an anonymous letter was sent to everyone saying that the church should not do this because all the people who have died from AIDS had broken God's laws against men sleeping with men. The good news was that most people were appalled by the letter because it showed such a lack of compassion.

"Also, the service planned for the upcoming Sunday focused on Advent as a season of looking for healing and wholeness, and I used this letter as the basis of my sermon. The prescheduled biblical reading was about Jesus being recognized as the Messiah because he had done work of healing, including people with leprosy. I remember when I started the sermon I had to hang on to the pulpit because I just started to shake I was so angry. It was, if I may say so myself, one hell of a sermon — just tearing into this letter, reading it out loud for people who hadn't heard it before, and simply saying there were just so many levels of ignorance in this letter that I didn't know where to start. I lambasted its biblical crap, saying that this person had no idea what they were talking about, that the Jesus that this letter writer was talking about seemed to have no relation to the Jesus that was in our gospel lesson for that day. I said that if Advent is supposed to be the season of healing, what can we do with this letter to get some healing? I said the first thing we can do is to carry this letter in our heads as we go into our neighborhood — and I mentioned the three hospitals in our general area which deal with people with AIDS. And I said, 'Let's go here and let's see the ministry of healing that's going on in these places; let's take our piety along with us so we can be changed by all this and see what the gospel is as all these people reach out to each other and become Christ to each other and real healing takes place.' The sermon was well received, and at the next council meeting we did approve the AIDS Pastoral Network's request to use the space. We survived that. There was a lot of homophobia running around, but at least we all lived to tell the tale."

Another UCC clergywoman I interviewed worked as a chaplain at a Roman Catholic hospital in the heart of steel mill country. She told me, "East Chicago's population breakdown reflects the range of clients I see and I deal with. About a third Eastern European, many of whom are first generation from Europe who came to work in the mills. Many of them speak no English or speak English as a second language. Eastern European is the primary language, be it Slavic, Czech, Polish, Hungarian, Lithuanian, you name it. About a third are African-American and about a third are Hispanic."

As a white, middle-class woman, she said the work is "definitely a challenge. Especially, if nothing else, because of the language barrier. It's a real challenge partly because what I know is that I've had opportunities that they cannot even begin to dream of, partly because of the color of their skin. So it's really interesting for me to try and get a handle on what I need to know about their backgrounds and to be sensitive about that. Even in terms of customs and practices at the time of a death. The Afro-American community — as does the Hispanic community — has a very different way of going through the whole grief process than do most white European folks. And it's not uncommon to have tons of people come to the hospital to see the body. I may be literally three or four hours with the family until everybody who is suppose to come has gotten there. I have had situations where there have been literally twenty to thirty people there. So it's very stressful on certain days and not so bad on other days."

I asked her to talk about her most difficult experiences. "I would say when I had just gotten there, the traumas that came into the emergency room, all of which were gunshot-wound-related, two of them kids in their early teens, mostly gang-related. Two of them were declared brain dead. We had to deal with organ donations, with the family and the whole revenge motive, and with their wanting to go out and take care of the people who did this."

I asked: "Why do you think you're good in this situation? What do you feel are your qualifications?" She replied: "Let me tell you, there are many days when I leave there and I think, 'What the hell am I doing here?' I guess I would say that part of it is my training and part of it is that I came here wanting and knowing that I would be able to get experience that I would not get in other basically white, middle-class suburban areas, as far as experience for my own ministry and for my own competency. But I think what has surprised me is I had no idea that it would be to the volume that it has been, because that is not what I was led to believe when I came here. So that's been amazing to me. Often I'm just amazed at the violence that I see. That's the part that throws me more than anything, because the whole idea of the sanctity of life does not seem to be a primary operative mode here in whatever form that may take. I've sat with folks while they've struggled with issues about whether or not they should have an abortion, what they should do or not do about the child they are carrying, and that kind of stuff. It's not that I am big time pro-life, that's not where I am at all, but it's just knowing that there's something bigger than yourself and that what happens to you affects other people around you. Things don't happen in isolation. That kind of awareness doesn't seem to be a primary awareness for a lot of these folks."

I asked why she thought that was so. "From the stories I've heard, I think part of it is because the majority of folks that I deal with so much here have had to struggle and scrape so hard just to make it day to day, they really can't or don't choose to think much beyond themselves because very literally there are days for these folks when they don't know where their next meal is coming from. So I think it is really hard to get a concept of something bigger than yourself when you don't have any food in your stomach. That would be my guess."

Employment Other Than Ordained Ministry

Ordained ministry is not the only form of employment within religious bodies. Laypeople are also employed in a variety of positions.

Local Church Positions

One-half of both UMC and UCC respondents in my survey had at some time been employed in local churches; and although most had been employed as pastors, many others had held positions as organists and music directors (23 percent, UMC; 11 percent, UCC), directors of education (12 percent, UMC; 5 percent, UCC), clerical and custodial workers (4 percent, UMC; 7 percent, UCC), and a variety of other positions (18 percent, UMC; 15 percent, UCC). About one-quarter (24 percent, UMC; 29 percent, UCC) had been out in those positions.

Positions on Denominational Levels

Small percentages of UMC and UCC respondents had also held staff positions on the province (5 percent, UMC; 2 percent, UCC) and national (7 percent, UMC; 5 percent, UCC) levels of their denomination. But whereas one-half of the UCC respondents have been out in their positions, only 11 percent of UMC respondents reported having been out on the province level, and none reported having been out on the national level.

One of the women I interviewed had been the director of the UCC's national peace advocacy agency. "I was traveling across the country setting up groups related to legislative issues in home towns of the members of the Congress or Senate who were on peace-related legislative committees. So I was doing a great deal of traveling, and I never ever said anything about the lesbian/gay issue, unless it came up in some legislative way. But I would speak about it in a professional, not a personal, way."

She then spoke about being at national meetings of the denomination: "If I was actively open about who I was and what I believed in, I could jeopardize my professional position, because I've been at meetings lots of times when I was working on peace issues or on corporate or social responsibility issues and things would get said about homosexuality. I could hear it among the people I was talking to. I could hear them complain about the church taking on issues like this. So I knew the climate out there was not open to anybody saying, 'Oh, by the way, I am one of them, so watch your language.' I usually was very circumspect about how I chose to address the issue. And if I did address it by calling somebody on the carpet, I would speak as a third person. I would say there are people that feel very strongly that that kind of remark is offensive."

Although her experience occurred in the early 1980s, she was not sure that the climate would be that much different now. "I think whether or not it would be any different would really depend on who the national staff leaders are at this point."

Randy Miller received his Master of Divinity degree from Emory University but decided not to seek ordination. "At the time that I came out, I was working or had just finished working at the UMC's Board of Discipleship in Nashville, Tennessee; and I came out with a bang. Then, in meeting people — you see the same people over and over again in church — I got very mixed reviews from people about my being gay; and I felt like a lot of the support I had given people was not returned by the church bureaucrats that I knew."

I asked him to give an example. "I went to the next General Conference, that would have been the 1988 conference, and half of the people that I had worked with and particularly people in Black Methodists for Church Renewal, people I had some camaraderie with, just ignored me. They pretended like I didn't exist. That was painful, but it also made me very angry."

I asked: "When you said you came out with a bang, do you mean in the church or with a bang period?" He responded: "I came out with a bang period. I worked on the National March on Washington for Lesbian and Gay Rights. It was my very next job, and I thought it was fantastic. Then I worked for Jesse Jackson as his National Gay and Lesbian Liaison in 1988, and in the context of that I did a lot of interviews with newspapers. When it came out in the papers, the *Washington Post,* the *Village Voice,* the Knight newspapers, which is a huge chain that appears in places like Birmingham, Alabama, that's how many of the people in the church found out. Between that and being very visible with Affirmation as well — I made no bones about it — people found out."

A UMC woman who worked as a program and staff coordinator on the province or conference level of her denomination said that identifying as a lesbian did not jeopardize her job because the conference has a protective clause for sexual orientation that includes a strong civil rights statement, an affirmative action statement, and a nondiscriminatory clause on policy and procedures for ministry. She explained how the province level could provide what the national level forbids: "Our last two bishops have been philosophically very supportive of gay and lesbian civil rights and issues. We've had legislation in our conference for the last four years that urges local churches to develop dialogue about and with lesbian/gay people and to consider becoming Reconciling Congregations. I get asked to visit and talk to churches that have decided to do that. I did one workshop last year at a local church in late May, and five people in that church then marched in the Portland Gay Pride Parade." The people who marched were non-gay people, and the Affirmation chapter in that area is made up mostly of non-gay people.

Preference and Discrimination

Employment Preference

Of my respondents who had ever been employed within any part of their denomination, about 3 percent (2 percent, UMC; 5 percent, UCC) said that their sexual orientation had been an asset in getting a position. Most of these positions involved consulting for or coordination of gay-related and AIDS-related programs.

Obstacles to Performing Liturgical Duties

Respondents more often reported experiences of discrimination than preference.

For example, 18 percent of gay clergy in my survey (15 percent, UMC; 21 percent, UCC) reported having encountered obstacles in performing liturgical duties because of their sexual orientation. Obstacles included being prevented from administering the sacraments and being prevented from preaching and were most often encountered by those who came out after their ordinations.

Employment Discrimination

One-quarter of lay and clergy respondents who had sought or held positions in the UMC and UCC reported various kinds of employment discrimination because of their sexual orientation (26 percent, UMC; 25 percent, UCC) (see table 13). More than one-tenth of UMC and UCC respondents who had sought any form of employment said they knew for certain that they had not been considered (16 percent, UMC; 17 percent, UCC) or had not been hired for a position (11 percent, UMC; 14 percent, UCC) because of their sexual orientation. About one-tenth of job-holders (11 percent, UMC; 8 percent, UCC) said they knew for certain that they had been fired from positions because they were gay or lesbian, and about 5 percent (7 percent, UMC; 2 percent, UCC) said they knew for certain that they had not been promoted because of discrimination.

Incidents in other denominations have also been reported. In 1995, for example, Abilene Christian University fired one of its summer theater directors after asking him to confirm rumors that he was gay. Previously, the young man had graduated third in his class from the university, had been praised by the alumni magazine, had been asked by the administration to write to prospective students, had been honored by *USA Today* as one of its "All-USA College Academic Team," and had gone on to pursue a master's degree elsewhere. The university is affiliated with the Church of God, a denomination that opposes homosexuality.[90]

Suspected Discrimination

Even more of my respondents suspected (see table 13), as opposed to knowing for certain, that they had been discriminated against because of their sexual orientation (43 percent, UMC; 38 percent, UCC). About one-quarter of UMC and UCC respondents suspected that they had not been considered (26 percent, UMC; 22 percent, UCC) or not been hired (22 percent, UMC; 26 percent, UCC), and about 5 percent suspected they had been fired (5 percent, UMC; 7 percent, UCC) for that reason. Almost one-quarter of UMC job-holders and one-tenth of UCC job-holders suspected that they had not been promoted (23 percent, UMC; 10 percent, UCC) because of discrimination.

TABLE 13

Percentages of UMC & UCC Respondents Who Said They Experienced, Did Not Experience, or Suspected Employment Discrimination Because of Their Sexual Orientation

kinds of discrimination	UMC (N=99)*		UCC (N=122)**	
	Yes	Suspect	Yes	Suspect
not considered	16%	26%	17%	22%
not hired	11%	22%	14%	26%
fired	11%	5%	8%	7%
not promoted	7%	23%	2%	10%
any of the above	26%	43%	25%	38%

* Of total 199 respondents, 99 answered employment discrimination questions; 86 reported that questions did not apply to them; and 14 left the questions blank.

** Of total 289 respondents, 122 answered employment discrimination questions; 146 reported that questions did not apply to them; and 21 left the questions blank.

Although suspected discrimination lacks the certainty and apparent seriousness of verifiable discrimination, gay people have often expressed the damaging effect of rumors, unspoken hostility, and unstated rejection. One closeted UMC clergy wrote:

> I will never have the advancement that I deserve because of innuendo and suspicion among my colleagues — some of whom, though married and presumed above suspicion, are also gay. Even colleagues who don't have personal problems with my life-style are

a little afraid to have me in a position of any prominence because I might cause "scandal" in the church.[91]

In James Wolf's study of gay Catholic priests, respondents also reported "active discrimination" less often than "a more nebulous form of passive discrimination." Because a bishop or major superior does not have to explain why a priest is passed over for promotion or suddenly reassigned to another position, the reasons for their decisions are rarely given.[92] Some of Carney and Davies's respondents reported that opposition to hiring gay candidates was increasingly being clothed in a general distrust of single people. One woman "was asked directly by a search committee member if she was lesbian. Although she denied it, she did not get the position she was seeking."[93]

Association of Discrimination with Being Out

Perhaps one of the more surprising findings from my survey is the similar percentages of employment discrimination reported by UMC and UCC employees. One may have expected to find discrimination reported less often within the pro-gay UCC. However, discrimination may be more strongly associated with outness than with denominational policies. For example, among UMC and UCC respondents, out pastors reported employment discrimination more often than those who were not out (22 percent out and 16 percent not out, UMC; 47 percent out and 13 percent not out, UCC). Perhaps gay employees in the UCC have felt encouraged by national policy to be out, but after coming out, have then experienced the discrimination typically directed at openly gay people within local congregations in all mainstream religious bodies.

Out gay employees in organized religion may also worry about and try to avoid discrimination less than those who are not out. In his study of gay priests, Wagner found that those who were out to other priests tended to be less concerned about discrimination than the more closeted respondents, even though the former were also the primary reporters of actual experiences of rejection and disapproval by other priests.[94]

Demographic Variables

Certain demographic variables, such as gender, sexual identity, age, and geographical region,[95] also appeared to be associated with differences in reported experiences of employment discrimination in my survey.

UMC and UCC men more often than women reported employment discrimination due to their sexual orientation (6 percent women and 15 percent men, UMC; 5 percent women and 15 percent men, UCC).[96]

By sexual identity, such employment discrimination was reported more often by UMC bisexuals (13 percent, bisexual; 11 percent, lesbian/

gay) and by UCC lesbians and gay men (0 percent, bisexual; 11 percent lesbian/gay).[97]

By age, such employment discrimination was reported most often by UMC respondents fifty years and older (14 percent, fifties; range of 10 percent to 12 percent, other age groups) and UCC respondents in their forties (13 percent, forties; range of 7 percent to 12 percent, other age groups).[98]

By geographical regions, such employment discrimination was reported most often by UMC respondents in the South (19 percent compared to range of 0 percent to 17 percent, other regions) and by UCC respondents in the South, Southwest, and West (33 percent compared to range of 2 percent to 18 percent, other regions).[99]

In the UMC and UCC, gay employees who were out, male, older, and/or from the South would appear to have experienced anti-gay discrimination more often than those who were not out, female, younger, and/or from other geographical regions. Bisexuals would seem to have fared worse than lesbians and gay men in the UMC but not in the UCC.

Conclusion

Findings from the various studies discussed above permit the following tentative conclusions.

Most gay clergy and lay employees within organized religion are not out. Coming out usually brings about the end of one's employment and/or ordained status. Not coming out usually fosters emotional stress and suffering. However, about one-quarter of gay clergy and lay employees in various religious bodies are completely out in their positions. The rates of outness were slightly higher for those in the more pro-gay religious bodies; and the positions in which gay people can be out were more often not as pastors but in other forms of ordained ministry outside the local church, such as counseling, teaching, chaplaincy, and administrative work, or as musical directors, directors of education, and custodial and clerical workers in the local church. Signs of improving conditions for gay people are their greater acceptance within some seminaries and the numbers of gay employees who are out, even within religious bodies that forbid being out. Some non-gay leaders within these bodies have exercised their power to protect and place gay people in certain kinds of positions.

Most gay clergy and lay employees find and hold on to the full range of traditional positions within organized religion by being completely closeted, by being out selectively to various trusted individuals, by camouflaging their orientation and relationships, and/or by compartmentalizing their social, affectional, and professional lives. As James

Wolf found, "with varying levels of frustration" most find that their work is satisfying and that their sexual orientation and professional lives "are not mutually exclusive." Others grow weary of secrecy, of leading double lives, and of hiding.

Even though the large majority of gay clergy and lay employees are not out, significant percentages report having been verbally harassed in seminary, prevented from carrying out their liturgical duties in local churches, and discriminated against in all forms of employment within religious bodies. Many remain closeted to avoid punishment and termination but do not always escape such treatment. A noticeable number have forgone the dubious safety of the closet to challenge anti-gay policies and practices. For them discrimination and unfair treatment are not to be suffered silently but to be faced directly and revealed plainly. They have made decisions (1) to come out and forfeit employment and ordained status within prohibitive religious bodies; (2) to recognize and prioritize their affectional relationships over getting and keeping positions; (3) to negotiate for and create options within those bodies; and (4) to continue working as religious leaders in alternative contexts. These decisions evidence a willingness, persistence, and resilience that have come to characterize a recognizable number of gay people within organized religion.

These characteristics, as well as those that apply to clergy and employees who are not out, lead to a question for continuing discussion in the next chapter. What are the beliefs and resources for support and community that sustain lesbian/bisexual/gay people in organized religion?

Chapter Six

Belief, Theology, Support, and Community

Belief

Strength of Belief

Available studies suggest that gay people do not differ from non-gay people in the strength of their religious beliefs. Over one-third of each (37 percent, non-gay; 36 percent, gay) reported strong attachment to their belief systems. Over 80 percent of gay men also claimed that their religious conviction was stronger than (37 percent) or the same as (45 percent) that of others. They also reported believing in life after death somewhat more often than non-gay people did (77 percent, non-gay; 85 percent, gay).[1]

In addition, James Wolf's comparison of gay and non-gay Roman Catholic priests showed that gay priests were about as likely as non-gay priests to have felt in the presence of God (97 percent, non-gay; 99 percent, gay), to have been afraid of God (40 percent, non-gay; 45 percent, gay), and to have felt loved by God (91 percent, non-gay; 98 percent, gay). Gay priests were more likely to have felt at one with God (82 percent, non-gay; 95 percent, gay), but more often have felt abandoned by God (21 percent, non-gay; 43 percent, gay) and less often have felt tempted by the devil (67 percent, non-gay; 49 percent, gay).[2]

Most gay people have reported that their own views of their sexuality have not affected their personal religious beliefs. In Alan Bell and Martin Weinberg's study of black, white, male, and female gay people, almost 60 percent reported that their sexual orientation had no effect; almost 10 percent reported that it had strengthened their religious feelings; and less than one-third reported that it had weakened their religious feelings.[3]

Organized religion's views of their sexuality, however, have led some gay people to seek "some kind of accommodation between religious beliefs and sexual orientation," some by refusing to relate homosexuality to religious doctrine and others by reinterpreting traditional religion as not violated by homosexuality.[4]

Shaping Belief

Some gay people have said that their homosexuality forced them to question, examine, formulate, and take their beliefs more seriously. As one of the UMC clergyman I interviewed said, "I think we've thought about our faith more than others. I think that for many people they can take their faith for granted. They don't have to think about things, and yet we have to deal with our Sunday school teachers teaching us 'Jesus loves me this I know' and then later finding out as adults that's not necessarily true. So there is a lot more thought that has to go into it. I don't think gay and lesbian persons have any kind of 'in' with truth. I think we've thought about it more though; and so if we do realize who God is, it would be more because we put more work into it."

Gay people from anti-gay religious bodies have probably had to engage in such accommodation and additional work more often than those from more liberal bodies. Scott Thumma's study of Good News, the gay evangelical parachurch in Atlanta, showed that gay men made contact with the organization to resolve the tension they felt between their conservative Christian backgrounds and their homosexuality.[5] Paul Bauer also spoke of how the Metropolitan Community Church (MCC) in Denver offered "a new belief system" to lessen the anxiety that members felt because of their negative experiences with their religious upbringing.[6] The members of Henry Rabinowitz's Talmud class at Congregation Beth Simchat Torah, the gay synagogue in New York, spoke of connecting rather than separating the various parts of their lives—of realizing that the "feeling of two conflicting identities, one gay and one Jewish, was a false consciousness."[7] And Karim Merchant wrote that he is "fairly closeted" in his mosque but that Trikone, the organization for gay and lesbian South Asians, had "empowered me to come to terms with being Muslim and gay" and that a newly formed group in Los Angeles called Salaam would further "offer me a safe space to begin my own reinterpretation of Islam on the issue of homosexuality."[8]

But these reinterpretations and "new belief systems" do not attempt to overturn old religious traditions as much as they seek to appropriate and find a place within them. For example, Good News focused on the traditional claim of conservative denominations to be the "elite of believers" and then identified the "difference of gayness" as an elite quality and criticized those denominations for not accepting gays into true Christian fellowship.[9] Bauer observed that the MCC also confirmed a belief in Jesus by interpreting his teachings as his love for people, including gay people.[10] And in Rabinowitz's study, one of the subjects from an Orthodox background said that just as his father had been "happy in his *shtibl* [learning center]," so he was happy in the gay synagogue: "In effect, Congregation Beth Simchat Torah is my *shtibl*."[11]

In my survey of UMC and UCC gay people, I observed a similar adherence to the traditional belief systems of their denominations as well as a tendency to be more liberal and creative than non-gay members within those systems. Such efforts to question, examine, formulate, and organize their beliefs fall under the rubric of theology.

Theology

Defining and Doing Theology

To theologize is to try to understand what is most important to oneself and/or to one's people. Within organized religion, "what is most important" has most often been conceived of as the ultimate power, force, or meaning in life and has been given such proper names as God, Adonai, Allah, Atma, and Bodhi.

Theology draws on four sources to understand more fully this ultimate power, force, or meaning. These sources are: (1) a particular tradition or established interpretation of that power, such as Judaism, Christianity, Islam, Hinduism, Buddhism, or any number of variations within those traditions; (2) scripture or a body of sacred literature about that power and its interaction with people, such as the Torah, Bible, Qur'an, Vedas, or Tripitaka; (3) the particular and current experience of the person or people doing the theologizing; and (4) the reasoning used by that person or people to select from, coordinate, and integrate their tradition, scripture, and personal experiences to understand "what is most important to them."[12] The ways in which these four sources — tradition, scripture, experience, and reason — are used and integrated distinguish various theologies from one another.

Kinds of Theology

Different kinds of theology place more or less emphasis on each of these sources. For example, liberal theologies tend to emphasize personal experience; moderate theologies try to adhere to a particular tradition; and conservative theologies usually emphasize a strict application of scripture to daily life. Among American Protestants, therefore, liberal theologies understand God as socially concerned, ecumenical, and visionary and God's people as those who think for themselves, make moral choices, and change society for the better; moderate theologies understand God as practical and orderly and God's people as those with simple faith and piety who maintain the middle-class way of life; and conservative theologies understand God as an authority who rules directly and literally from the Bible and God's people as those who preserve an older, biblical way of life.[13]

Theologically, the UMC is a moderate denomination, and the UCC is a liberal denomination; and in my survey UMC respondents did report having moderate theologies somewhat more often (14 percent, UMC; 11 percent, UCC) and liberal theologies somewhat less often (85 percent, UMC; 88 percent, UCC) than UCC respondents, but by very small differences. Compared with a survey of non-gay delegates to the 1992 General Conference of the UMC, my UMC respondents were considerably more liberal (48 percent, non-gay; 85 percent, gay).[14] Although UMC respondents mirror somewhat the theological position of their denomination, they seem to have more in common with the gay UCC respondents than with non-gay UMC delegates.

Understanding God

When I interviewed gay people in the UMC and UCC about their own understanding and imaging of God and Jesus, their responses were similar, complementary, and mostly liberal. A few did speak of God in such conventional or conservative terms as "almighty" and "all-knowing," but as an immanent power "among us" not as a transcendent ruler "above us." One UCC woman said, "I believe God is omnipotent, all over, in everything, in talking to someone, and in getting a glimpse of real understanding." Another said God is "a higher power that is all forgiving, a source of strength and security for me. There are no boundaries and limits to the love and peace. God is there for everyone, and it doesn't matter who or what we are. You're accepted, and we were all created in God's image." A UMC woman also spoke of God as creator, but as one who values gay people as among its creations: "I really believe in creation theology and that God created all things and God is a God of goodness. I mean, you look at the world and think of God as the creator, nothing goes to waste, everything is recycled in creation, and it doesn't make any sense to me that God would create and waste a portion of the people."

A UMC woman and man used biblical references for God. Tim Tennant-Jayne said, "The passage I use now is when Moses is at the burning bush and he says, 'Who shall I tell the people has sent me?' and God responds with, 'I am that I am.' God is very much a presence here and now." He went on to say that he experienced this presence at all kinds of times: "It could be riding my bike to work and just seeing the sunrise over downtown or somebody saying 'Hi' to me on the streets, running into somebody that I haven't seen for a few months, doing some readings, maybe from science fiction, maybe from a meditation, just something clicks." The woman liked the image of God as the loving parent in the Book of Hosea, where God says, "Don't you know that it was I who bent over you and cared for you and taught you to walk and fed you and lifted you up." She said that she has "a personal and developing sense of God, that God and I change because of our interaction with each other, rather than a sense of God as an unmoved first cause kind of thing."

Two others also used parental imagery. A UMC woman remembered "as a small child my father saying to me, 'You know how much I love you?' and I would say, 'Yes'; and my father would say, 'You know God loves you more than I could ever love you in your wildest imagination.' My parents also gave me a sense of 'It's OK to question God, it's OK to tell God if you're angry, it's OK to be honest with God'; and so I've done that a lot. I'm not afraid to ask questions or challenge authority." Margarita Suárez said, "The image of the eagle is becoming more and more powerful for me, the image of the eagle soaring, being in a high place, kicking the eaglets out of the nest when it's time for them to start flying, not nudging but throwing them out of the nest, removing all of the comfort of the nest. When the eagle mother first makes the nest, she puts comforting things in, like soft grass; and when she wants the eaglets to begin to fly, she takes the comfortness out of the nest and then pushes them off the edge to make them fly, but she doesn't let them die. If they don't fly well enough and they're looking like they aren't going to make it, she swoops down, catches them on her wing, and brings them back. She does that again and again until they get it."

Only two of the people I interviewed referred to God in the conventional trinitarian terms of Father, Son, and Holy Ghost. One UCC woman said, "God, the Holy Spirit, and Jesus are all one. There's three parts of it, but the one I like and feel is most important when I talk about God being present is the Holy Spirit." Another UCC woman said that she too was "more focused on the Holy Spirit than I am probably on God or Jesus Christ." She described the Holy Spirit as "an in-dwelling presence" that was an "advocate, counselor, and a guide."

Two UMC men talked about conventional male images of God. B. J. Stiles said, "I think in my worst days I still have all the traditional imagery of God's being grandfatherly and 'up there.' And in my better days I think of God as the source of the life energy that is around me moment by moment, and, therefore, God is the totality, fulfillment, and complexity of life, the source of challenges and issues that I confront inside myself, inside my relationship, and out on the street when I'm dealing with poverty and homelessness and racism." Randy Miller said, "I have been experimenting over the last four years with imaging God as a female, actually as a black woman. I think the father figure is great, as well; but in my life I think I need—and I think it's part of being gay—some healing around female energy. So I've been exploring that and not just intellectually, but seeing how I could, in terms of my theology, live my life and pray and in a very deep way try to experience how that feels. I sort of image God as a woman with embracing arms, of course heavy set, and with the power that heals people and embraces them and makes them whole. I'm really focusing on the graceful aspects of God in terms of offering grace and mercy and healing. I think so many gay and lesbian people, including myself, need to hear that. For us, for right now, we don't need necessarily to know about the transcendence of God or God as a judge."[15]

All of the interviewees spoke of interacting personally and intimately with God. Several described this relational intimacy as both personal and communal. A UCC clergyman said, "I have a relational theology where we find God in each other"; and a UMC clergyman said, "I image God as the force of community, a community of people together. I have an image of the community of people at my church ending the service with Communion. People are standing in a circle; and I see almost this dome of light covering and encircling this community that is the power of God, that's present in all of these people who have come together in a spirit of love and caring for one another." A UCC woman said, "My image of God is a loving, evolving spirit struggling with us—something that I don't completely understand. A spirit moving with us."

Understanding Jesus

Just as my interviewees tended to challenge or avoid the conventional images of a transcendent, trinitarian, male God in favor of an immanent, changing, personally creative and interactive God, they also spoke of Jesus less as the divine son of God and more as a fellow human: "a companion," "my best friend," "someone who is accompanying me." A UCC woman said Jesus is "one who is walking with you, at your side at all times, and who, when you are at your low point, carries you through." A UMC clergywoman said, "Jesus is first of all a human being. I think Jesus was the son of God in the same sense that I think that all of us are sons and daughters of God. The difference was that I think he clearly realized that about himself, and I think many do not clearly realize that about themselves. It's one thing for me to know it, and it's another thing to have gone through the spiritual journey enough to realize it. I experience Jesus as a sage, as a teacher of the spiritual path who is wise and wonderful. In some sense he shares a heritage with many other religious teachers, so that he is not necessarily unique at that point."

Other people I interviewed emphasized this latter image of Jesus as a teacher, example, or standard more than as a personal friend. They referred to him as "a prophetic leader," "a landmark or a pointer to the way," "the tour guide along the way," "the model of compassion and love," "a transformer who changes people's lives," and "that cutting-edge-type person who taught us how to be a part of God's family." One UCC woman said, "The road that he walks is the road I attempt to walk; and so I get encouraged on how to handle that." Selena Blackwell said that Jesus is "a model of God, but a model that we can simulate, one in which we are to show our love to God by how much we need each other and how we dream the earth and the life therein. One where we're not supposed to sit around in judgment of each other so much as to reach out and help each other and, if it comes down to it, to die for each other. One of trying to become less ego-centered and more concerned about people and things around you."

Others, however, did speak of Jesus in the more conventional theological language of his being both divine and human. One UCC man said that "for me Jesus was the fleshed, person form of God who was here and ends up being our example of the kind of person I would like to be." Two UMC clergymen found Jesus' divinity and humanity grounded in the Bible. One said that he was "a historical figure, Jesus Christ in Bethlehem of Judaea, God showing just how far love will go, that God's love goes all the way, and as Paul put it, 'There is nothing that can separate us from God.' Jesus lived that love; Jesus was that love." The other said, "For me I'd have to say Jesus is that very personal way God has walked through the lives of humanity and is still present to us in those stories in the Bible and how we use those stories. I want to say that Jesus is the very intimate or very personal way God has come to us."

A UMC woman agreed that "Jesus remains the greatest example of God's revelation" but insisted that "the institutional church and Jesus are not synonymous." She thought that Jesus has been "misused by the church," and she did not "see anything in Jesus that gives the church any excuses for its behavior throughout history in terms of inquisitions, witch-hunts, and the persecution of lesbians and gay men."

Others were also critical of the ways in which the church has idolized, masked, and restricted Jesus.[16] For example, Mark Ehrke, who was raised in the UCC and became active in the Religious Society of Friends, maintained that "being gay does something to sensitize you to contradictions out there. It certainly has been my experience in this issue of Christianity and being gay. All the trappings, all the talk about Jesus, this and that and everything else, gets in the way of the common message, of that compassion and understanding that Jesus put forth; but other great religions, other great people have put forth the same message. But this worshiping of Jesus gets in the way of the message, of its commonality with others and for all. One of the things I've always loved about Quakers is the silence; and I find most Christian religions just love to yammer. Just all this talk, all this busyness gets in the way of spirituality. My perspective of spirituality is that understanding the message is something so basic, so simple; and all this other stuff gets in the way for me."

Mary Gaddis agreed. She said, "I've been fed up with the church for years. Part of why I'm not as connected to the church is what I can remember since I was eight or ten years old: I have been saying I don't understand this Jesus stuff. I don't understand why someone thinks Jesus had to die for my sins; and there's no reason whatsoever that somebody should have to hang on the cross because I did something bad. I don't understand that concept at all. I used to try to understand it. It's like when you grow up you'll understand three plus two equals five, when you grow up you'll understand why two thousand years ago some guy hung on a cross for sins that I'm doing. Forget it, it doesn't make sense. Now, what I've concluded is that it doesn't have to make sense. It simply doesn't have any meaning for me. The Christ part is what I don't understand. Jesus is a guy who came along and said we better pay attention to all of the people because all of the people are children of God, and we better treat each other justly, and we better treat each other in Godlike ways. That makes a whole lot of sense to me. Liberation theology and understanding Jesus as that kind of liberator is wonderful; but that other stuff, the Christ stuff, doesn't make any sense. It used to be I wanted to figure it out; now it's like I don't have to. It doesn't have to make sense. For the people it makes sense to, that's fine."

Conservative Views

Some gay Christians, however, consider themselves to be theologically conservative and criticize "an extremely liberal theological view where 'anything goes,'" where "Jesus is not so much a savior as a political martyr, and any kind of god is OK to worship, even if that 'god' is yourself." Gay Pentecostals, for example, often speak of adhering more strictly to the Bible and bringing forth its "Apostolic truth." But their views are themselves imbued with liberal premises and interpretations, such as the oft-repeated claim that "Jesus loves us no matter what."[17]

Thumma, too, reported that gay evangelicals in his study no longer "believe in the inerrancy of the Bible" but still insisted with a certainty characteristic of their evangelical, conservative heritage that theirs was the "proper" interpretation. Focusing on the image of God as creator in the Psalms, Good News reasoned that "since God made me the way I am, why shouldn't I express my sexuality?" and "Why would God ask me to change something I can't?"[18]

Indeed, the theologies of most gay Christians, whether they consider themselves to be liberal, moderate, or conservative, seem to rest on the traditionally liberal view of God and Jesus as not "judging" but "accepting and loving all of their children."[19] As one of the leaders of Good News said, "God loves us and stays with us, forever offering forgiveness, healing, and wholeness. We live and move and have our being—including our sexual being—within the sphere of God's love."[20]

Faith

Theologian Paul Tillich defined "faith" as "the state of being ultimately concerned."[21] With theology we try to understand what concerns us ultimately, whereas with faith "we embrace, take seriously, and share with others" those ultimate concerns.[22] Findings from my survey about the faith of respondents provided further evidence of similarities among UMC and UCC gay people (see table 14). For example, about three-quarters of both UMC and UCC respondents (75 percent, UMC; 71 percent, UCC) said that the Bible was especially important to who they are and what they do as persons of faith; of those respondents, over two-thirds (68 percent, UMC and UCC) said that a particular biblical theme was central to their faith, and for about one-half of them the important themes were social justice (32 percent, UMC; 21 percent UCC) or love (22 percent, UMC; 28 percent, UCC). Over one-half of both UMC and UCC respondents (53 percent, UMC; 59 percent, UCC) also said that the center or basis of their faith was other than biblical; and each group of respondents named the same sources with similar frequency. The nonbiblical sources most often reported were personal experience (27 percent, UMC; 25 percent, UCC), spiritual connection (14 percent, UMC; 18 percent, UCC), community or fellowship (10 percent, UMC; 11 percent, UCC), and creation (6 percent, UMC; 8 percent, UCC).

Comparisons of my findings with those from a study of non-gay UMC members showed that the bases of faith for gay UMC respondents were more like those of gay UCC respondents than of non-gay UMC members. For example, 89 percent of non-gay UMC members, compared to 75 percent of my gay UMC respondents, said that the Bible was especially important to their faith. Concerning nonbiblical resources for faith, 64 percent of the non-gay UMC members said that they used church tradition, their own reasoning, and their own experience equally, whereas 53 percent of my gay UMC respondents said they used personal experience, spiritual connection, community, and creation in that order of preference.[23]

The similarities concerning the bases and resources of faith reported by my UMC and UCC respondents suggest that gay people across religious bodies may have more in common with each other than with their fellow non-gay church members. Other data support this notion. In 1990, for example, ten gay religious organizations responded

TABLE 14

Percentages of UMC and UCC Respondents Reporting That the Bible Is Especially Important for Their Faith; That a Particular Biblical Theme Is Important for Their Faith and Which Themes Are Important; and That Their Faith Depends on Nonbiblical Sources and Which Sources Are Important

	UMC (N=198)	UCC (N=282)
Bible especially important	75%	71%
Important biblical theme	68%	68%
social justice	32%	21%
love	22%	28%
other themes	46%	51%
Nonbiblical source of faith	53%	59%
personal experience	27%	25%
spiritual connection	14%	18%
community, fellowship	10%	11%
creation	6%	8%
various other sources	43%	38%

to the anti-gay campaign of the Christian Right with this collectively written letter:

> Our experiences as persons of faith have taught us that the God who created us, sustains us and calls us to live out the command to "do justice, love mercy and walk humbly with God" is the same God who condemns all those human conditions that would separate us from each other and God. Our experience has shown us that the fear and hatred of persons with same sex orientation, called homophobia, [are] contrary to the love and will of the Creator. Many of our traditions teach us that those behaviors and attitudes, like homophobia, and the actions that accompany them that separate us one human being from the other, are called SIN.
>
> We join over 26 other gay and lesbian religious coalitions from all the major faith groups in America to unite with one voice in saying that we see no inconsistency between our sexual orientation and our faith traditions. We stand as persons strengthened by our relationship to our God to continue a ministry of love to fight for the elimination of all barriers that separate God's children whether

they be barriers of race, gender, nationality, economic class or sexual orientation.[24]

The signers of the letter represented the organizations of gay Eastern Orthodox Christians, Presbyterians, Christian Scientists, Pentecostals, Seventh-Day Adventists, Jews, Brethren and Mennonites, Roman Catholics, Episcopalians, and members of the UCC. The letter's contents were similar to the responses in my survey of and interviews with UMC and UCC people in the following ways: (1) the emphasis on personal experience and on personal relationships with God; (2) the emphasis on the love of God and the goodness of God's creation; (3) biblical references to love and social justice; (4) the reinterpretation of religious traditions to assert that homophobia, not homosexuality, is sinful; and (5) the repeated call to eliminate separation and barriers within society and religious bodies and to find or make community.

Eric Law, a gay Episcopal priest, summarized these concerns when he wrote elsewhere that "spirituality to me is the ability to make connection: connection with myself, especially parts of myself that I dislike and deny; connection with others, not just those who are like me but also those who are different and even my enemies." He said further that making these connections required him "to stretch, to step out of my boundaries, to take risks."

It would be difficult not to see that gay people affiliated with mainstream religious bodies are "ultimately concerned" about relationship, connection, community, and creation. However, these were the concerns also expressed by those who have left mainstream bodies and been attracted to gay churches and synagogues formed independently of them. A number of examples follow.

Thumma found that for people at the evangelical parachurch in Atlanta, "religious acceptance by God, a community, and a heritage" replaced the alienation and rejection they had experienced in their home churches.[25]

According to Michelle Thomas, a pastor in one of the Apostolic churches of the National Gay Pentecostal Alliance, there is a "huge network" of gay Pentecostals across the country in spite of the anti-gay hostility of most televangelists. She wrote, "I've been able to tap into this network, to worship God with fellow Gays and Lesbians openly and proudly, just as we are. Believe me, no one has really lived till one is in a room full of Gays and Lesbians hooting and hollering for Jesus!"[26]

At Denver's MCC, Bauer observed that "in addition to a feeling of acceptance by God, there is a strong community support system at work"; and as "members gain the impression that fellow worshippers share their own perceptions and feelings, a common basis for communication, concerning both sexual and religious problems, is provided."[27]

One of Rabinowitz's subjects said that "Judaism has to be practiced in a community" and "if homosexuality could be totally accepted as just another difference," there would be no need for a gay synagogue. He claimed that most Americans lead atomized lives and lack community, but at the gay synagogue they have this community. Another person said, "I need to be part of a Jewish community," and for him that community is Congregation Beth Simchat Torah. One man who did not live near the gay synagogue said that in his own neighborhood he *davened* (prayed) at large Orthodox synagogues where he could be anonymous, but "for holiday celebrations I'd be missing very much if I didn't have my *hevrah* [community] in Congregation Beth Simchat Torah."[28]

Paul Foster also found in his study of gay Catholic men in Toronto that his respondents often distinguished between the "official church" and their own self-formed groups by noting the injustice of the former and saying that "their real faith community is not this institution that wants to keep them shut out of power; their faith community is wherever they have been able to find acceptance."[29]

Faith Communities

One's "faith community" can be defined as the place, center, or source of one's own support, power, nurture, comfort, and meaning, as "where I find God and God finds me, where my life becomes most meaningful."[30] When I asked respondents in my survey to identify their primary faith communities (see table 15), they cited their local churches or congregations most often (23 percent, UMC; 28 percent, UCC) and their lovers, partners, and families[31] next (16 percent, UMC; 20 percent, UCC).

The Christian church in general (11 percent, UMC; 9 percent, UCC), colleagues within the denomination (11 percent, UMC; 9 percent, UCC), the gay organization within the denomination (11 percent, UMC; 4 percent, UCC), people within their local congregations (9 percent, UMC; 8 percent, UCC), the denomination itself (4 percent, UMC; 4 percent, UCC), and gay people outside the denomination (4 percent, UMC; 4 percent, UCC) were identified as primary faith communities less often; other groups of people and organizations, including ecumenical organizations, various support groups, campus groups, Alcoholics Anonymous, the MCC, and friendship networks, were also identified (11 percent, UMC; 14 percent, UCC).

These latter categories of faith communities — ecumenical organizations, support groups, and campus groups — will be discussed before the more often reported categories of lovers/partners/family and gay organizations within religious bodies. The local congregation — the faith

TABLE 15

Percentages of UMC and UCC Respondents Identifying Various Primary Faith Communities

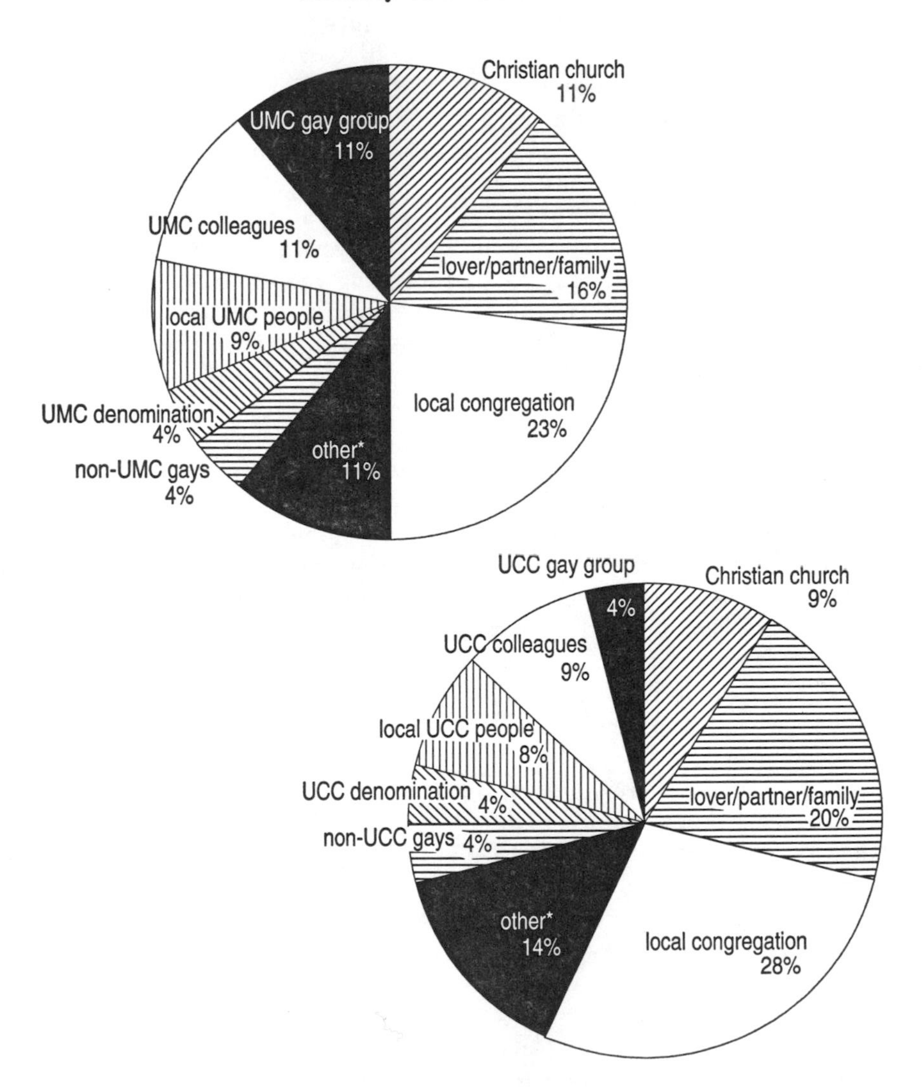

*Ecumenical activities, various support groups, campus groups, Alcoholics Anonymous, Metropolitan Community Church, and friendship networks

community reported most often—will then be discussed under the major headings of "The Black Church" and "Welcoming Congregations."

Ecumenical Organizations and Support Groups

Katie Sanetra told me she felt the unconditional welcome of community at an ecumenical service for Gay Pride Week sponsored by the Interfaith Alliance of Seattle. "It was like I wasn't sitting in church and having to shake my head 'no.' It was something that I could feel completely around me, surrounding me, and it wasn't something I had to reject. The words were inclusive. They blessed the space. We shared bread, but it was not the body of Christ. It was a blessing of the earth, which is what I have to do when I go up for Communion in my church when they say, 'Body and blood of Christ,' and I'm going, 'No, this is blessings of the earth from God.' They didn't mention Christ very much at all. They spoke about God instead and spoke of being together and communicating and being one with the earth."

One of the UCC clergyman I interviewed said, "I have a number of support networks, but the most important group is one that I formed this year on my own initiative. It consists of myself, another UCC clergyperson, an American Baptist clergyperson, a United Methodist clergyperson, and a Lutheran clergyperson. I deliberately picked all men—all gay men and all clergy. I thought that that common denominator would give us some basis for discussion and support. We focus on issues of friendship and relationships and have really opened up to each other on a wide range of topics like fidelity and faithfulness, including sexual fidelity in relationships. We learned a lot when two of the people were going through the endings of their relationships. A lot of intimate details were shared, and we all really have opened up in the context of this group. Part of my issue in forming the group was to make it a support group and secondly to concentrate on issues of friendship and relationship, which to me are central issues as a gay clergyperson."

Mark Ehrke, a UCC layperson, said, "When I stop and think about it, I have a community of people. I have a very dear Catholic friend. Whenever we need prayer support, we call each other and we pray for each other. I have other friends. When I'm going through a hard time, I have four, five, or six people that I can call for prayer support. You know, this is my true community. It goes beyond any sort of denominational thing. My community right now are largely people that I know through my UCC associations, the Quakers, this Catholic woman who is a former co-worker of mine, and my lover whom I met through the Friends."

Another UCC clergyman said, "I've had some incredibly close friends who were very, very important to me. I belonged to a men's group for people who were gay and straight. That group of men was incredibly important in my own coming out, when I felt very much alone." And a UCC woman said her primary support group was the lesbian community outside of the church. "Particularly what I'm closest to right now is SAGE, Senior Action in a Gay Environment, where I go to a fifty-plus support discussion almost every Friday evening. We have a wonderful sort of holdover from the early days of feminism, a kind of consciousness-raising support group. I've met a lot of good, helpful, supportive interesting people through SAGE. So I feel that it is my strongest source of support; and as a result, my church ties have become less and less strong."

A UMC woman said she drew her support from a variety of people and groups inside and outside the church. "I came out in the late 70s when the gay rights movement was at its height. Portland had a very strong lesbian community. There was a lesbian educational forum going on at the time. I had a number of lesbian friends. Within the church there was sort of an underground church for a long time made up of people who believed in social justice. I was very much a part of it. My best friend at the time was a nonchurched gay man. Also, because I didn't make a decision to come out—I mean really deal with my sexuality—until I was nearly forty and because I was in a professional therapy support group, I didn't have to deal with a lot of the fear and anxiety of people abandoning and leaving me. I was independent; I was raising my children alone; I knew I could take care of myself; and so what other people thought of me was much less important than it is when you're coming out at twenty. So it was a relatively easy process for me."

James Wolf also reported that for many of the priests in his survey, groups of gay clergy were a "major source of support." One said, "We meet once a month as a means of support in sharing our lives with regard to sexuality, spirituality, and ministry." Another said, "There are a number of people 'out' in my [religious] community, and this network of friends is vital. Without it I could not survive, nor would I choose to do so." And another said, "I most appreciate the opportunities for informal sharing among other gay priests and religious. Here I find affirmation and a special sense of confidence and community." Some said that their religious superiors supported the formation of such groups, and others said that they had formed "small clandestine support groups" because of their superiors' "active discrimination" or "passive neglect to address the problem of prejudice."[32]

Campus Groups

Gay students on university and college campuses have often expressed the lack of and need for community, and some have begun to find it.[33] Chad Heilig, for example, wrote about coming out as an undergraduate at a state university in the South. He said he was fortunate to have the support of several gay men at his local church and of a select group of friends on campus, but neither the church nor the campus ministry ever sponsored public programs about sexuality and spirituality. As a result, he said that he "felt uncomfortable being myself, both at church and at the student center," and "carried with me the aching desire to see a more intentionally inclusive, church-based ministry to lesbigay students." As a graduate student at the University of California at Berkeley, he did find "a church home" in a local "welcoming" or Reconciling Congregation (RC) that sponsored a parish-based campus ministry program, but he also found the local gay community to be "largely cynical and resentful of the church." He said that he suspected and hoped that other gay students shared his "thirst for full inclusion in the family of faith," but finding those students was frustrating and proved to be more difficult than he expected.[34]

At Illinois Wesleyan University, the Methodist Student Fellowship decided to become part of the RC movement as a way to fulfill its purpose of creating "a nurturing community for all people interested in working together with Christ." Andrew Ulman, one of the organizers, said, "We easily formed natural alliances with the lesbian and gay organization on campus, with whom we are now sponsoring joint projects."[35]

Mary Council-Austin, a UMC campus minister at Howard University, helped sponsor "The Circle of Friends," a bimonthly, coffeehouse-style ministry to provide "a visible sign of God's love and care" for gay people. She wrote about one student who had been harassed by young men in his neighborhood and then kicked out of his off-campus housing because of his sexual orientation: when such "realities" as the sight of this young man "sitting in the middle of his belongings weeping and screaming" present themselves, "suddenly warnings from others to avoid offering ministries for gay, lesbian, and bisexual students pale into insignificance," and "the profound search for community amid deep and hurtful divisions takes on a new urgency."[36]

When Stephen Schneider, Norman Farberow, and Gabriel Kruks conducted their study of suicidal behavior in gay college men, they found that "significantly more of the suicidal than of the nonsuicidal gay men reported no religious affiliation." Although 49 percent of respondents with Jewish, Catholic, Protestant, and other religious affiliations reported suicide attempts or suicidality, 72 percent of nonaffiliated respondents did so. The association of suicidal behavior with religious nonaffiliation found in this study draws further attention to the supportive role that organized religion could play in the lives of gay people.[37]

Odette Lockwood-Stewart, another UMC campus minister, gathered information from Christian students on various campuses throughout the United States and summarized her findings as follows: (1) some gay students find spiritual and social support in informal networks of friends and in organized groups on campus and in the surrounding community; (2) some students, but not the majority, find support in campus ministry programs, local churches, and individual chaplains; (3) anti-gay groups dominate or intimidate the religious communities and campus ministries on some campuses; (4) some campus ministry programs have addressed the issue of homosexuality but have not ministered to gay students themselves; and (5) gay students in state or secular colleges felt more secure about their civil rights than did students from church-affiliated colleges.[38]

In 1995 at Yeshiva University in New York City, a group of Orthodox rabbis condemned gay student groups in an open letter to the university's president. They wrote that "what Judaism tells us is an abomination should find no welcome in our institution" and urged the president "to explore every possible avenue to obviate this blemish." The letter and similar efforts by other professors and students arose after a graduating student of the law school acknowledged his male partner in a commencement address.[39]

Odette Lockwood-Stewart also reported that students in her study "talked of increased violence and hate language"; some were "demoralized by the visible limitations and fragility of tolerance and of student coalitions"; and others "were demoralized by the atmosphere of homophobia which they felt is shaped by the religious right and fostered by the silence of the majority of Christians." But most, she found, "still carried hope," which "came from their own commitments to engage with those who differed from themselves."[40]

The support of some campus ministry programs has affected how some gay people relate to their local churches after college. David Ward, a member of the Presbyterian Church (U.S.A.), wrote that being out as a gay Christian "has always been relatively easy for me," since "the first person I ever spoke to about being gay was my college minister and he affirmed me and my sexuality." Because the minister "never faltered in his acceptance and love" and told him that he "was welcome and needed in the church," David says that he has "never been willing to accept 'second class' status in the church."[41]

Lovers/Partners/Family

The reporting of faith communities in my survey provided some noticeable differences according to the gender of respondents (not in table 15). Women from the UMC and UCC identified their primary faith communities as their lovers, partners, and families more often than UMC and UCC men (32 percent women and 12 percent men, UMC; 25 percent women and 15 percent men, UCC). Further, UMC men identified the denominational gay organization more often than UMC women (4 percent, women; 14 percent, men); and UCC men identified the Christian church in general more often than UCC women (6 percent, women; 13 percent, men). Women more often than men would appear to have found their primary faith communities outside of institutional and formal religious organizations. As one UMC clergywoman has written:

> Our childhood God despises homosexuals; our church family denies our very existence; our traditional theology openly condemns us; our denominations and churches believe we are sick individuals who choose to alienate ourselves from God by refusing to ask for forgiveness for our sinful ways.
>
> This is my experience, from the heart of a wounded Christian lesbian, unable and unwilling to relinquish my Christianity, looking for an overflowing cup in the midst of a seemingly endless drought. Over the years, my reflections, my stunted spiritual growth, and my weariness at working so hard to be part of — indeed a leader of — a denomination that has not accepted me, called me to step away from it. Doing so has led me on an inward journey, striving to find the theology of fullness for which I long.
>
> Contemplating the times in my life when I have felt spiritually whole, when I have felt God's love filling me to overflowing, I recall the tender embrace of my lover.... It is through relationships, intimate friendships, and lover relationships that we can experience God's love at work in our lives.
>
> Together, my lover and I have seen God's gentleness in our most intimate moments, God's compassion when we comfort one another. It is through the joys and pains of this relationship that I have felt God's spirit entwined with my own, filling me with unconditional love.[42]

This statement of "faith through personal relationship" is not without its counterpart by women in other religious bodies. A Mormon woman has also written that she learned through her own experience and much spiritual searching that "God has not created me to be lonely and miserable but led me to women like myself so we can help bear one another's burdens and find peace and fulfillment." She claimed to "have achieved a unity with God" as "my spouse and I continue to find enlightenment" and to "feel blessed that our relationship embraces every aspect of a good marriage — spiritual, emotional, and temporal growth."[43]

Although men did not identify their relationships and families as their primary faith communities as often as women, they did so with as much seriousness and intensity. For example, when I asked Peter Ilgenfritz what was the center or main source from which he drew support, comfort, and power, he said, "Certainly from my relationship. It's really from Dave. Our relationship and our life together is one of the core center places." Peter said that although the denomination and local church "used to be incredibly important to me, right now the UCC is not such a vital place in my life as it used to be. I feel some sadness about that, because I would like it to be again. Right now sometimes I think, 'Why am I even involved? Why do I even stay with this?' and yet there's part of me that is maybe obstinate enough that I say, 'Well, I still think I can find a place in this church; I still think I can find a place in this denomination.' But I'm not finding myself fed very much by the church or the denomination." As discussed in the previous chapter, after my interview with Peter, he and Dave did find a position as copastors at a UCC church in Seattle.

B. J. Stiles also identified family and friend as his community of nurture, support, and comfort. Having come out as a gay man in middle-age, he said that his "daughters were extraordinarily caring and have been wonderfully supportive. I think I especially am absolutely dependent upon the emotional support of my children. For both me and my partner, our families are critical to our day-to-day emotional support. We also have many really dear friends; most of them are gay men. I think our most immediate support system are our gay male friends here in the city."

Gay Organizations within Religious Bodies

The UMC respondents identified their denominational gay organizations as their primary faith communities more often than the UCC respondents did (11 percent, UMC; 4 percent, UCC; see table 15).[44]

One UMC clergyman told me, "I think for most people who find Affirmation a place of community and support—an assurance about who they are and where Christ is really found in a community of faithful, committed Christians — to have the general church say you're unacceptable really hurts. But it doesn't change the reality of what we've experienced with other people in Affirmation, which has told us, 'Yes, God really loves you, and you're really a good person, and it really doesn't matter what these people say.' "

Randy Miller said that he has been committed to Affirmation because it is "a group that I really feel an amazing debt to because I came to them after I came out. I was battered and wounded in some ways and I think that there was just some fantastic people who were just themselves and were just free, and they embraced me, and slowly I felt like that was the place where I finally could tell my whole story and didn't have to leave any pieces out. I got a lot of power from them. They have been my primary faith community."

Gay people in other religious bodies have also expressed their appreciation for and reliance on their gay organizations. In Neil Miller's interview with Bill Dorn, the excommunicated Catholic priest recalled the final Dignity Mass at the Newman Center at the University of Minnesota, from which the organization had been expelled by the bishop. At the end of the service, people carried the ceremonial ornaments across the street to the Episcopal university center, where future services would be held. Bill said, "There was a joyful sense that we are here and we will stay and our fate isn't dependent on the church..., a feeling that we are a church in our own way..., a realization that we don't need the church to validate who we are."[45]

Lorry Sorgman, the president of the World Congress of Gay and Lesbian Jewish Organizations, wrote about her group's participation in the 1987 National March for Lesbian and Gay Rights in Washington, D.C. As the group joined the parade with their banner, the other religious groups gave them "a huge reception of applause and celebration." Lorry said that "tears nearly blinded my eyes" when "I saw a man wearing a *yarmulke* and his family with him as they joined in the *simchas* [joy] of the moment." She asked, "Could it be that the true spirit of being Jewish is one of acceptance and respect? For the first time in my life I witnessed what it felt like to be truly welcomed as a Lesbian Jew."[46]

A closeted Presbyterian minister also expressed his appreciation for the participation of Presbyterians for Lesbian and Gay Concerns (PLGC) at the march. He wrote, "Thanks to PLGC's participation, it was one of the key Christian experiences of my life. I thought about all the delegations I could have marched with—old, new friends from states, regions, etc., yet here was my church so visible." He marched at the front of the PLGC delegation with five or six others carrying the group's banner.[47]

A Mennonite woman wrote about her reluctance to attend the denomination's annual meeting, since at the previous meeting "it was questioned whether lesbians and gay men could even be considered 'God's people.'" But because she knew that the Brethren/Mennonite Council for Gay and Lesbian Concerns (BMC) would be there, she did attend and "found a great comfort in BMC's presence." For her the "focal point of each day" was BMC's worship service, where people shared their own stories with each other. In her view, BMC effectively worked to bring the gay issue "down to a personal level, rather than an issue to be discussed on the delegate floor. And I believe that this personalizing of the discussion is the way for many diverse people to become God's people."[48]

Non-gay people too are welcome to join and participate in these gay organizations. One "straight, open-minded male" high school student said he and his non-gay parents started worshiping with Lutherans Concerned when he was twelve or thirteen: "That was an interesting point of my life because I was still naive about many things, but I was made to feel mature and 'grown-up' because of my lack of prejudice."[49]

But these organizations are not without their problems, and many have had to work at being more open to women, bisexuals, and people of color.

Problems within Organizations

Gender. As discussed in chapter 4, Leonard Primiano's study of a Dignity chapter found that "as hard as its administrators tried to attract women to the chapter by changing its liturgy's sexist language or cajoling its visiting priests and congregation to include women and their concerns in their general attitudes, Dignity still represented an enclave of male culture in a male environment." Primiano observed, for example, that "the lesbian community was often erased" because the folklore of the group, such as the humor, metaphors, and personal anecdotes used in services, "was about the male experience of being gay, the male body and male sexuality." One woman said, "I really have to get myself psyched up to go to Dignity because I know sometimes I will be the only woman there. Sometimes, I'm going to be offended by the language, or I'm going to be offended by the body language of some of the men, and I have to almost put myself in a frame of mind that you are willing to go down there and deal with that." She added that she made "conscious decisions" not to attend when she was tired because then she would be "quick to shout out and react." Another woman discontinued her affiliation with the chapter because "the men there failed to realize that lesbians did not express their sexuality in the same way as men." She thought that Dignity's whole meaning and purpose were predicated on "a masculine interest in having gay sexuality blessed by the Church," which for her was too "narrow" and something they should "evolve out of." Although her lesbianism was "sometimes extremely important" to her, "in the scheme of things... the amount of time I am a sexual person... is minimal." Emphasizing her "gayness over the femaleness, or the Irishness, or any other aspect" did not make sense to her.[50]

Mary Gaddis recalled that her first contact with Affirmation was at one its national gatherings, "which had forty or fifty men and five women. They were really excited that five women were there. They had never had that many women there before. One of the first things that we talked about was how we had to have gender parity in whatever we do with the leadership of the organization. So we started off right then doing that. We said we wanted to have a ten-person coordinating committee and that half of them had to be women. If there were only five women in the whole group, on one level you're a leader, but on the other level you're sort of there by default; you're there simply because you are a member."

Another UMC woman worried that the people in Affirmation may become a one-issue people. She said, "Homosexuality has become such an issue for them that I don't see them at other sessions of General Conference, like when abortion was being discussed or continued funding for women's programs. I have a lot of issues that are important to me and that I work on, but they don't seem to be that important to others in Affirmation." She did admit, however, that gay people may not be welcome at these other sessions during national meetings.

Bisexuality. Most gay organizations have also tried to respond to the increased visibility and demands of bisexuals.[51] After many years as an active lesbian in the United Church Coalition for Lesbian/Gay Concerns (UCCL/GC), Margarita Suárez decided to come out as a bisexual and was "terrified of being rejected" by what she described as "my own people," "my gay/lesbian friendship network," "my family." But she found that "for my Coalition friends all over the country whom I have been participating with and loving and knowing and working with for the last ten or twelve years, this was not an issue. They still love me."[52]

Other bisexuals — including Unitarian Universalists, Friends, Jews, and Methodists — have also written about the fear of coming out and being excluded from these gay organizations.[53] Peggy Gaylord, for example, wrote about attending the 1988 national gathering of Affirmation:

> In an early warm-up exercise, we went around the room to say, "I am [gay/lesbian/straight] and what I really like about being that is..." I was two-thirds of the way from the starting point in a circle of 90 people. Each person in turn said "I am lesbian..." or "I am gay...." My hands were sweating; my heart and head were pounding; I couldn't breathe. Was I going to have to say "lesbian" and deny my self once more, in a room where I had hoped for so much? Talk about internalized biphobia! Then, the man just before me said, "I am bisexual," giving me permission to be myself, whatever the consequences.

Peggy said that she went on to meet more bisexuals in subsequent meetings, to speak up to gay and straight people about the need to be more inclusive, and to take part in the organization's decision in 1991 to change its name to include "Bisexual" — "Affirmation: United Methodists for Lesbian, Gay, and Bisexual Concerns."[54] Other organizations followed suit. For example, in 1993 "Unitarian Universalists for Lesbian and Gay Concerns (UULGC)" became "Interweave: Unitarian Universalists for Lesbian, Gay and Bisexual Concerns."[55]

Race. Three of the people I interviewed also spoke of their experiences as people of color in predominantly white denominations and gay organizations. Randy Miller said, "I think Affirmation has placed itself publicly through our spokespersons and through the papers and releases we put out as very supportive of African-American stances. We have been very deliberate in putting whatever support we can in with the agenda of African-American folks. When ethnic minority concerns were a priority[56] for our denomination and were under attack, Affirmation was very visible as one of the progressive caucuses that really supported continuing to focus on those concerns. It didn't come out totally the way that we wanted it to come out, but we were very visible and very supportive. So we've done that sort of thing, and we've had programs on racial issues. There's always been this sort of visible, vocal support for people of color out of Affirmation, even though Affirmation hasn't been able to attract significant numbers of people of color to belong to or participate in its own organization."

When I asked Margarita Suárez what UCC gay people needed to do around issues of race, she said, "Truly acknowledge there is difference and that we aren't necessarily one happy family, one happy community. I think that we tend to try to move directly to the commonalities; and then what happens is that we avoid affirming the difference." Margarita thought that in order for more gay people of color to become more visible and active, "an entirely other kind of group had to be formed that is for people of color, that is a place where gay, lesbian, and bisexual men and women of color can have their own space, something that comes out of people of color, something that comes from one 'out' person or 'semi-out' person in the black community who's willing to begin this organization and to promote it within the black church. There are a lot more out gay and lesbian people who are white than there are gay and lesbian people of color in the UCC. So, I think there needs to be something specific in the communities of color by people of color; and once there is, then I think there can be some kind of commonality work done with both gay/lesbian people of color and white gay/lesbian people. But as long as the Coalition [UCCL/GC] is almost exclusively white, it's going to be the rare person of color who takes a chance to venture into it. And that rare person of color is probably going to be someone like myself who grew up in a more upper-middle-class, white type of environment and consciousness. I didn't have the same kind of cultural issues to deal with as if I had come out of a ghetto kind of community. I had more ease at feeling comfortable in a predominantly white denomination and group; and it was actually only after I had been in it for five, six or seven years that my own consciousness as a Latina became strong enough for my own self that I could from inside the system begin to challenge what I saw as its cultural unilateralism. But even now it's difficult for me to do because the Coalition is my family; it's hard to confront your family with stuff that's hard. And yet I saw that that was part of what I needed to do after a certain point. And I don't know if what I've said is the only way for lesbian/bisexual/gay people of color to become active, but simply saying, 'OK let's become interracial,' isn't going to work, isn't going to bring them in."[57]

Selena Blackwell, another UCCL/GC member, said that she too had been "in predominantly white situations ever since I was five, so I'm used to being the only one," but she did observe and was bothered by some differences with other members. She said she thought that "it's common for other nonblack, white folks, to look at homophobia as a separate issue — like, 'I think we should be about fighting homophobia; I'm not so sure I want to be about fighting racism,' or something like that. For me it's not a separate thing because it's part of a lot of personal experiences that keep me fired up, keep me fueled. Whether its homophobia, heterosexism, sexism, or racism, it's linked by oppression. It's hard for me to separate it all out. I can't help but see the interconnection." She was also a member of the UCC's province-level Committee on Racism, which she was finding "a real comfortable place because I can be who I am in my totality there." She said that when she and her partner had a commitment ceremony, "just about the whole Committee on Racism came. So I find them personally supportive on that level. I think probably they know other gay and lesbian people among their families and friends, so this groundwork might've been laid already, and I think they see the connection a little bit better. I don't get blank stares as much when I talk about it with them."

The problems reported by gay people within predominantly black religious bodies were not less severe.

The Black Church

"The black church" is a general term that refers to Protestant denominations with predominantly African-American memberships as well as to African-American congregations within predominantly white religious bodies.[58]

Source of Pain and Sadness

When James Sears interviewed young gay people in the South, he found that while both white and black subjects "reported varying degrees of animosity expressed in their churches toward homosexuality," all of the

fierce allies at General Conference. They can't be intimidated in the same ways I think that some white liberals can be.

"Nobody publicly accuses African-Americans in our denomination of lack of fortitude. They accuse white liberals of forsaking their faith and running off, but in the United Methodist Church a lot of African-American clergy and laypeople are known to be people of amazing faith. Part of it is a social justice thing. I think that African-Americans have a long history of struggle in faith or social justice, so that when they support lesbian/gay people, it's seen as a result of very positive faith. And conversely, when an African-American or an African person stands up and condemns gay and lesbian people, it has a much more powerful effect than when some old white conservative stands up and does it."

Randy explained that "at every General Conference, Affirmation asks the delegates we have supporting us to stand up, and it's very clear that a lot of African-American delegates stand up and make their support clearly known. The first time I saw it, I found it very amazing; the second time I saw it I just accepted it. From talking with my African-American friends in the church, I think that somehow they can get it that gay people ought to be treated fairly. They're not so sure about all the rest of it, but they get it that this is a basic issue about justice. I had a great experience when they were setting up the Study Committee on Homosexuality in 1988. This older black woman turned to me — I just happened to be sitting beside her — and she said, 'They're going to do a study. You and I know what that means. We've been through this before.' She must have been seventy, and she could easily see that I was gay; and it was great. I wish I had had a camera and paper because it was a great story of the connection. I didn't have to explain this whole lesbian/gay business; I was wearing my pink triangle, and she just got it. I think that's the way it's been with some African-American people on lesbian/gay issues."

Communities for Other People of Color

Other gay people of color have also spoken about dealing with racism, homophobia, and other prejudice. Shaffiq Essajee, for example, wrote that Muslims "are viewed with great suspicion, constantly discriminated against, and openly called barbaric warmongers and oppressive tyrants," even though from his point of view most "are gentle, noble, peaceful people, and our societies are tolerant and charitable." As a gay Muslim, he has learned that "the same people who would discriminate against me because of my sexuality would also do so because of my religion" and that other gay people "are the first to stand by me when others accuse me of belonging to a religion that advocates the subjugation of women or terrorist bombing attacks." But while he has found that gay people "understand that prejudice and ignorance are universal adversaries, whether the issue is religious freedom or sexual freedom," he admitted sadly that "many leaders within the Muslim community have not made the same connection."[68]

Eric Law, a Chinese-American Episcopalian, remembered trying unsuccessfully to find his identity within various communities: "When it came to race relations, the gay community, which I dreamed would accept me, was no more than a micro version of the straight world." Since arriving in the United States, he also found that "there was too much individualism in me" to "buy totally into the Chinese culture, with its emphasis on group, not personal identity and behavior." Eric said that after pushing himself "too hard to choose one group over another," he "snapped and lost connections with all groups." He recalled, however, that he was "lucky to have a very supportive Christian community that did not perceive me as a lost person wandering from community to community" but "affirmed my marginality and nurtured me to a point where I could use this marginality creatively and constructively." Although he "might never fit in" to the Chinese community, the mainstream gay community, or dominant American culture, he felt that his "experiences of being in between" them enabled him to support, work with, and challenge them.[69]

Welcoming Congregations

Welcomed as Gay or Ex-Gay?

A woman who was an administrator on the province level of the UMC told me that with the exception of "welcoming" or Reconciling Congregations the denomination had not made any effort to draw in gay people. She pointed out that a local church in her area had become a Reconciling Congregation, and gay people joined as a result: "Once the church puts its mind to saying, 'This is a safe place,' gay and lesbian people will seek that out." She went on to explain that "one of the illustrations that I like to use in workshops about the importance of a church declaring, even advertising, what it does and stands for is this: if you walk into a public building and you have to go to the bathroom, and there are no signs on any of the doors, it's very scary to walk down a hallway and just start opening doors to see where you belong or don't belong. And that's the way it is with church. If there is a sign on the church or an advertisement that says 'everybody' is welcome here, that's one thing; but if the church goes out of its way to say 'lesbians and gay men' are welcome, that's another thing, because historically lesbians and gay men know that 'everybody' doesn't necessarily include us. 'Everybody' is like a hallway with blank doors, and going down the hallway opening them is uncertain and nervous-making for lesbians and gay men. We probably won't bother to make the effort for fear of not finding a friendly room."[70]

Another movement within the UMC consists of Transforming Congregations. This woman explained that a Transforming Congregation is "a church that's involved in a process of publicly supporting and working with people who wish to become ex-gays." They are open to gay and lesbian people who want to change, and "there are many people who have claimed that they have." She added that "part of me thinks that the Transforming Congregation is an OK movement because at least it's real clear to me that that congregation says what it is, has put a sign on the door, and told me that it's not a place I want to worship. But there are some people who may feel very strongly that that's exactly where they want to worship, and that's OK with me."

A UMC clergyman, however, was saddened by "the kind of really self-deprecating and self-hating kinds of theologies that groups like the Transforming, ex-gay-type movements try and push, because they sucker in some folks and some folks lose their lives because of the kind of crap that those people put out. Rather than giving people hope, it's really forcing them into some kind of agenda that is going to hurt them and continue to hurt them."

I asked why he thought the Transforming Congregations appealed to some gay people, and he said: "They have some easy answers, like, 'You do this and you'll be fine.' They reinforce some of the cultural biases that some people have been brought up believing. One of the appeals for somebody who might have some personal ambiguity about their orientation, or might not have found a good relationship in the gay community, or might have some other problems, like they were sexually abused or have alcohol or drug problems or other stuff that's really screwing them up, is that homosexuality gets mixed in with it and is seen as the way out of the other problems. The Transforming folks say, 'If you come along with us, we'll solve all those problems'; and they give them a lot of attention and caring that they didn't find at a bar or in the drug community or in a back alley; and so they haven't looked to the Reconciling Congregation kind of place. They've looked in an unaccepting place, and when they haven't found acceptance, then they think they've found it with the Transforming people. It's very deluding, but they think they've found a quick fix."

Acceptance, Confidence, and Pride

The UMC and UCC respondents identified their local congregations most often as their primary faith communities (23 percent, UMC; 28

percent, UCC; see table 15), but those congregations that had officially declared themselves to welcome gay people seemed to merit and receive the most strongly felt appreciation and participation, as evidenced by these three findings:

1. As reported in chapter 3, over three-quarters of respondents who belonged to welcoming churches, compared to about one-quarter who belonged to nonwelcoming churches, were out.

2. When I asked respondents to recall a specific event within the past five years that made them feel proud to be affiliated with their denominations, most cited local churches' decisions to be become welcoming congregations (29 percent, UMC; 35 percent, UCC).[71]

3. Those who belonged to welcoming congregations identified their local congregations as their primary faith communities more often than those who did not belong to welcoming congregations (27/20 percent, welcoming/nonwelcoming, UMC; 34/21 percent, welcoming/nonwelcoming, UCC).

Just how personally important and meaningful a welcoming congregation can be for a gay person was expressed by one woman who wrote anonymously to ask her local Church of the Brethren to become a part of the Supportive Congregation Network sponsored by the Brethren/Mennonite Council for Gay and Lesbian Concerns. She said that she had worked with the pastor of the church "a lot in the past couple of years to deal with some of my fears and anxieties about God, religion, and my role as a lesbian member of the church." She explained that "religion is something that is important in my life" and that she wanted "to be able to be open with my church because the church is an extended family for me." She added that she had gay friends who would like to belong to a church "where they don't have to wear masks and hide their true selves," and said, "I feel the same way." For her the Supportive Congregation Network was important because by becoming part of it "my church family could help me feel accepted in a world that is often unaccepting."[72]

One of the UCC men I interviewed said that belonging to a welcoming or Open and Affirming (ONA) congregation provided him with confidence and pride at his place of employment outside of the church. He worked as a truck driver for the city newspaper where "a lot of folks are surprised that I have a faith home. People say, 'You're kidding; you're out at your church and everybody knows?' And I say, 'Yes!' And people are very surprised that there is someplace like mine. They'll say, 'We know there's a couple of gay people in our church, but nobody knows it; people who do know know because they're friends, and they wouldn't dream of letting everybody know, because, heaven forbid, who knows what the church would do?' And I'm glad I don't have to worry about what the church is going to do to me."

Decision as Process

Other people have described their local church's decision to become a welcoming congregation as a process in which their faith grew and was strengthened in community with others. Pat Long, a member of Pullen Memorial Baptist Church in Raleigh, wrote that "my own journey began the day after the 1988 Gay Pride March," in which she discovered her pastor, Mahan Siler, had also participated. She sent him an anonymous letter "asking whether those of us the church forced into hiding were really the children of God or merely the skeletons in the family closet." He read the letter as part of a sermon and said that it was "cruel of the church to judge as an abomination what God has given in the creation of a person." For Pat "that sermon was the beginning of my self-acceptance as a lesbian." In 1990 Mahan talked with her about whether Pullen might become a welcoming congregation. "I went to the Board of Deacons to propose that we begin the process. That night I came out to people who had known me for eleven years but did not know I was lesbian. They responded positively. The deacons did not favor a formal process but encouraged our extending an open invitation to discussions on homosexuality and the church. We did." Pat said that "what evolved was a mixed group" of "gay and straight, young and old, single and coupled" people who participated in an ongoing program of open forums, worship services, and classes. Most of the church did not become involved until Mahan brought to the deacons a gay couple's request for him to bless their union.[73]

Pat said that "as the only openly gay deacon" she "immediately became a resource person." To show them "why it matters that the church recognize us as couples," she told them that "nine years earlier my lover, a Pullen member, died. We were out to no one." After many discussions, educational sessions, and meetings involving all members, the church voted to perform same-sex unions and to welcome officially the full inclusion of gay members. Pat recalled:

> So many memories — so many special people who spoke up for what they believed — bared souls, honest questions, delightful surprises. At one session, with chairs filled and folks sitting wall-to-wall on the floor, a tiny lady in her late 70's took a handful of pages from her purse and said she'd done some research at the library. As far as she could see, homosexuality was natural and

> there wasn't anything wrong with it. The couple next to her nodded in agreement. A father holding his infant son said he wanted his kids to grow up in a church where all people are welcome. A father of three said he'd be pleased if his kids grew up to be like the lesbians he'd met at Open Forum. A dozen or more lesbians and gay men came out in the meetings, sharing their pain and their joy.[74]

After the vote, the Southern Baptist Convention pressured the church to reverse its vote. But this local congregation remained faithful to its gay members, and after 109 years of belonging to the denomination was expelled by it.

This story is not an isolated example of the welcoming church movement's power to change, enliven, and strengthen a local church. When I asked UCC clergywoman Diane Darling what had been the best thing that had happened to her church during her twelve years as its pastor, she said, "Without a doubt the Open and Affirming process. I don't mean the decision, but the whole process, the process that began maybe when they first accepted me as a lesbian. It's still going on in the sense of what kind of community we have here. I believe that every person in this congregation will tell you the same thing, if they're still here, and most are. It was an incredible time; it was a spiritual, rich, exciting, challenging, scary time. People who have been in this church for twenty-five years say they never before have ever felt that sense of the spirit of God moving across the face and being of a church in their lives. And this is a pretty lively bunch. I mean there's a lot of spirit in this church. They laugh well, they celebrate well, they play well, they argue well, they know how to get through conflict. So some of this prepared them for dealing with the ONA process, even though they did want to hide their face in the sand for a while. But the experience of people coming together and really talking was very powerful. What it has unleashed is a sense of what it means to be a community in church. So much of a sense of church has been affected by what we went through with the Open and Affirming process."

About Us, Not about Them

Diane said that going through the process provided "a feeling of 'Isn't-it-amazing?' So many life-altering moments for people and I'm sitting right here watching it happen, like people coming out for the very first time right there in church. A nineteen-year-old boy in our church came right out. He said, 'I know you all say that everyone is welcome, but the truth is I know for sure what the Baptist church down the street thinks about me, but I don't really know if I'm really welcome here.' And it became very clear to people that this whole thing wasn't about just Diane or some strange people. Instead, 'It's about our Robbie. Diane will come and go, but this is one of our own; we remember when he was born; we've seen him in church; we're proud of him; he's preached sermons in the baccalaureate Sunday; we love him, and now he's telling us he needs us to say this.'

"Another woman in the community who choked on the *l* word, she just couldn't say it, didn't think the ONA process was important and didn't know why people had to be out, etc.; and then I'm sitting there in one of these open discussion meetings and I hear her say, 'I'd like to say something as a lesbian woman.' It just kind of went on, and nobody else in that room had an inkling of how hard and how many years and what it took for her to say that and make that identification. Everybody knew she is lesbian, but for her finally to say it was a first.

"The biggest surprise was with this guy who never comes to church and had just dropped out. He stayed on as a member, once in a while sending money, was always considered as part of the church, but did not want to have anything to do with it or the clergy. He and his wife have a very good friend who attends this church. The wife and this woman were college roommates, and the three of them have traveled together. She's a lesbian, and they didn't know it. She never felt right telling them. When he found out about this ONA business, he came to one of these meetings about it and let everyone know what he thought of it. He couldn't believe that the church had a lesbian minister, he couldn't believe that we were talking about stuff like this, 'What the hell is happening to the church?' and he's going to vote 'no!' The friend heard about his remarks and weeks later on the morning of the ONA vote went to their house and came out to them. So then he comes to the meeting — and nobody had known this had happened except me and a couple of other people — and everyone thinks, 'Here's one "no" vote for sure.' (By the way, when you talk about this issue, it's a great way to get big attendance at your congregational meetings.) There he is, and we get to talking, and he finally gets up to have his say. He goes, 'A lot of you have heard me go on about how awful I think this Open and Affirming stuff is; and I've been struggling with it, and I asked what would my grandpa do — he was kind of my hero and a wise man — and I didn't get any answer. While I'm trying to figure this out, a friend of mine comes over to the house and tells us she thinks it's real important and she wants us to vote on this because she's a lesbian. I wondered why she never told us, and I still don't understand it; but I understand about friendship and about love, and I love this friend of ours; and it's important to her, so I'm going to vote "yes" on this damn thing.' Then he sits down, and there's not a dry eye in the house."

Becoming More Faithful

"That's how those things happen, how people change, and how people come out, one by one. There's nothing more powerful than that experience of having someone you love say, 'Guess what?' Here was this church that thought Open and Affirming was just about me and Elaine and a few other folks, and it suddenly realizes that instead it is *us*, these are our friends. So the vote was being taken, and someone started singing 'Amazing Grace,' and everybody started singing and stood up arm in arm. It didn't seem to matter anymore what the vote was, what the result was, because we were doing church. That was the feeling, that that's what this was about — about struggling, wrestling, and listening for what God wants us to do and what God wants us to be even when it's scary.

"You know so much of what we do — and frankly I think everyone would admit it — is to maintain the institution. We have fun together, and sometimes we do something good for someone else, and we try to help the poor in the community; but with the ONA process there was a feeling about being a part of a historical moment in history, being part of a movement in history that's bigger than us, but through which we can be used. That excitement, there's nothing like it. They're kind of proud of themselves. 'We did it.' We did something that counts because people's lives have been radically changed.[75] So this whole community has been impacted by that. And then the big thing also is that you don't have to be afraid of anything anymore. There's no fear about handling conflict."

Not Just for Gay People

Diane said that the ONA process did not change only the lives of gay people; nor were non-gay people changed only in their outlook on gay people. "For instance, this incident happened shortly after the 'yes' vote on Open and Affirming. A couple, where the man had sexually forced himself upon his wife numerous times early in their marriage, had finally gone into counseling with me and a professional counselor and had done some real healing; and they wanted to do a renewal of vows and healing service on their upcoming twentieth anniversary. They really saw that it was possible because of what the church had been through with Open and Affirming. Part of what they used in the healing service, a service really for forgiveness, was a section of our Open and Affirming statement, the part that says, 'Sexuality is a gift from God and it's good.' It was fascinating because during the process there had been many conversations about how our Open and Affirming statement would be used, and the first time it was used publicly was in this straight couple's healing service.

"And then there's another couple in the church that is dearly loved. They're in their young thirties with two beautiful, wonderful, bright, talented children; and everyone pictured them as the perfect family. They got divorced about a year ago, and they wanted to stay in the church. They wanted their kids to stay there, and they wanted to learn how to share this space. So we used and adapted the service out of the UCC Book of Worship about recognition of the end of a marriage; and I just tried to lead into it by saying that the church is important, that it's not enough just to have made their vows in a church, and it's not enough to have them end in a lawyer's office. They needed to be reminded that nothing can separate them from the love of God. They need us to embody that while they go through the guilt and changes that people go through when they get divorced. So they came up during worship and said that. And the congregation and people said these incredible words: 'We love you, and we don't always understand or didn't always know what to do or say, but we give you our support; and we may not understand your decision, but we love you and the children. We'll be with you and give you our blessing, and we'll do what we can to remind you that nothing can separate you from the love of God.' Powerful, powerful, powerful time. Everybody in that congregation that had ever been divorced or thought of it was weeping. The long and short of this being to say I think when you start talking about one thing that's hard like Open and Affirming, it opens the door to say we've got to try to be a truthful community about what life is and know where the hard places are. The issue isn't about being gay or married or divorced but how we just live together.

"Those have been some incredible moments, and they've been impacted and made more possible because of the Open and Affirming process. They're passing moments, but they're the moments everyone will remember because this is what church is about. This couple is still in this church, and right now this weekend we're doing this big, intergenerational musical, and there they are working side by side on this play. It's a healing community."

Conclusion

Lesbian/bisexual/gay people within organized religion not only have religious beliefs as strong as those of non-gay people but have taken upon themselves the responsibility for examining, assessing, and understanding what is most important to them and for leading lives that are faithful to their ultimate concerns. Studies show that gay people across various religious bodies — both mainstream and alternative — are ultimately concerned about experiencing connection, fellowship, and community with different kinds of people. Without generalizing too hastily to all gay people within organized religion, the similarity of findings and statements about how they understand, approach, and apply their religious traditions, the Bible, God, and other sources of faith would suggest that gay people across various religious bodies do have a lot in common — perhaps more in common with each other than with non-gay people within their respective religious bodies.

Rejection of gay people by some religious bodies has not made gay people less adept and resourceful at finding and making communities in which they feel valued, since their lovers, partners, and families were identified as their primary faith communities almost as often as local congregations within mainstream bodies were. They have also formed their own ecumenical groups, support groups, campus ministry programs, and gay organizations within almost all religious bodies.

Of all developments within organized religion, the "welcoming" congregation movement has received the strongest endorsement and appreciation of gay people and given them a solid basis for hope; and as such, it provides an apt transition to the final chapter, which considers how gay people evaluate their religious bodies and why they remain within them. Before moving on, however, it should be noted that "welcoming" congregations have not had the singular effect of making gay people feel more accepted but have provided non-gay people with the opportunity and means to examine, change, and take more seriously their own lives. Also, as mentioned in chapter 3, the "welcoming" congregation movement represents an exceedingly small number of local congregations within religious bodies (for example, less than 1 percent of congregations in the UMC; about 2 percent of congregations in the UCC). As the next chapter will show, the high regard in which lesbian/bisexual/gay people hold this movement does not necessarily apply to their religious bodies when considered more broadly.

Chapter Seven

Evaluations, Feelings, Reasons, and Challenges

In chapter 2 I explained that I wanted my study to shift away from organized religion's view of gay people to gay people's view of organized religion. Relying on numerous studies by gay and non-gay researchers, on my own survey, and on my screening of newsletters of various gay religious organizations, I have sought to examine and compare the experiences of gay people within many different religious bodies. Chapters 3, 4, and 5 presented those experiences under the rubrics of membership, participation, and employment in organized religion. Chapter 6 shifted from concrete experiences to expressions of belief, theology, and faith. Here in this final chapter, gay people's feelings about, evaluations of, and reasons for remaining in their respective religious bodies will be discussed. In closing, I shall recognize and offer a theory of gay experience within organized religion that is drawn and developed from the findings presented in this and earlier chapters.

Gay and Non-gay Views

When Thomas O'Brien conducted his survey of gay Catholics, he contacted people through local chapters of the gay Catholic organization, Dignity. For a control group of non-gay Catholics, he used the young adult prayer and Bible study group in his local parish. He found that both groups held similar attitudes about their own sexuality: 82 percent of gay respondents and 86 percent of non-gay respondents accepted it very positively; 18 percent of the former and 14 percent of the latter were neutral about it; and none of the non-gay group and less than 1 percent of the gay group wished that their sexuality were different. Both groups were also similar in reporting that the kinds of relationships that were most fulfilling were long-term and permanent (80 percent, non-gay; 90 percent, gay); and both described their relationships as "a sign of God's love," "good," "natural," "loving," "fulfilling," "growth-filled," "complementary," "happy," and "life-giving."[1]

But O'Brien also found that the two groups differed in their descriptions of the church's attitude toward their sexuality. The gay responses, as a rule, perceived that attitude as negative, while the control group's perceptions were mostly positive. Three percent of gay respondents compared to 71 percent of non-gay respondents said the church accepts their sexuality, while 84 percent of gay respondents compared to 10 percent of non-gay respondents said the church negates their sexuality.[2] Such negativity by gay people was also found in other studies.

For example, in a national survey of gay couples with various religious affiliations, Partners Task Force of Seattle found that of the various sources of support sought out by their respondents only the "mainstream church" was rated as more hostile than supportive. The gay church, on the other hand, was rated as strongly supportive.[3]

Scott Thumma's study of the gay evangelical parachurch in Atlanta, Paul Bauer's study of the Metropolitan Community Church (MCC) in Denver, and Henry Rabinowitz's study of the gay synagogue in New York have shown that these are the kinds of settings in which gay people do not have to separate their social lives and relationships from their religious lives. As Bauer observed, in mainstream religion even "the liberal churches, in making specific policy statements on homosexuality, identify the individual as first a homosexual and second a possible Christian." And Rabinowitz concluded that gay synagogues are "the only terrain" where the contradiction between Jewish identity and sexual identity is lessened.[4]

But many gay people, of course, remain within mainstream religious bodies with varying degrees of success and satisfaction. However, they have tended to view their treatment by these bodies differently than have non-gay members. For example, O'Brien found wide discrepancy between gay and non-gay responses to the "Letter to the Bishops of the Catholic Church on the Pastoral Care of Homosexual Persons," which was issued in 1986 by the Vatican.[5] Eighty percent of the gay respondents compared to 20 percent of the non-gay respondents said they had read the letter. A majority of both characterized the statement as negative, but the percentage of gay respondents to do so was much greater than non-gay respondents (50 percent, non-gay; 94 percent, gay). A much greater percentage of gay respondents said the letter would lead to a significantly decreased understanding of gay Catholics (33 percent, non-gay; 76 percent, gay). The majority of non-gay respondents (67 percent) said the letter would have no effect or would lead to a slightly increased or decreased understanding of gay Catholics.[6]

Lawrence Reh also found noticeable differences between gay and non-gay responses in his survey of members of the Presbyterian Church (U.S.A.) who wanted the denomination's anti-gay policy changed. Non-gay respondents thought that positive changes would occur sooner than did gay respondents. For example, 84 percent of non-gay respondents predicted that denominational prohibitions against the ordination of openly gay candidates would be reversed by the year 2000, whereas 61 percent of gay respondents thought so. In addition, 92 percent of non-gay respondents thought that even if denominational prohibitions were not reversed the first ordination of an openly gay candidate would occur within one of the districts by the year 2000, whereas 61 percent of gay respondents thought so. Reh concluded that the "more pessimistic" responses of gay people when compared to those of non-gay people "may reflect closer contact with the issue, and consequent disillusionment on the part of lesbian and gay people over what is possible or likely."[7]

But some non-gay people have experienced very close contact with gay issues and have spoken candidly and personally from their feelings and experience. Wayne Schow, for example, is a Mormon who lost his gay son to AIDS. Claiming neither theological nor psychological expertise, he wrote, "I only know that elements in my life that matter greatly to me — my son, my responsibility as a parent, my commitment to my church, my faith in the moral vision of Christianity — have been thrust into confrontation in a way that challenges my deeply held convictions about life and its meaning." "Haunted by a vision of what might have been" for his son, he said he "think[s] of all those who need consolation, love, a chance to overcome alienation, a chance to talk openly without being condemned." Although he "sincerely hope[s] the future will not continue to find Latter-day Saints and their church deficient in openness and charity towards this significant minority," his "critical assessment" was that "the church not only fails to comfort many of its own members who need a radically different kind of assistance, it also fails to promote tolerant understanding in the greater society."[8]

Feelings

When I asked respondents in my survey of gay people in the United Methodist Church (UMC) and in the United Church of Christ (UCC) to name the feelings that best describe their affiliation with their denominations (see table 16), "hopeful" was the feeling most often reported, but more so by UCC than UMC respondents (54 percent, UMC; 74 percent, UCC).[9]

Other feelings reported by both sets of respondents were "committed" (39 percent, UMC; 48 percent, UCC), "challenged" (31 percent, UMC; 46 percent, UCC), and "uncertain" (36 percent, UMC; 29 percent, UCC).

TABLE 16
Ten Feelings Most Often Reported by UMC and UCC Respondents, in Rank Order

UMC (N=196)		UCC (N=278)	
hopeful	51%	hopeful	74%
angry	50%	encouraged	50%
discouraged	46%	committed	48%
marginalized	44%	welcomed	47%
sad	41%	challenged	46%
committed	39%	loved	41%
uncertain	36%	valued	41%
challenged	31%	affirmed	39%
ignored	30%	involved	38%
unwelcome	26%	uncertain	29%

Percentages add to more than 100 because some respondents reported more than one feeling.

Feelings unique to UCC respondents were "encouraged" (50 percent), "welcomed" (47 percent), "loved" (41 percent), "valued" (41 percent), "affirmed" (39 percent), and "involved" (38 percent).

Feelings unique to UMC respondents were "angry" (50 percent), "discouraged" (46 percent), "marginalized" (44 percent), "sad" (41 percent), "ignored" (30 percent), and "unwelcome" (26 percent).

The responses from UCC respondents were mostly positive, and those from UMC respondents were mostly negative. Within each group of respondents a number of variations were noticeable.

Demographic Variables

Gender

Among UMC respondents, women reported more often than men that they felt hopeful (66 percent, women; 49 percent, men), committed (50 percent, women; 34 percent, men), and challenged (39 percent, women; 27 percent, men).

Among UCC respondents, women reported more often than men that they felt committed (52 percent, women; 40 percent, men) and involved (41 percent, women; 31 percent, men), but less often than men that they felt welcomed (40 percent, women; 50 percent, men).

Sexual Identity

Among UMC respondents, bisexuals more often than lesbian/gay people reported that they felt marginalized (58 percent, bisexual; 43 percent, lesbian/gay), angry (58 percent, bisexual; 49 percent, lesbian/gay), and challenged (42 percent, bisexual; 30 percent, lesbian/gay).

Among UCC respondents, bisexuals more often than lesbian/gay people reported that they felt committed (61 percent, bisexual; 43 percent, lesbian/gay) and challenged (52 percent, bisexual; 42 percent, lesbian/gay).

Age

In the UMC, respondents in their twenties reported less often than those in other age groups that they felt sad (30 percent, twenties; 40 percent, thirties; 49 percent, forties; 38 percent, fifty and above) and marginalized (33 percent, twenties; 46 percent, thirties; 48 percent, forties; 41 percent, fifty and above).

In the UCC, respondents in their twenties reported less often than those in other age groups that they felt valued (29 percent, twenties; 34 percent, thirties; 51 percent, forties; 43 percent, fifty and above); and respondents fifty and older reported more often than those in other age groups that they felt loved (31 percent, twenties; 37 percent, thirties; 36 percent, forties; 49 percent, fifty and above).

Geographical Regions

The UMC respondents from the South reported more often than those from other regions that they felt unwelcomed (11 percent, New England; 10 percent, Middle Atlantic; 13 percent, Upper Midwest; 33 percent, Lower Midwest; 56 percent, South; 15 percent, Southwest/West; 11 percent, West Coast).

The UCC respondents from the West Coast reported more often than respondents from other regions that they felt welcomed (45 percent, New England; 44 percent, Middle Atlantic; 46 percent, Upper Midwest; 38 percent, Lower Midwest; 39 percent, South/Southwest/West; 48 percent, West Coast).

Welcoming Congregations and Outness

The UMC respondents who were members of "welcoming" churches or who were "fully out" to their local congregations reported more often than those who were not that they felt angry (60/46 percent, welcoming/nonwelcoming; 54/46 percent, out/nonout), marginalized

(51/39 percent, welcoming/nonwelcoming; 50/39 percent, out/nonout), and sad (62/35 percent, welcoming/nonwelcoming; 49/35 percent, out/nonout), but also more often committed (49/39 percent, welcoming/nonwelcoming; 43/37 percent, out/nonout).

The UCC respondents who were members of "welcoming" churches or who were "fully out" to their local congregations reported more often than those who were not that they felt welcomed (68/39 percent, welcoming/nonwelcoming; 58/36 percent, out/nonout), affirmed (52/34 percent, welcoming/nonwelcoming; 52/24 percent, out/nonout), and valued (52/36 percent, welcoming/nonwelcoming; 47/36 percent, out/nonout).

Although UCC respondents who were out to their local congregations or members of "welcoming" churches reported positive feelings more often than those who were not, the same was not found for those who were out or members of "welcoming" churches among UMC respondents. Outness and membership in "welcoming" churches for UMC respondents would seem to be associated with feelings of anger, sadness, and marginalization, but also with feeling committed to the denomination.

A Preponderance of Negative Feelings

The preponderance of negative feelings found among UMC respondents in general was also reported among gay people in other religious bodies.

From his study of gay Mormons, Christopher Alexander reported that "some of the men who wrote me harbor considerable anger and blame the church." One explained, "The biggest agony I went through was my attempt to understand the suffering, my own and that of my friends. During a one week period I was able to count thirty friends who had seriously contemplated suicide because of their feelings about being gay. The Mormon church was the biggest factor, so I thought, in the origins of these suicidal feelings and fantasies."[10]

Scott Thumma reported that of the gay men from conservative Christian denominations attracted to Good News, "many expressed anxiety, despair, and the feeling that they had come to 'the end of the rope.' Religious acceptance by God, a community, and a heritage were perceived as a potential way to relieve the sense of alienation and rejection."[11]

Even in reputedly pro-gay denominations such as the Unitarian Universalist Association (UUA), gay people express negative feelings. One man with AIDS expressed his confusion at feeling "largely deserted in the midst of a community that has done more than most to aid in a horrible crisis." He went on to say, "I wish I weren't so angry and sometimes so very depressed. I know that this has confused, angered and hurt some of my best Unitarian Universalist friends, gay and non-gay. I haven't yet left the church, though a dozen times I've come close. What do I want? How much do I have the right to ask? Why can't I accept that Unitarian Universalists are human and striving for improvement like other good people? Probably more than most other people. Do I dare compare the issues of AIDS and homophobia to those of slavery, the holocaust, abortion, the civil rights movement or Vietnam? Do I have the right to demand the same concern and action that Unitarian Universalists produced in past crises?"[12]

Conflicting Feelings

Anger and despair would seem to characterize the feelings that many gay people have about the religious bodies in which they were raised and to which they belong. As Kirsten Peachey wrote, "Assess the status of gay and lesbian people in the church.... Why? What is there to assess? Ask almost any gay or lesbian person and you'll get a ready assessment— one invariably full of pain, anger, and caution." But Kirsten was quick to add that "you'll also hear an almost foolish hopefulness, a yearning for a time when there will be justice for and inclusion of those of us who are different,...for the community which we know as home but which hasn't had the courage to love us back." Even after being rejected by a Mennonite seminary and feeling "driven even further outside the Mennonite church circle," she said that "for some unknown reason, I still hold on to a foolish optimism, a yearning that grows out of a nagging love of the Mennonite community. I trust, ultimately, that the people of the church will put aside their fear and begin to listen."[13]

When Deborah Carney and Susan Davies asked respondents in their survey "how they felt about being a lesbian or bisexual woman in the church," they found "a combination of pain, strength, and affirmation. Responses ranged from 'like a fence sitter' to 'I feel good about myself; I'm mad as hell at the church.'" Although "all found strength, healing, and joy in acknowledging their identity,...none were happy about being closeted or about its effects on their relationship, but one spoke for many when she said, 'Now I feel strong, my skills are strengthened. I have more compassion and confidence, joy, humor. I can speak my mind and take risks.'"[14]

Susan Kramer, a Presbyterian, also wrote about her opposing or conflicted feelings: "Sometimes I become discouraged as a lesbian within the church. Sometimes I feel crazy remaining in the church and even crazier that I returned. What's the sense of it? What's the worth of it? Particularly that seems true when I am told both covertly and overtly, 'Susan, we want your gifts, but Susan, we don't want who you are.'" She recognized that the balance for these negative feelings was not always found within her own denomination: "Other times I feel hopeful about being in the church. These times occur often serendipitously and in the most unlikely places. For instance, when reading the newspaper and expecting only discouraging, depressing news. There amazingly, I read that the Reformed Jews have voted to allow lesbians and gay men into the rabbinate. I pause. I breathe deeply. I am grateful that another major religious group in North America is including lesbians and gay men in full membership."[15]

A Preponderance of Hope

Studies other than my own have also found that "hope" is a feeling widely expressed by gay people within religious bodies. In her research on gay religious leaders, for example, Clare Fischer found that "optimism" and a "belief in the efficacy of religious leadership" were characteristic of her subjects and were illustrated by the fact that "in spite of institutional disappointment and personal experiences with church bigotry, none...chose to work outside of the religious traditions to which they felt a deep belonging."[16] James Wolf also found that "in trying to resolve the frustration they feel as gay men and Catholic priests," the majority of his respondents "have decided to follow their conscience and hope for change."[17]

Leaders of the various gay organizations within religious bodies have also encouraged fellow gay members to remain hopeful. For example, when Keith Kron was elected chairman of the Unitarian Universalist organization in 1993, he said, "I feel, more than anything else, an incredible sense of hope." He went on to claim that "hope tells me we believe that our organization makes a difference, that we are a vital, vibrant, incredible group of people, that we have become stronger individuals because we are part of something greater. Hope tells me we have a future and that we can positively change the larger whole."[18] Chris Glaser of Presbyterians for Lesbian and Gay Concerns, however, qualified his own advice about hope in view of the more anti-gay record of his denomination: "I don't believe it's helpful to get our hopes up about the results" of the current discussion about homosexuality, "but I do believe that the hope that has kept us going during these past two decades will sustain us until God's dream comes true. That is the hope to which we are called."[19]

Bases for Hope

Leaders have also cited the bases for hope, and these have varied across religious bodies. Keith Kron proudly and confidently stated that "by our work and presence in our larger communities, we make a difference" and then cited the organization's cosponsorship of the 1983 Gay Rights

March on Washington, its leadership of the denomination in a protest of sodomy laws, its training of leaders to serve in congregations, and its educational programs throughout the denomination.[20]

In response to Neil Miller's question about remaining active in a denomination with anti-gay national policies, Nick Wilkerson, an elder of Central Presbyterian Church in Louisville, said that he "was very much an optimist." As Miller reported, for Nick "the fact that people in his own church were so supportive tended to negate anything the national church said or did," and "even if church policy didn't change, Nick thought that as an openly gay church official he was making an important contribution to gay people in Louisville. 'When you are gay and twelve years old in a small town in western Kentucky like where I grew up,' he observed, 'you don't know anyone else who is gay. The only [gay] people you hear about or read about tend to be unsavory. . . . Being a positive role model for gays is important.' "[21]

In one of my interviews with a UMC clergyman, I found that hope often rests on small indicators of progress. After the 1992 General Conference affirmed its anti-gay position, I asked Tim Tennant-Jayne how he was feeling about that action. He said, "Real bleak. The phrase that keeps running through my head lately is a recognition that 'at heart the United Methodist Church is an institution' and is very concerned with institutional things like self-preservation. However, I think there is still a very strong spirit within it and an opening for God to work." I asked why he thought so, and he said, "The percentages are getting better. We didn't change the *Discipline* this time; however, from all I can understand it seems to be that instead of three-quarters of the people being against change, it's like 70 percent or something. Or maybe from 80 percent opposed, it's down to 75 percent opposed. So that seems to be getting better."[22]

Another UMC clergyman said that what happened at the 1992 General Conference was "probably as good a result as could be anticipated. I didn't go into it with real high expectations." He thought it was significant, however, that "the conservatives were not able to deep-six the Study Report [on Homosexuality]" that had been commissioned by the denomination and presented to conference delegates. Although its pro-gay proposals were defeated, except for a statement in support of civil rights, that the report itself was "going to be offered to the whole church as a study document" was for him "a positive step forward." He said, "I see hope in the whole denomination being asked to study this issue over the next four years. From this study report there is a continual education process going on."

A UMC province-level staff person who attended the 1992 General Conference said being there "was mostly very painful. Part of that was because I spent most of my time with the Affirmation people. And I saw the pain and the anguish that was there. So mostly it was hard; but again it's like I have an amazing amount of support. Even in that place there were people from my own area and from the national church who know who I am, know I'm a lesbian, who came to me and gave me support; so I just have a real strong support system. I was really glad to be there, and it was really hard to be there."

Changing Feelings

Feelings, of course, change and are affected by developments in one's personal life and in the religious body with which one is affiliated. For example, from their counseling work with adolescent and young adult Mormons, Ron Schow and Marybeth Raynes summarized the personal history of one man who grew up in the Mormon church and became homosexually active when he was fifteen. He had confided in his bishop who advised fasting, prayer, and abstinence. By the time he turned nineteen, his several years of abstinence qualified him to go on a mission,[23] even though he told his bishop that his homosexuality still troubled him. His sexual desires persisted, and his mission president advised him to marry quickly after his mission ended. He married within six months of returning home, but he was able to have sex with his wife only by thinking of men. Schow and Raynes report: "Discouraged, depressed, and devastated by guilt, he divorced and turned to substance abuse. Soon he was an alcoholic. Only after years of therapy, participation in Alcoholics Anonymous, and development of a stable committed relationship with another gay Mormon has he been able to put his life together. He says that through prayer he found that the Lord loves him. He no longer hates himself or considers his life sinful."[24]

Gay people's feelings about their religious affiliations change not only in the context of personal struggles and professional counseling but in the more public context of participating in denominational politics. For example, in his regular column in the newsletter of the American Baptist gay organization, Rick Mixon chronicled the responses of gay members to their denomination's increasing anti-gay hostility.[25]

When the denomination first discussed a resolution to "affirm that the practice of homosexuality is incompatible with Christian teaching," Rick commented "on the questions raised by some of our friends and supporters to the gentle response of lesbians and gay men present at the gay bashing that occurred." Agreeing that "some ugly and abusive things were uttered from the podium," he reminded readers that "we have heard it all before," and "after so much abuse, one finds ways to turn off the shouting and the hatred as a simple means of survival." He said that hearing such remarks "infuriates and saddens me," but he "felt embarrassment and pity for my sisters and brothers who spew such ignorance and bitterness." He preferred instead to "sit quietly and maintain my dignity because my mind and heart are tuned in elsewhere," especially into "the warmth of the loving and supportive things that were being said from that same podium where we were being bashed."

A vote later that year to defeat the resolution was cause for "some rejoicing," but he felt that the closeness of the vote "says there is much work to be done to help American Baptists understand, accept and value their lesbian, gay and bisexual members."

Subsequent reconsideration and passage of the same resolution were, he wrote, "disheartening" and "evoke[d] sadness and anger in many of us." But Rick also noted that "the passage of the resolution has renewed the energy of many of us (fueled by our anger and our grief) to re-double our efforts," for "ironically, it is the animosity of our adversaries that has helped me to see how important it is to continue to bear faithful witness here and now."

These new feelings of commitment were encouraged by "two hopeful signs" at a later national meeting of the denomination: the passage of a resolution calling for dialogue on human sexuality and the formation of a commission on human sexuality. Rick now encouraged gay members to build on these new developments and to "demand the right to be heard and respected as full members of the American Baptist family."[26] Within the three-year period of the denomination's discussion and resolutions, some of its gay members would appear to have become less passive and more assertive; and from feelings of disappointment, sadness, anger, and grief emerged feelings of commitment, renewal, and hope.

Seeing how and why gay people feel as they do about the religious bodies with which they are affiliated leads to considering how they evaluate those bodies.

Evaluations

In addition to expressing their personal feelings about organized religion, gay people have also analyzed and provided critiques of the religious bodies to which they belong. Their evaluations of these bodies will be discussed next.

Regressing and Progressing on Gay Issues

In 1993, the National Gay Pentecostal Alliance (NGPA) criticized fellow non-gay Pentecostal and Apostolic Christians for supporting the Christian Right. They accused them of forsaking their traditional biblical fundamentalism: "You won't find any scriptural mention of the Apostles running for political office or attempting to influence legislation in any way. They never asked the government to enforce Christian moral standards. The Apostles never picketed an adult bookstore, bombed an abortion clinic, or lobbied for laws to imprison or execute people whose moral standards were different. Yet the church today does those things." Citing passages from the Book of Revelation, they accused the mainstream Pentecostal and Apostolic churches of following "the church of Laodicea (Rev. 3:13–22), which means 'people of judgment,'" instead of "the church of Philadelphia (Rev. 3:7–13), which means 'brotherly love.'"[27]

Reports from gay people who attended the local churches of such denominations as the United Pentecostal Church International (UPC) provided NGPA leaders with what they have said is "strong evidence" that "most of the Apostolic church has become bound by a spirit of judgment." Noting that "something rather odd has begun taking place in every UPC where one of our people attends," they reported that "all of a sudden, pastors who never before spoke the word homosexuality from the pulpit, are unable to preach anything else. Every sermon has become an anti-Gay diatribe." They observed, however, that this regressive surge on gay issues has been softened by the occasional "report we have received of a UPC minister who has invited openly Gay people to be part of the congregation, refusing to condemn or judge them."[28] The NGPA leaders had also observed that countering the "homophobic tirades" of many televangelists such as Jerry Falwell, other "pastors around the country" and one televangelist in the South "have suddenly said that God told them that the next big revival will include Gays."[29]

Small progress has also been reported by gay people in other religious bodies. Clergyman B. J. Stiles told me that within the UMC he did not "see much evidence of institutional change, with the exception of the Reconciling Congregation movement," but that he was "inundated with personal encounters of individual change." For him, the greatest progress was in "the sheer visibility of the men and women who, whether they are gay or not, are gay supportive. And the visibility of that handful of us provides encouragement and some degree of modeling for other people who are fearful or closeted, who don't themselves know how to cope with the fact that either they are gay or that a member of their family is gay."

A province-level UMC staff person described what she saw as regressive signs within the denomination. "I had an experience with a man at General Conference who came to me and said that he had come a long way on lesbian/gay issues, but that he was real angry about the demonstration that was going on by Affirmation.[30] 'So, I'm not sure I'm going to vote for you. I've come a long way, but I think this is inappropriate.'

He said that I needed to acknowledge that the church had come a long way; and I responded, 'No, we, as a church, need to acknowledge our addiction to power and prestige. We need to acknowledge that people have been dropped and lost, that we've been preoccupied with thinking that we're right, and that we haven't accepted the harm that we've really done.' "

I interviewed a former UCC staff person who saw the progress in the UCC as both "significant and glacial." She said, "I think it's very significant on a national level. There's that inevitable split that happens on all progressive issues — the national staff is ready and eager, the local churches are slower and less enthusiastic. I think that it is more glacial on gay issues than, for example, peace issues, where I was working, because this is a much tougher issue for the churches. An awful lot of stuff from the Bible talks to us about peace. It is very clear. John the Baptist never said you shouldn't be at peace. There's none of the biblical disapproval attached to peace-making that there is to homosexuality. As a result the mountains that we have to climb on the issue of homosexuality are much higher and they are more difficult to surmount in changing people's minds."

She said that "hopeful things" about the UCC were "that it's given Bill Johnson a national position and that some of the local churches have been willing to ordain openly gay and lesbian people." In 1972, Bill Johnson had been the first openly gay man to be ordained in the UCC or in any other mainstream religious body; and in 1990, he was appointed to direct the AIDS Ministry Program of the United Church Board for Homeland Ministries. "I think it is a real credit to the denomination that Bill finally has a position on the national staff of some substance. It's taken years and he has really plowed the earth on the subject single handedly on a national level."

She also thought that "the UCC deserves some credit for pioneering on women's issues" and said "there is no question in my mind" that gay and feminist issues are connected. "I do not think there would have been a gay rights resolution in General Synod [national meeting] without feminism having raised the basic issues about gender identity and stereotypical male/female roles. So, feminism for me is the bedrock of the UCC's and my own understanding and involvement in lesbian/gay issues."

In addition to these different anecdotal accounts by UMC and UCC gay people about progressive and regressive change on gay issues within their denominations, significant statistical differences were found between my UMC and UCC respondents in their evaluations of their denominations (see table 17). Seventy percent of UCC respondents, compared to 20 percent of UMC respondents, reported that they consider their denomination to be progressing on gay issues; and 3 percent of

TABLE 17

Percentages of UMC and UCC Respondents Who Rated Their Denominations as Progressing, Maintaining the Status Quo, or Regressing in Gay Issues

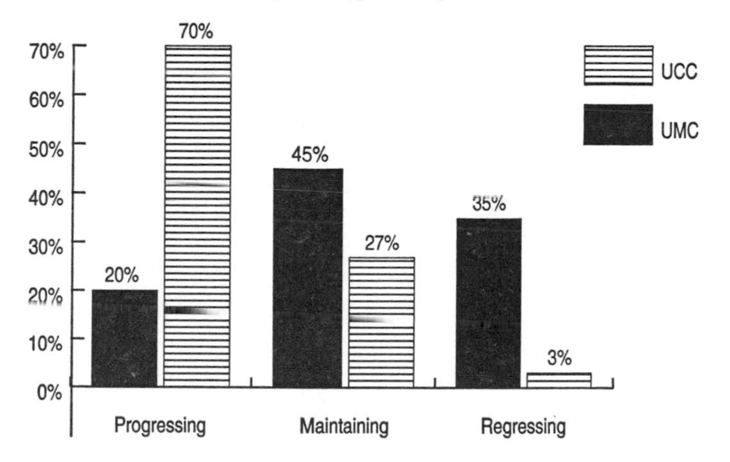

UCC, compared to 35 percent of UMC, reported that they consider their denomination to be regressing on these issues.

In a Unitarian Universalist Association (UUA) study, gay evaluations of the denomination were similar to those of UCC respondents in my survey. Seventy percent evaluated the UUA's outreach to gay people as positive, and about 30 percent "said they experience limited acceptance within the UUA" (not in table).[31]

These differences between UMC, UCC, and UUA respondents can be examined in more detail by considering their evaluations of the various levels within each denomination.

Denominational Levels

As discussed in chapter 2, UMC and UCC polities differ. The UMC is top-down, and its national level mandates programs and policy for lower levels. The UCC is bottom-up, and its national level makes recommendations to the lower levels. The UUA's polity and gay stance are similar to those of the UCC and will be used to make some comparisons.

I asked my UMC and UCC respondents to rate each level of their denominations (local, district, province, national meeting, national)[32] on gay issues (see table 18). On a scale of excellent, good, fair, or poor, a plurality[33] of UCC respondents consistently gave each level at least a "good" rating (27 percent, local/excellent; 33 percent, district/good; 40 percent, province/good; 58 percent, meeting/good; 53 percent, national/

TABLE 18
Percentages of Most-Often-Reported Rating (Excellent, Good, Fair, or Poor) of Each Denominational Level by UMC and UCC Respondents

Denominational level	UMC rating (N=172)	UCC rating (N=284)
local	32% poor	27% poor/27% excellent
district	55% poor	33% good/33% fair
province	54% poor	40% good
national meeting	76% poor	58% good
national	81% poor	53% good

good), and a plurality of UMC respondents consistently gave each level a rating of "poor" (32 percent, local; 55 percent, district; 54 percent, province; 76 percent, national meeting; 81 percent, national).

Local Levels, National Meetings, and National Levels

Data not shown in table 18 provide for more comparisons of the evaluations of denominational levels.

For example, of demographic variables, only responses according to geographical regions showed noticeable differences in evaluations, especially of the local level. For instance, a plurality of UMC and UCC respondents from the Upper Midwest (36 percent, UMC; 38 percent, UCC) and from the West Coast (35 percent, UMC; 39 percent, UCC) evaluated their local levels as "excellent," compared to "poor" and "fair" ratings by at least a plurality of respondents from other regions (for UMC — 71 percent poor, New England; 36 percent fair, Middle Atlantic; 41 percent poor, Lower Midwest; 36 percent poor, West/Southwest; 35 percent poor, South; and for UCC — 37 percent poor, New England; 40 percent fair, Middle Atlantic; 59 percent poor, Lower Midwest; 31 percent fair, South/Southwest/West).

Concerning local evaluations, I also found that 41 percent of UMC and 48 percent of UCC respondents gave their local congregations either an "excellent" or a "good" evaluation (21 percent excellent and 20 percent good, UMC; 27 percent excellent and 21 percent good, UCC). These findings would suggest that the local congregations of UCC respondents more often than those of UMC respondents have dealt satisfactorily with gay issues, but other findings show that UCC respondents rated their local congregations less favorably than their national levels (good/excellent: 48 percent, local; 69 percent, national meeting; 61 percent, national) and that UMC respondents rated their local levels more favorably than their national levels (good/excellent: 41 percent, local; 4 percent, national meeting; 2 percent, national).

This UCC pattern of less favorable local evaluations and more favorable national evaluations was mirrored by respondents in the UUA study. Forty-one percent of the latter said that the UUA's national goals and programs for people were good, but not shared by individual congregations.[34] UMC evaluations, however, reversed the pattern.

Among UMC respondents, favorable evaluations decreased significantly with greater proximity to the levels that make and adjudicate the denomination's anti-gay policy. Among UCC and UUA respondents, favorable evaluations increased significantly with greater proximity to the level responsible for making the denomination's pro-gay policy. Even though the greatest percentage of UMC respondents selected "poor" as a rating for their local congregations (21 percent, excellent; 20 percent, good; 27 percent, fair; 32 percent, poor), "poor" evaluations were given less often to local than to upper levels (as presented above in table 18). UMC respondents did not rate their local congregations as favorably as UCC respondents, but they would appear to rely on them more urgently as the best refuge from anti-gay national law and enforcement.

A UMC clergyman explained to me why for him the local level was more important than the national quadrennial meeting or the national level: "There are still a lot of good folks who are part of the denomination who see the church's stand on gay/lesbian folks as unjust and are committed to investing energy and challenging that unjust stand. When I see kids, teenagers at my local church, who have been in a Reconciling Congregation for five or six years, who are now heading off to college or are in college, and they meet somebody gay or lesbian, it's just like no big deal to them except that they understand that the prejudices and biases of the larger society are really just not acceptable and it grates at them. That's an amazing and wonderful thing. It says things can change. This whole generation of kids are growing up knowing something different. They're growing up in a church where they know that these two guys sitting next to Mom and Dad are a couple who have been together for ten years and they're just like any other adult couples in the church. They're really cool about it. So there's a lot of hope in that."

John Lardin, one of the UCC people I interviewed, spoke of his appreciation for the openness within each of the various denominational levels: "The thing that gives me the most hope is the openness for dialogue and discussion that I have experienced locally, at the association [district] level, at the conference [province] level, and at the national level. As long as people are willing at least to listen, not necessarily to hear, but who will give time to listen and to try and understand and look at where lesbian, gay, and bi folks are coming from, I think there is hope there, and that keeps it going for me. We're not getting shot out of the saddle by people saying we don't have time for you; and I haven't experienced that anywhere at any level of the UCC." John, a former Roman Catholic, said, "The UCC helped me to understand better and see how we can come from very many different places and all be connected. I think the UCC lets us examine what we believe and why, and that happens both within local church settings and other areas where we can really see how we are connected to one another and how we interwork, and that makes the UCC something very special that I don't think a lot of other denominations are necessarily keyed into as well."

John thought that the UCC polity, in which no one level has power over the other, was partially responsible for this openness to dialogue, but he thought it had "more to do with the whole discussion aspect, that the church is there and they will listen to a whole bunch of folk and no one has got the only answer. It's the feeling that the larger denomination tries to listen and hear what everyone's concerns are and not shut people out because people don't agree." John extended his appreciation of openness and dialogue to those groups within the UCC with whom he usually disagreed, such as the Biblical Witness Fellowship. "They can be a real pain, and they aren't necessarily trying to go to the same place we are, but they offer us a chance to do some real learning and constantly are making people reexamine who they are. They force us to keep struggling at times; and it's not just Biblical Witness that does that: a lot of groups force us to keep struggling. Certainly some groups are hurt more than others and are listened to more than others, but at least we all can have our input."

For Margarita Suárez, on the other hand, the UCC's structured openness to dialogue and the nonlegislative role of national meetings were frustrating at times. When I asked what bothered her most about the denomination, she said, "The talk, talk, talk, talk, and talk. Like I'm tired of talking. There's a part of me that wants democratic process, but not at the expense of never doing what needs to be done. Sometimes I wish we would just do it, instead of asking fifteen thousand people what they think because we feel like we have to get everyone in the process in order for the process to be valid. Let's just forget that sometime and just say, 'This is right, this is just, this is what we need to do,' and do it. Sometimes I get frustrated by all this democracy, diversity, everybody-is-in-the-family-of-God garbage. I understand all the arguments for it, but I still don't buy why we have to do that. So there is a part of me that says, 'If you don't like it, good-bye.' We take stands and make resolutions, but it's very frustrating for me that we don't do enough by them. I believe in the process, and yet it's uncomfortable because we can never tell anybody anything; we can only suggest. Sometimes I want to tell them, sometimes I want to say, 'Yes, this is the gospel mandate, the road to justice, period. I'm sorry if you think otherwise. You are wrong.' "

Margarita was more inclined to base her positive evaluation of the denomination on particular people she knew throughout the various levels of the UCC rather than on the various levels themselves and the UCC form of governance. "I guess I have found the perfect group of people who really care about the same kinds of things that I care about. Some of them are in the gay/lesbian/bisexual community, some of them are the progressives, like Valerie Russell;[35] some are just individuals around about, the various individual people whom I've found in the struggle, whom I might see once every two years, but when I see them I get a little burst of energy, I get hope." Margarita's comments provide the opportunity to ask more specifically about the reasons that gay people have for staying or remaining within organized religion.

Reasons for Staying

Four Themes: Suffering, Risking, Fighting, Leaving

From Ralph McFadden's interviews with gay members of the Church of the Brethren, these four themes emerged:

1. I am sometimes sad and lonely because of the church's attitudes, but I see no other option than being secretive and silent about my life;
2. I am going to keep involved in the life of the church and keep trying because I have gifts and skills, and I am somewhat optimistic about the church;
3. I am angry about the church's attitude, and I am going to stay in and really fight it out; and
4. I am angry about the church's attitude, and I am going to leave the church.[36]

These same themes were apparent among gay people in other religious bodies.

Suffering

A "closeted" UMC clergyperson, for example, wrote, "I believe that those of us who choose to stay in the Church (instead of leaving it for 'perfect freedom') have chosen 'the way of suffering' and in that act have become more keenly united not only to Christ but also to those for whom Christ died. It is what enables us to comprehend the

Gospel in the deepest places of our hearts, blesses us in the fulfillment of our ministries, and sends us forth into the world with a daring and tender love."[37]

Risking

On the other hand, David Ward, a Presbyterian, advocated staying under different conditions and found a different message from Jesus for doing so: "Take some risks. The result may be far more significant and fruitful than playing it safe. Jesus took the ultimate risk on the cross, he risked that we'd forget about him, that we would turn our backs on God. No commitment is made without risk." On the music staff of a large, wealthy suburban church, David said, "I never hesitated to share my gift of life with this church, to risk being open." He recounted, "I freely shared my grief over loss of friends to AIDS and reached out to this church for financial and moral support in this crisis. They always responded.... These people now give money to AIDS-related organizations, the ministers pray for people with AIDS and the Senior Pastor even mentions gay-related issues from the pulpit compassionately and with insight into the direction that the church needs to move." He admitted that this local church was "no Nirvana" and "certainly is not a candidate for More Light status" (the Presbyterian name for a "welcoming congregation"), but he claimed that "if we are going to have any further significant impact on the life of the church we must take the risk to be open, sharing our spirituality, our sexuality and our integrity as gay and lesbian Christians."[38]

Fighting

Beverly Brubaker of the Church of the Brethren added that staying within the church meant fighting for equality: "The Church will be as complacent about an issue as its involved members allow it to be. I think that it is time that we more aggressively (assertively, if you prefer!) raise the issue of equal rights for gays, lesbians, and bisexuals."[39] Rabbi Sharon Kleinbaum expressed similar sentiments in 1993 when Congregation Beth Simchat Torah (CBST) was banned from marching in the annual Salute to Israel Parade in New York because of Orthodox fundamentalist pressure. The gay synagogue held its own celebration of Israel Independence Day that same afternoon; and thirty Reconstructionist, Reform, and Conservative rabbis, as well as the governor of the state, the mayor of the city, and many supporters from the greater New York Jewish community attended. Sharon told the gathering, "Today is a victory for CBST because we are making clear that though we have been excluded from the parade, we have not been silenced. Today we stand here to say to Israel that despite the hatred shown towards us, despite the bigotry, we will fight for our right to stand up proudly, openly, and say that Israel should be safe and peace should prosper in her gates."[40]

Leaving

But Michael Dickens, after finding in his study that gay people in the black church were often "forced to remain closeted for the most part and also must endure repeated condemnation from the pulpit," concluded that this situation was "unhealthy," "intolerable," and "too compromising." He went on to explain that "many of us opt to leave the church rather than stay and try to reconcile our sexuality with our faith. Many choose this path, even though they are giving up the church which has played a very significant role in their affirmation as African-American people."[41]

Leaving versus Staying

For some gay people, leaving the religious body with which they have been affiliated does not mean leaving organized religion. Some have left mainstream bodies to become active in alternative gay religious organizations and churches. Leaders of the National Gay Pentecostal Alliance (NGPA) have advised gay people who attend mainstream Pentecostal and Apostolic churches to "Be careful!" and, if they are the only one in their church, to "Get out!" They have warned that these churches "will not hesitate to use physical means to harm you" and that "in some areas this has already begun and our people have been the targets." The NGPA has also offered "a safe place" in their own churches: "Please understand that by asking people to leave, we are not advocating surrender. This is simply a tactical retreat. We cannot stand on the front lines of battle with no weapons or protection. The tactical retreat will give us an opportunity to properly train you to wage spiritual war." The NGPA leadership has also been clear in stating that the war is against the "spirit of judgment behind the people" in the oppressive churches not against the people themselves.[42]

Other gay people have left one religious body but remain active within organized religion by joining another more welcoming mainstream body. For example, after being refused admission to the Mennonite seminary, Kirsten Peachey "found other contexts in which to pursue my faith, educational goals, and interests in ministry — places in which there is more room for me to be a whole person." She said, "The Mennonite church has lost me," and she entered instead the

UCC-affiliated Chicago Theological Seminary and pursued ordination in the UCC.[43]

Bet Hannon, a Presbyterian, also transferred her membership to the UCC. Having begun the ordination process for the second time in the Presbyterian Church (U.S.A.) (PCUSA) and seeing that it would fail again, she decided to end the process and to leave the denomination. She said that the reasons for leaving were the same as those for leaving a harmful relationship: "It has become clear to me once again just how much my relationship to the PCUSA was an abusive relationship. I never really understood why abused women (and men) stayed with their partners who abused them, but I think now I have some inkling. When I worked with abused women who were not ready to leave their partners, I always asked them, 'Will you know when you've reached your limit? when you've had enough?' I have reached my limit with the PCUSA, and I know that I don't need to be beaten up one more time to feel justified in leaving."[44]

However, other gay people have chosen to remain in spite of the hostility, opposition, and rejection. When Diane Vezmar-Bailey decided to come out as a bisexual Presbyterian clergy and thereby relinquish her ordained status, she did so "with the hope that the church will change its policy" and said that "in the meantime" she would join a More Light congregation and "continue to work toward the day when *all* persons who believe in Jesus Christ can fully participate in the life of the Presbyterian Church (U.S.A.)."[45]

Chris Glaser, a regular contributor to the Presbyterian gay newsletter, argued that for gay people "leaving is not an option, because we *are* the church. Abandoning the institutional church is abandoning lesbian, gay, and bisexual members that are being born in the moments it takes to write or to read this column." Chris also observed that "as ossified and calcified as the church may be as an institution, it is still where we most easily may meet others attempting to embody Christ.... We in PLGC [Presbyterians for Lesbian and Gay Concerns] would never have met one another were it not for the Presbyterian Church."[46]

In fact, many gay people do remain within mainstream religious bodies. James Wolf's survey of Catholic priests, for example, showed that "gay religious do not necessarily leave when they cannot find acceptance; the great majority of our respondents appear to have every intention of remaining in the priesthood." The future plans of non-gay and gay priests did not differ much. Similar percentages of both said they were likely to stay (89 percent, non-gay; 82 percent, gay), uncertain about staying (8 percent, non-gay; 13 percent, gay), and likely to leave (3 percent, non-gay; 5 percent, gay). As one priest asked metaphorically, "When you have a fight in the family, do you leave the family?"[47]

Reasons for Staying: Quantified, Ordered, Compared

In Paul Foster's study of gay Catholic men in Toronto, respondents reported that they remained within the church for three reasons (in this order of reported frequency): (1) because of a strong attachment to the tradition of the church, meaning that they had been raised in the church and/or they valued the familiar sacraments and rituals of the church; (2) because of a sense of hope resulting from the support of particular leaders within the church and from the nurture of their local faith community, a gay Catholic group; and (3) because they have been able to make a distinction between the official church, which they mistrust, and their local faith community, in which they have been able to find acceptance. Foster concluded that "remaining Catholic, it would appear, allows gay men to continue to belong to the community in which they were raised and which they feel connected to and familiar with."[48]

The reasons for staying found by Foster — familiarity, family background, particular people, local support, and being able to establish a tangential relationship with the institutionalized church — will be explored further and added to by the findings from my survey (see table 19).

TABLE 19

Percentages of UMC and UCC Respondents Reporting Various Reasons for Remaining Affiliated with Their Denominations

UMC (N=198)		UCC (N=273)	
committed to change	35%	record on gay issues	28%
familiarity/home	22%	familiarity/home	19%
tangential relationship	22%	polity	18%
family background	16%	social justice record	18%
local congregation	14%	committed to change	16%
polity	11%	family background	15%
keep job/clergy status	11%	tangential relationship	13%
theological tradition	11%	local congregation	11%
particular people	8%	particular people	9%
social justice record	6%	keep job/clergy status	6%

Percentages add to more than 100 because some respondents reported more than one reason.

Similarity of Reasons

When respondents in my survey explained why they remained affiliated with their respective denominations, the differences between UMC and UCC responses did not provide the clear-cut comparisons that their feelings about and evaluations of their denominations did (see tables 16, 17, 18).

The reasons for staying that were similar for both UCC and UMC respondents in frequency and rank order were: because the denomination is a familiar home (UMC 22 percent, 2d; UCC 19 percent, 2d), because of one's family background and upbringing within the denomination (UMC 16 percent, 4th; UCC 15 percent, 6th), because of particular people and leaders within the denomination (UMC 8 percent, 9th; UCC 9 percent, 9th).

As a UMC clergywoman told me, "I come from three or more generations of United Methodists. My grandfather was at the Uniting Conference in '39 as a member of the Methodist Protestant Church. It's my church. There is no compelling thing, it's just my church. None of the churches are perfect out there. As long as I can do it, be healthy and spiritually fed, and live with integrity, I will be there." She said another part of why she stays is because "I've been blessed with knowing gay men and lesbians who are a part of the church for a long time. I was involved with some of the very early meetings and gatherings of Affirmation many, many years ago. I feel that I'm part of a tradition that's there, that we are there whether we are visible or not, whether I see them often or not. I've been fairly isolated in recent years, so I don't have a lot of contact with those folks, but I know that they are there. I know I'm not alone. I know that I'm a part of a movement that is clearly healing. There's a sense of belonging to that, whether it's through contact with an Open and Affirming church or a Reconciling Congregation or whether it's contact with a group of Affirmation folks or whether it's contact with folks through a gathering together of Affirmation folks with Dignity and Integrity, MCC, or whatever. There is a spirit among those gatherings that's the spirit of inclusive church in the twenty-first-century church. It's quite contagious. It's clear to me that the spirit of God is there. I have been blessed by that spirit on a number of occasions, and it's enough to let me know I am part of something blessed."

When I asked Margarita Suárez why she remains in the church, she said, "Why do I stay Christian? It's not because I necessarily believe Jesus is the *only Son* of the *only God* and the *only way*. It's because that's what I know; that's how I grew up; that's what is so comfortable for me; and I would not say that I believe it 100 percent. It's not that I don't think that there's power in Buddhism or in Judaism or in the Presbyterians, Methodists, and Disciples, but they're not whom I got attracted to; they're not who brought me in; they're not who took my hand and walked me through the system and helped give me a sense of my own power. So I stay because I love a lot of what I see, and I have terrific respect for a lot of people with whom I am in community around the country. And I guess ultimately I still have hope that the revolution is going to come."

Differences in Reasons

The UMC respondents reported some reasons for staying more and less often than the UCC respondents. Such reasons involved staying because of denominational polity, because of the denomination's record on social justice issues, because of the support of local congregations, and because of being able to maintain a tangential relationship with the denomination, that is, by maintaining a certain distance from and not personally investing in the denomination's approval of gay people. The most noticeable contrast, however, was between the reason given most often by each group of respondents: UMC respondents said they stayed because they were committed to changing the denomination, and UCC respondents said they stayed because of the denomination's pro-gay record. All of the above differences will be discussed further below.

Polity and Social Justice Issues. Slightly higher percentages and rankings were given by UCC than by UMC respondents to denominational polity (UMC 11 percent, 6th; UCC 18 percent, 3d) and to the denomination's record on various social justice issues (UMC 6 percent, 10th; UCC 18 percent, 4th) as reasons for staying. But UCC people whom I interviewed were cautious, too, in banking too much on the denomination's polity. When I asked Charlotte Stacey what she considered to be the most negative and the most positive feature about the UCC, she said, "Interestingly enough, probably the exact same thing for both, which is the polity. I've been at General Synod and I've seen the wonderful things that have happened in General Synod and then come back and realized the local church in most cases couldn't care less about what gets passed there. This is the negative and the positive. In other words, going back to the year we passed the Open and Affirming resolution in '85, to remember the wonderful process that occurred in General Synod from committee to the body voting overwhelmingly for that issue, and then to come back to the present and realize that here it is seven years later and we've got some sixty churches that are Open and Affirming and a lot of churches that couldn't care less about the issue and probably have never discussed it. An example being, that year when we came back, the representatives from our Hartford Association [district] never even mentioned in their report that that resolution was passed even though they knew other associations did.

"Now, to give you the other side of it, the wonderful part. Look at the Methodists and Lutherans. When their local churches want to be the equivalent of what we call Open and Affirming, their hierarchical polity tells them they can't. The same with the Catholic Church; their hierarchy tells them they can't. That's the positive side of UCC. I probably wouldn't want it any other way, but it's like anything else — when it goes the way you'd like it to, it's wonderful; and when it works against you, you don't think it's that great."

Selena Blackwell agreed: "What makes me feel the most positive about the UCC is that its corporate head is in the right place; that the social action and social justice is there along with the traditional, theological, scriptural stuff; that they do act on social justice and inclusivity with national resolutions and pronouncements. What makes me feel bad about the denomination is that because of the polity the resolutions aren't enforceable. A lot of the local churches don't implement them. At times I wish that there were a way for the high-level or middle-level instrumentalities to make the local churches more receptive or responsible, or at least to make the resources more available. It's kind of like the same thing that makes me feel good about it makes me feel bad about it. Generally it's the polity that makes the UCC strong, but it's also the polity that is so frustrating."

Local Congregations. Slightly higher percentages and rankings were given by UMC respondents to a local congregation's support for gay people (UMC 14 percent, 5th; UCC 11 percent, 8th) as a reason for staying. (See the above discussion about evaluation of denominational levels [pp. 215–219] and the discussion in the previous chapter about welcoming congregations [pp. 193–200].)

Tangential Relationship. The UMC respondents more often than the UCC respondents reported that they were able to stay by maintaining a tangential relationship with the denomination (UMC 22 percent, 3d; UCC 13 percent, 7th).

The UMC respondents from the Lower Midwest reported more often than respondents from other regions that they remained affiliated with the denomination because they have a tangential relationship with it (33 percent compared to average of 20 percent for other regions, with respondents from the South next highest, 28 percent; not in table). By contrast, none of the UMC respondents from the West Coast reported that they remain affiliated because they have a tangential relationship. Among UCC respondents, those from the South/Southwest/West reported more often than those from other regions that they remained affiliated with the denomination because they have a tangential relationship with it (22 percent compared to average of 11 percent for other regions; not in table).

Record on Gay Issues. The UCC respondents most often reported that they stay because of the denomination's record on gay issues (28 percent, 1st). This reason was not given by any UMC respondents.

One UCC clergywoman had the following to say about the importance for her of the denomination's record and reputation on gay issues: "If people in general look at our denomination (if they really know who we are and don't confuse us with Church of Christ; I spend a lot of time explaining who we're not), they make comments like, 'That's right, you're those liberal folks, etc.,' and usually if we talk for any length of time they may bring up something about, 'You ordain all those homosexuals.' I'll talk about what some of that means in terms of the way we are structured, but what I find helpful is that at least there's some reputation, and whether it's totally accurate or not (because Biblical Witness people would really have something else to say about all that), what I know is that at least that's helpful to me because it means the whole world does not turn out to be Southern Baptists. And that really in a way makes me proud to be who I am in terms of the denomination and why I stay."

Peter Ilgenfritz, a UCC clergyman, agreed that "the support for gays and lesbians by the denomination as a whole" is "very important." He said he knew it felt very different for his partner in the Presbyterian Church who "has a hard time going to worship in a Presbyterian church and thinking, 'I don't know how I can belong to this denomination; I don't know how I can call myself a Presbyterian minister.' I don't have those same dilemmas with the UCC."

Committed to Change. Most UMC respondents reported that they remain affiliated with the denomination because they are committed to changing it and making it a more welcoming and nurturing environment for gay people (35 percent, 1st). This reason was given much less often by UCC respondents (16 percent, 5th).

After the 1992 quadrennial meeting of the UMC I asked a lesbian church administrator how the vote to reaffirm the denomination's antigay policy would affect Affirmation. She answered, "I don't think it's going to cave in. I think there are some people who are burned out and they'll back off, but I don't think that'll hold or dominate. What I saw happen in Affirmation was that a new national council was elected, and those people are enthusiastic, excited, committed, and determined."

Another UMC woman expressed disappointment with the denomination but said one could not simply abandon it. "For a long time I've been frustrated with the church. There's a part of me that sees that the church is going to do whatever it does, and I've got plenty of other things to do. The other side of me recognizes that organized religion has been around longer than government; it's been around longer than any kind of organized whatever; and if we can get religion to change, if we can get that organization to change and understand what justice and inclusion is all about, then we're going to make major improvement. And change isn't going to happen until the religious institutions change, so it's going to happen slowly."

This sense of responsibility and obligation to change what one inherits was echoed by Randy Miller. "I think that if I had been born a Catholic or grew up a Catholic or Baptist, then that would be the context or the portion where I was placed to do battle. My whole image of staying with the church is about love for the church and that's true. I love and respect some of the traditions and practices. I also feel as though it's what I've been given, as a grandmother of a friend used to say, 'This is your portion.' The portion that I have been given is to do battle in the United Methodist Church around issues of inclusiveness and to make sure that the face of God is not obscured by all of this junk that people want to put on the church. I really do feel very strongly that I have an obligation, that I have a calling to do battle within the United Methodist Church, to transform it or revolutionize it. But I also think that a lot of the homophobia in society comes from the church. Because I am a person of faith, part of my obligation or vocation is to do battle to change the church, so that society will be changed. I could just walk away and go to some other part of the country where the church didn't have very much effect, but that wouldn't obliterate the church. Soon or at some point the evil or homophobia would find me wherever I am, even in San Francisco. I think that's part of the whole history of being African-American. You take up a four-hundred-year struggle where you are and know that it might not change in your lifetime. You've got to do battle where you are, because the evil or slavery or whatever will always find you."

Summary

Most UCC respondents said that they felt good about belonging to their denomination and that they remained affiliated with it because of the denomination's record on gay issues, because of the denomination's bottom-up polity, and because of the denomination's record on social justice issues.

Most UMC respondents said that they did not feel good about their affiliation with the denomination and that they stayed because they want to change the denomination's anti-gay policy and practice. Some said they are able to stay because of supportive local congregations. Others said they stayed by maintaining a tangential relationship with the denomination.

In both denominations, many respondents said they stayed because their denomination is their familiar home. Reasons for staying were bolstered by strong feelings of hopefulness by both UMC and UCC respondents, but more so by the latter.

The similarity of the experiences of UMC and UCC respondents reported in previous chapters — as measured by their participation, leadership roles, disclosure of sexual orientation, employment, and ordination within each denomination — contrasts with the difference in their feelings about and evaluations of their respective denominations. Evidence of the restrictive UMC policy's affect on gay people was less apparent in the actual experiences of UMC respondents than in their feelings about and evaluations of the denomination. If it were not for the extreme negativity of their evaluations and feelings, one may be tempted to conclude that the restrictive policy has little impact.

That staying is indeed more difficult for UMC respondents than for UCC respondents was signaled most clearly by the reported feelings of those who were out to their local congregations or belonged to welcoming congregations. Although such respondents in the UCC enjoyed feeling welcomed, valued, affirmed, involved, and loved, those in the UMC said they felt angry, marginalized, and sad. The consequence for trying to create the best situations and to find the best settings in the UMC would seem to be not greater happiness but ongoing conflict, rejection, and unhappiness.

That UCC respondents, therefore, more often than UMC respondents said they felt *committed to their denomination* is not surprising. But perhaps more significant to the study of gay people in organized religion is the finding that most UMC respondents reported that they remained affiliated with their denomination because they are *committed to changing their denomination.*

The reasons reported for remaining affiliated with their denominations were similar for UCC and UMC respondents, but the most frequent reason among and the most noticeable difference between UCC and UMC respondents had to do with the policy and practice of their denomination concerning gay people — that is, UCC respondents stay because of those policies and practices; and UMC respondents stay to change them. In simple and perhaps contradictory language, gay people remain with the church whether it mistreats them or treats them well. One may wonder if gay people are perhaps very tenacious or simply masochistic, and also if mainstream religion would be better advised to accept the fact that some gay people are going to stay regardless of its policies and practices and those who stay are committed and prepared to endure hardship.

Conclusion

Findings from Previous Chapters

Unlike the non-gay population, the majority of gay people are either not affiliated with any religious body or affiliated with nonmainstream, alternative religious bodies.

Most gay people who remain within established religious bodies, however, are highly active as lay ministers, leaders, and officials within them. Studies of gay and non-gay people in three religious bodies showed that the gay members participate on local boards and committees more often than non-gay members.

Although openly gay participation has been more difficult within anti-gay as opposed to pro-gay religious bodies, the reported differences have not been wide. For example, in my survey UMC respondents were out to their local congregations almost as often as UCC respondents; and although they encountered resistance to their membership and participation more often, they received support and were welcomed as often.

Findings about ordination and employment were also similar across religious bodies. For example, nearly identical percentages of UMC, UCC, and Catholic clergy said that they came out after ordination, and UMC respondents as often as UCC respondents reported that they were currently employed and that they had experienced employment discrimination.

Other sources of information have also revealed that gay people within reputedly pro-gay religious bodies, such as the Religious Society of Friends, Reformed Judaism, and the Unitarian Universalist Association, have experienced opposition, discrimination, and rejection; and gay people within reputedly anti-gay religious bodies, such as Conservative Judaism, the Presbyterian Church (U.S.A.), and the Southern Baptist Convention, have found support, approval, and acceptance within some settings. Within most bodies certain local congregations have welcomed gay people and managed to neutralize somewhat national anti-gay policies.

Geography and outness, more than policy, seemed to be more directly associated with the frequency of problems encountered by gay people. Among both UMC and UCC respondents, for example, those living in the South and Lower Midwest reported problems most often, and those from the West Coast and Upper Midwest reported problems least often.

Those who were out reported problems more often than those who were not out.

The importance of policy, however, cannot be ignored. In spite of the similar findings about the frequency of outness among UMC and UCC gay people, for example, the percentages of their outness as members, as participants on boards and committees, in leadership positions, and as pastors and employees were always slightly, and occasionally significantly, greater for UCC respondents. One-tenth of UCC clergy in my survey had also been ordained as openly gay people, a finding for which there are counterparts only in the Unitarian Universalist Association, Reform and Reconstructionist Judaism, the Metropolitan Community Church, the United Church of Canada, some Buddhist denominations, and some districts of the Episcopal Church.

But in spite of different policies and demographic variables, the finding that prevailed throughout the various studies of gay people within various religious bodies was the fact that they are present, visible, and active within organized mainstream religion. Among the gay people in my survey, for example, 90 percent of both UMC and UCC respondents reported that they were fully out or out to some people within their local churches.

Some observers have said that without the presence of gay people in mainstream religious bodies, those bodies would be free to enact antigay measures stricter than the ones they have. Others have said that the presence of gay people has provoked these bodies to take stricter measures than they would have if left alone. But one cannot deny that the presence and activism of gay people in these bodies have had the effect of drawing public attention and news media coverage on a regular and often spectacular basis.

Actual changes have occurred with greater success in some religious bodies than in others, but a movement for change by gay people has been felt in almost of them. The newsletters of gay organizations, various empirical studies, and coverage by the news media have documented such efforts by members of the restrictive as well as the progressive bodies.

However, receiving little or no attention in the news media, but readily available in studies of and newsletters by these gay people, were their theologies and faith statements.

Theology, Faith, Vision, View

Gay people have engaged in the serious examination and critique of the official beliefs, laws, and teachings of their respective religious traditions. They have tended not only to adhere to the traditions of their religious bodies but also to find within their traditions a source, means, or basis for embracing and affirming gay people.

By examining and appropriating their various religious traditions, gay people have often transcended the peculiarities of those traditions and come to understand, define, and articulate their faith in ways that are similar for gay people across religious bodies. Their collective theology and faith would read as follows: We take most seriously our personal experience and personal relationships as a resource for ordering our lives and understanding their ultimate meanings; living a "good" life means accepting and loving ourselves as physical, sexual, affectional beings; living a good life in the world involves understanding, contributing to, and changing others around us; we must help ourselves and others understand that homophobia, not homosexuality, is a problem; and our ultimate concern is to relate to others across social barriers, to accept and value human differences, and to build inclusive community as equals.

The various parts of this collective statement are probably familiar to most people within the wider gay community, but their arrangement, integration, and presentation offer a vision for comprehending and living out of concerns that others have perhaps not communicated so succinctly and completely.

Perhaps because gay people within mainstream religion find themselves amidst and contending with non-gay people on a regular basis, they can envision the necessity and difficulty of building community across human differences better than gay people whose main support and arena for working on change is the secular gay community.

Perhaps, also, because gay people have so often been rejected and demeaned by mainstream religion, they are among the most likely and most qualified to remind their fellow non-gay members that all major religious traditions share at their deepest levels the view that "each living being is a swirl in the flow, a formal turbulence, a 'song,' " and that their task is not to forget but "to hark again to those roots, to see our ancient solidarity, and then to the work of being together."[49] This view is how many gay people within organized religion understand themselves and religion — as necessary and important members of a diverse and inclusive community.

Theory: A Practical and Public View

The literary and historical scholar Wlad Godzich has written that the term "theory" is derived from the ancient Greek verb *theorein,* meaning to view, to contemplate, to examine. He has also observed that in Greek "it does not enter into an opposition with praxis," and it "does not designate a private act carried out by a cogitating philosopher but a very public one with important social consequences."[50]

The theory or view of gay people within organized religion put forth above is personal and communal, traditional and prophetic. It has emerged from an examination, critique, and affirmation of their personal experiences, of their religious traditions, and of current practices of their religious bodies. It allows for, recognizes, and has been developed from the similarities and differences of their experiences, feelings, evaluations, and reasoning. It is more than an abstraction or idea: its practical dimension is evident in its suggestions and prescriptions; and its social dimension is evident in its attempts to require and reach out for the participation of non-gay people to implement the suggestions and prescriptions.

That gay people have understood and embraced the alliance rather than opposition of theory and practice has been illustrated in studies showing that they more often than their fellow non-gay members participate in ecumenical and interfaith activities. Inclusive community has not been simply an idea but the practice that characterizes and distinguishes gay people within organized religion. Perhaps they can serve as role models for non-gay people who need to reach beyond what is secure and familiar, if inclusive community and social change are to happen. But most gay people would acknowledge that such role reversal is not about to happen soon. In line with the Greek root of the word "theory," gay people understand the social consequences of their view or theory for organized religion and for themselves.

Persistence, Danger, and Freedom

Gay people are the first to admit that remaining within mainstream religious bodies requires both hope and foolishness. Gain and reconciliation have been offset by loss and alienation. Progress has been slow or nonexistent. They agree with critics of mainstream religion that they have chosen to remain within oppressive situations and should not be surprised by the bad treatment they receive. Given that, I would still suggest that rather than trying to decide if gay people should stay within mainstream religious bodies or criticizing gay people for remaining within them, it is better instead to recognize that some gay people have remained and to try to understand their experience.

From the research I have done, I do not think their experience can be understood conclusively as positive or negative, good or bad, hopeful or hopeless. What has emerged from the research is not only the similarity of gay experience across religious bodies, as noted above, but the inseparability of change and permanence and the interaction of hope and pain.

Like many gay people in North America, gay people within mainstream religion were inspired by the Stonewall Rebellion to become more visible within their respective social institutions. Gay people have sought greater visibility and acceptance within their religious bodies because historically they were rejected and silenced by them. Efforts to bring about these changes have resulted in bruising battles, some gradual acceptance, but most often the taking and solidification of anti-gay positions by religious bodies. In response to these defeats and "glacial progress" many gay people have tended to insist even more on change, to create alternatives, to remain actively involved, and to come out where it is forbidden. In these circumstances, the greater visibility of gay people as well as their rejection by religious bodies have swelled dramatically in relationship to each other. Those whose feelings are the most negative and whose evaluations are the most critical are also the ones to reason most often that they should remain within their religious bodies to change them.

The courage, persistence, and greater visibility of gay people have been one part of their experience. Their rejection, defeats, and injury have been the other. None of the studies permits the appreciation or prioritization of only one part. To underscore the inseparability and interaction of both parts I shall close with a poem about the suicide of Phyllis Athey, which was discussed in chapter 5.

STANDING WITNESS

by Patricia Broughton

Phyllis is dead.

Shot herself to death Monday afternoon.

You remember Phyllis:
    the lesbian who wanted to be ordained in the
        United Methodist Church (God knows why).
Wanted to be a minister in a church that told her quite clearly:
    "No queers allowed here"
        (Only they said it much nicer than that, of course.)

Still, Phyllis persisted (God knows why)
    insisted she had a call to ministry,
    insisted she'd be less than whole
        proclaiming the Gospel of Jesus Christ
            from the vantage point
                of a closet.

Somehow she clung to the notion that she, too,
    was made in the image of God (God knows why),

even while being battered by the church,
even while her gifts and graces were being trashed.

Well, Phyllis is dead now.
She's not around to bother you anymore, Church.
Not around to stand before you,
insisting you see her
and hear her
and know her.

No, Phyllis isn't around anymore.
And all you have left to contend with, Church,
is a host of witnesses—
angelic and otherwise—
who stand expectantly before you.

And not a closet in sight.

Personally, I would prefer that lesbian/bisexual/gay people "demand assertively of" rather than "stand expectantly before" the church, but I think the poet probably more accurately grasps our collective experience within and practical expectations of organized religion. As a people, we have needed to stand and expect in between and in preparation for the occasions when our strength, numbers, and confidence would encourage us to attack and demand. Since the Southern Baptist Convention took 150 years to repent of its stand on slavery and over 30 years to apologize for its opposition to the civil rights movement of the 1960s,[51] a lot more standing than attacking may be needed to survive and endure until full acceptance and equality are ours. That many of us are visibly active precisely where we are forbidden to be suggests that we have the resources and reserve to see those goals through.

As gay people contemplate the future, we should know that if mainstream religion becomes more humane, charitable, and welcoming of all people, such changes will depend significantly on us. If we choose to take responsibility to advocate for and participate in those changes, we should also know that our lives will be marked with some moments of exhilarating freedom and hope as well as unrelenting if not crushing defeats and humiliation.

Appendix A

Largest Religious Bodies in North America

TABLE A.1

The following gives rank order of the sixty-five largest Christian and Jewish religious bodies in the United States, by number of adherents, including number of adherents of Islam, Buddhism, and Hinduism.[1]

Roman Catholic Church	52,900,126
Southern Baptist Convention	18,940,682
United Methodist Church	11,091,032
National Baptist Convention, U.S.A., Incorporated	8,200,000
Church of God in Christ	5,499,875
Evangelical Lutheran Church in America	5,226,798
Presbyterian Church (U.S.A.)	3,553,335
Church of Jesus Christ of Latter-day Saints (Mormon)	3,540,820
National Baptist Convention of America	3,500,000
African Methodist Episcopal Church	3,500,000
Lutheran Church–Missouri Synod	2,603,725
Reform Judaism	2,548,557
Progressive National Baptist Convention, Incorporated	2,500,000
National Missionary Baptist Convention of America	2,500,000
Episcopal Church	2,445,286
Conservative Judaism	2,237,466
Assemblies of God	2,161,610
United Church of Christ	1,993,459
American Baptist Churches in the U.S.A.	1,873,731
Churches of Christ	1,681,013
Baptist Bible Fellowship International	1,500,000
Jehovah's Witnesses	1,381,000
Christian Churches and Churches of Christ	1,213,188
African Methodist Episcopal Zion Church	1,142,016
Christian Church (Disciples of Christ)	1,037,757
Seventh-Day Adventists	903,062
Church of the Nazarene	888,123
Islam	877,200
Christian Methodist Episcopal Church	718,922

Buddhism	701,760
Church of God (Cleveland, Tennessee)	695,074
United Pentecostal Church International	550,000
Unitarian Universalist Association	502,000
International Council of Community Churches	500,000
Pentecostal Assemblies of the World	500,000
Wisconsin Evangelical Lutheran Synod	419,928
Orthodox Church in America	400,000
Orthodox Judaism	394,847
Reformed Church in America	362,932
Hinduism	350,880
National Association of Free Will Baptist	293,448
Baptist Missionary Association of America	289,969
Christian and Missionary Alliance	271,865
Wesleyan Church	259,740
International Church of the Foursquare Gospel	255,092
American Baptist Association	250,000
Antiochian Orthodox Christian Archdiocese of North America	250,000
Church of God (Anderson, Indiana)	232,876
Christian Reformed Church	226,163
Christian Reformed Church in North America	223,617
Presbyterian Church in America	221,392
Byzantine Ruthenian Catholic Church	215,753
Church of Christ, Scientist	214,000
Conservative Baptist Association of America	200,000
Church of the Brethren	186,588
Evangelical Free Church of America	181,692
Coptic Orthodox Church	180,000
Baptist General Conference	167,874
General Association of Regular Baptist Churches	160,123
Pentecostal Holiness Church	157,728
Mennonite Church	154,259
Reorganized Church of Jesus Christ of Latter-day Saints	150,143
International Pentecostal Holiness Church	131,674
Religious Society of Friends	130,484
Salvation Army	127,577

TABLE A.2

The following gives the rank order of the forty-eight largest Jewish and Christian religious bodies in Canada by number of adherents.[2]

Roman Catholic Church in Canada	11,852,350
United Church of Canada	1,984,307
Anglican Church in Canada	848,256
Presbyterian Church in Canada	233,335
Greek Orthodox Diocese of Toronto	230,000
Evangelical Lutheran Church in Canada	203,937
Pentecostal Assemblies of Canada	194,972
Conservative Judaism	135,400
Canadian Baptist Federation	131,349
Church of Jesus Christ of Latter-day Saints in Canada (Mormon)	130,000
Ukrainian Orthodox Church of Canada	120,000
Jehovah's Witnesses	106,052
Antiochian Orthodox Christian Archdiocese of North America	100,000
Salvation Army in Canada	99,658
Christian Reformed Church in North America	86,231
Reform Judaism	85,516
Christian and Missionary Alliance in Canada	80,681
Lutheran Church — Canada	79,645
United Baptist Convention of the Atlantic Provinces	66,484
Fellowship of Evangelical Baptist Churches in Canada	61,572
Baptist Convention of Ontario and Quebec	44,713
Seventh-Day Adventist Church in Canada	42,083
Conference Mennonites in Canada	37,008
Orthodox Judaism	33,850
Pentecostal Assemblies of Newfoundland	33,700
Canadian Conference of Mennonite Brethren Churches	28,250
Baptist Union of Western Canada	20,660
North American Baptist Conference	17,943
Unitarian Universalist Association	17,928
Mennonite Church	14,861
Apostolic Church of Pentecost of Canada, Incorporated	14,500
Evangelical Free Church of Canada	13,699
Canadian and American Reformed Churches	13,536
Reorganized Church of Jesus Christ of Latter-day Saints	11,111
Church of the Nazarene	10,915
Associated Gospel Churches	9,284
Romanian Orthodox Episcopate of America (Jackson, Michigan)	8,600
Christian Churches and Churches of Canada	7,500
Free Methodist Church in Canada	7,479
Churches of Christ in Canada	7,181
Russian Orthodox Church in Canada, Patriarchal Provinces	7,000
Canadian Convention of Southern Baptists	6,743

Church of God (Cleveland, Tennessee)	6,670
Estonian Evangelical Lutheran Church	6,478
Evangelical Mennonite Conference	6,358
Reformed Church in Canada	6,236
Baptist General Conference of Canada	6,066
Wesleyan Church of Canada	5,256

Appendix B

Chronology of Gay-Related Events within Organized Religion from World War II to 1972

The following chronology has been assembled with reference to a variety of sources.[1]

1943 In his book *On Being a Real Person,* Reverend Harry Emerson Fosdick, founding minister of New York City's Riverside Church, calls attention to the poor preparation of clergy to deal with homosexuality. He is the first well-known church leader to do so.

1946 In Atlanta, George Hyde, a minister in the independent Catholic movement, organizes the first church for homosexuals. Services are first held in a gay bar on Christmas Eve for eighty-five people, who subsequently take for their congregation the name Eucharistic Catholic Church. This church is the forerunner of the gay church movement.

1948 Henry Hay founds the Mattachine Society, a male homosexual emancipation group, in Los Angeles with the help of a sociologist, a psychologist, and a Unitarian minister.

Henry Van Dusen, president of Union Theological Seminary, writes that Kinsey's findings are evidence of a "degradation in American morality approaching the worst decadence of the Roman era."

1953 The Mattachine Society holds a national convention in Los Angeles at the First Universalist Church. The church's minister, Wallace Maxey, is a board member. Five hundred gay people attend.

The *American Anthropologist* publishes Nancy O. Lurie's article "Winnebago Berdache."

1954 An autobiography, *Baba of Karo: A Woman of the Muslim Hausa,* transcribed from interviews by Mary F. Smith and published by Faber and Faber, gives an account from Nigerian village life of *'yandauda,* men who "become like women."

1955 Eight homosexual women in San Francisco form the Daughters of Bilitis. Originally founded as a social organization, DOB soon broadens its role to that of educating the public and changing attitudes about lesbianism. Chapters in other cities subsequently form. Two of the founders, Phyllis Lyon and Del Martin, will be founding members of the Council on Religion and the Homosexual in 1964.

Derrick Sherwin Bailey's book *Homosexuality and the Western Christian Tradition* (Longmans, Green) is published. It is the first scholarly work to challenge comprehensively traditional interpretations of biblical passages allegedly related to homosexuality.

The *American Anthropologist* publishes "A Note on Berdache," Henry Angelino and Charles Shedd's 1951 study of the American Indian individual who is viewed by her or his tribe "as being of one sex physiologically but as having assumed the role and status of the opposite sex."

Father Edward Lucitt, head of the Catholic Holy Name Society in Camden, New Jersey, leads a protest against naming a new bridge after Walt Whitman because he was a "homoerotic."

1956 Reverend Robert Wood's article "Spiritual Exercises" is published in *Grecian Guild Pictorial,* a physique magazine, with a photograph of the author in clerical collar.

1957 *The Wolfenden Report: Report of the Committee on Homosexual Offenses and Prostitution,* issued in Great Britain, cites Derrick Sherwin Bailey's study *Homosexuality and the Western Christian Tradition* and leads to the repeal of sodomy laws there and in the United States.

The archbishop of Westminster, Great Britain, Roman Catholic Church, issues a statement saying "Catholics are free to make up their own minds" about whether criminalizing or decriminalizing private acts of homosexuality between consenting adults "harms the common good."

1959 At a midwinter meeting of leaders of the United Church of Christ, Reverend Hermann Reissig challenges the denomination to respond to the homosexual. Subsequently, the denomination's Council for Christian Social Action begins private discussions about homosexuality.

Spencer W. Kimball and Mark E. Petersen, apostles and elders of the Church of Jesus Christ of Latter-day Saints (Mormon), are assigned to be in charge of sexual cases. During the next decade they will counsel many homosexuals and provide them with the opportunity to "repent" before being dismissed and excommunicated. Kimball also begins his book *The Miracle of Forgiveness,* in which he will formulate the ideas about homosexuality that will dominate church policy.

1960 Reverend Robert Wood, a United Church of Christ clergyman, publishes his book *Christ and the Homosexual (Some Observations)* (Vantage Press). He is the first homosexual to use his real name and church affiliation when writing about homosexuality; and his book is the first to claim that one need not be heterosexual to be Christian.

1961 The National Council of Churches (NCC) sponsors the "North American Conference on Church and Family" (Green Lake, Wisconsin). Homosexuality is included on the agenda. Subsequently, Reverend William H. Genne, chair of the Family Life Division, and his wife, Elizabeth S. Genne, edit the NCC's publication *Foundations for Christian Family Policy,* which includes a discussion of homosexuality.

1962 Reverend Robert Wood is invited to give a talk, "The Church's Ministry with the Homosexual," at Union Theological Seminary in New York City. The seminary's president denounces his speech and threatens expulsion for practicing homosexuals, but the faculty does not back him.

Reverend A. Cecil Williams and Reverend Ted McIlvena of Glide Memorial Methodist Church, San Francisco, begin ministry to "castoffs," including homosexuals, in Tenderloin area. Project is called Glide Urban Center.

1963 Friends Home Service Committee, London, issues *Towards a Quaker View of Sex.* The report urges the church to "come of age" and to take "a fresh look at homosexuality."

1964 Reverend Ted McIlvena of the Glide Urban Center organizes four-day consultation between gay activists in San Francisco and sixteen Protestant ministers from several denominations, including some from other cities. Ministers leave committed to work with homophile groups in their areas.

The San Francisco contingent forms Council on Religion and the Homosexual (CRH) to promote continuing dialogue between the church and homosexuals. The council lasts until 1974 as the main organization for educating clergy and introducing them to concerns of gay Christians. It spawns councils in Dallas, Los Angeles, Washington, and Seattle and will meet with leaders and decision-making bodies of the United Church of Christ, Episcopal Church, Lutheran Church in America, and Methodist Church.

In his work *The Ethics of Sex* (Harper and Row), German Protestant theologian Helmut Thielicke complains of the lack of attention given to homosexuality by church leaders and theologians. He criticizes the church's doctrinaire, dogmatic, and fundamentalist dismissal of homosexuality and urges instead an understanding based on a "pastoral encounter" with homosexual persons.

John Lassoe, priest and legal strategist for the Episcopal Diocese of New York, testifies in favor of decriminalizing sodomy at the State Assembly's hearings on criminal code revision.

In his book *The Kaska Indians: An Ethnographic Reconstruction* (Yale University Press), J. J. Honigmann reports on the role and behavior of homosexual women.

1965 The Board of Trustees of the Council on Religion and the Homosexual, San Francisco, releases a "Brief of Injustices," which indicts society's discriminatory treatment of homosexuals. The "brief" follows from incidents of harassment and arrest by police at a dance sponsored by the council, is sent to San Francisco's Human Rights Commission, and has the effect of changing police harassment in homosexual bars.

Thirty people picket at Grace Cathedral in San Francisco to protest removal of Reverend Canon Robert W. Cromey by the Episcopal Diocese of California for signing the "Brief of Injustices" as a CRH Board member.

Twenty-four people picket the Federal Civil Service Commission in Washington, D.C., to protest discrimination against homosexuals in government hiring. One of the picketers is Reverend Robert Wood, who wears his clerical collar.

The Roman Catholic Church successfully lobbies the New York State legislature to defeat a repeal of its sodomy law.

In a speech at Duke University, Episcopal bishop James Pike urges the repeal of laws against the sexual behavior of consenting adults.

A resolution opposing discrimination against homosexuals is prepared for the Union of American Hebrew Congregations (UAHC) convention but is never presented. National Federation of Temple Sisterhoods passes a parallel resolution but does not implement it because UAHC does not pass its own resolution.

1966 The National Council of Churches (NCC) sponsors seminar entitled "The Church and Homosexuals" for thirty-six participants. Public media are not informed, and a follow-up report is not made.

In New York, Judson Memorial Church led by Reverend Howard Moody sponsors a public meeting to discuss and oppose police entrapment of homosexuals.

The Phoenix Society for Individual Freedom in Kansas City forms a Council on Religion and the Homosexual after the San Francisco model.

In his book *Toward a Christian Understanding of the Homosexual,* H. Kimball-Jones recommends that the church recognize the validity of mature homosexual relationships without endorsing homosexuality.

1967 Episcopal priests from the Northeast hold a symposium in New York and urge that homosexuality be considered morally neutral and that homosexual relationships be judged by the same standards as heterosexual relationships.

The Diocesan Council of the Episcopal Church in California urges an end to entrapment, unfair treatment in gay bars, and training for police who encounter homosexuals.

Anglican theologian Norman W. Pittenger argues for full acceptance of homosexuals by the church in his book *Time for Consent: A Christian Approach to Homosexuality,* published by SCM Press of London.

Two periodicals, *Social Action,* of the United Church of Christ, and *Social Progress,* of the United Presbyterian Church, feature the same forty-eight-page special issue devoted to the civil liberties of homosexuals.

Newsweek publishes an article titled "God and the Homosexual."

1968 Reverend Troy Perry founds the Universal Fellowship of Metropolitan Community Churches in Los Angeles. It is the first Christian denomination for predominantly homosexual congregations.

Staff representatives of the United Church of Christ meet in Philadelphia with East Coast leaders of the increasingly active and vocal homophile movement.

The Council on Religion and the Homosexual, Kansas City, persuades Kansas City's Metropolitan Inter-church Agency to establish a task force on homosexuality.

1969 The Stonewall Rebellion in June in New York's Greenwich Village prompts the beginning of the gay liberation movement.

Spencer W. Kimball, elder of the Church of Jesus Christ of Latter-day Saints, publishes his book *The Miracle of Forgiveness,* the definitive source for Mormon policy on homosexuality, which is described as "an ugly sin, repugnant to those who find no temptation in it, as well as to many past offenders who are seeking a way out of its clutches."

The Pilgrim Press publishes an anthology, *The Same-Sex: An Appraisal of Homosexuality,* edited by Ralph W. Weltge. It is the first book to present views of the homophile community by homosexual people themselves.

The Council for Christian Social Action of the United Church of Christ adopts a statement entitled "Resolution on Homosexuals and the Law." It is the first social policy statement by a religious denomination to oppose and urge repeal of laws that make private relations between consenting adults a crime.

Solomon B. Freehof's *responsum* or legal opinion in *Current Reform Responsa* is the earliest Reform Jewish statement on Judaism and homosexuality. It upholds the traditional view of homosexual behavior as sinful.

In their anthology of anthropological studies, *Spirit Mediumship and Society in Africa,* editors John Beattie and John Middleton point out that mediums "are usually shrewd, intelligent, and accepted members of society" and that spirit possession is primarily the province of women and associated in some cultures with male homosexuality.

1970 The Biennial Convention of the Lutheran Church of America adopts a statement opposing prejudice, discrimination, and laws against homosexuals and claiming that homosexuals are "entitled to understanding justice in church and community."

The General Assembly of the Unitarian Universalist Association of Churches in North America resolves to end discrimination against homosexuals and bisexuals by opposing legal regulations and by initiating programs of sex education within their churches.

In his article "The Christian Male Homosexual" (published in the Catholic clerical journal *Homiletic and Pastoral Review*), John J. McNeill, a Jesuit theologian, argues for the acceptance of monogamous homosexual relationships as a lesser evil than promiscuity

Spencer W. Kimball's 1969 book, *The Miracle of Forgiveness,* is condensed into a nine-page manual, *Hope for Transgressors,* as a publication of the Church of Jesus Christ of Latter-day Saints.

Michael F. Valente's book *Sex: The Radical View of a Catholic Theologian* is published by Macmillan. Valente argues for tolerance and a new vision in theology that would recognize homosexuality as natural and good.

Doubleday publishes John G. Milhaven's book *Toward a New Catholic Morality,* in which Milhaven maintains that homosexual behavior is "wrong and unChristian."

1971 The First National Conference on Religion and the Homosexual is held at the Interchurch Center in New York. With seventy participants from eleven denominations, it is the most broadly based consultation on homosexuality and religion ever convened. The event is covered by the secular media, including the *New York Times, Washington Post, Time* magazine, and *Ladies Home Journal.*

Twelve members of the New York chapter of the Daughters of Bilitis attend Central Presbyterian Church's showing of *The*

Fox, part of its weekly film program, and engage those attending in a discussion about the oppression of gay people and their mispresentation in film.

The New York chapter of the Daughters of Bilitis organizes a demonstration at St. Patrick's Cathedral in support of the controversial and highly publicized speech by feminist activist Ti-Grace Atkinson against the Catholic Church's oppression of women.

Reverend Richard Nash and Elgin Blair found the Unitarian Universalist Gay Caucus.

The Church of Jesus Christ of Latter-day Saints publishes *New Horizons for Homosexuals,* written in the form of a "letter to a dear friend" and signed by Spencer Kimball, the church elder who wrote *The Miracle of Forgiveness* in 1969.

The major motion picture *Little Big Man* is released. It includes the positive depiction of one character in the role of the Cheyenne *heemaneh,* a biological male who takes on the role of a woman.

Roman Catholic ethicist Charles Curran offers a mediating position between total condemnation and total acceptance of homosexual behavior in his article "Homosexuality and Moral Theology: Methodological and Substantive Considerations," appearing in *The Thomist.*

Westminster Press publishes an anthology of essays, *Is Gay Good? Ethics, Theology, and Homosexuality,* edited by W. Dwight Oberholtzer.

1972 The Golden Gate Association of the Northern California Conference, United Church of Christ, ordains William Johnson into Christian ministry. It is the first ordination of an openly gay person in the history of the Christian church. Subsequently, Reverend Johnson founds the United Church of Christ's Gay Caucus.

The San Francisco Board of Rabbis, representing three movements of Judaism, votes to support legalization of private sexual acts between consenting adults.

Beth Chayim Chadashim, a gay synagogue, is founded in Los Angeles and applies for membership in the Union of American Hebrew Congregations.

In *Lame Deer, Seeker of Visions: The Life of a Sioux Medicine Mane* (Simon and Schuster), John Lame Deer discusses the respected position and sacred power of the Lakota *winkte,* a biological male who takes on a woman's role.

Evangelical Christian minister Ralph Blair issues his pamphlet, *An Evangelical Look at Homosexuality.* Blair argues that Christian evangelism and homosexuality are not contradictory.

Appendix C

Profiles of Twenty Respondents from UMC and UCC Survey

The following sketches are of persons I interviewed in my survey of gay members of the UMC and UCC.

UMC Respondents

A (UMC clergy) This thirty-four-year-old ordained clergy works as an administrative assistant for a UMC-related institution. He and his partner are active in a small, urban UMC church that has been a Reconciling Congregation for six years. He has been a longtime member of Affirmation and has written gay-related articles for religious periodicals.

C (UMC clergy) This forty-one-year-old UMC clergywoman had been removed from clerical duties because she identified openly as a lesbian. She subsequently pursued and received an advanced degree in another profession and is now practicing in that profession. After reviewing and editing the transcript of her interview, she decided not to return it to me. She wrote: "It helped me realize how much I had moved through, and that I no longer need to dwell on the people or pain. So, while I apologize for not following through with the process, I am grateful to you for helping me to understand better than I might otherwise, some significant periods in my life."

Mary Gaddis (UMC laity) At the time of the interview, Mary Gaddis was forty-two years old and living with her partner, Judy. Both of her children were away at college. She works as a steam fitter and teaches at a nonprofit organization that she started to teach women construction skills. She infrequently attends two urban United Methodist churches. One is a Reconciling Congregation.

H (UMC clergy) This UMC clergywoman is a campus minister at a state university. In addition to her responsibilities on campus and related activities in the surrounding community, she attends a small United

Methodist church that is not a Reconciling Congregation. At the time of the interview she was forty-five years old.

L (UMC laity) At the time of the interview, this woman was fifty-one years old. She is an elementary school teacher with two college-age children of her own. She and her partner were not living together, and since the interview have separated. In follow-up correspondence, she writes, "I'm fine and she is doing better — it was for the best, but not easy." She is active in a six-hundred member, urban United Methodist church. It is not a Reconciling Congregation.

Randy Miller (UMC laity) At the time of the interview, Randy Miller was thirty-three years old and employed as the program director of an AIDS agency. He had received a Master of Divinity degree from Emory University, had worked on the UMC national staff, and had been active in Black Methodists for Church Renewal. He was attending an inner-city, fifteen hundred-member United Methodist church. It is not a Reconciling Congregation but has a history and practice of welcoming and supporting lesbian/bisexual/gay people.

S (UMC laity) This UMC laywoman is an associate director of one the denomination's regional jurisdictions. She lives with her partner and recently changed her local membership from a one-thousand-member church to a seventy-five-member church. Both are located within the same city, and the smaller church recently became a Reconciling Congregation. At the time of the interview, she was just turning fifty years of age.

Katie Sanetra (UMC laity) For nine years, Katie Sanetra has been attending a small, urban United Methodist church that is a Reconciling Congregation. She chooses not to be a member because her theology is not Christ-centered. At the time of the interview, she was thirty-eight years old and holding down two jobs, one in shipping and receiving and the other as a security guard.

B. J. Stiles (UMC clergy) At the time of the interview, B. J. Stiles was fifty-nine years old. He lives with his partner of eight years and has two grown daughters and one grandchild. He is a UMC clergyman but is employed as the executive director of a nonprofit, national AIDS organization not affiliated with the denomination. He attends a fifteen-hundred-member, urban United Methodist church that is not a Reconciling Congregation.

Tim Tennant-Jayne (UMC clergy) At the time of the interview, Tim Tennant-Jayne was thirty-seven years old and living with his lover. Previously, he had been employed as a UMC minister and was now working in a stained glass studio. He was attending two different inner-city

United Methodist churches, each with 200 to 250 members. One is a Reconciling Congregation.

UCC Respondents

Selena Blackwell (UCC laity) At the time of the interview, Selena Blackwell was thirty-six years old. She had been employed as a computer adviser for a major insurance company but was about to begin studying for the Master of Divinity degree at Yale. She lives with her partner, and her children are with her half-time. She is African-American and active in a one-thousand-member, suburban, predominantly white UCC church. It is not an Open and Affirming congregation.

Diane Darling (UCC clergy) Diane Darling is an ordained UCC clergywoman who has been pastoring the same local church in Modesto for twelve years. It is an Open and Affirming congregation. She began as a seminary intern for nine months and was asked to stay on as associate pastor. Two years later she was appointed as cominister and served for five years in that position. In the fall of 1989, the church voted to make her its sole pastor. Her partner, Elaine, is the organist and director of the children's choir. Since the time of the interview, Diane has moved to become the pastor of Sayville Congregational Church on Long Island.

Mark Ehrke (UCC laity) At the time of the interview, Mark Ehrke was thirty-four years old, working as an educational assistant with the public school system, and in the process of getting his licensure in elementary school education. He was raised in the UCC but has become active in the Religious Society of Friends, where he subsequently met his current lover.

Peter Ilgenfritz (UCC clergy) Peter Ilgenfritz, a UCC clergyman, received his Master of Divinity degree from Yale Divinity School, where he met his partner, Dave. After graduation they each served local churches in different geographical areas before moving to Chicago together. At the time of the interview, Peter was thirty years old and employed as the executive director of an AIDS service organization in Evanston, Illinois, and Dave was enrolled in the social work school at the University of Chicago. They attended an Open and Affirming UCC congregation. Subsequent to the interview, Peter and his partner were hired to share a job as associate minister at University Congregational Church in Seattle.

J (UCC clergy) At the time of the interview, this thirty-one-year-old UCC clergywoman had recently received her Master of Divinity degree from Eden Seminary and had been working for one year as a hospital chaplain at a Roman Catholic hospital in the steel mill area outside of Chicago. Since the time of the interview, she became the director of pastoral care at another hospital, where in addition to direct patient care, she now has management responsibilities. She attends a local UCC church that is not Open and Affirming.

John Lardin (UCC) At the time of the interview, John Lardin was twenty-eight years old, living with his lover, and working as an administrative assistant. He is an active lay leader in a 120-member, suburban UCC church and in the United Church Coalition for Lesbian/Gay Concerns (UCCL/GC). He chaired the task force that developed the process for his local church to become an Open and Affirming congregation.

M (UCC clergy) At the time of the interview, this ordained clergyman was thirty-eight years old. He had recently received his Master of Divinity degree from Chicago Divinity School and was serving as the pastor at a local inner-city church of 130 members. It is not an Open and Affirming congregation. Previously he did administrative work at a large university in the Chicago area. He and his partner have been together for twenty years.

P (UCC laity) At the time of the interview, this UCC laywoman was fifty-four years old and unemployed. She had worked for many years as a public policy advocate and administrator in nonprofit organizations, including several national agencies of the UCC. She currently belongs to a small, interracial, suburban UCC church that is not an Open and Affirming congregation.

Charlotte Stacey (UCC laity) At the time of the interview, Charlotte Stacey was forty-one years old and employed as a district manager for a major insurance company. She has lived with her partner, Marge, for seven years. Both are active in a small-town, two-hundred-member UCC church, in which Charlotte is the organist and choir director. Her church is not an Open and Affirming congregation.

Margarita Suárez (UCC clergy) At the time of the interview, Margarita Suárez was thirty-four years old, had recently married, and was pregnant with her first child. She is Latina and identifies as bisexual. A UCC clergywoman, she had been serving as the pastor of a sixty-member, inner-city church for two years. It was an Open and Affirming congregation. Since the time of the interview, Margarita gave birth to a son; her church has had to close officially for financial reasons; and she has become the associate pastor at a UCC church in Evanston.

Appendix D

Newsletters of Gay Religious Organizations Screened for This Study

TABLE D.1

Newsletters of Gay Religious Organizations Screened from 1988 to 1995

Publication	Organization	Religious Body/Tradition	Affiliation
*Waves**	United Church Coalition for Lesbian/Gay Concerns	United Church of Christ	recognized
Affirmation	Affirmation: United Methodists for Lesbian & Gay Concerns	United Methodist Church United Methodist Church	not recognized not recognized
Open Hands	Reconciling Church Program	United Methodist Church	not recognized
*Voice of the Turtle**	American Baptists Concerned for Lesbian, Gay & Bisexual People	American Baptist Churches in the U.S.A.	not recognized
*More Light Update**	Presbyterians for Lesbian & Gay Concerns	Presbyterian Church (U.S.A.)	recognition rescinded
*Dialogue**	Brethren/Mennonite Council for Lesbian & Gay Concerns	Mennonite Church, Church of the Brethren, related denominations	not recognized
Interweave World (formerly *UULGC World*)	Unitarian Universalists for Lesbian, Gay & Bisexual Concerns	Unitarian Universalist Association	recognized and funded
FLGC Newsletter	Friends for Lesbian & Gay Concerns	Religious Society of Friends, Friends United Meeting (YUM)	unofficial group (YUM)
World Congress Digest	World Congress of Gay & Lesbian Jewish Organizations	various movements of Judaism, with some member organizations affiliated with Union of American Hebrew Congregations (Reform) or Federation of Reconstructionist Congregations	independent
*Apostolic Voice**	National Gay Pentecostal Alliance	Pentecostal tradition	independent
Trikone	Trikone: Gay & Lesbian South Asians	Islam	independent

*Issues to 1995 also used.

Notes

Preface

1. See Dean Hamer and Peter Copeland, *The Science of Desire: The Search for the Gay Gene and the Biology of Behavior* (New York: Simon and Schuster, 1994); Simon LeVay, *The Sexual Brain* (Cambridge, Mass.: MIT Press, 1993); and Warren J. Blumenfeld and Diane Raymond, *Looking at Gay and Lesbian Life,* rev. ed. (Boston: Beacon, 1993), 115–46.

2. See Patricia Beattie Jung and Ralph F. Smith, *Heterosexism: An Ethical Challenge* (Albany: State University of New York Press, 1993), 16–31; Jim Bailey, "Deathblow for So-Called 'Ex-Gay' Ministries?" *More Light Update* (Presbyterians for Lesbian and Gay Concerns), April 1995, 11 (reprinted from *Second Stone,* January/February 1995); and David L. Wheeler, "A Researcher's Claim of Finding a Biological Basis for Homosexuality Rekindles Debate over Link between Brain Morphology and Behavior," *Chronicle of Higher Education,* 4 September 1991, 9, 15.

3. For the origin and use of these terms in church policy, see Sally B. Geis and Donald E. Messer, eds., *Caught in the Crossfire: Helping Christians Debate Homosexuality* (Nashville: Abingdon, 1994), 197–202; Garlinda Burton, "Statement Defines 'Self-Avowed Practicing,'" *Christian Social Action,* February 1991, 34–35; and J. Gordon Melton, ed., *The Churches Speak on Homosexuality: Official Statements from Religious Bodies and Ecumenical Organizations* (Detroit: Gale Research, 1991). The terms "self-avowed," "self-acknowledged," "self-accepting," and "noncelibate" are also used.

4. Leonard Patterson, "At Ebenezer Baptist Church," in Michael J. Smith, ed., *Black Men/White Men: A Gay Anthology* (San Francisco: Gay Sunshine, 1983), 163–66.

5. Ibid., 164.

6. Ibid., 165, 236.

7. See James H. Cone, *For My People: Black Theology and the Black Church* (Maryknoll, N.Y.: Orbis, 1984), 96–98. Cone says that the black churches have tended to be as conservative as white churches on gay issues because — unlike Martin Luther King Jr. — the black churches did not use and develop the tools of social and economic analysis. Cone notes that the "integrity of [King's] commitment and the depth of his analysis" were what enabled him to see beyond immediate concerns and grasp the importance of other social issues. See also Cornel West, "Black Sexuality: The Taboo Subject," in *Race Matters* (New York: Vintage, 1994), 119–31; and James Waller, "Go West," *Out,* October 1994, 90.

8. See Melton, ed., *The Churches Speak on Homosexuality,* 202, 260.

9. "PNBC Takes Landmark Stand," *Voice of the Turtle* (American Baptists Concerned), winter 1995, 1; and Calvin O. Butts III, "Report of the Resolutions Committee to the 33rd Annual Session of the National Baptist Convention, Inc." (Memphis: August 1994), 11–13.

10. Barry A. Kosmin and Seymour P. Lachman, *One Nation under God: Religion in Contemporary American Society* (New York: Harmony, 1993), 2, 15–17, 142–46. Also, an estimated forty-seven thousand Native Americans practice ancestral tribal religions. This number accounts for less than 3 percent of the Native American population and much less than 0.1 percent of the total American population. For the most part, the religious affiliations of Native Americans resemble those of other Americans.

Jews usually belong to a local synagogue that is affiliated with one of the four "movements" of Judaism—Reconstructionist, Reform, Conservative, or Orthodox. Each movement has a national organization to which its local synagogues belong. These organizations are the Federation of Reconstructionist Congregations, the Union of American Hebrew Congregations, the United Synagogue of Conservative Judaism, and the Union of Orthodox Jewish Congregations. See Barry A. Kosmin et al., *Highlights of the CJF 1990 National Jewish Population Survey* (New York: Council of Jewish Federations, 1991), 32; and Martin B. Bradley et al., *Churches and Church Membership in the United States 1990: An Enumeration by Region, State and County Based on Data Reported for 133 Church Groupings* (Atlanta: Glenmary Research Center, 1992), 3, 451.

11. Those who identify as non-Catholic and non-Protestant Christians make up less than 3 percent of the population. Most of them belong to (1) the Eastern Orthodox Church, which has its origins in the Eastern Roman Empire rather than the Western Roman Empire, the latter being the seedbed of the Roman Catholic Church; or (2) the Church of Christ, Scientist; the Church of Jesus Christ of Latter-day Saints; or the Jehovah's Witnesses, which have their independent origins in America and lack direct ties to the Protestant Reformation of sixteenth-century Europe. The Unitarian Universalist Association, on the other hand, is independent of but recognizes its Christian and Protestant origins. See Lyman A. Kellstedt et al., "Religious Traditions and Religious Commitments in the USA" (paper prepared for the Twenty-Second International Conference of the International Society for the Sociology of Religion, Budapest, 19–23 July 1993), 7; Wade Clark Roof and William McKinney, *American Mainline Religion: Its Changing Shape and Future* (New Brunswick, N.J.: Rutgers University Press, 1987), 97–99, 253–56; and Kosmin and Lachman, *One Nation under God,* 228.

12. The worldwide Catholic Church is divided into eight "rites"—Armenian, Byzantine, Chaldean, Latin (or Roman), Maronite, Melkite-Greek, Romanian Byzantine, and Ukrainian Byzantine. Each of the rites is present in the United States, but the Latin rite far exceeds the others. Over 97 percent of local Catholic parishes are of the Latin rite; and over 99 percent of Catholics belong to the Latin rite. See Kosmin and Lachman, *One Nation under God,* 130–42; and Bradley et al., *Churches and Church Membership,* 1.

13. Within Protestantism in the United States there are over 130 national or international "denominations" to which local churches belong. The sizes of these denominations vary greatly. For example, close to thirty-eight thousand local churches belong to the Southern Baptist Convention and as few as two belong to the General Six Principle Baptists. Keeping track of Protestant denominations is complicated, not only because of the large number of them but because of the ongoing formation of new denominations and the merging of older ones. Since 1980, approximately fifty new denominations have formed, and two major mergings — one of three different Lutheran denominations and the other of two Presbyterian denominations — have occurred.

Perhaps what is most confusing is that such names for different kinds of Protestants as "Baptist" or "Pentecostal" are nonspecific and do not describe a single denomination but an informal "family" or cluster of independent denominations. The various family names for these clusters of independent Protestant denominations are the following: Adventist, Baptist, Brethren, Christian (Churches of Christ), Churches of God, Friends, Lutheran, Mennonite, Methodist, Moravian, Pentecostal, Presbyterian, and Reformed. Different denominations that share a common history or tradition but have different practices, beliefs, or organizational structure may share one of these family names and may use it as part of a longer name. Within the Pentecostal family, for example, there are about thirty independent denominations, such as the Pentecostal Holiness Church and the United Pentecostal Church International. There are also some non-Protestant Christian families, such as Latter-day Saints, with four denominations, and the Eastern Orthodox, with over twenty.

Some Protestant denominations (such as the Episcopal Church, Congregational Christian Churches, and the Universal Fellowship of Metropolitan Community Churches) and other non-Protestant denominations (such as the Church of Christ, Scientist; Jehovah's Witnesses; and the Unitarian Universalist Association) do not have a family group.

There are also two thousand independent, nondenominational Christian churches, each with at least three hundred adherents and together totaling over two million adherents, in the United States. Depending on their style of worship, these are usually categorized as independent charismatic or independent noncharismatic churches. See Kosmin and Lachman, *One Nation under God,* 130–42, 291–98; Bradley et al., *Churches and Church Membership,* xiii, 1–3, 453; Kellstedt et al., "Religious Traditions and Religious Commitments in the USA," 2–8; Roof and McKinney, *American Mainline Religion,* 85–99, 253–56; and Kenneth B. Bedell, ed., *Yearbook of American and Canadian Churches, 1994* (Nashville: Abingdon, 1994), 49, 81, 96, 133–35, 161–62.

14. Such organizations are the Buddhist Churches of America, the Islamic Center of Washington, the Federation of Islamic Associations in the United States and Canada, the Council of Muslim Communities of Canada, and the Vedanta Societies of the Ramakrishna Mission. See Bedell, ed., *Yearbook of American and Canadian Churches, 1994,* 163–64; Kosmin and Lachman, *One Nation under God,* 125–26, 135, 151–53, 287–88; Robert C. Lester, *Buddhism: The Path to Nirvana* (San Francisco: Harper and Row, 1987), 140–43; and Fred-

erick M. Denny, *Islam and the Muslim Community* (San Francisco: Harper and Row, 1987), 109–17.

Chapter 1: Historical Overview

1. For a historical overview of organized religions and homosexuality within Western civilization and the world, see Warren J. Blumenfeld and Diane Raymond, *Looking at Gay and Lesbian Life,* rev. ed. (Boston: Beacon, 1993), 152–217; John Boswell, *Christianity, Social Tolerance, and Homosexuality: Gay People in Western Europe from the Beginning of the Christian Era to the Fourteenth Century* (Chicago: University of Chicago Press, 1980); and Arlene Swidler, ed., *Homosexuality and World Religions* (Valley Forge, Pa.: Trinity International, 1993).

2. See Jonathan Katz, *Gay American History: Lesbian and Gay Men in the U.S.A., A Documentary* (New York: Thomas Y. Crowell, 1976; Harper Colophon, 1985), 19–23, 569–70 n. 20; Louis Crompton, "Homosexuals and the Death Penalty in Colonial America," *Journal of Homosexuality* 1 (1976): 277–93; Robert Oaks, "Perceptions of Homosexuality by Justices of the Peace in Colonial Virginia," *Journal of Homosexuality* 5 (fall–winter 1979/80): 35–41; and Robert Oaks, "Defining Sodomy in Seventeenth-Century Massachusetts," in Salvatore J. Licata and Robert P. Petersen, eds., *The Gay Past: A Collection of Historical Essays* (New York: Haworth, 1986), 79–83.

3. *Encyclopedia of Crime and Justice,* 1st ed., s.v. "Homosexuality and Crime," by Anthony Russo and Laud Humphreys. See also Chris Bull, "Citing the Bible, Federal Judge OK's Ban on Marriage," *Advocate,* 11 February 1992, 20; Walter Barnett, *Sexual Freedom and the Constitution: An Inquiry into the Constitutionality of Repressive Sex Laws* (Albuquerque: University of New Mexico Press, 1973), 75; and John D'Emilio, *Sexual Politics, Sexual Communities: The Making of a Homosexual Minority in the United States 1940–1970* (Chicago: University of Chicago Press, 1983), 13–14.

4. See Alfred C. Kinsey, Wardell B. Pomeroy, and Clyde E. Martin, *Sexual Behavior in the Human Male* (Philadelphia: W. B. Saunders, 1948), 465, 487; Sara Harris, *The Puritan Jungle: America's Sexual Underground* (New York: Putnam, 1969), 169–75; Barnett, *Sexual Freedom and the Constitution,* 91–92 n. 48; William Paul, "Minority Status for Gay People: Majority Reaction and Social Context," in William Paul et al., eds., *Homosexuality: Social, Psychological, and Biological Issues* (Beverly Hills: Sage, 1982), 364; and Donald C. Knutson, introduction to *Homosexuality and the Law,* special issue of *Journal of Homosexuality* 5 (fall–winter 1979/80): 5–24.

5. *Bowers v. Hardwick* (excerpts from *Bowers v. Hardwick,* 106 U.S. 2841 [1986]), in Christine Pierce and Donald VanDeVeer, eds., *AIDS: Ethics and Public Policy* (Belmont, Calif.: Wadsworth, 1988), 219–29.

6. Ron Schow, Wayne Schow, and Marybeth Raynes, eds., *Peculiar People: Mormons and Same-Sex Orientation* (Salt Lake City: Signature Books, 1991), xxiv. In fact, without being sexually explicit records do show "strong emotional ties" among male church leaders and "considerable affection toward members

of the same sex" by both men and women. Such "homosocial" relationships were less frequently reported with the increasing influence of Victorian mores.

7. Katz, *Gay American History,* 33–34.

8. See Adam Clayton Powell Sr., *Against the Tide: An Autobiography* (New York: Richard R. Smith, 1938), 215–17; and George Chauncey, *Gay New York: Gender, Urban Culture, and the Making of the Gay Male World, 1890–1940* (New York: Basic Books, 1994), 254–56.

9. Walter L. Williams, *The Spirit and the Flesh: Sexual Diversity in American Indian Culture* (Boston: Beacon, 1988), 175–200. See also Evelyn Blackwood, "Sexuality and Gender in Certain Native American Tribes: The Case of Cross-Gender Females," *Signs: Journal of Women in Culture and Society* 10 (1984): 39–40; and Barry A. Kosmin and Seymour P. Lachman, *One Nation under God: Religion in Contemporary American Society* (New York: Harmony, 1993), 144. *Berdache* is itself a Western term used here to encompass the many terms used by various tribes for this alternate-gender role; see Williams, *Spirit and the Flesh,* 9–10. For a list tribes and their various terms, see Will Roscoe, "North American Tribes with Berdache and Alternative Gender Roles," in Roscoe, ed., and Gay American Indians, comp., *Living the Spirit: A Gay American Indian Anthology* (New York: St. Martin's, 1988), 217–22.

10. Robert W. Wood, *Lesbians and Gays in the UCC: Recollections of the Early History* (Athens, Ohio: United Church Coalition for Lesbian/Gay Concerns, n.d.), 1.

11. D'Emilio, *Sexual Politics, Sexual Communities,* 24–29, 32–33, 38, 58.

12. Kinsey, Pomeroy, and Martin, *Sexual Behavior in the Human Male,* and Alfred C. Kinsey et al., *Sexual Behavior in the Human Female* (Philadelphia: W. B. Saunders, 1953); *The Wolfenden Report: Report of the Committee on Homosexual Offenses and Prostitution,* authorized American ed. (New York: Stein and Day, 1963); D'Emilio, *Sexual Politics, Sexual Communities,* 33–37, 41–43, 48–49, 144–45; and Katz, *Gay American History,* 91–105.

13. Harry Emerson Fosdick, *On Being a Real Person* (New York: Harper and Brothers, 1943), viii, 184; and Henry P. Van Dusen, "The Moratorium on Moral Revulsion," *Christianity and Crisis,* 21 June 1949, 81. See also D'Emilio, *Sexual Politics, Sexual Communities,* 36; and, for an account the clinical pastoral education movement, see Richard Hasbany, ed., *Homosexuality and Religion* (New York: Haworth, 1990), 12–13.

14. Derrick Sherwin Bailey, *Homosexuality and the Western Christian Tradition* (London: Longmans, Green, 1955).

15. Robert W. Wood, *Christ and the Homosexual (Some Observations)* (New York: Vantage, 1960), and idem, *Lesbians and Gays in the UCC,* 2–3.

16. Alastair Heron, ed., *Towards a Quaker View of Sex* (London: Friends Home Service Committee, 1963); H. Kimball-Jones, *Toward a New Understanding of the Homosexual* (New York: Association, 1966); Norman W. Pittenger, *Time for Consent: A Christian Approach to Homosexuality* (London: SCM, 1967); "Civil Liberties and Homosexuality," *Social Action,* December 1967, and *Social Progress,* November–December 1967; *Christian Century,* 5 June 1968, 744–45; and D'Emilio, *Sexual Politics, Sexual Communities,* 215.

17. Ralph W. Weltge, ed., *The Same-Sex: An Appraisal of Homosexuality* (Philadelphia: United Church Press, 1969); and Solomon B. Freehof, "Homosexuality," *Current Reform Responsa* (Cincinnati: Hebrew Union College Press, 1969): 236–38.

18. See Schow, Schow, and Raynes, eds., *Peculiar People,* xxv.

19. John J. McNeill, "The Christian Male Homosexual," *Homiletic and Pastoral Review* 70 (1970): 667–77, 747–58, 828–36; Michael F. Valente, *Sex: The Radical View of a Catholic Theologian* (New York: Macmillan, 1970); and John G. Milhaven, *Toward a New Catholic Morality* (New York: Doubleday, 1970).

20. Charles Curran, "Homosexuality and Moral Theology: Methodological and Substantive Considerations," *The Thomist* 35 (1971): 447–81; W. Dwight Oberholtzer, ed., *Is Gay Good? Ethics, Theology, and Homosexuality* (Philadelphia: Westminster, 1971); for Blair, see Gay Task Force, *A Gay Bibliography,* 6th ed. (Philadelphia: American Library Association, 1980), and Gerald T. Sheppard, "The Use of Scripture within the Christian Ethical Debate concerning Same-Sex Oriented Persons," *Union Seminary Quarterly Review* 40 (1985): 32, 35 n. 43.

21. See, for example, Margaret Mead, *Male and Female: A Study of the Sexes in a Changing World* (New York: William Morrow, 1949); Clellan Ford and Frank Beach, *Patterns of Sexual Behavior* (New York: Harper, 1951); Nancy O. Lurie, "Winnebago Berdache," *American Anthropologist* 55 (1953): 708–12; Henry Angelino and Charles Shedd, "A Note on Berdache," *American Anthropologist* 57 (1955): 121–26; and Sue-Ellen Jacobs, "Berdache: A Brief Review of the Literature," *Colorado Anthropologist* 1 (1968): 25–40.

For reports and studies of cross-gendered women, see Alice Joseph, et al., *The Desert People* (Chicago: University of Chicago Press, 1949), 227; Edwin Thompson Denig, *Five Indian Tribes of the Upper Missouri* (Norman: University of Oklahoma Press, 1961), 195–200; John J. Honigmann, *The Kaska Indians: An Ethnographic Reconstruction* (New Haven: Yale University Press, 1964), 129–30; Claude Schaeffer, "The Kutenai Female Berdache: Courier, Guide, Prophetess, and Warrior," *Ethnohistory* 12 (1965): 195–216; and George Devereux, *Mohave Ethnopsychiatry* (Washington, D.C.: Smithsonian Institution, 1969), 262, 416–20.

22. Stuart Miller and Arthur Penn, producers, *Little Big Man* (Cinema Center Films, 1971); and John (Fire) Lame Deer and Richard Erdoes, *Lame Deer, Seeker of Visions* (New York: Simon and Schuster, 1972).

23. J. Gordon Melton, ed., *The Churches Speak on Homosexuality: Official Statements from Religious Bodies and Ecumenical Organizations* (Detroit: Gale Research, 1991), xviii.

24. Katz, *Gay American History,* 408, 417; D'Emilio, *Sexual Politics, Sexual Communities,* 101–7, 193–95, 204; and Del Martin and Phyllis Lyon, "Lesbian Liberation Begins: Early Days of the DOB," *Harvard Gay and Lesbian Review* winter 1995, 15–18.

25. D'Emilio, *Sexual Politics, Sexual Communities,* 193–95.

26. Ibid., 192–95, 202, 214–15.

27. Wood, *Lesbians and Gays in the UCC,* 7.

28. Edward Batchelor Jr., *Homosexuality and Ethics* (New York: Pilgrim, 1980), 239–40; and D'Emilio, *Sexual Politics, Sexual Communities,* 146.

29. Schow, Schow, and Raynes, eds., *Peculiar People,* xxv.

30. Wood, *Lesbians and Gays in the UCC,* 3, 4–5.

31. Batchelor, ed., *Homosexuality and Ethics,* 136–37.

32. Toby Marotta, *The Politics of Homosexuality* (Boston: Houghton Mifflin, 1981), 37; and D'Emilio, *Sexual Politics, Sexual Communities,* 215.

33. Yoel H. Kahn, "Judaism and Homosexuality: The Traditionalist/Progressive Debate," in Hasbany, ed., *Homosexuality and Religion,* 78 n. 10.

34. See D'Emilio, *Sexual Politics, Sexual Communities,* 227; and Kenneth B. Bedell, ed., *Yearbook of American and Canadian Churches, 1994* (Nashville: Abingdon, 1994), 130–31, 160.

35. Gary David Comstock, *Violence against Lesbians and Gay Men* (New York: Columbia University Press, 1991), 21–22.

36. Batchelor, ed., *Homosexuality and Ethics,* 237, 240–41.

37. Wood, *Lesbians and Gays in the UCC,* 8–11; "Personal News," *Waves* (United Church Coalition for Lesbian/Gay Concerns), June 1992, 5; and "Historic Ordination 20 Years Ago" and Byron Hiller Light, "Confessions of a Recovering Homophobic," *United Church News,* June 1992, 3.

38. Aaron Cooper, "No Longer Invisible: Gay and Lesbian Jews Build a Movement," in Hasbany, ed., *Homosexuality and Religion,* 84–85. Beth Chayim Chadashim was voted into membership by the Union of American Hebrew Congregations the following year, 1973.

39. See Seward Hiltner, "Homosexuality and the Churches," in Judd Marmor, ed., *Homosexual Behavior: A Modern Appraisal* (New York: Basic Books, 1980), 222–23.

40. Batchelor, ed., *Homosexuality and Ethics,* 235–42. See also James G. Wolf, *Gay Priests* (San Francisco: Harper and Row, 1989), 13–15; and Vincent J. Genovesi, "Human Rights and Civil Rights for Gays and Lesbians," *America,* 22 April 1995, 15–20.

41. See Randall Frame, "The Issue That Won't Go Away," *Christianity Today,* 5 March 1990, 28; Kenneth S. Kantzer, "Homosexuals in the Church," *Christianity Today,* 22 April 1978, 8; and James Davison Hunter, *Culture Wars: The Struggle to Define America* (New York: Basic Books, 1991), 189.

42. Mearle L. Griffith and C. David Lundquist, *Survey of Delegates to the 1992 General Conference of the United Methodist Church* (Dayton: Office of Research, General Council on Ministries, United Methodist Church, 1992).

43. For a comprehensive presentation of official positions, see Melton, ed., *Churches Speak on Homosexuality.*

For a bibliographic listing of reports, resolutions, and statements by denominations, see Ray Mesler, "One View of the Current Status of Homosexual Persons in Various Church Denominations in the United States" (M.Div. thesis, Union Theological Seminary, New York City, 1984), 155–63. In his survey of Christian denominations Mesler finds that 75 percent have taken official positions ("One View," 73–90). See also Batchelor, ed., *Homosexuality and Ethics,* 235–42.

For analyses of positions, studies, reports, and debates, see Richard L. Smith, *AIDS, Gays, and the American Catholic Church* (Cleveland: Pilgrim, 1994); Jeffrey S. Siker, ed., *Homosexuality in the Church: Both Sides of the Debate* (Louisville: Westminster/John Knox, 1994); Sally B. Geis and Donald E. Messer, eds., *Caught in the Crossfire: Helping Christians Debate Homosexuality* (Nashville: Abingdon, 1994); Albert R. Jonsen and Jeff Stryker, eds., *The Social Impact of AIDS in the United States* (Washington, D.C.: National Academy Press, 1993), 117–57; Patricia Beattie Jung and Ralph F. Smith, *Heterosexism: An Ethical Challenge* (Albany: State University of New York Press, 1993), 115–65; Blumenfeld and Raymond, *Looking at Gay and Lesbian Life,* 152–217; Arlene Swidler, ed., *Homosexuality and World Religions* (Valley Forge, Pa.: Trinity International, 1993), 124–27, 149–79; Hunter, *Culture Wars,* 91–95, 192–94; Robert Nugent and Jeannine Gramick, "Homosexuality: Protestant, Catholic, and Jewish Issues: A Fishbone Tale," in Hasbany, ed., *Homosexuality and Religion,* 19–28; symposium entitled "Homosexuals and Homosexuality: Psychiatrists, Religious Leaders and Laymen Compare Notes," *Judaism* 32 (1983): 390–443; and James B. Nelson, *Embodiment: An Approach to Sexuality and Christian Theology* (Minneapolis: Augsburg, 1978), 180–210.

44. See, for example, Nancy Bartley, "When Religion and Sexuality Collide; Some Fear Issue Will Tear Presbyterian Church Apart," *Seattle Times,* 22 May 1993, C7; Larry Witham, "Church Writings on Sex May Spark Revolt from Pews," *Washington Times,* 21 January 1992, A1; Paul Hornick, "Articles Reveal the Real Threat to Churches," *Houston Chronicle,* 6 December 1991, A37; David Firestone, "Churches' Struggle on Accepting Gays," *New York Newsday,* 24 November 1991, 7; "Homosexuality Is a Divisive Issue within Churches, Report Says," *Los Angeles Times,* 16 November 1991, F15; Russell Chandler, "A Sexual Agenda at Church; Major Denominations Are Reappraising Their Positions on Everything from Homosexuality to Premarital Sex," *Los Angeles Times,* 6 June 1991, A1; Thomas J. Billitteri, "Divisions in the Church," *St. Petersburg Times,* 25 May 1991, 4E; Ron McCracken, "Why the Surprise in Decline of Church Attendance?" *Toronto Star,* 4 May 1991, G11; Monica Copeland, "New Group Leaves Church: 'Apartheid' Cited in Catholicism," *Washington Post,* 7 April 1990, C14; "Episcopal Synod Could Divide Church," *Chicago Tribune,* 4 June 1989, 32C; Peter Steinfels, "New Group Fights Episcopal Changes," *New York Times,* 3 June 1989, sec. 1, 8; "Some Fear Homosexuality Dominating Methodist Meeting," *Chicago Tribune,* 29 April 1988, 5C; John Dart, "Methodist Church Hurt by Diversity of Beliefs, Bishop from L.A. Says," *Los Angeles Times,* 27 April 1988, sec. 1, 3; Julia Duin, "Mainline Methodists Denounce Liberal Trends," *Christianity Today,* 5 February 1988, 51–52; "Catholic Dissenters Draw Blame for Church's Woes," *Los Angeles Times,* 6 September 1986, section 2, 5; and Marjorie Hyer, "Liberal-Conservative Fights Wrench Protestant Denominations," *Washington Post,* 29 May 1981, C12.

45. Harlan W. Penn, "Ordination in the Presbyterian Church (U.S.A.): Unjustified and Hysterical Fears," *More Light Update,* December 1989, 13–14 (reprinted from *The Presbyterian Outlook,* 4–11 September 1989).

46. Mark Bowman, Reconciling Church Program, Inc., telephone conversation, 8 February 1994.

47. William B. Abernethy, "The Wellesley Congregational Church, UCC," *Open Hands,* winter 1993, 16. See also James B. Nelson, *Body Theology* (Louisville: Westminster/John Knox, 1992), 55–57.

48. See D'Arcy Jenish, "Empty Pews, Angry Members: Churches Confront the Decline," *Maclean's,* 12 April 1993, 48; Michael McAteer, "United Church Membership Drops by 22,000," *Toronto Star,* 27 May 1992, A15; Bob Harvey, "Churches Split Over Gays' Role, *Ottawa Citizen,* 7 December 1991, C10; Nancy Hardesty, "Holy Wars: Gays and Lesbians Fight Organized Religion," *Advocate* (Los Angeles), 4 December 1990, 37; Anne M. Squire, "Homosexuality, Ordination, and the United Church of Canada," *Queen's Quarterly* 98 (1991): 338–52; and Charles Moorhouse (Letter from United Church of Canada member), *More Light Update* (Presbyterians for Lesbian and Gay Concerns), December 1989, 11–12.

49. See David A. Roozen and C. Kirk Hadaway, eds., *Church and Denominational Growth: What Does (And Does Not) Cause Growth or Decline?* (Nashville: Abingdon, 1993), 208–9, 234, 239, 346–57; and Robin D. Perrin, "American Religion in the Post-Aquarian Age: Values and Demographic Factors in Church Growth and Decline," *Journal for the Scientific Study of Religion* 28 (1989): 75–89.

50. See Hunter, *Culture Wars,* 10–11, 91–95, 192–93; Mary Nemeth, Nora Underwood, and John Howse, "God Is Alive: Despite Common Assumptions about the Decline of Religion, Most Canadians Are Committed Christians," *Maclean's,* 12 April 1993, 32; and Joe Wakelee-Lynch, "Should I Stay or Should I Go? Christian Gays and Lesbians Debate Their Place in the Church," *Utne Reader,* January–February 1992, 40, 42.

51. Mary E. Hunt, "A Four Word Letter (Not to Be Confused with a Four Letter Word)," *More Light Update* (Newsletter of Presbyterians for Lesbian and Gay Concerns), August 1991, 4–8.

52. Pat Long, "Pullen Memorial Baptist Church: An Inside Look at a Journey of Affirmation," *Voice of the Turtle* (Newsletter of American Baptists Concerned for Lesbian, Gay and Bisexual People), fall 1992, 5–6.

53. The following list of articles provides a sampling of coverage by mainstream newspapers in North American: David W. Dunlap, "Gay Writer Fasts in Jail, Seeking Talk with Pat Robertson," *New York Times,* 5 March 1995, sec. 1, 24; Peter Steinfels, "Rabbis Draw Up Ethics of Nonmarital Sex," *New York Times,* 30 April 1994, 8; Gayle White, "Clinton Worries Religious Right; Evangelicals Take Aim at Social Agenda," *Atlanta Journal and Constitution,* 20 February 1993, E6; "American Baptists' Vote to Condemn Gays Fails," *Los Angeles Times,* 27 June 1992, B5; Douglas Todd, "Anglican Minister Says She'll Seek Justice for Fired Gay Priest," *Vancouver Sun,* 28 April 1992, A3; Don Lattin, "Church Should Reassess Homosexuality, Says Evangelical Lutheran Report," *San Francisco Chronicle,* 6 December 1991, A27; James L. Franklin, "Orthodox Stay Out of Church Body: Greek Clerics Cite Discord over Women, Homosexuality," *Boston Globe,* 12 September 1991, 31; Sue Ellen Christian, "Nominee Faces Battle in Disciples of Christ; Issues of Sexuality Dividing Church," *Chicago Tribune,* 2 August 1991, 8C; Gerald Renner, "Episcopalians Avoid Confrontation in Vote on Ordaining Homosexuals," *Hartford*

Courant, 20 July 1991, B6; Maria Puente, "Presbyterians Reject New Sexual Ethics," *USA Today,* 11 June 1991, 1A; Michael McAteer, "United Church [of Canada] in Critical Debate on Homosexuality," *Toronto Star,* 19 August 1990, A11; R. Gustav Niebuhr and Wade Lambert, "Lutherans Suspend Congregation for Hiring Lesbians as Ministers," *Wall Street Journal,* 19 July 1990, B4; Phyllis Winfield, "Views on Gay Rabbis Mixed: Reform Jews Vote to Let Homosexuals Join the Clergy," *Seattle Times,* 30 June 1990, A14; C. H. White, "[Southern] Baptists Attack Homosexuality in Stinging Resolution," *Houston Chronicle,* 17 June 1989, 22A; Dyan Zaslowsky, "Buddhists in U.S. Agonize on AIDS Issue," *New York Times,* 21 February 1989, A14; Jeanne Pugh, "Methodists Again Reject Homosexuality," *St. Petersburg Times,* 3 May 1988, 1A; Joan Barthel, "Dissent into Darkness: The Vatican and Catholic University's Father Charles Curran Disagreed over What a Priest Could Teach about Abortion, Contraception and Homosexuality," *Washington Post,* 22 March 1987, W15; "Tapes Cite Three Homosexual Acts by Bakker; Falwell Says Church Leaders Received Testimony on Encounters," *Los Angeles Times,* 28 May 1987, sec. 1, 2; "AIDS Victim Excommunicated by Mormon Church Court Dies," *Los Angeles Times,* 19 March 1986, sec. 2, 2; "Methodists File Charges against Homosexual Pastor," *Chicago Tribune,* 25 June 1985, 8C; "Unitarian Universalist Association Approves Religious Blessings of Homosexual Unions," *New York Times,* 29 June 1984, sec. 1, 10; Edward A. Gargan, "Rights Issue Perils City–Salvation Army Pact," *New York Times,* 22 December 1983, A1; Marjorie Hyer, "Panel to Probe Charge against Methodist Bishop," *Washington Post,* 8 May 1982, B6; "Mormon Church Elder Calls Homosexuality an Addiction," *New York Times,* 6 April 1981, A12; Marjorie Hyer, "United Church of Christ Produces New 'Study Guide on Ordination and Sexuality,'" *Washington Post,* 10 October 1980, B10; "Brigham Young University Official Confirms Stake Out of Homosexual Bars," *New York Times,* 27 September 1979, 16; Constance d'au Vin, "Orthodox Jewish Leader Set to Fight against 'Gay Rights,'" *Washington Post,* 19 May 1978, C16; "General Assembly of Christian Church Accepts Study to Work for Civil Rights for Homosexuals," *New York Times,* 24 October 1977, 56; and "Seventh-Day Adventist Church President Condemns Homosexual Behavior," *New York Times,* 22 August 1977, 17.

54. For discussion of efforts by organized religion to oppose and support gay rights, see Ted G. Jelen and Clyde Wilcox, "Religion in America: The Christian Right in the 1990s," *Public Perspective,* March–April 1993, 10; and Hunter, *Culture Wars,* 3–12.

55. For news media coverage of the legal proceedings, see Joyce Purnick, "Court Overrules Order by Koch on Sexual Bias," *New York Times,* 29 June 1985, sec. 1, 1; Alan Finder and Albert Scardino, "Court Upholds Mayor's Order on Homosexuals," *New York Times,* 12 May 1985, sec. 4, 6; Alan Finder and Katherine Roberts, "Koch's Order on Homosexual Bias Overturned," *New York Times,* 9 September 1984, sec. 4, 6; Marcia Chambers, "Judge Bars City from Enforcing Bias Order," *New York Times,* 30 June 1984, sec. 1, 28; Michael Goodwin, "Koch Eases Edict on Homosexuals Pending Church Court Challenge," *New York Times,* 21 June 1984, A1; and Michael Goodwin, "Salvation

Army Losing City Pacts for Stand on Hiring Homosexuals," *New York Times,* 3 March 1984, sec. 1, 1.

56. "African-American Clergy Speak Out for Gay Rights," *Voice of the Turtle* (Newsletter of American Baptists Concerned for Lesbians and Gay Men), fall 1991, 7.

57. See the following articles by John Gallagher in the *Advocate:* "Pride and Prejudice: Facing Tough Battles over Ballot Initiatives, Activists in Missouri and Idaho Scramble to Avoid Past Mistakes" and "Initiatives: A Black-and-White Issue in Missouri?" 12 July 1994, 32–34, 36–39; "Partnership Disagreement: The Bid to Repeal a Domestic-Partnership Law in Austin, Tex., Was Expected to Fail; So Why Did It Win Big?" 14 June 1994, 22; "Us vs. Them: State of the Union," 2 November 1993, 41–51; "Taking the Initiative: Battles over Gay Rights Intensify in Ohio, Florida, Colorado, and Oregon" and "Troubled Alliance: A Hot Debate in San Francisco Complicates the Tense Relationship between the Gay and Black Civil Rights Movement," 5 October 1993, 24–27, 36–40; "The Awful Truce: Oregon Tries to Ban Antigay Initiatives, but the Courts Will Have the Last Word," 7 September 1993, 30–31; "Shoutout in Oregon: Six Localities Pass Measures that Ban Enactment of Gay Rights Laws," 10 August 1993, 30; "Bracing for the Battle: Antigay Initiatives in Five States Are a Call to Arms for Activists Fearful of Colorado-Style Repeats," 29 June 1993, 50, 52–54; "Colorado Goes Straight to Hell," 23 February 1993, 34–42; "A Tale of Two Strategies: Campaigns in Two States Each Beat Back Antigay Ballot Measures but Have Few Other Similarities," 12 January 1993, 54–55; "The Rise of Fascism in America: How Antigay Hate Became a Fact of Political Life in Oregon," 3 November 1992, 37–43; and with Katrin Show, "The Right's New Strategy: In Oregon Hate Rages in the Name of 'Family Values,'" 30 July 1992, 46–49.

58. See Chris Bull, "A Family That Prays Together: Pam Walton Seeks a Truce with a Leading Figure on the Religious Right — Her Father," *Advocate,* 13 December 1994, 46–47; and "'Homosexuality Makes God Vomit': A Fundamentalist Leader's Antigay Viewpoint" (interview with Jay Grimstead, director of Coalition on Revival), *Advocate,* 20 October 1992, 42–43.

59. Lyman A. Kellstedt et al., "Religious Traditions and Religious Commitments in the USA" (paper prepared for the Twenty-Second International Conference of the International Society for the Sociology of Religion, Budapest, 19–23 July 1993), 6–7.

For information showing that many conservative, evangelical, and fundamentalist Christians are not against gay rights, see Michael Penn-Strah, "An Evangelical Heart Talks about Sexual Orientation," *Growingplans* (United Church Board for Homeland Ministries, Division of Evangelism and Local Church Development), spring 1995, 18–19; Tom Griffith, "Give a Cheer for Our Evangelical Brothers and Sisters," *Open Hands,* winter 1995, 22; Richard L. Berke, "Christian Right Defies Categories: Survey Discloses Diversity in Politics and Religion," *New York Times,* 22 July 1994, A1, A16; Andrew M. Greeley, "Religion and Attitudes towards AIDS Policy," *Sociology and Social Research* 75 (April 1991): 126–32; Randall L. Frame, "The Evangelical Closet: Conservative Christianity's Struggle with Homosexuality May Be More Common Than Many Like to Admit," *Christianity Today,* 5 November 1990, 56–57; and Chris

Bull, "Rights Bill Looks Secure: Massachusetts Measure Is Saved by Religion," *Advocate* (Los Angeles), 30 January 1990, 13.

60. See Richard L. Berke, "Christian Coalition Unveils 'Suggestions,'" *New York Times,* 18 May 1995, B13, and idem, "Two Top Republicans Soften Their Tone: Quayle and Bennett Are among Speakers at Christian Conference," *New York Times,* 17 September 1994, 9; and Ralph Reed Jr., "The Religious Right Reaches Out," *New York Times,* 22 August 1993, section 4, 15.

61. See, for example, Genovesi, "Human Rights and Civil Rights for Gays and Lesbians," 15–20.

62. Sue Levi Elwell, "The Lesbian and Gay Movement: Jewish Community Responses," in Christie Balka and Andy Rose, eds., *Twice Blessed: On Being Lesbian or Gay and Jewish* (Boston: Beacon, 1989), 230.

63. Marjorie Hyer, "Bible 'Inaccurate' Guide to Sexual Mores Today," *Washington Post,* 4 July 1977, A3.

64. I alter the typology of stances (rejecting-punitive, rejecting-nonpunitive, qualified acceptance, and accepting) offered by Nelson, *Embodiment,* 188–99, because, as Nelson himself admits, the assumption "that it is possible to reject ...and still be nonpunitive" is flawed. See also David Kelsey, "Homosexuality and the Church: Theological Issues," *Reflection* 80 (1983): 9–12.

65. For those religious bodies that have arrived at conclusive positions, the process has often involved in-depth study, protracted committee work, and complex legislative procedures. See, for example, Yoshio Fukuyama, "The United Church of Christ and Human Sexuality: The Life Cycle of a Social Concern," *Chicago Theological Seminary Register* 76 (fall 1986): 1–10.

66. See Kim Byham, "Episcopal Church Begins Study of Union Blessings," *Second Stone,* September/October 1994, 1, 10; Sam A. Portaro, "Homosexuality as Vocation," *Witness,* June 1991, 18–19, 25; Hardesty, "Holy Wars," 35; Nugent and Gramick, "Homosexuality," in Hasbany, ed., *Homosexuality and Religion,* 23–24.

67. Schow, Schow, and Raynes, eds., *Peculiar People,* xxv–xxviii. See also Vern Anderson, "Homosexuals Struggle to Find Acceptance within Their Faith Lifestyle: More Often, the Pressure to Conform to the Church's Heterosexual Ideal Fosters Marriages, Duplicity, Profound Guilt, Anger and Despair," *Los Angeles Times,* 28 December 1991, F16; and in the *Advocate,* see Robert I. McQueen's articles, "Mormons Show Fear," 18 June 1975, 15; "BYU Inquisition" and "Dogma according to Kimball," 13 August 1975, 14–15; and other articles, "Mormons Excommunicate Editor of *Advocate,*" 9 August 1979, 10–11, and "Gay Mormons Organize," 2 November 1977, 30.

68. Lutheran Church in America, *A Study of Issues concerning Homosexuality* (Division for Mission in North America, 1986), 38.

69. See Mesler, "One View."

70. See Judith Berns, "The Making of a Jewish, Lesbian Buddhist," *Sinister Wisdom* 54 (winter 1994/95): 22–28; Erin Culley, "Get Thee to a Monastery," *Out,* October 1994, 88; "Dalai Lama in *Out,*" *Trikone: Gay and Lesbian South Asians,* April 1994, 13; Margaret Miller and Lee Moriwaki, "A Lesson on Life, Happiness—Anyone Can Achieve It, Says Dalai Lama to Seattle Crowd," *Seattle Times,* 29 June 1993, B1; Sandy Boucher, *Turning the Wheel: American*

Women Creating the New Buddhism, rev. ed. (Boston: Beacon, 1993), 43, 169–70, 177, 180, 243–44, 255, 319, 343; José Ignacio Cabezon, "Homosexuality and Buddhism," in Swidler, ed., *Homosexuality and World Religions,* 94; Rita Gross, "The Householder and the World Renunciant: Two Modes of Sexual Expression in Buddhism," *Journal of Ecumenical Studies* 22 (winter 1985): 83, 96; and Tensho David Schneider, "Accidents and Calculations: The Emergence of Three AIDS Hospices," *Tricycle: The Buddhist Review* 1 (spring 1992): 78–83.

71. About Islam and homosexuality in the United States little has been written. For accounts of anti-gay statements and action by Muslim spokesmen, organizations, and individuals, see Katherine S. Mangan, "Conservative Students Challenge Support for Campus Gay Organizations," *Chronicle of Higher Education,* 27 January 1995, A38; James C. McKinley Jr., "Man Accused in Terror Plot Bombed Gay Bar, U.S. Says," *New York Times,* 14 January 1995, 26; Chris Bull, "Farrakhan under Fire: The Nation of Islam Leader Catches Heat over a Deputy's Anti-Semitic Remarks; But What about the Aide's Antigay Comments?" *Advocate,* 8 March 1994, 25–26; Jon Nordheimer, "Divided by a Diatribe: College Speech Ignites Furor over Race," *New York Times,* 29 December 1993, B1, B6; and Peter Steinfels, "U.S. Muslims, Despite World Spotlight, Focus on the Personal," *New York Times,* 7 May 1993, A20.

Several gay people have begun the task of appropriating the Muslim tradition and developing a Muslim apologetic for same-gender sexuality. See, for example, Shahid Dossani, "Gay by the Grace of Allah," *Trikone: Gay and Lesbian South Asians,* July 1994, 1, 7, 8; Khalid Duran, "Homosexuality and Islam," in Swidler, ed., *Homosexuality and World Religions,* 181–97; Rakesh Ratti, ed., *A Lotus of Another Color: An Unfolding of the South Asian Gay and Lesbian Experience* (Boston: Alyson, 1993); and Arno Schmitt and Jehoeda Sofer, eds., *Sexuality and Eroticism among Males in Moslem Societies* (Binghamton, N.Y.: Harrington Park, 1992).

72. In *Trikone,* see Shaffiq Essajee, guest editorial, April 1994, ii; and Karim Merchant, "Gay and Lesbian Muslim Voices," July 1994, 8.

73. See Curtis Harris and Leota Lone Dog (interview by Deborah Blincoe), "Two Spirited People: Understanding Who We Are as Creation," *New York Folklore* 19 (1993): 155–65; Joe Rio, "What Do Indians Think About?" in Loraine Hutchins and Lani Kaahumanu, eds., *Bi Any Other Name: Bisexual People Speak Out* (Boston: Alyson, 1991), 37–39; Randy Burns, preface to Roscoe, ed., *Living the Spirit,* 1–5; Williams, *The Spirit and the Flesh,* 201–29; Paula Gunn Allen, *The Sacred Hoop: Recovering the Feminine in American Indian Traditions* (Boston: Beacon, 1986), 194–208, 245–61; Robert Lynch, "Seeing Twice," *Southern Exposure,* November–December 1985, 90–93; and Judy Grahn, *Another Mother Tongue: Gay Words, Gay Worlds* (Boston: Beacon, 1984), 49–72.

74. For overviews, see Robert Goss, *Jesus Acted Up: A Gay and Lesbian Manifesto* (San Francisco: HarperSanFrancisco, 1993), 118–21; Marvin M. Ellison, "Homosexuality and Protestantism," in Swidler, ed., *Homosexuality and World Religions,* 149–79; Nugent and Gramick, "Homosexuality," in Hasbany, ed., *Homosexuality and Religion,* 7–46; and Beverly Wildung Harrison, *Making*

the Connections: Essays in Feminist Social Ethics, ed. Carol S. Robb (Boston: Beacon, 1985), 135–51.

75. Jim Gittings, "Clergy and Sexuality: The Pot Still Simmers," *Christianity and Crisis,* 20 July 1992, 251.

76. *Special Conference Issue* of *Affirmation* (United Methodists for Lesbian, Gay and Bisexual Concerns), summer 1992.

77. Morris L. Floyd, "If You Had Asked...," *Reporter* (United Methodist Church), 26 July 1991 (reprinted in *Affirmation,* fall 1991, 3).

78. Mesler, "One View," 149–51. See also J. Giles Milhaven, "How the Church Can Learn from Gay and Lesbian Experience," in Jeannine Gramick and Pat Furey, eds., *The Vatican and Homosexuality: Reactions to the "Letter to the Bishops of the Catholic Church on the Pastoral Care of Homosexual Persons"* (New York: Crossroad, 1988), 216–23.

79. Surveys typically do not break down Jewish respondents by their Orthodox, Conservative, Reformed, and Reconstructionist identities.

80. See Lynn E. Kunkel and Lori L. Temple, "Attitudes towards AIDS and Homosexuals: Gender, Marital Status, and Religion," *Journal of Applied Social Psychology* 22 (1992): 1030–40; John K. Cochran and Leonard Beeghley, "The Influence of Religion on Attitudes toward Nonmarital Sexuality: A Preliminary Assessment of Reference Group Theory," *Journal for the Scientific Study of Religion* 30 (1991): 45–62; and Bradley R. Hertel and Michael Hughes, "Religious Affiliation, Attendance, and Support for 'Pro-Family' Issues in the United States," *Social Forces* 65 (1987): 858–82.

81. See Wade Clark Roof and William McKinney, *American Mainline Religion: Its Changing Shape and Future* (New Brunswick, N.J.: Rutgers University Press, 1987), 211–13; and Jeannine Gramick, "Homosexuality to Be a Burning Catholic Issue" (letter), *New York Times,* 11 July 1992, 18.

82. Common Vision Planning Committee, *Report and Recommendations of the Common Vision Planning Committee to the Board of Trustees, Unitarian Universalist Association* (Boston: Unitarian Universalist Association, January 1989).

83. John Dart, "Majority in the Survey Say Gays Should Not Be Barred from Serving in the Clergy," *Los Angeles Times,* 5 January 1992, 25A.

84. Frances Green, ed., *Gayellow Pages,* U.S./Canada edition, no. 19 (New York: Renaissance House, 1988), 44–45, lists national religious organizations. For discussion of denominations' treatment of caucuses, see Goss, *Jesus Acted Up,* 122–23; Denise Carmody and John Carmody, "Homosexuality and Roman Catholicism"; Ellison, "Homosexuality and Protestantism," in Swidler, ed., *Homosexuality and World Religions,* 144–45, 152; Richard D. Mohr, *Gay Ideas: Outing and Other Controversies* (Boston: Beacon, 1992), 82–83; and Elwell, "The Lesbian and Gay Movement," in Balka and Rose, eds., *Twice Blessed,* 228–35.

85. Ina Mae Murri, "Lesbian and Mormon," in Schow, Schow, and Raynes, eds., *Peculiar People,* 39–40.

86. Merchant, "Gay and Lesbian Muslim Voices," *Trikone,* July 1994, 8.

87. See *Welcoming Churches: A Growing Ecumenical Movement,* special issue of *Open Hands,* winter 1993.

88. See Robert L. Kuyper, ed., *Transforming Congregations* (newsletter), Bakersfield, Calif.; and *The Loving Opposition, Our Response to the Homosexual Crisis,* special issue of *Christianity Today,* 19 June 1993.

For critiques of the ex-gay movement, see Keith Clark, " 'Ex-Gay' Ministries and 'Curing' Homosexuality," *More Light Update* (Presbyterians for Lesbian and Gay Concerns), April 1995, 10–13; Sara Miles, "Soul to Soul," *Out,* October 1994, 94–97; video documentary by Teodoro Maniaci and Francine M. Rzeznik, codirectors, *One Nation under God* (New York: 3Z/Hourglass Productions, 199[illegible]); *Ex-gay Movement,* special issue of *Dialogue* (Brethren/Mennonite Council for Gay and Lesbian Concerns), April 1990; Frederic Millen, "Exodus Cofounders Tell Ex-gay Movement to Get Real," *Advocate,* 4 December 1990, 39; Sylvia Pennington, *Ex-gays: There Are None!* (Hawthorne, Calif.: Lambda Christian Fellowship, 1989); and Ralph Blair, *Ex-gay* (New York: Homosexual Community Counseling Center, 1982).

89. For a discussion of the movement to create gay synagogues, see Lewis John Eron, "Homosexuality and Judaism," in Swidler, ed., *Homosexuality and World Religions,* 124, 126; Aliza Maggid, "Joining Together: Building a Worldwide Movement," and Janet R. Marder, "Getting to Know the Gay and Lesbian Shul: A Rabbi Moves from Tolerance to Acceptance," in Balka and Rose, eds., *Twice Blessed,* 157–70, 209–27; Kahn, "Judaism and Homosexuality," and Aaron Cooper, "No Longer Invisible: Gay and Lesbian Jews Build a Movement," in Hasbany, ed., *Homosexuality and Religion,* 58–60, 65, 83–94; Henry Rabinowitz, "Talmud Class in a Gay Synagogue," *Judaism* 32 (1983): 433–43; Barry D. Schwartz, "Homosexuality: A Jewish Perspective," *United Synagogue Review Quarterly* 30 (1977): 27; J. Stern, "Report of the Ad Hoc Committee on Homosexual Congregations," *CCAR Yearbook* 84 (1974): 28–29; and Sanford Ragins, "An Echo of the Plea of Our Fathers," *CCAR Journal* 20 (1973): 45.

For a discussion of Faith Temple, an independent evangelical, charismatic church with a predominantly African-American congregation in Washington, D.C., see Neil Miller, *In Search of Gay America: Women and Men in a Time of Change* (New York: Atlantic Monthly, 1989; Perennial Library, 1990), 241–56; and James S. Tinney, "Why a Black Gay Church?" in Joseph Beam, ed., *In the Life: A Black Gay Anthology* (Boston: Alyson, 1986), 70–86.

For a study of an independent, conservative, evangelical Christian organization in Atlanta, see Scott Thumma, "Negotiating a Religious Identity: The Case of the Gay Evangelical," *Sociological Analysis* 52 (1991): 333–47.

For the formation of Goddess worshiping groups by lesbians, see Lillian Faderman, *Odd Girls and Twilight Lovers: A History of Lesbian Life in Twentieth-Century America* (New York: Columbia University Press, 1991), 227–28; and Grahn, *Another Mother Tongue.* For accounts of pagan groups formed by gay men, see Mark Thompson, ed., *Gay Spirit: Myth and Meaning* (New York: St. Martin's, 1987), 260–78, 292–302.

See *Trikone,* September 1988, 6; July 1988, 6; and January 1988, 2, for announcements about Radha Krishna Seva Sangha, an association of Lesbian and Gay Vaudiya Vaishnavas that organized regular kirtan evenings, festivals, cultural programs, and had a special outreach for those with AIDS.

90. See, for example, Greg Grisa, "Deliberately Diverse: The Sojourner Truth Congregation," *UULGC World* (Unitarian Universalists for Lesbian and Gay Concerns), January 1993, 4; Joseph Hanania, "New Leader for Family of Gay Worshippers; Rabbi Marc Blumenthal Hopes Mainstream Judaism Will Soon Accept His Congregation into Its Spiritual Home," *Los Angeles Times,* 27 September 1992, J1; "UCC Admits Gay Church," *Christian Century,* 30 May to 6 June 1990, 563; "Spirit of the Lakes Received into the UCC," *Waves* (United Church Coalition for Lesbian/Gay Concerns), May 1990, 1, 2–3; "Reconstructionists Admit Gay/Lesbian Synagogue," *World Congress Digest* (World Congress of Gay and Lesbian Jewish Organizations), fall 1989, 2; "Nation's Reform Jews Accept Gay Temple," *Advocate,* 11 September 1974, 24; and Erwin L. Herman, "A Synagogue for Jewish Homosexuals?" *Central Conference of American Rabbis* 20 (summer 1973): 33–40.

91. Schneider, "Accidents and Calculations," 78–83.

92. As of fall 1993, member organizations were from Arizona, California, Colorado, Connecticut, the District of Columbia, Florida, Georgia, Illinois, Indiana, Kentucky, Maine, Massachusetts, Michigan, Minnesota, Missouri, Nebraska, New York, Ohio, Pennsylvania, Texas, and Washington and from Australia, Austria, Belgium, Canada, England, France, Hungary, Israel, Netherlands, South Africa, and Sweden. In its newsletter, *World Congress Digest,* see "World Congress Has a Busy, Productive Spring," and "World Congress Member Organizations," fall 1993, 1, 4; "1972–1992: Twenty Years of Gay and Lesbian Jewish Community," summer 1992, 1–5; and "World Congress Grows to 5 Continents," spring 1992, 1.

93. See Bedell, ed., *Yearbook of American and Canadian Churches, 1994,* 130–31, 160; Troy D. Perry, *The Lord Is My Shepherd and He Knows I'm Gay: The Autobiography of the Reverend Troy D. Perry* (New York: Bantam, 1972); Troy D. Perry and Thomas L. P. Swicegood, *Don't Be Afraid Anymore: The Story of Reverend Troy Perry and the Metropolitan Community Churches* (New York: St. Martin's, 1990); and Ronald M. Enroth, "The Homosexual Church: An Ecclesiastical Extension of a Subculture," *Social Compass* 21 (1974): 355–60.

94. See Perry and Swicegood, *Don't Be Afraid Anymore,* 230–68.

95. Williams, *Spirit and the Flesh,* 210–12; Burns, preface to Roscoe, ed., *Living the Spirit,* 1–5; Beth Brant, "Recovery and Transformation: The Blue Heron," in Lisa Albrecht and Rose M. Brewer, eds., *Bridges of Power: Women's Multicultural Alliances* (Philadelphia: New Society, 1990), 118–21; and Harris and Lone Dog, "Two Spirited People," 155–64.

96. [Kevin Gordon], *Homosexuality and Social Justice: Reissue of the Report of the Task Force on Gay/Lesbian Issues, San Francisco,* updated and expanded ed. (San Francisco: Consultation on Homosexuality, Social Justice, and Roman Catholic Theology, 1986).

97. Division for Church in Society, Department for Studies of the Evangelical Lutheran Church in American, *First Draft of a Social Statement, The Church and Human Sexuality: A Lutheran Perspective* (Chicago: Evangelical Lutheran Church in America, 1993), 12.

Chapter 2: Methodology and Studies

1. United Methodist Church, "Report of the Committee to Study Homosexuality" (Dayton: General Council on Ministries, 1992), from "Report on the Study of Homosexuality," *Daily Christian Advocate,* petition no. FM-10865-3000-A, 1992, 5 May 1992, 265–81; see 268.

2. Evangelical Lutheran Church in America, *Human Sexuality and the Christian Faith: A Study for the Church's Reflection and Deliberation* (Minneapolis: Division for Church in Society ELCA, 1991), 41; and Presbyterian Church U.S.A., *Presbyterians and Human Sexuality 1991,* 203rd General Assembly response to the report of the Special Committee on Human Sexuality, including a "Minority Report" (Louisville: Office of the General Assembly PCUSA, 1991), 45–46, 48, 55–56.

An earlier and pioneering study by the United Church of Christ, *Human Sexuality: A Preliminary Study* (New York: United Church Press, 1977), may have been precedent-setting for the format and content of the later studies. It relies on the work of scholars and experts to discuss the Bible, ethics, psychology, public policy, and sex education. It also acknowledges the "important contributions" by members of the gay caucus to the study: "Their insights into the nature of sexuality are profound, living as they have on the boundary of human acceptance and defining the nature of personhood, intimacy, masculinity, and femininity in the context of their own experience." But the study makes no effort to utilize experiential or anecdotal data from gay or non-gay people in the report.

3. In Presbyterian Church U.S.A., *Presbyterians and Human Sexuality 1991,* see 8, 16–17, 45–46, 48, 55–56 for its treatment of lesbian/gay issues, and 1–42 for its critique of patriarchal gender inequality and development of gender/sexual justice. In United Methodist Church, "Report of the Committee to Study Homosexuality," see 268 for anecdotal data from gay men, lesbians, ex-gays, ex-lesbians, parents, other relatives, friends, church officials, pastors, and church members; and 275–79 for concluding answers to the question "What can the church teach responsibly?" and for discussion of the implications of those answers for the life and ministry of the church. In Evangelical Lutheran Church in America, *Human Sexuality and the Christian Faith,* see 41 for anecdotes about lesbian/gay people; 12–27, 43–44 for discussion of biblical passages; and 31–32, 45–46 for development of a "neighbor love" ethic.

4. United Methodist Church, "Report of the Committee to Study Homosexuality," 274.

5. Ibid., 274, 275.

6. Xavier John Seubert, "The Sacramentality of Metaphors: Reflections on Homosexuality," *Cross Currents* 14 (spring 1991): 52–68. See also Ann Thompson Cook, *And God Loves Each One: A Resource for Dialogue about the Church and Homosexuality* (Washington, D.C.: Dumbarton United Methodist Church, 1988), for an example of a local church's effort to disagree with denominational policy and affirm gay people by collecting information about the range of their experiences; Andrew Sullivan, "Virtually Normal," *South Atlantic Quarterly* 93 (summer 1993): 659–73, for a discussion of homosexuality that integrates the author's personal experience, official statements by the Catholic

Church, and the church's traditional teachings; and J. Giles Milhaven, "How the Church Can Learn from Gay and Lesbian Experience," in Jeannine Gramick and Pat Furey, eds., *The Vatican and Homosexuality: Reactions to the "Letter to the Bishops of the Catholic Church on the Pastoral Care of Homosexual Persons"* (New York: Crossroad, 1988), 216–23, for a non-gay theologian's articulation of the need for the church to learn from gay people.

7. Paulo Freire, *Pedagogy of the Oppressed,* trans. Myra Bergman Ramos (New York: Continuum, 1970, 1985).

8. See, for example, Gustavo Gutiérrez, *A Theology of Liberation* (Maryknoll, N.Y.: Orbis, 1974); Cornel West, Caridad Guidote, and Margaret Coakley, eds., *Is Liberation Theology for North America? The Response of First World Churches* (New York: Theology of the Americas, 1978); Robert McAfee Brown, *Theology in a New Key: Responding to Liberation Themes* (Philadelphia: Westminster, 1978); Justo L. González and Catherine Gunsalus González, *Liberation Preaching: The Pulpit and the Oppressed,* Abingdon Preacher's Library (Nashville: Abingdon, 1980); Carter Heyward, *Our Passion for Justice: Images of Power, Sexuality, and Liberation* (New York: Pilgrim, 1984); Dorothee Soelle with Shirley A. Cloyes, *To Work and to Love: A Theology of Creation* (Philadelphia: Fortress, 1984); Beverly Wildung Harrison, *Making the Connections: Essays in Feminist Christian Social Ethics,* ed. Carol Robb (Boston: Beacon, 1985), 235–63; John J. McNeill, *Taking a Chance on God: Liberating Theology for Gays, Lesbians, and Their Lovers, Families, and Friends* (Boston: Beacon, 1988); Robert Goss, *Jesus Acted Up: A Gay and Lesbian Manifesto* (San Francisco: HarperSanFrancisco, 1993); Ada María Isasi-Díaz, *En la Lucha/In the Struggle: A Hispanic Women's Liberation Theology* (Minneapolis: Fortress, 1993); and Richard Cleaver, *Know My Name: A Gay Liberation Theology* (Louisville: Westminster/John Knox, 1995).

9. See, for example, Harrison, *Making the Connections,* 206–34.

10. Beverly Wildung Harrison, *Our Right to Choose: Toward a New Ethic of Abortion* (Boston: Beacon, 1983), 95.

11. Donna Haraway, *Simians, Cyborgs, and Women: The Reinvention of Nature* (New York: Routledge, 1991), 183–201.

12. Ibid., 196.

13. Ibid., 183–201. See also Jean Baker Miller, *Toward a New Psychology of Women* (Boston: Beacon, 1986), 10–11, for a discussion of the kind of knowledge that members of subordinate social groups have and members of dominant groups do not.

14. Troy D. Perry, *The Lord Is My Shepherd and He Knows I'm Gay: The Autobiography of the Reverend Troy D. Perry* (New York: Bantam, 1972); Troy D. Perry and Thomas L. P. Swicegood, *Don't Be Afraid Anymore: The Story of Reverend Troy Perry and the Metropolitan Community Churches* (New York: St. Martin's, 1990); Carter Heyward, *A Priest Forever: The Formation of a Woman and a Priest* (New York: Harper and Row, 1976); Chris Glaser, *Uncommon Calling: A Gay Man's Struggle to Serve the Church* (New York: Harper and Row, 1988); McNeill, *Taking a Chance on God;* Rose Mary Denman, *Let My People In: A Lesbian Minister Tells of Her Struggles to Live Openly and Maintain Her Ministry* (New York: Harper and Row, 1990); Antonio A. Feliz,

Out of the Bishop's Closet: A Call to Heal Ourselves, Each Other, and Our World (San Francisco: Aurora, 1988; Alamo Square, 1992); James Ferry, *In the Court of the Lord: A Gay Priest's Story* (New York: Crossroad, 1994); and Mel White, *Stranger at the Gate: To Be Gay and Christian in America* (New York: Simon and Schuster, 1994).

15. Barbara Zanotti, ed., *A Faith of One's Own: Explorations by Catholic Lesbians* (Trumansburg, N.Y.: Crossing Press, 1986), xi, xvi.

16. Rosemary Curb and Nancy Manahan, eds., *Lesbian Nuns: Breaking Silence* (Tallahassee: Naiad, 1985).

17. Christie Balka and Andy Rose, eds., *Twice Blessed: On Being Lesbian or Gay and Jewish* (Boston: Beacon, 1989), ix, 7.

18. Will Roscoe, ed., and Gay American Indians, comp., *Living the Spirit: A Gay American Indian Anthology* (New York: St. Martin's, 1988), 5.

19. Ron Schow, Wayne Schow, and Marybeth Raynes, eds., *Peculiar People: Mormons and Same-Sex Orientation* (Salt Lake City: Signature Books, 1991).

20. Wayne Schow, "Homosexuality, Mormon Doctrine, and Christianity: A Father's Perspective," in Schow, Schow, and Raynes, eds., *Peculiar People,* 127.

21. Loraine Hutchins and Lani Kaahumanu, eds., *Bi Any Other Name: Bisexual People Speak Out* (Boston: Alyson, 1991), 89–123.

22. Rakesh Ratti, ed., *A Lotus of Another Color: An Unfolding of the South Asian Gay and Lesbian Experience* (Boston: Alyson, 1993), 21–33, 81–84, 92–97, 113–32, 252–59.

23. See, for example, Andrew Sullivan, "Alone Again, Naturally," *New Republic,* 28 November 1994, 47, 50, 52, 54, 55; Judith Plaskow, "Lesbian and Gay Rights: Asking the Right Questions," *Tikkun* 9 (1994): 31–32; *Christians and Homosexuality: Dancing Toward a New Light,* special issue of *The Other Side,* 1994; Thomas H. Stahel, " 'I'm Here': An Interview with Andrew Sullivan," *America,* 8 May 1993, 5–11; Roseanne Leipzig and Judy Mable, "Lesbian Wedding," *Lilith,* fall 1992, 11–14; Melanie Morrison, "A Love That Won't Let Go: The Experience of Grace for Lesbians and Gay Men," *Sojourners,* July 1991, 12–16; Dan Grippo, "Why Lesbian and Gay Catholics Stay Catholic," *U.S. Catholic,* September 1990, 18–25; George DeStefano, "Gay under the Collar: The Hypocrisy of the Catholic Church," *Advocate,* 4 February 1986, 43–48; Louie Crew, "Gays as an Occasion of Grace," *Christianity and Crisis,* 2 November 1981, 290, 302–4; "Must Homosexuals Be Jewish Outcasts?" *Sh'ma,* 3 October 1978, 303–5; and Barry Alan Mehler, "Gay Jews: One Man's Journey from Closet to Community," *Moment,* February–March 1977, 22–24.

24. For a list and the addresses of newsletters, see Frances Green, ed., *Gayellow Pages 1989,* no. 17 (New York: Renaissance House, 1988), 44–45.

25. Goss, *Jesus Acted Up,* xiv–xv.

26. Haraway, *Simians, Cyborgs, and Women,* 190, 191. Carter Heyward, *Touching Our Strength: The Erotic as Power and the Love of God* (San Francisco: Harper and Row, 1989), does develop a lesbian/gay theological ethics by prefacing each of her chapters with an experiential statement by one of her students; and McNeill, *Taking a Chance on God,* is a psychotherapist who aims "to provide a spirituality based in the revelatory experience of lesbian and gay

Christians, a spirituality designed to meet their spiritual needs and inform their pastoral action in the world."

27. See, for example, John K. Cochran and Leonard Beeghley, "The Influence of Religion on Attitudes toward Nonmarital Sexuality: A Preliminary Assessment of Reference Group Theory," *Journal for the Scientific Study of Religion* 30 (1991): 45–62; Patricia L. Jakobi, "Medical Science, Christian Fundamentalism, and the Etiology of AIDS," *AIDS and Public Policy Journal* 5 (1990): 89–93; Bradley Hertel and Michael Hughes, "Religious Affiliation, Attendance, and Support for 'Pro-Family' Issues in the United States," *Social Forces* 65 (1987): 858–80; Stephen D. Johnson, "Factors Related to Intolerance of AIDS Victims," *Journal for the Scientific Study of Religion* 26 (1987): 105–10; E. Wilbur Bock, Leonard Beeghley, and Anthony J. Mixon, "Religion, Socioeconomic Status, and Sexual Morality: An Application of Reference Group Theory," *Sociological Quarterly* 24 (1983): 545–59; and Theodore C. Wagenaar and Patricia E. Bartos, "Orthodoxy and Attitudes of Clergymen towards Homosexuality and Abortion," *Review of Religious Research* 18 (1977): 114–25.

28. Michael C. Dickens, "An Analysis of Societal Racism and Homophobia and Their Effect upon Gay and Bisexual Men of African Descent" (M.A. thesis, Wesleyan University, 1994). Of the twenty-three subjects, twenty identified as African-American, two as West Indian, and one as Kenyan/European-American.

29. Odette Lockwood-Stewart, "A Report of Conversations with Students," *Open Hands,* fall 1994, 9.

30. Alissa Nelyn Steelman, "The Effect of the Organized Christian Church on Gay and Lesbian Spirituality," *Proceedings of Sixth National Conference on Undergraduate Research* 6 (1992): 615–20.

31. Paul Foster, "Why We Stay: Gay Men in the Roman Catholic Church" (Independent Research Project, Department of Sociology, University of Toronto, 1992).

32. Thomas O'Brien, "A Survey of Gay/Lesbian Catholics concerning Attitudes toward Sexual Orientation and Religious Beliefs," *Journal of Homosexuality* 21 (1991): 29–44.

33. Ralph G. McFadden, "If We Would Just Turn Purple," *Brethren Life and Thought* 36 (winter 1991): 35–41 (earlier version published as "If We Would Just Turn Purple: Church of the Brethren Experience," *Dialogue* (Brethren/Mennonite Council for Gay and Lesbian Concerns), January 1990, 1–3). McFadden does not provide a number for his sample of interviewees. I arrived at the number twelve by counting the different interviews referred to and discussed.

34. R. Jan Stout, "Sin and Sexuality: Psychobiology and the Development of Homosexuality"; Ron Schow and Marybeth Raynes, "Difficult Choices for Adolescents and Adults"; and Christopher J. Alexander, "Suicidal Behavior in Gay and Lesbian Mormons," in Schow, Schow, and Raynes, eds., *Peculiar People,* 168–88, 189–208, 257–63. Stout is an assistant professor of psychiatry at the University of Utah School of Medicine and a past president of the Utah Psychiatric Association. His article first appeared in *Dialogue: A Journal of Mormon Thought* 20 (summer 1987): 29–41. Schow and Raynes describe their sample

as "actual clients" or "composites" of clients whose names and identities have been changed: "Some are teenagers or young adults wondering how to build a life in a world of homophobia. Others are adult women and men who have struggled for years with their attraction and are in various stages of acceptance or ambivalence about their identity. Still others are partners in heterosexual marriages. Some hoped or expected that their homosexuality would disappear with marriage; some want marriage and an acceptable life regardless of the cost; some are living a double life." Alexander's research was conducted from 1985 to 1987, and his article first appeared in the November 1989 issue of Affirmation's newsletter, *Affinity.*

35. Deborah H. Carney and Susan E. Davies, "Yours in Sisterhood: A Lesbian and Bisexual Perspective on Ministry," in Susan E. Davies and Eleanor H. Haney, eds., *Redefining Sexual Ethics: A Sourcebook of Essays, Stories, and Poems* (Cleveland: Pilgrim Press, 1991), 75–83.

36. Kent Franks et al., "Exploration of Death Anxiety as a Function of Religious Variables in Gay Men with and without AIDS," *Omega: Journal of Death and Dying* 22 (1990–91): 43–50. The researchers write: "An apparent methodological limitation is that participation was based upon informal contacts and availability, rather than on any procedure that approached randomization or representation with respect to gay men with and without AIDS in San Francisco."

37. A. W. Richard Sipe, *A Secret World: Sexuality and the Search for Celibacy* (New York: Brunner/Mazel, 1990), 8–14, 103–38.

38. James G. Wolf, *Gay Priests* (San Francisco: Harper and Row, 1989); compared with the study conducted by the National Opinion Research Center, commissioned by the Ad Hoc Committee on Pastoral Research and Practices, National Conference of Catholic Bishops (NCCB), and analyzed by Andrew M. Greeley and R. Schoenerr, *The Catholic Priest in the United States: Sociological Investigations* (Washington, D.C.: United States Catholic Conference, 1972), and with study conducted by Eugene C. Kennedy and Victor J. Heckler, *The Catholic Priest in the United States: Psychological Investigations* (Washington, D.C.: United States Catholic Conference, 1972).

39. Clare B. Fischer, "A Bonding of Choice: Values and Identity among Lesbian and Gay Religious Leaders," *Journal of Homosexuality* 18 (1989/90): 145–74 (also in Richard Hasbany, ed., *Homosexuality and Religion* [New York: Haworth, 1990]).

40. Neil Miller, *In Search of Gay America: Women and Men in a Time of Change* (New York: Atlantic Monthly, 1989; Perennial Library, 1990), 10–12, 211–56.

41. Lawrence A. Reh, "More Light Churches," *More Light Update* (Presbyterians for Lesbian and Gay Concerns), September 1989, 1–16.

42. Common Vision Planning Committee, *Report and Recommendations of the Common Vision Planning Committee to the Board of Trustees, Unitarian Universalist Association* (Boston: Unitarian Universalist Association, 1989); and F. Jay Deacon, " 'Common Vision' Survey Finds Mixed Views of Gay/Lesbian Inclusion in Unitarian Universalism," *Ethics and Action,* June 1988, 1, 3, 18.

43. Leonard Norman Primiano, " 'I Would Rather Be Fixated on the Lord': Women's Religion, Men's Power, and the 'Dignity' Problem," *New York Folklore* 19 (1993): 89–103.

44. Sheila Murphy, "Counseling Lesbian Women Religious," *Women and Therapy* 5 (winter 1986): 7–17.

45. Walter Williams, *The Spirit and the Flesh: Sexual Diversity in American Indian Culture* (Boston: Beacon, 1988), 2, 4, 6–7 (the number of informants with tribal affiliation are: twenty-eight Lakota, seven Omaha, six Crow, four Cheyenne, four Navajo, three Hupa, three Cherokee, three Creek, two Micmac, and one each for Choctaw, Laguna Pueblo, Pomo, Sac and Fox, Paiute, Chippewa, Mohawk, Haliwa-Saponi, Lumbee, Gros Venture, Otoe, and Osage); and Curtis Harris and Leota Lone Dog (interview by Deborah Blincoe), "Two Spirited People: Understanding Who We Are as Creation," *New York Folklore* 19 (1993): 155–65.

46. James T. Sears, *Growing Up Gay in the South: Race, Gender, and Journeys of the Spirit* (New York: Harrington Park, 1991). Of the thirty-six subjects, 56 percent were Southern Baptist, 8 percent Jehovah's Witness, 8 percent Catholic, 8 percent Lutheran, 6 percent African Methodist, 6 percent Episcopal, 3 percent Methodist, and 6 percent no formal religious background.

47. Scott Thumma, "Negotiating a Religious Identity: The Case of the Gay Evangelical," *Sociological Analysis* 52 (1991): 333–47; and idem, "Straightening Identities: Evangelical Approaches to Homosexuality" (master's thesis, Emory University, 1987).

48. Henry Rabinowitz, "Talmud Class in a Gay Synagogue," *Judaism* 32 (1983): 433–43.

49. Richard Wagner, *Gay Catholic Priests: A Study of Cognitive and Affective Dissonance* (San Francisco: Specific Press, 1981).

50. Paul F. Bauer, "The Homosexual Subculture at Worship: A Participant Observation Study," *Pastoral Psychology* 25 (1976): 115–27.

51. Alfred C. Kinsey, Wardell B. Pomeroy, and Clyde E. Martin, *Sexual Behavior in the Human Male* (Philadelphia: W. B. Saunders, 1948), 483, 631, 636, and Alfred C. Kinsey et al., *Sexual Behavior in the Human Female* (Philadelphia: W. B. Saunders, 1953), 463–66, 497, 498. Interviews with women and men were conducted in all states, with highest concentrations of women in New York, Pennsylvania, Illinois, Indiana, California, New Jersey, Ohio, Florida, Massachusetts, and Maryland, and highest concentrations of men in Indiana, New York, Pennsylvania, Illinois, Ohio, Kentucky, New Jersey, Michigan, Massachusetts, and Kansas.

52. Martin S. Weinberg and Colin J. Williams, *Male Homosexuals: Their Problems and Adaptations* (New York: Oxford University Press, 1974), 93–96, 248–59, 283–84. In addition to being all-male, Weinberg and Williams' sample was 96 percent white and 65 percent urban. By age, 18 percent was under twenty-six years, 30 percent was twenty-six to thirty-five, 28 percent was thirty-six to forty-five, and 24 percent was over forty-five. The researchers distributed a uniform questionnaire for their survey instrument and obtained a comparable sample from the general population.

53. Alan P. Bell and Martin S. Weinberg, *Homosexualities: A Study of Diversity among Men and Women* (New York: Simon and Schuster, 1978), 26–48, 149–54, 277–80, 363–66. Of the sample, 30 percent was female, and 70 percent was male; 18 percent was black, and 82 percent was white. The researchers conducted telephone interviews and obtained a comparable sample from the general population.

54. Jerrold Greenberg, "A Study of Male Homosexuals (Predominantly College Students)," *Journal of the American College Health Association* 22 (1973): 56–60.

55. Karla Jay and Allen Young, *The Gay Report: Lesbians and Gay Men Speak Out about Sexual Experiences and Lifestyles* (New York: Summit Books, 1979), 6–11, 719–21, 810–11.

56. Stephen G. Schneider, Norman L. Farberow, and Gabriel N. Kruks, "Suicidal Behavior in Adolescent and Young Adult Gay Men," *Suicide and Life-Threatening Behavior* 19 (winter 1989): 381–94 (reprinted in Gary Remafedi, ed., *Death by Denial: Studies of Suicide in Gay and Lesbian Teenagers* [Boston: Alyson, 1994], 107–22).

57. Partners Task Force for Gay and Lesbian Couples, *Partners' National Survey of Lesbian and Gay Couples,* special issue of *Partners: Newsletter for Gay and Lesbian Couples,* May/June 1990. The report states: "The survey drew a total of 1,749 responses, representing 1,266 couples—706 lesbian couples (56 percent) and 560 male couples (44 percent).... Represented in the survey were residents of 48 states, Puerto Rico and the District of Columbia. Geographic distribution was remarkably even, with the best represented state, California, accounting for only 3 percent of the responses" (2–4).

58. Gary Remafedi et al., "Demography of Sexual Orientation in Adolescents," *Pediatrics* 89 (1992): 714–21. The authors state: "The sample included 34,706 students (grades 7 through 12) from diverse ethnic, geographic, and socioeconomic strata."

59. Martin S. Weinberg, Colin J. Williams, and Douglas W. Pryor, *Dual Attraction: Understanding Bisexuality* (New York: Oxford University Press, 1994), 315, 365–66. The study was conducted in the San Francisco Bay Area at three different periods, 1983, 1984–85, and 1988.

60. Edward O. Laumann et al., *The Social Organization of Sexuality: Sexual Practices in the United States* (Chicago: University of Chicago Press, 1994), 303, 305, tables 8.1 and 8.2. The researchers' study is based on their National Health and Social Life Survey that used ninety-minute, face-to-face interviews conducted in 1992. Their area probability sample of 3,432 English-speaking adults between the ages of eighteen and fifty-nine consisted of 1,921 women and 1,511 men; overselected blacks and Hispanics; and did not include those living in correctional facilities, colleges dormitorics, military barracks, and homeless shelters (see 35–73 and 549–70 for more information about the design of the study, sampling procedures, and data collection).

61. See Bennett L. Singer and David Deschamps, *Gay and Lesbian Stats: A Pocket Guide of Facts and Figures* (New York: New Press, 1994), 9–12; Felicity Barringer, "Measuring Sexuality through the Polls Can Be Shaky," *New York Times,* 25 April 1993; James T. Spears, *Growing Up Gay in the South: Race,*

Gender, and Journeys of the Spirit (New York: Harrington Park, 1991), 432–36; and Gary David Comstock, *Violence against Lesbians and Gay Men* (New York: Columbia University Press, 1991), 32.

62. See Kenneth B. Bedell, ed., *Yearbook of American and Canadian Churches, 1994* (Nashville: Abingdon, 1994), 125–27; United Church of Christ, *History and Program: The United Church of Christ* (Cleveland: United Church, 1991); United Church Coalition for Lesbian/Gay Concerns, comp., *United Church of Christ Social Policy regarding Lesbian, Gay and Bisexual Concerns, a Compendium of Actions by: The Council for Christian Social Action (1969), the Executive Council (1973, 1980, 1981), and General Synods 10, 11, 14, 15, 16* (Athens, Ohio: United Church Coalition for Lesbian/Gay Concerns, n.d.); Gary David Comstock, "Aliens in the Promised Land? Keynote Address for the 1986 National Gathering of the United Church of Christ's Coalition for Lesbian/Gay Concerns," in Hasbany, ed., *Homosexuality and Religion,* 133–44; W. Evan Golder, "Homosexual Candidates for Ministry Challenge UCC Ordination Polity," *United Church News,* February 1988, 8; and William Johnson, "United Church of Christ," *Open Hands,* summer 1986, 16–17.

63. The generic term "episcopal" refers to a governing order of bishops. Other denominations with episcopal governance have included the term as a proper noun within their names, for example, Episcopal Church, African Methodist Episcopal Church, and African Methodist Episcopal Zion Church.

64. For a very brief but remarkably clear and helpful summary statement about UMC governing structure, see "United Methodist Polity," *Open Hands,* summer 1986, 11. The UMC polity is often referred to as a "connectional" system, in which the church hierarchy can overrule the local church. See Bedell, ed., *Yearbook of American and Canadian Churches, 1994,* 127–29; United Methodist Church, *Manual on Conference and District Councils on Ministries of the United Methodist Church* (Nashville: United Methodist Communications, 1989–92), 1; idem, *General Agencies of the United Methodist Church, Organization Charts* (Nashville: United Methodist Communications, 1991); 1; idem, *Come Share Rejoice: The Structure of the United Methodist Church* (Nashville: United Methodist Communications, n.d.); United Methodist Church, *Report of the Committee to Study Homosexuality* (Dayton: General Council on Ministries, 1992); and "Our History: Affirmation Time Line," *Affirmation* (newsletter of Affirmation: United Methodists for Lesbian and Gay Concerns), summer 1989, 1, 3, 4–5.

65. *Waves* (national newsletter of the United Church Coalition for Lesbian/Gay Concerns) 17, no. 2 (May 1990): 11; and *Affirmation* (newsletter of Affirmation) 16, no. 2 (summer 1991): 1.

66. Suggested changes had to do with clarification of a few terms and the addition of a few questions about lay leadership and ministry.

67. I compared the percentages of respondents from states and regions to data for non-gay denominational memberships, as reported by Martin B. Bradley et al., *Churches and Church Membership in the United States in 1990: An Enumeration by Region, State and County Based on Data Reported for 133 Church Groupings* (Atlanta: Glenmary Research Center, 1992).

68. Four men and six women were interviewed from each denomination. Of each group of ten, five were ordained (UCC two men, three women; UMC three men, two women) and five were laypeople (UCC two men, three women; UMC one man, four women).

Four of the five ordained UCC interviewees were currently employed in clergy positions (three pastors, one hospital chaplain), while the other was an executive director of an AIDS agency. One of the five UMC ordained interviewees was currently employed in a clergy position as a college chaplain, while the others were a seminary staff member, an executive director of a national AIDS organization, a stained-glass worker, and a law student. Of all UCC and UMC people holding clergy positions, two were out about their sexual orientation (both UCC), and three were not (one UCC, two UMC).

Of the five ordained UCC and UMC people who were not currently holding clergy positions, three had left or were removed from such positions because of their sexual orientation (one UCC, two UMC), and two (both UMC) had chosen alternative employment to avoid hostility or to seek a more welcoming working environment.

The ten lay interviewees were employed as a program director of an AIDS agency, a church administrator on the regional level, an elementary school teacher, a steam fitter, a security guard, an educational assistant, an administrative assistant, a computer adviser, a public policy advocate for nonprofit organizations, and a district manager for a major insurance company.

The ages of people interviewed ranged from twenty-eight to fifty-nine with an average age of thirty-nine and a median age of 37.5.

69. The UMC interviewees who agreed to be identified by name are Chip Aldridge, Mary Gaddis, Nancy Law, Randy Miller, Katie Sanetra, Barbara Sawyer, B. J. Stiles, and Timothy D. W. Tennant-Jayne. One woman asked that her name not be used. Another woman, after reviewing and editing the transcript of her interview, decided not to return it to me. She wrote: "It helped me realize how much I had moved through, and that I no longer need to dwell on the people or pain. So, while I apologize for not following through with the process, I am grateful to you for helping me to understand better than I might otherwise, some significant periods in my life."

UCC interviewees who agreed to be identified by name are Selena L. Blackwell, Diane Darling, Mark Ehrke, Peter Ilgenfritz, Susan L. Jelinek, John W. Lardin, Wayne MacPherson, Charlotte Stacey, and Margarita Suárez. One woman asked that her name not be used: "I regret that I do not dare have my name openly attached to my remarks. The development of strong anti-gay organizations that can put their agendas into state referenda in Oregon and Colorado, for example, remind me how virulent the hatred of us is in this country. I just don't feel safe being myself except in specific situations of my own choosing."

Chapter 3: Belonging, Switching, Leaving, and Shopping

1. Alfred C. Kinsey, Wardell B. Pomeroy, and Clyde E. Martin, *Sexual Behavior in the Human Male* (Philadelphia: W. B. Saunders, 1948), 625.

2. Ibid., 469–87, 509, 525, 540, 569–71, 583, 589, 631, 636.

3. Alfred C. Kinsey et al., *Sexual Behavior in the Human Female* (Philadelphia: W. B. Saunders, 1953), 154–58, 203–5, 247–49, 304–7, 359–60, 381–82, 424, 463–66, 497, 498, 515–16, 521–24, 686–87.

4. The greater percentage of Jewish respondents in the homosexual sample may be due to the concentrated Jewish population in the surveyed areas, but among those respondents there is a disproportionate percentage of Orthodox Jews compared to that within the general Jewish population (23 percent, 7 percent).

5. Martin S. Weinberg and Colin J. Williams, *Male Homosexuals: Their Problems and Adaptations* (New York: Oxford University Press, 1974); Karla Jay and Allen Young, *The Gay Report: Lesbians and Gay Men Speak Out about Sexual Experiences and Lifestyles* (New York: Summit Books, 1979); and Martin S. Weinberg, Colin J. Williams, and Douglas W. Pryor, *Dual Attraction: Understanding Bisexuality* (New York: Oxford University Press, 1994).

6. Weinberg and Williams, *Male Homosexuals,* 249–50, 254–56.

7. James T. Sears, *Growing Up Gay in the South: Race, Gender, and Journeys of the Spirit* (New York: Harrington Park, 1991), 37–39.

8. Ibid., 50, 52.

9. Ibid., 52.

10. Ibid., 56, 58–59.

11. Jay and Young, *Gay Report,* 719–21.

12. Sandip Roy, "An Indian Original: Gutsy and Provocative, Ashok Row Kavi Has Always Challenged the Status Quo," *Trikone: Gay and Lesbian South Asians,* October 1993, 6. I include this comment by a non–North American because he is a frequent visitor and lecturer in the United States and Canada, where his work is well known by South Asian gay people, and because the Ramakrishna Mission is the primary Hindu organization in North America.

13. Sharmeen Islam, "Gay and Lesbian Muslim Voices," *Trikone: Gay and Lesbian South Asians,* July 1994, 1.

14. Alan P. Bell and Martin S. Weinberg, *Homosexualities: A Study of Diversity among Men and Women* (New York: Simon and Schuster, 1978), 363–64.

15. Edward O. Laumann et al., *The Social Organization of Sexuality: Sexual Practices in the United States* (Chicago: University of Chicago Press, 1994), 305.

16. Bell and Weinberg, *Homosexualities,* 363–64.

17. Jerrold Greenberg, "A Study of Male Homosexuals (Predominantly College Students)," *Journal of the American College Health Association* 22 (1973): 58.

18. Kent Franks et al., "Exploration of Death Anxiety as a Function of Religious Variables in Gay Men with and without AIDS," *Omega: Journal of Death and Dying* 22 (1990–91): 46.

19. Weinberg, Williams, and Pryor, *Dual Attraction,* 365–66.

20. Ibid., 365. Percentages calculated from table 12.1, "Demographic and Background Data, 1984 and 1985 Questionnaire Sample: Religiosity."

21. Gary Remafedi et al., "Demography of Sexual Orientation in Adolescents," *Pediatrics* 89 (1992): 714–21.

22. Weinberg, Williams, and Pryor, *Dual Attraction,* 365; and Franks et al., "Exploration of Death Anxiety," 46.

23. Jay and Young, *Gay Report,* 810–11.

24. Alissa Nelyn Steelman, "The Effect of the Organized Christian Church on Gay and Lesbian Spirituality," *Proceedings of Sixth National Conference on Undergraduate Research* 6 (1992): 618–19. For a journalistic account of various forms of alternative spirituality and religion, see Edward M. Gomez, "If the Spirit Moves You," *Out,* October 1994, 84–85, 87, 89, 91, 93, 130.

25. The exception is Orthodox Judaism, but the difference is smaller than the difference between lesbians and gay men in any other religious body or grouping.

26. Wade Clark Roof and Mary Johnson, "Baby Boomers and the Return to the Churches," in David A. Roozen and C. Kirk Hadaway, eds., *Church and Denominational Growth* (Nashville: Abingdon, 1993), 299; and Barry A. Kosmin and Seymour P. Lachman, *One Nation under God: Religion in American Society* (New York: Harmony Books, 1993), 210–14. I realize that the respondents in these studies may include lesbian, bisexual, and gay members, but I choose to use the term "non-gay" in my discussion for the sake of establishing terms that will clarify comparison. These studies do not attempt to report data by sexual orientation of respondents.

27. Kosmin and Lachman, *One Nation under God,* 213–14.

28. Ibid., 214. For discussion of alternative religious formation, see Nett Hart, "Radical Lesbian Spirituality," *Lesbian Ethics* 3 (spring 1988): 64–73; and Denise Nadeau, "Lesbian Spirituality," *Resources for Feminist Research* 12 (1983): 37–39.

29. Michael C. Dickens, "An Analysis of Societal Racism and Homophobia and Their Effect upon Gay and Bisexual Men of African Descent" (M.A. thesis, Wesleyan University, 1994), 51.

30. Walter L. Williams, *The Spirit and the Flesh: Sexual Diversity in American Indian Culture* (Boston: Beacon, 1986), 207–15, 224–27; and Will Roscoe, "Gay American Indians: Creating an Identity from Past Traditions," *Advocate,* 29 October 1985, 45–49.

31. Franks et al., "Exploration of Death," 46.

32. "Liberal," "moderate," and "conservative" refer to the general and prevailing theological/social characteristic of these denominations. The term "liberal" does not necessarily apply to a denomination's lesbian/gay policy. Examples of liberal Protestant denominations are the Episcopal Church, Presbyterian Church (U.S.A.), and the United Church of Christ. Moderate Protestant denominations would be Disciples of Christ, Evangelical Lutheran Church of America, United Methodist Church, Northern Baptists, and Reformed Church of America. Conservative Protestant denominations are Assemblies of God, Churches of Christ, Churches of God, Seventh-Day Adventists, evangelicals/fundamentalists, Nazarenes, Pentecostals/Holiness, and Southern Baptists. Black Protestants are concentrated in the United Methodist, Northern Baptist, and Southern Baptist denominations. See Wade Clark Roof and William McKinney, *American Mainline Religion: Its Changing Shape and Future* (New Brunswick, N.J.: Rutgers University Press, 1987), 162–72, 253–56.

33. In the UCC, the General Synod is the representative body of delegates that meets every two years. Delegates are chosen by local churches, regional organizations, and agencies. See United Church of Christ, *The Constitution and Bylaws, United Church of Christ* (Cleveland: Executive Council for the United Church of Christ, 1991), 8.

34. William J. McKinney Jr., *Findings from the Membership Inventory,* New Conversations Supplement (New York: United Church Board for Homeland Ministries, n.d.). I realize that the respondents in McKinney's study may include lesbian, bisexual, and gay members, but I choose to use the term "non-gay" in my discussion for the sake of establishing terms that will clarify comparison. McKinney's study does not attempt to report data by sexual orientation of respondents.

35. The General Conference is the representative, decision-making body of the UMC. It meets every four years. See "United Methodist Polity," *Open Hands,* summer 1986, 11.

36. Timothy J. Gilbride, Mearle L. Griffith, and C. David Lundquist, *The Survey of United Methodist Opinion: A Research Tool for Informed Decision Making* (Dayton: Office of Research, General Council on Ministries, United Methodist Church, 1990), 5. I realize that the respondents in Gilbride, Griffith, and Lundquist's study may include lesbian, bisexual, and gay members, but I choose to use the term "non-gay" in my discussion for the sake of establishing terms that will clarify comparison. Their study does not attempt to report data by sexual orientation of respondents.

37. Roof and Johnson, "Baby Boomers," 300.

38. Jay and Young, *Gay Report,* 810–11.

39. For recent studies and anthologies on bisexuality, see Weinberg, Williams, and Pryor, *Dual Attraction;* Elizabeth Reba Weise, ed., *Closer to Home: Bisexuality and Feminism* (Seattle: Seal, 1992); Loraine Hutchins and Lani Kaahumanu, eds., *Bi Any Other Name: Bisexual People Speak Out* (Boston: Alyson, 1991); Thomas Geller, ed., *Bisexuality: A Reader and Sourcebook* (Chicago: Times Change, 1990); and Fritz Klein and Timothy J. Wolf, eds., *Bisexualities: Theory and Research* (New York: Haworth, 1985).

40. Jay and Young, *Gay Report,* 810–11.

41. Wade Clark Roof, "Multiple Religious Switching: A Research Note," *Journal for the Scientific Study of Religion* 28 (1989): 533.

42. Roof and McKinney, *American Mainline Religion,* 172–75.

43. For comparison, see Gilbride, Griffith, and Lundquist, *Survey of United Methodist Opinion,* 1; and McKinney, *Findings from the Membership Inventory,* n.p.

44. Dickens, "Analysis of Societal Racism and Homophobia," 51.

45. Tracy Archibald, "And from Kansas" (letter), *More Light Update,* February 1992, 12–13.

46. R. Jan Stout, "Sin and Sexuality: Psychobiology and the Development of Homosexuality," in Ron Schow, Wayne Schow, and Marybeth Raynes, eds., *Peculiar People: Mormons and Same-Sex Orientation* (Salt Lake City: Signature Books, 1991), 183.

47. Christopher J. Alexander, "Suicidal Behavior in Gay and Lesbian Mormons," in Schow, Schow, and Raynes, eds., *Peculiar People,* 261.

48. Jean Burgess, "And Then There Was Light," in Schow, Schow, and Raynes, eds., *Peculiar People,* 82–90.

49. Ibid., 82–90.

50. Bob Jenkins, "The Pain Grows" (letter), *Open Hands,* summer 1992, 21.

51. Neil Miller, *In Search of Gay America: Women and Men in a Time of Change* (New York: Atlantic Monthly, 1989; Perennial Library, 1990), 241.

52. Paul F. Bauer, "The Homosexual Subculture at Worship: A Participant Observation Study," *Pastoral Psychology* 25 (1976): 115, 118–19, 120. See also Bedell, ed., *Yearbook of American and Canadian Churches, 1994,* 130–31, 160; John Gallagher, "Is God Gay?" *Advocate,* 13 December 1994, 40–46; and Michael S. Piazza, *Holy Homosexuals: The Truth about Being Gay or Lesbian and Christian* (Dallas: Sources of Hope, 1994).

53. Scott Thumma, "Negotiating a Religious Identity: The Case of the Gay Evangelical," *Sociological Analysis* 52 (1991): 333–47.

54. Ibid.

55. Ibid.

56. Miller, *In Search of Gay America,* 241–50.

57. Ibid., 248–49.

58. Ibid., 251–56.

59. In *Apostolic Voice* (National Gay Pentecostal Alliance), see Brother Carey, "God's Unconditional Love," June–July 1993, 1, 3–4, 8–9; and idem, "NGPA: Eleven Years, and Not Looking Back," October–November 1991, 1–2.

60. Henry Rabinowitz, "Talmud Class in a Gay Synagogue," *Judaism* 32 (1983): 433–43.

61. Ibid., 440.

62. Ibid., 441.

63. Ibid.

64. Ibid., 434.

65. Ibid., 434–35.

66. Ibid., 442. See Mayer Rus, "Next Year in the Village," *Out,* October 1994, 86.

67. "Jewish Communities Sponsor Dialogues on Gay and Lesbian Issues," *World Congress Digest* (World Congress of Gay and Lesbian Jewish Organizations), winter 1991, 2.

68. Roy Dahl, "The Best of Times and the Worst of Times," *Dialogue* (Brethren/Mennonite Council for Gay and Lesbian Concerns), June 1993, 4–5.

69. Ibid. See also Reta Halteman Finger, "A Burden or a Gift?" *Daughter of Sarah,* May/June 1988, 29–32.

70. Dahl, "Best of Times," 4–5.

71. See, for example, these accounts of pro-gay congregations expelled by the Southern Baptist Convention for defying anti-gay denominational policy: William Booth, "A Renegade Congregation Mourns 'Emotional' Severing of Baptist Ties: Members Defend Church's Blessing of Gay Relationship, New Openness," *Washington Post,* 15 June 1992, A9; Gayle White, "Baptists Drop Two Churches over Gays; Homosexuality Mainly 'a Choice,' Quayle Suggests,"

Atlanta Journal and Constitution, 10 June 1992, A2; Richard Vara and Cecile Holmes White, "Baptists Vote for Houston Pastor as Leader: Two Churches Kicked Out over Gay Issue," *Houston Chronicle,* 10 June 1992, A10; Adelle M. Banks, "Baptists Take Stand against Homosexuality: The Denomination Votes to Oust Two North Carolina Churches That Supported the Union or Ordination of Gay Man," *Orlando Sentinel Tribune,* 10 June 1992, A1; "Sanctioning Gay Lives, Two Churches Feel Wrath," *New York Times,* 2 May 1992, section 1, 11; "Church Stance on Gays Stirs Southern Baptists; The Denomination Considers a New Method to Remove Congregations after the Licensing of a Homosexual for the Ministry in Chapel Hill," *Los Angeles Times,* 11 April 1992, B5; and "Baptist Church Defies Denomination, Makes Gay Man a Minister," *Orlando Sentinel Tribune,* 11 April 1992, D8.

72. Coming out for many is a process, both tentative and progressive. A UMC lesbian, who is the mother of two grown children and was fifty-one years old when I interviewed her, had the following to say about her experiences in her local church: "I've come out to quite a number of people, more people now than I would have thought I ever would have. It hasn't upset anybody yet. I guess I've had some sort of intuitive sense about who's OK to be open with. One of my friends that I've come out to is the mayor of our city, and she was very supportive. Another is someone that I worked with and with whom I'd established a close friendship. I said to her, 'There's something I want to tell you'; and she looked up and thought I was going to give her an interesting piece of gossip. I said, 'I want to tell you that I'm a lesbian; I want you to know it, and I don't want you to hear it from someone else.' She said, 'Is that all, is that it?' And then she said, 'I thought so.' Sometimes I get that kind of response."

73. I calculated the percentages of "welcoming" congregations within each denomination and the rates of increase in the number of "welcoming" congregations nationwide from information provided in the newsletters *Affirmation* (Affirmation: United Methodists for Lesbian and Gay Concerns) and *Waves* (United Church Coalition for Lesbian/Gay Concerns) from 1986 to 1993.

74. Affirmation Council, "Is It Time for a New Beginning?" *Affirmation,* spring 1993, 1.

75. Lawrence A. Reh, "More Light Churches," *More Light Update* (Presbyterians for Lesbian and Gay Concerns), September 1989, 1–16.

76. As in many religious bodies, clergy within the UMC may be employed in other than parish positions. These positions may be referred to as "special appointment" or "appointed beyond the local church" (ABLC).

77. Roof and Johnson, "Baby Boomers," 306–7.

78. Greg Grisa, "Deliberately Diverse: The Sojourner Truth Congregation," *UULGC World* (Unitarian Universalists for Lesbian and Gay Concerns), January 1993, 4.

Chapter 4: Service, Participation, Leadership, and Advocacy

1. See Ronald M. Green, *Religion and Moral Reason: A New Method for Comparative Study* (New York: Oxford University Press, 1988), 162–94.

2. See John (Fire) Lame Deer and Richard Erdoes, *Lame Deer, Seeker of Visions* (New York: Simon and Schuster, 1972; Washington Square, Pocket Books, 1976), 144–63; Vine Deloria Jr., *God Is Red* (New York: Grosset and Dunlap, 1973), 209–24; Jamake Highwater, *The Primal Mind: Vision and Reality in Indian America* (New York: Harper and Row, 1981; New American Library, Meridian, 1982), 168–89; Beth Brant, "Introduction: A Gathering of Spirit," in Brant, ed., *A Gathering of Spirit: A Collection by North American Indian Women* (Ithaca, N.Y.; Firebrand, 1988), 8–15; Dhyani Ywahoo, "Renewing the Scared Hoop," and Carol Lee Sanchez, "New World Tribal Communities," in Judith Plaskow and Carol P. Christ, eds., *Weaving the Visions: New Patterns in Feminist Spirituality* (San Francisco: Harper and Row, 1989), 274–80, 344–56.

3. Walter L. Williams, *The Spirit and the Flesh: Sexual Diversity in American Indian Culture* (Boston: Beacon, 1988), 210–11.

4. Ibid., 209, 225. See also Beth Brant, *Food and Spirits* (Ithaca, N.Y.: Firebrand, 1991), 49–66.

5. Will Roscoe, "The American Indian Berdache as Artist and Priest," *Southwestern American Indian Society* 12 (spring 1988): 127–50; Williams, *Spirit and the Flesh*, 224–25; Randy Burns, preface to Will Roscoe, ed., *Living the Spirit: A Gay American Indian Anthology* (New York: St. Martin's, 1988), 1–2, 217–22; and Will Roscoe, "Bibliography of Berdache and Alternative Gender Roles among North American Indians," *Journal of Homosexuality* 14 (1987): 81–171; Walter L. Williams, "Persistence and Change in the Berdache Tradition among Contemporary Lakota Indians," in Evelyn Blackwood, ed., *Anthropology and Homosexual Behavior* (New York: Haworth, 1986), 191–200.

For other studies done since 1975, see Curtis Harris and Leota Lone Dog (interview by Deborah Blincoe), "Two Spirited People: Understanding Who We Are as Creation," *New York Folklore* 19 (1993): 155–64; Raymond E. Hauser, "The *Berdache* and the Illinois Indian Tribe during the Last Half of the Seventeenth Century," *Ethnohistory* 37 (1990): 45–65; Roscoe, ed., *Living the Spirit*, 32–47, 64–76; Paula Gunn Allen, *The Sacred Hoop: Recovering the Feminine in American Indian Traditions* (Boston: Beacon, 1986); Beverly Chinas, "Isthmus Zapotec 'Berdaches,'" *Newsletter of the Anthropological Research Group on Homosexuality*, May 1985, 3–4; Evelyn Blackwood, "Sexuality and Gender in Certain Native American Tribes: The Case of Cross-Gender Females," *Signs: Journal of Women in Culture and Society* 10 (1984): 27–42; Beatrice Medicine, "'Warrior Women'—Sex Role Alternatives for Plains Indian Women," in Patricia Albers and Beatrice Medicine, eds., *The Hidden Half: Studies of Plains Indian Women* (Washington, D.C.: University Press of America, 1983), 269; Charles Callender and Lee Kochems, "The North American Berdache," *Current Anthropology* 24 (1983): 443–56; Harriet Whitehead, "The Bow and the Burden Strap: A New Look at Institutionalized Homosexuality in Native North America," in Sherry Ortner and Harriet Whitehead, eds., *Sexual Meanings: The Cultural Construction of Gender and Sexuality* (Cambridge: Cambridge University Press, 1981), 86, 90–93; James S. Thayer, "The Berdache of the Northern Plains: A Socioreligious Perspective," *Journal of Anthropological Research* 36 (1980): 287–93; Harald Broch, "A Note on Berdache among the Hare Indians of Northwestern Canada," *Western Canadian Journal of Anthropology* 7 (1977):

95–101; Robert Stoller, "Two Feminized Male American Indians," *Archives of Sexual Behavior* 5 (1976): 529–38; Maurice Kenney, "Tinselled Bucks: An Historical Study in Indian Homosexuality," *Gay Sunshine,* winter 1975–76, 15–17; Donald Forgey, "The Institution of Berdache among the North American Plains Indians," *Journal of Sex Research* 11 (1975): 1–15.

For journalistic accounts about and personal statements by contemporary gay Indians, see Jennifer Juarez Robles, "Tribes and Tribulations: Despite Columbus Day Unity, Native American Gays and Lesbians Do Battle with Straights for Acceptance," *Advocate,* 17 November 1992, 40–43; Joe Rio, "What Do Indians Think About?" in Loraine Hutchins and Lani Kaahumanu, eds., *Bi Any Other Name: Bisexual People Speak Out* (Boston: Alyson, 1991), 37–39; Jane Caputi, "Interview with Paula Gunn Allen," *Trivia* 16/17 (1990): 50–67; Beth Brant, "Recovery and Transformation: The Blue Heron," in Lisa Albrecht and Rose M. Brewer, eds., *Bridges of Power: Women's Multicultural Alliances* (Philadelphia: New Society, 1990), 118–21; Neil Miller, *In Search of Gay America: Women and Men in a Time of Change* (New York: Atlantic Monthly, 1989; Perennial Library, 1990), 190–96; Ramón A. Gutiérrez, "Must We Deracinate Indians to Find Gay Roots?" *Out/Look,* winter 1989, 61–67; Robert Lynch, "Seeing Twice," *Southern Exposure,* November–December 1985, 90–93; Will Roscoe, "Gay American Indians: Creating an Identity from Past Traditions," *Advocate,* 29 October 1985, 45–49; Beth Brant, "Reclamation: A Lesbian Indian Story," in Trudy Dartee and Sandee Potter, eds., *Women-Identified Women* (Palo Alto: Mayfield, 1984), 97–104; Martin Duberman, "1965 Native American Transvestism," *New York Native,* 21 June 1982, 12, 46; Edmund White, *States of Desire: Travels in Gay America* (New York: E. P. Dutton, 1980), 99–101; Dean Gengle, "Reclaiming the Old New World: Gay Was Good with Native Americans," *Advocate,* 28 January 1976, 40–41; and Bob Waltrip, "Elmer Gage: American Indian," *One Magazine,* March 1965, 6–10.

6. Allen, *Sacred Hoop,* 1, 13–14.

7. Williams, *Spirit and the Flesh,* 215–24; and Will Roscoe, "Living the Tradition: Gay American Indians," in Mark Thompson, ed., *Gay Spirit: Myth and Meaning* (New York: St. Martin's, 1987), 74–75.

8. Williams, *Spirit and the Flesh,* 218–19.

9. Ibid., 227.

10. Burns, preface, and Erna Pahe, "Speaking Up," in Roscoe, ed., *Living the Spirit,* 3, 5, 109; Roscoe, "Living the Tradition," in Thompson, ed., *Gay Spirit,* 71–72; and Williams, *Spirit and the Flesh,* 211.

11. Pahe, "Speaking Up," in Roscoe, ed., *Living the Spirit,* 109; Roscoe, "Living the Tradition," in Thompson, ed., *Gay Spirit,* 76; and Robles, "Tribes and Tribulations," *Advocate,* 17 November 1992, 43.

12. Robles, "Tribes and Tribulations," 41–43; Robert Allen Warrior, *Tribal Secrets: Recovering American Indian Intellectual Traditions* (Minneapolis: University of Minnesota Press, 1995), 122; and Clyde H. Farnsworth, "AIDS Is Brought Sadly Home to Canada's Indians," *New York Times,* 3 January 1995, A4.

13. Harris and Lone Dog, "Two Spirited People," 162–63.

14. Ibid., 159; Williams, *Spirit and the Flesh,* 227; Roscoe, "Living the Tradition," in Thompson, ed., *Gay Spirit,* 76; Pahe, "Speaking Up," in Roscoe, ed., *Living the Spirit,* 110; and Robles, "Tribes and Tribulations," 41–43.

15. Allen, *Sacred Hoop,* 62.

16. Williams, *Spirit and the Flesh,* 217.

17. James S. Tinney, "Struggles of a Black Pentecostal," in Michael J. Smith, ed., *Black Men/White Men: A Gay Anthology* (San Francisco: Gay Sunshine, 1983), 169. This "estimate" may not be as extreme as it may appear. In 1929 in New York City, Reverend Adam Clayton Powell spoke of the pervasive presence of homosexual parishioners and clergy in Harlem's churches and of the support for their participation by knowing congregations. See George Chauncey, *Gay New York: Gender, Urban Culture, and the Making of the Gay Male World, 1890–1940* (New York: Basic Books, 1994), 254–56; and Adam Clayton Powell, *Against the Tide: An Autobiography* (New York: Richard R. Smith, 1938), 57–59, 206, 209–20. See also Michael C. Dickens, "An Analysis of Societal Racism and Homophobia and Their Effect upon Gay and Bisexual Men of African Descent" (M.A. thesis, Wesleyan University, 1994), 43–49.

18. *Prologue* (Provo, Utah: Prometheus, 1978), 56. See discussion in Jan Stout, "Sin and Sexuality: Psychobiology and the Development of Homosexuality," in Ron Schow, Wayne Schow, and Marybeth Raynes, eds., *Peculiar People: Mormons and Same-Sex Orientation* (Salt Lake City: Signature Books, 1991), 178.

19. Stout, "Sin and Sexuality," in Schow, Schow, and Raynes, eds., *Peculiar People,* 178.

20. I use the terms "service" and "ministry" synonymously to mean giving care, aiding, and attending to those in need, contributing to the comfort and happiness of others.

21. "Caring for Children," *Dialogue* (Brethren/Mennonite Council for Lesbian and Gay Concerns), November 1990, 5.

22. Janie Spahr, "Rainbow's End: Creating a Safe Place," *Open Hands,* winter 1991, 6–7.

23. Tinney, "Struggles of a Black Pentecostal," in Smith, ed., *Black Men/White Men,* 169.

24. Stout, "Sin and Sexuality," in Schow, Schow, and Raynes, eds., *Peculiar People,* 178.

25. "Coming Out to My Session," *More Light Update* (Presbyterians for Lesbian and Gay Concerns), December 1988, 2–3.

26. Mark O'Keefe, "Members Often Reluctant to Accept Gays at Church," *Dallas Morning News,* 12 June 1993, 39A.

27. L. Loreen Fox-Shipley, "Experiencing God's Love in a Painful Situation," *Dialogue* (Brethren/Mennonite Council for Lesbian and Gay Concerns), June 1993, 3.

28. Tim Tyner, "Evangelism in the Gay/Lesbian Community: One Affirmation Group Story," *Affirmation* (United Methodists for Lesbian and Gay Concerns), winter 1988, 7–8.

29. Paul F. Bauer, "The Homosexual Subculture at Worship: A Participant Observation Study," *Pastoral Psychology* 25 (1976): 115–27.

30. Henry Rabinowitz, "Talmud Class in a Gay Synagogue," *Judaism* 32 (1983): 433–43.

31. Leonard Norman Primiano, " 'I Would Rather Be Fixated on the Lord': Women's Religion, Men's Power, and the 'Dignity' Problem," *New York Folklore* 19 (1993): 89–103.

32. *FLGC Newsletter* (Friends for Lesbian and Gay Concerns), summer 1992, 4.

33. "Affirming Steps: Lakeshore Avenue Baptist Church," *Voice of the Turtle* (American Baptists Concerned), fall 1990, 1.

34. "Justice Issues" and "Personal News," *Waves* (United Church Coalition for Lesbian/Gay Concerns), March 1993, 5, 8.

35. The outright denial of membership to gay people may be rare, but it does occur. See, for example, "Introducing Coalition Council Member Alice O'Donovan," *Waves* (United Church Coalition for Lesbian/Gay Concerns), June 1991, 7.

36. Mearle L. Griffith and C. David Lundquist, *An Analysis of Major Issues Addressed by the 1988 General Conference and a Comparison with Beliefs and Attitudes of Local Church Members* (Dayton: Office of Research, General Conference of Ministries, United Methodist Church, 1990), 1, 7–8, 15, 17. I realize that the findings for Griffith and Lundquist's study may include lesbian, bisexual, and gay members, but I choose to use the term "non-gay" in my discussion for the sake of establishing terms that will clarify comparison. Their study did not attempt to report data by sexual orientation of respondents.

37. For resolutions concerning gay issues passed by the Executive Council and General Synod, see United Church Coalition for Lesbian/Gay Concerns, comp., *United Church of Christ Social Policy regarding Lesbian, Gay and Bisexual Concerns, a Compendium of Actions by: The Council for Christian Social Action (1969), the Executive Council (1973, 1980, 1981), and General Synods 10, 11, 14, 15, 16* (Athens, Ohio: United Church Coalition for Lesbian/Gay Concerns, n.d.).

38. Hans Holznagel, "Synod and Assembly to Deal with Gay Issues," *United Church News,* June 1993, 13; and Andy Lang, "Clinton Rapped on Military Gays" and "Youth Hear Straight Talk about Gay Concerns" and "General Synod Summary of Actions," *United Church News,* July/August 1993, CG-5, CG-9, CG-10.

39. "Church Shows Independence in Survey on Social Issues," *United Church News* (UUC New York Conference Linkage edition), May 1990, 12.

40. Average of percentages for three categories of problems and two categories of advantages.

41. Griffith and Lundquist, *Analysis of Major Issues,* 13, 15. See also Ted Selen, "Sources of Political Intolerance: The Case of the American South," in Laurence W. Moreland, Tod A. Baker, and Robert P. Steed, eds., *Contemporary Southern Political Attitudes and Behavior: Studies and Essays* (New York: Praeger, 1982), 73–91. In his sample of 3,796 non-Southerners and 1,780 Southerners, Selen found 65 percent of the former tolerant of homosexuals compared to 46 percent of the latter.

42. Martin B. Bradley et al., *Churches and Church Membership in the United States 1990: An Enumeration by Region, State and County Based on Data Reported for 133 Church Groupings* (Atlanta: Glenmary Research Center, 1992), 4–11. Using data from Bradley et al., I calculated that of a total 37,238 local UMC churches, 19,540 (52 percent) are in the South, and of a total 6,260 local UCC churches, 788 (13 percent) are in the South.

43. Average of percentages for three categories of problems and two categories of advantages.

44. William J. McKinney Jr., *Findings from the Membership Inventory,* New Conversations Supplement (New York: United Church Board for Homeland Ministries, n.d.). I realize that the findings for McKinney's study may include lesbian, bisexual, and gay members, but I choose to use the term "non-gay" in my discussion for the sake of establishing terms that will clarify comparison. His study did not attempt to report data by sexual orientation of respondents.

45. Calculated from figures provided by Timothy J. Gilbride, Mearle L. Griffith, and C. David Lundquist, *The Survey of United Methodist Opinion: A Research Tool for Informed Decision Making* (Dayton: Office of Research, General Council on Ministries, United Methodist Church, 1990), 13. I realize that the findings for Gilbride, Griffith, and Lundquist's study may include lesbian, bisexual, and gay members, but I choose to use the term "non-gay" in my discussion for the sake of establishing terms that will clarify comparison. Their study did not attempt to report data by sexual orientation of respondents.

46. Thomas O'Brien, "A Survey of Gay/Lesbian Catholics concerning Attitudes toward Sexual Orientation and Religious Beliefs," *Journal of Homosexuality* 21 (1991): 29–44.

47. Gilbride, Griffith, and Lundquist, *Survey of United Methodist Opinion,* 13.

48. The UCC name for local churches, agencies, and provinces within the denomination that declare themselves as officially "welcoming" gay people.

49. Average of percentages for four levels of participation, chairing, and outness.

50. Average of percentages for four levels of participation, chairing, and outness.

51. See *Bisexuality: Perceptions and Realities,* an issue of *Open Hands,* fall 1991.

52. F. Jay Deacon, "Stonewall Plus 20: A Welcoming UUA," *UULGC World* (Unitarian Universalists for Lesbian and Gay Concerns), September 1989, 2–3.

53. Wheadon United Methodist Church Reconciling Congregation Task Force, "One Church's Journey Toward Including Bisexuals," *Open Hands,* fall 1991, 16.

54. Average of percentages for four levels of participation and outness.

55. Average of percentages for four levels of participation, chairing, and outness.

56. Thomas J. Lueck, "Homosexuals Turn Mass into Silent Protest of Pastoral Letter," *New York Times,* 30 August 1993, B1.

57. "RTP Responds to Local Crisis at Eugene Synagogue," *Right to Privacy Inc. Newsletter* (Eugene, Oregon), April 1994, 5.

58. See Aaron Cooper, "No Longer Invisible: Gay and Lesbian Jews Build a Movement," in Richard Hasbany, ed., *Homosexuality and Religion* (New York: Haworth, 1989), 74–77, 88–89; and in *World Congress Digest* (World Congress of Gay and Lesbian Jewish Organizations), see "JNF Inscribes Our Plaque," fall 1992, 1, and "UAHC to JNF: Inscribe Gay Plaque," summer 1988, 1.

59. Lev Raphael, "Letter from Israel," *Lambda Book Report,* November/December 1994, 8–10; "Memorial Service at Yad Vashem Disrupted by Protest," *World Congress Digest* (World Congress of Gay and Lesbian Jewish Organizations), fall 1994, 1; "Hatred, Then and Now," *Advocate,* 12 July 1994, 15; and "They Also Died," *New York Times,* 31 May 1994, A3.

60. Ed Kobee, "UU's and the 1993 March on Washington for Lesbian, Gay and Bisexual Equal Rights," *UULGC World* (Unitarian Universalists for Lesbian and Gay Concerns), January 1993, 3; and "We Are Marching!" *Interweave World* (Unitarian Universalist for Lesbian, Gay and Bisexual Concerns), 15 April 1993, 1.

61. See also *Special General Conference Issue,* issue of *Affirmation* (United Methodists for Lesbian, Gay and Bisexual Concerns), summer 1992.

62. Michael Purintun, "The Baltimore Demonstration," *More Light Update* (Presbyterians for Lesbian and Gay Concerns), May 1991, 11–3. See also Jim Anderson, "An Assembly We Will Never Forget," *More Light Update* (Presbyterians for Lesbian and Gay Concerns), August 1991, 1–2.

63. In *Voice of the Turtle* (American Baptists Concerned), see Chris Boisvert, "General Board Adopts Resolution Calling for Dialog on Sexuality" and "AB-Concerned Has Positive Presence at Biennial"; Rick Mixon, "Reflections on San Jose, San Francisco and Geyserville"; and Jo Bower, "Pride and Spirit," summer 1993, 1, 2, 3, 9, 11.

64. Claire Simon, "A Kinder, Gentler F.U.M.," and Bruce Grimes, "FUM Restricts 'Unofficial Quaker Groups,'" *FLGC Newsletter* (Friends for Lesbian and Gay Concerns), winter 1992, 1–2.

65. Beverly Brubaker, "Support and Advocacy," *Dialogue* (Brethren/Mennonite Council for Gay and Lesbian Concerns), March 1991, 4–5.

66. See *Commitment Ceremonies,* special issue of *Dialogue* (Brethren/Mennonite Council for Gay and Lesbian Concerns), fall 1994; *Same-Sex Unions,* special issue of *More Light Update* (Presbyterians for Lesbian and Gay Concerns), September 1994; *Holy Unions,* special issue of *Christian Social Action,* October 1990; and *Confronted by Love: The "Holy Union" Controversy,* special issue of *Open Hands,* fall 1990.

For a sampling of news media coverage from 1984 to 1994 in North America, see Peter Steinfels, "Unmarried Couples; Single-Sex Couples; Triads and Quintets; Why Bother with Marriage Norms?" *New York Times,* 14 May 1994, 28; Brian Kroeker, "For and against Same-Sex Marriages as Models of Commitment," *Ottawa Citizen,* 9 January 1993, A11; Linda Wheeler, "Mass Wedding Marries Tradition and Protest," *Washington Post,* 25 April 1993, A17; Michael McAteer, "United Church Avoids Stand on Same-Sex Marriage Issue," *Toronto Star,* 21 August 1992, A28; Bob Harvey, "Pentecostals Find Old-Style Morality Wins New Adherents," *Ottawa Citizen,* 15 August 1992, C7; Roy Bragg, "Lesbian Marriage Notice Stirs Up Debate in Austin," *Houston Chronicle,* 15 July 1992, A18; Larry Witham, "Rabbis Vote on Gay Blessings," *Washington Times,* 14 March 1992, B4; Michael McAteer, "Bless Gay Couples, United Church Urged," *Toronto Star,* 3 March 1992, A1; James L. Franklin, "Jewish Movement Backs Gay Rights," *Boston Globe,* 20 February 1992, 42; "Jewish Group Urges Full Equality for Homosexuals; Reconstructionism, the Proposal Includes Allowing Rabbinical Sanctions for Same-Sex Marriages," *Los Angeles Times,* 15 February 1992, F17; Laura Sessions Stepp, "Jewish Branch Adopts Liberal Rules for Gays: Reconstructionists' Action Could Allow Marriages," *Washington Post,* 8 February 1992, B7; "Judge in D.C. Rules Out Church Wedding for Gays," *Orlando Sentinel Tribune,* 25 January 1992, D8; "Gay Wedding Rites on Increase: Panel Studying," *Atlanta Journal and Constitution,* 5 October 1991, B1; Elizabeth Rhodes, "New Ties That Bind: Same-Sex Couples Challenge the System to Gain Legal Recognition of Their Commitments to Each Other," *Seattle Times,* 21 July 1991, K1; Gayle White, "Phoenix Convention Anoints Same-Sex Unions: Church for Gays Meets in Same City as Episcopalians," *Atlanta Journal and Constitution,* 19 July 1991, A8; Gayle White, "Bishops Waiting for '94 to Decide on Gay Episcopalians: Proposals for Same-Sex Unions, Homosexual Ordinations on Hold," *Atlanta Journal and Constitution,* 16 July 1991, A4; Holly Morris, "Gays Doubt Episcopal Ordination: Convention Also to Mull Same-Sex Marriage Issue," *Atlanta Journal and Constitution,* 13 July 1991, E6; Tom Harpur, "Why the Anglican Church Should Bless Gay Unions," *Toronto Star,* 23 June 1991, B7; Clarence Page, "A Nontraditional Way to Say 'I Do,'" *Chicago Tribune,* 8 October 1989, C3; and Edward A. Gargan, "Homosexual Weddings Stir Dispute," *New York Times,* 5 September 1984, B4.

67. See Steven R. Durant, "Holy Unions or Marriage," *More Light Update* (Presbyterians for Lesbian and Gay Concerns), October 1993, 14; Jeff Johnson, "An Old Fashioned Gay Relationship," *Voice of the Turtle* (American Baptists Concerned), winter 1992, 4; "Naming Same-Sex Unions: Homewood Friends Reach Greater Clearness," *FLGC Newsletter* (Friends for Lesbian and Gay Concerns), spring 1990, 2; Suzanne Sherman, ed., *Lesbian and Gay Marriage: Private Commitments, Public Ceremonies* (Philadelphia: Temple University Press, 1992), 1–8; and Becky Butler, ed., *Ceremonies of the Heart: Celebrating Lesbian Unions* (Seattle: Seal, 1990), 41.

68. See "Reconstructionist Movement Approves 'Commitment Ceremonies,'" *World Congress Digest* (World Congress of Gay and Lesbian Jewish Organizations), fall 1993, 3; Yoel H. Kahn, "Judaism and Homosexuality: The Traditionalist/Progressive Debate," in Hasbany, ed., *Homosexuality and Religion,* 74–77; Eric Schuman, "Unitarian Universalist," *Open Hands,* summer 1986, 12–13; Office for Lesbian and Gay Concerns, *A Planning Guide for Same-Sex Services of Unions* (Boston: Unitarian Universalist Association); Barry A. Kosmin and Seymour P. Lachman, *One Nation under God: Religion in Contemporary American Society* (New York: Harmony Books, 1993), 230; and Bruce Grimes, ed., *Religious Society of Friends: Inclusive Minutes on Marriage* (Sumneytown, Pa.: Friends for Lesbian and Gay Concerns, May 1993).

69. For Presbyterians, see in *More Light Update* (Presbyterians for Lesbian and Gay Concerns): Chris Glaser, "Walk with Me: A Ceremony of the Heart,"

March 1995, 1–4; "General Assembly 1994, Wichita, Kansas, June 10–17: Highlights," August 1994, 1; special issue, *Same-Sex Unions,* September 1994; and Jim Anderson, "An Assembly We Will Never Forget," 2.

For Episcopalians, see "Episcopal Priest Relieved of Duties after Officiating at Same-Sex Ceremony," *Second Stone,* July/August 1995, 6; "A Sexual Showdown: Will the Bishops of the Episcopal Church Tacitly Embrace the New Morality?" *Time,* 15 August 1994, 38; and "Episcopals Find God in Gay Relationships," *New York Native,* 8 August 1994, 11–12.

70. Scott Harris, "Blessing of a Covenant: Gays United in Rites at Prominent Pasadena Church," *Los Angeles Times,* 25 January 1992, B1.

71. Kit Ketchum, "An Open Letter of Thanks," *UULGC World* (Unitarian Universalists for Lesbian and Gay Concerns), November 1990, 3.

72. Ann Brenoff, "Jewish Paper in San Diego Tackles Difficult Subject: Reaction of Readers Has Been Mixed to Decision to Publish Announcement of Lesbian Couple's Commitment Ceremony," *Los Angeles Times,* 4 August 1992, E1. See also "Jewish Lawyer Denied Job Because of Lesbian Marriage," *World Congress Digest* (World Congress of Gay and Lesbian Jewish Organizations), spring 1992, 3; "Marriage: Quaker Couple Gets High Profile," *FLGC Newsletter* (Friends for Lesbian and Gay Concerns), summer 1992, 3; George B. Pyle, "A Man Marries a Man? Print It!" *New York Times,* 11 August 1993; and David W. Dunlap, "For Better or Worse, A Marital Milestone: Ithaca Officials Endorse a Gay Union," *New York Times,* 27 July 1995, B1, B5.

73. "Entreat Me Not to Leave Thee," *Dialogue* (Brethren/Mennonite Council for Gay and Lesbian Concerns), November 1990, 4.

74. See Rick Harding, "Methodists Clash over Gay Marriage: Washington, D.C., Congregation Faces Hot Water, Bishop Warns," *Advocate,* 19 June 1990, 14; "UMC and Gay Unions," *Christian Century,* 27 June to 4 July 1990, 626–27; and Graeme and Jane Donovan, "Holy Union: One Church's Experience," *Open Hands,* fall 1990, 7–8.

75. For legal concerns, see William B. Rubenstein, ed., *Lesbians, Gay Men, and the Law,* Law in Context Series Reader 2 (New York: New Press, 1993), 377–474; Patricia V. Long, section 10, "Legal Considerations and a View toward the Future," in Task Force on Same-Gender Covenants, *Task Force Report: Celebration of Same Gender Covenants* (Raleigh, N.C.: Pullen Memorial Baptist Church, 1993), 25–27; Nan D. Hunter, Sherryl E. Michaelson, and Thomas B. Stoddard, *The Rights of Lesbians and Gay Men: The Basic Guide to a Gay Person's Rights,* American Civil Liberties Union Handbook Series (Carbondale: Southern Illinois University Press, 1992), 74–117; Johnette Duff and George G. Truitt, *The Spousal Equivalent Handbook: A Legal and Financial Guide to Living Together* (New York: Plume, 1992); Diane Whitacre, *Will You Be Mine? Domestic Partnership, San Francisco City Hall; February 14, 1991* (San Francisco: Crooked Street, 1992); Lambda Legal Defense and Education Fund, *Domestic Partnership Issues and Legislation* (New York: Lambda Legal Defense and Education Fund, 1990); Editors of the Harvard Law Review, *Sexual Orientation and the Law* (Cambridge, Mass.: Harvard University Press, 1990), 93–119; and Hayden Curry, Denis Clifford, and Robin Leonard, *A Legal Guide for Lesbians and Gay Couples,* 7th ed. (Berkeley: Nolo Press, 1993).

For other concerns in general, see Lawrence A. Kurdek, ed., *Social Services for Gay and Lesbian Couples* (New York: Harrington Park, 1994); D. Merilee Clunis and G. Dorsey Green, *Lesbian Couples: Creating Healthy Relationships for the 1990s* (Seattle: Seal, 1993); Susan E. Johnson, *Staying Power: Long Term Lesbian Couples* (Tallahassee: Naiad, 1991); John H. Driggs and Stephen E. Finn, *Intimacy between Men: How to Find and Keep Gay Love Relationships* (New York: Plume, 1991); Tina Tessina, *Gay Relationships; For Men and Women: How to Find Them, How to Improve Them, How to Make Them Last* (Los Angeles: Jeremy P. Tarcher, 1989); Celeste West, *A Lesbian Love Advisor: The Sweet and Savory Arts of Lesbian Courtship* (San Francisco: Cleis, 1989); Eric Marcus, *The Male Couple's Guide: Finding a Man, Making a Home, Building a Life* (New York: Harper and Row, 1988); Betty Berzon, *Permanent Partners: Building Gay and Lesbian Relationships That Last* (New York: Plume, 1988); John DeCecco, *Gay Relationships* (New York: Harrington Park, 1988); Phyllis Jean Kinheart Athey and Mary Jo Kinheart Osterman, *The Lesbian Relationship Handbook* (Evanston, Ill.: Kinheart, 1984); and David P. McWhirter and Andrew M. Mattison, *The Male Couple: How Relationships Develop* (Englewood Cliffs, N.J.: Prentice-Hall, 1984).

76. Partners Task Force for Gay and Lesbian Couples, *Partners' National Survey of Lesbian and Gay Couples,* special issue of *Partners: Newsletter for Gay and Lesbian Couples,* May/June 1990, 16, found that "relationship rituals" were one of the factors significantly associated with "high-quality relationships."

77. See Sally B. Geis and Donald E. Messer, eds., *Caught in the Crossfire: Helping Christians Debate Homosexuality* (Nashville: Abingdon, 1994); and John Dart, "Support Grows among Clergy for 'Weddings' of Gay Couples," *Los Angeles Times,* 7 December 1987, 3.

For a philosophical defense of same-sex unions, see Richard D. Mohr, *A More Perfect Union: Why Straight America Must Stand Up for Gay Rights* (Boston: Beacon, 1994), 31–53; for a theological discussion and debate, see Robert Williams, "Toward a Theology for Lesbian and Gay Marriage" (with responses by Ann C. Lammers, "Whom God Joins, the Church Should Bless"; Margaret R. Miles, "Beyond Biological Determination"; Joseph Monti, "The Norm of Heterosexual Marriage"; David A. Scott, "The Hermeneutics of Marriage"; and Louis Weil, "The Church Does Not Make a Marriage"), *Anglican Theological Review* 71 (spring 1990): 134–74; and for a historical defense, see John Boswell, *Same-Sex Unions in Premodern Europe* (New York: Villard, 1994).

78. Ketchum, "Open Letter of Thanks," 3. For problems in another otherwise pro-gay, liberal denominations, see Nancy M. Erikson, "Should the Church Bless This Union?" *United Church News,* May 1995, 10; and in *FLGC Newsletter* (Friends for Lesbian and Gay Concerns), "Friends United Meeting to FLGC," winter 1990, 4; "Letter to Friends United Meeting," July 1989 (insert); and "Summary of Business of Midwinter Gathering," spring 1989, 2.

79. See Task Force on Same-Gender Covenants, *Task Force Report;* Mahan Siler, "The Blessing of a Gay Union: Reflections of a Pastoral Journey," *Baptists Today,* 19 March 1992, 11; and Kosmin and Lachman, *One Nation under God,* 230.

80. See "Did Gay Weddings, Says New ELCA Bishop," *Second Stone,* March/April 1995, 5.

81. For examples, see Sid Hall, "Same-Sex Unions: Perspectives from a Clergy Ally," *Open Hands,* spring 1993, 24; and Rick Harding, "Methodists Clash over Gay Marriage," 14. In *Affirmation* (United Methodists for Lesbian, Gay and Bisexual Concerns), see "More Midwest Mischief" and Jeanne Knepper, "Pro-Active Congregations," winter 1992, 5, 7–8; and "Clergywoman Withdraws" and Jean Caffey Lyles, "Bishop to Indiana Clergy: No More Gay Union Liturgies," fall 1992, 3–5.

For similar conflict in the United Church of Christ, see John T. McQuiston, "Lesbian Banns Divide Church, and a Minister Loses His Job: Close Vote Ousts Cleric Who Defied Advice," *New York Times,* 2 August 1995, B4; in the Episcopal Church, see "Episcopal Priest Relieved of Duties after Officiating at Same-Sex Ceremony," *Second Stone,* July/August 1995, 6; in the Church of the Brethren, see Deanna Brown, "Sticks and Stones and Words," *Dialogue* (Brethren/Mennonite Council for Gay and Lesbian Concerns), winter 1995, 4–5; and in the Presbyterian Church (U.S.A.), see "Holy Union Leads to Pastor's Resignation," *More Light Update* (Presbyterians for Lesbian and Gay Concerns), October 1993, 13, and Pyle, "A Man Marries a Man?" A15.

82. Partners Task Force, *Partners' National Survey of Lesbian and Gay Couples,* 1.

83. For accounts of various ceremonies that have taken place and advice for planning ceremonies, see Cherry Kittredge and Zalmon Sherwood, eds., *Equal Rites: Lesbian and Gay Worship, Ceremonies, and Celebrations* (Louisville: Westminster/John Knox, 1995); Tess Ayers and Paul Brown, *The Essential Guide to Lesbian and Gay Weddings* (San Francisco: HarperSanFrancisco, 1994); Sherman, ed., *Lesbian and Gay Marriage;* Elizabeth Stuart, *Daring to Speak Love's Name* (London: Hamish Hamilton, 1992); and Butler, ed., *Ceremonies of the Heart;* Paul Horowitz and Scott Klein, "A Ceremony of Commitment," in Christie Balka and Andy Rose, eds., *Twice Blessed: On Being Lesbian or Gay and Jewish* (Boston: Beacon, 1989), 126–32; and Larry J. Uhrig, *The Two of Us: Affirming, Celebrating and Symbolizing Gay and Lesbian Relationships* (Boston: Alyson, 1984).

For research on historical precedents for same-sex ceremonies, see Butler, ed., *Ceremonies of the Heart,* 3–41; John Boswell, *Same-Sex Unions in Premodern Europe,* and *1500 Years of the Church Blessing Lesbian and Gay Relationships: It's Nothing New,* videotape of address (Washington, D.C.: Integrity, 1988).

84. "Mary and Marcia," *Open Hands,* fall 1990, 13.

Chapter 5: Seminary, Ordination, Ministry, and Employment

1. The terms for "clergy" used by different religious bodies vary. Roman Catholic and Episcopalian clergy are called priests; Protestant clergy are called ministers or pastors; and Jewish clergy are called rabbis. Roman Catholic women cannot become priests, but many enter Christian ministry by joining religious orders and are called nuns or religious.

2. Neil Miller, *In Search of Gay America: Women and Men in a Time of Change* (New York: Atlantic Monthly, 1989; Perennial Library, 1990), 211–56.

3. Dismissals have occurred with some regularity since 1970, when the gay liberation movement encouraged gay clergy to be more open and outspoken. For an account of one of these earlier events, see F. Gene Leggett, "Whose Life Is Disrupted?" *Open Hands,* summer 1986, 20–21; and Peter Madison, "Gene Leggett 1935–1987," *Affirmation* (United Methodists for Lesbian, Gay and Bisexual Concerns), winter 1988, 16–19.

Non-gay clergy have also been fired and denied ministerial standing for taking pro-gay positions. See, for example, Deanna Brown, "Sticks and Stones and Words," and Helen Wells Quintela, "Redemption in the Storm," *Dialogue* (Brethren/Mennonite Council for Gay and Lesbian Concerns), winter 1995, 4–6; Jan Griesinger, "They Fired My Pastor Today," *Waves* (United Church Coalition for Lesbian/Gay Concerns), December 1994, 4, 8; Fran Myers, "Where the Spirit Blows," *Voice of the Turtle* (American Baptists Concerned), summer 1994, 11; "Holy Union Leads to Pastor's Resignation," *More Light Update* (Presbyterians for Lesbian and Gay Concerns), October 1993, 13; Sid Hall, "Same-Sex Unions: Perspectives from a Clergy Ally," *Open Hands,* spring 1993, 24; "Clergywoman Withdraws" and Jean Caffey Lyles, "Bishop to Indiana Clergy: No More Gay Union Liturgies," *Affirmation* (United Methodists for Lesbian, Gay and Bisexual Concerns), fall 1992, 3–5; "More Midwest Mischief" and Jeanne Knepper, "Pro-active Congregations," *Affirmation* (United Methodists for Lesbian, Gay and Bisexual Concerns), winter 1992, 5, 7–8; John Nelson, "A Plague of Homophobia: One Case in Point," *Waves* (United Church Coalition for Lesbian/Gay Concerns), June 1991, 9; and Rick Harding, "Methodists Clash over Gay Marriage: Washington, D.C., Congregation Faces Hot Water, Bishop Warns," *Advocate,* 19 June 1990, 14.

4. Bet Hannon with Bruce Grimes, "Iowa Yearly Meeting Forces Lesbian Pastor Out," *FLGC Newsletter* (Friends for Lesbian and Gay Concerns), winter 1991, 1, 3–5.

5. Dick Hasbany, "Scott Anderson's Story: A Tale of Homophobia, Betrayal, Anger, and Wholeness," *More Light Update* (Presbyterians for Lesbian and Gay Concerns), August 1990, 1–5. See also Barbara Roche, "Ministry, Not Martyrdom: Presbyterians Lose a Gay Pastor," *Christianity and Crisis,* 18 June 1990, 194–96.

6. Chris Boisvert, "Gay Lutheran Pastor Defrocked," *Voice of the Turtle* (American Baptists Concerned), spring 1994, 1, 4. See also "Lutheran Bishop Gives Nod to Gay Pastor," *Second Stone,* March/April 1995, 3. Later developments provided the bishop with two options: either to suspend the congregation from the denomination or to reverse the defrocking. He did neither and chose instead to let the congregation keep Merkel as a defrocked pastor.

7. In *Voice of the Turtle* (American Baptists Concerned), see: Mark Crosby, "Gay Candidates Status Frozen: A Personal Response and Sharing of Feelings," winter 1995, 1, 4; "Witch Hunts Begin in Earnest," fall 1994, 1, 3; Irving Cummings and Jeffrey Long-Middleton, "Mark Crosby's Appeal Denied," summer 1994, 7; "Openly Gay Pastoral Counselor Denied Endorsement by ABC/USA Board: Two Conflicting Resolutions Cause Confusion," spring 1994, 1; Susan

Vanderburgh, "Lesbian and Gay Persons in the Church," winter 1994, 5–6; Rick Mixon, "Rick's Report: Can We Talk?" spring 1993, 2–3; Mark Crosby, "One of the Witches Is in Our Midst!" winter 1993, 8; and "News Alert! Attacks on the Ordinations of Lesbian and Gay Clergy," fall 1992, 9.

8. Chris Boisvert, "First Openly Lesbian ABC Minister Called," *Voice of the Turtle* (American Baptists Concerned), winter 1992, 1, 4.

9. J. Gordon Melton, ed., *The Churches Speak on Homosexuality: Official Statements from Religious Bodies and Ecumenical Organizations* (Detroit: Gale Research, 1991), 209, 259–60, 268–69; "Reconstructionist Movement Approves 'Commitment Ceremonies,'" *World Congress Digest* (World Congress of Gay and Lesbian Jewish Organizations), fall 1993, 3; and Arlene Kelly, "AFSC and Affirmative Action," *FLGC Newsletter* (Friends for Lesbian and Gay Concerns), winter 1991, 1, 2–3.

10. See Kelly, "AFSC and Affirmative Action," 1, 2–3.

11. Within the UCC, for example, a noticeable increase in the hiring of gay clergy is often offset by dismissals and rejections. For hiring, see in *Waves* (United Church Coalition for Lesbian/Gay Concerns): April Allison, "Small West Virginia Church Calls an Openly Lesbian Pastor" and "Pastoral Calls," December 1994, pp, 1, 10; and "Sayville (NY) Church Retains John Geter," June 1991, 1–2. For discrimination and firing, see "Justice Issues," March 1993, 5; "Personal News," December 1992, 5–6; Alice O'Donovan, "On Saying Goodbye" and "Personal News," December 1991, 1–26; "Bitter Division at Andover, NH," June 1991, 8; and Wendy Taylor and Ellen Sweetin, "Miracle in Missoula," February 1990, 5–6. See also "Historic Church Picks Lesbian Pastor," *Second Stone,* March/April 1995, 5.

See also Common Vision Planning Committee, *Report and Recommendations of the Common Vision Planning Committee to the Board of Trustees, Unitarian Universalist Association* (Boston: Unitarian Universalist Association, 1989), 10, 12.

12. National polls find that less than half of surveyed Americans think gay people should be hired for the clergy. Polls show a growing acceptance of gay clergy, but never by as much as 50 percent. Reported percentages vary regionally, for example, from a pro-gay high of 62 percent in parts of California to an anti-gay high of 69 percent in Kentucky. Support for hiring gay clergy also decreases dramatically from those who attend religious services infrequently to those who attend regularly. And among Catholics, Protestants, and Jews, the latter are by the far the most supportive. See John Dart, "Majority in the Survey Say Gays Should Not Be Barred from Serving in the Clergy," *Los Angeles Times,* 5 January 1992, 25A; Don Lattin, "Churchgoers Do Not Want Gay Clergy," *San Francisco Chronicle,* 23 May 1990, A1; and "You Can Be Gay and Christian in Kentucky," *Second Stone,* November/December 1994, 6.

13. See in *Voice of the Turtle* (American Baptists Concerned): "Witch Hunts Begin in Earnest," 1, 3; and Vanderburgh, "Lesbian and Gay Persons," 5–6.

14. James G. Wolf, *Gay Priests* (San Francisco: Harper and Row, 1989), 45–46.

15. A. W. Richard Sipe, *A Secret World: Sexuality and the Search for Celibacy* (New York: Brunner/Mazel, 1990) 8–14, 103–38.

16. Ibid., 118–29.
17. Ibid., 126–27, 133.
18. Sheila Murphy, "Counseling Lesbian Women Religious," *Women and Therapy* 5 (winter 1986): 10.
19. Sipe, *A Secret World,* 129, 134.
20. Ibid., 107.
21. Ibid., 107–8.
22. Ibid., 108.
23. Ibid., 133–37. The priests in the last group usually feel guilty about their homosexual activities, try to control their behavior, and tend to seek professional help. Unlike other gay priests, they have not established a pattern of homosexual behavior or fixed sexual identity. Some get caught in police traps at highway rest areas because of their inexperience at seeking sexual partners. Sipe observed that "many in this group are pained by their sense of loneliness, and they desire most of all simply 'to be held,' or to 'have someone accept me as I am.' " They naively look for such affection and relationships with hustlers and in areas known for impersonal sex.
24. Wolf, *Gay Priests,* 7, 38, 41–42; and Richard Wagner, *Gay Catholic Priests: A Study of Cognitive and Affective Dissonance* (San Francisco: Specific Press, 1981).
25. Wolf, *Gay Priests,* 7, 38, 41–42; and Wagner, *Gay Catholic Priests.*
26. Wolf, *Gay Priests,* 26; compared with the study conducted by the National Opinion Research Center, commissioned by the Ad Hoc Committee on Pastoral Research and Practices, National Conference of Catholic Bishops (NCCB), and analyzed by Andrew M. Greeley and R. Schoenerr, *The Catholic Priest in the United States: Sociological Investigations* (Washington, D.C.: United States Catholic Conference, 1972), and Eugene C. Kennedy and Victor J. Heckler, *The Catholic Priest in the United States: Psychological Investigations* (Washington, D.C.: United States Catholic Conference, 1972).
27. Wolf, *Gay Priests,* 45–48; and Wagner, *Gay Catholic Priests.* Wolf reported that in his and Wagner's samples "there appears to be evidence of more concern for the development of long-term relationships with other men and less acceptance of promiscuous sexual activity than would be found in the general population of gay men." He went on to say: "Of the various topics written about by our respondents, comments regarding sexual activity were the most numerous. On this issue two themes that surfaced repeatedly were concerns about the morality of homosexual activity and the problems inherent in promiscuity." To make comparisons with gay men in the general population, Wolf used data from Alfred C. Kinsey, Wardell B. Pomeroy, and Clyde E. Martin, *Sexual Behavior in the Human Male* (Philadelphia: W. B. Saunders, 1948). In Wolf see also T. Thompson, "A Christian Spirituality," 126, and R. Roberts, "The Fears of a Gay Priest," 148.
28. Wolf, *Gay Priests,* 29.
29. Murphy, "Counseling Lesbian Women Religious," 8, 12, 17.
30. Wolf, *Gay Priests,* 28, 63–64.
31. Ibid., 7, 28.
32. Ibid., 34.

33. Deborah H. Carney and Susan E. Davies, "Yours in Sisterhood: A Lesbian and Bisexual Perspective on Ministry," in Susan E. Davies and Eleanor H. Haney, eds., *Redefining Sexual Ethics: A Sourcebook of Essays, Stories, and Poems* (Cleveland: Pilgrim Press, 1991), 76.

34. Murphy, "Counseling Lesbian Women Religious," 9.

35. Wolf, *Gay Priests,* 35.

36. Carney and Davies, "Yours in Sisterhood," in Davies and Haney, eds., *Redefining Sexual Ethics,* 76, 79–80.

37. Nancy Carter, "Ignorance vs. Education: The UMC Funding Ban," *Open Hands,* summer 1986, 8–9.

38. Susan Kramer, "Birthing," *More Light Update* (Presbyterians for Lesbian and Gay Concerns), September 1990, 3–4.

39. Kirsten Peachey, "Unwilling Alienation: A Mennonite Church Experience," *Dialogue* (Brethren/Mennonite Council for Gay and Lesbian Concerns), January 1990, 1, 3–4.

40. Murphy, "Counseling Lesbian Women Religious," 7, 10.

41. Carney and Davies, "Yours in Sisterhood," in Davies and Haney, eds., *Redefining Sexual Ethics,* 76, 78.

42. Sipe, *A Secret World,* 112–13.

43. Wolf, *Gay Priests,* 35–36; compared with study conducted by the National Opinion Research Center.

44. Carney and Davies, "Yours in Sisterhood," in Davies and Haney, eds., *Redefining Sexual Ethics,* 82.

45. Sipe, *A Secret World,* 110. For a description of more restrictive earlier times, see R. Roberts, "The Fears of a Gay Priest," in Wolf, *Gay Priests,* 144–45.

46. Virginia Wolf, "Seminary Community or Closet?" *Open Hands,* fall 1994, 10.

47. Ibid.

48. Ibid.

49. Wolf, *Gay Priests,* 36.

50. Carney and Davies, "Yours in Sisterhood," in Davies and Haney, eds., *Redefining Sexual Ethics,* 79.

51. Miller, *In Search of Gay America,* 237–40.

52. Wolf, *Gay Priests,* 34, 45. The earlier study by Wagner, *Gay Catholic Priests,* found a smaller percentage of its sample (50 percent) reporting awareness of sexual orientation at the average age of ordination (see Wolf, *Gay Priests,* 34). The difference may reflect the social change that occurred within seminary settings and among gay seminarians between the 1970s and 1980s (see Sipe, *A Secret World,* 110).

53. Carney and Davies, "Yours in Sisterhood," in Davies and Haney, eds., *Redefining Sexual Ethics,* 76.

54. "Coming out" or "coming out of the closet" is usually understood by most gay people as a long and ongoing process that can occur at any stage of life. See Warren J. Blumenfeld and Diane Raymond, *Looking at Gay and Lesbian Life* (Boston: Beacon, 1993), 85–92. Anthologies of coming out stories are readily available. One of the earlier ones, which was also issued as a documentary film, is Nancy Adair and Casey Adair's *Word Is Out: Stories of Some of*

Our Lives (San Francisco: New Glide/Delta, 1978). For discussions of coming out in spiritual, theological, and religious terms, see, for example, Robert H. Hopcke, Karin Lofthus Carrington, and Scott Wirth, eds., *Same-Sex Love and the Path to Wholeness* (Boston: Shambhala, 1993); *In, Out, In Between: The Closet Dilemma,* special issue of *Open Hands,* summer 1989; and Carter Heyward, "Coming Out: Journey without Maps," *Christianity and Crisis,* 11 June 1979, 153–56. For an anthropological study of coming out, see Gilbert Herdt, " 'Coming Out' as a Rite of Passage: A Chicago Study," in Gilbert Herdt, ed., *Gay Culture in America: Essays from the Field* (Boston: Beacon, 1992), 29–67.

55. See also W. Evan Golder, "Homosexual Candidates for Ministry Challenge UCC Ordination Polity," *United Church News,* February 1988, 8.

56. Carney and Davies, "Yours in Sisterhood," in Davies and Haney, eds., *Redefining Sexual Ethics,* 76.

57. The terms used for the geographical structure of religious bodies vary. Most, however, have four levels that increase in size from the local congregation to regional and national organizations. For convenience and simplicity, I shall use the following common terms when referring to the structural levels of any religious body: local, district, province, national.

58. Carney and Davies, "Yours in Sisterhood," 76.

59. Carney and Davies, "Yours in Sisterhood," in Davies and Haney, eds., *Redefining Sexual Ethics,* 79.

60. See Ruth Frost, "Part of the Rainbow: A Lutheran Pastor Shares Her Views," *Voice of the Turtle* (American Baptists Concerned), fall 1990, 4; Jan David Tobias, "A New Day: Ordination of Lesbian and Gay Persons," *Entree* (Campus Ministry Communications, Evangelical Lutheran Church in America), April–May 1990, 21–22; and David Perry, "Lutheran Seminarians Face 'New Inquisition,' " *Advocate,* 5 July 1988, 37–39.

For mainstream news media coverage, see Russell Chandler and John Dart, "Two Churches Suspended for Homosexual Ordinations," *Los Angeles Times,* 19 July 1990, A3; R. Gustav Niebuhr and Wade Lambert, "Lutherans Suspend Congregation for Hiring Lesbians as Ministers," *Wall Street Journal,* 19 July 1990, B4; Jane Gross, "Lutherans Punish Two Churches for Gay Ordinations," *New York Times,* 19 July 1990, B6; Don Lattin, "Two SF Churches Suspended — Gay Clergy; Discipline Board's Action Includes Trial," *San Francisco Chronicle,* 19 July 1990, A1; John Dart and Russell Chandler, "Churches Give Gay Clergy Emotional Greeting; Despite a Warm Welcome of Lesbian Couple and a Gay man, a Fight Looms in the Evangelical Lutheran Church to Punish, or Possibly Expel, Their Two Congregations," *Los Angeles Times,* 22 January 1990, A3; Jane Gross, "Milestone in Church: Gay Clergy Ordained," *New York Times,* 22 January 1990, A10; Russell Chandler and John Dart, "Church Defied as Three Gays Are Ordained," *Los Angeles Times,* 21 January 1990, A1; and Don Lattin, "Gays and Lesbians Challenge Clergy," *San Francisco Chronicle,* 19 January 1990, A4.

61. Bill Johnson, "Cheryl Harrell Ordained in Massachusetts," *Waves* (United Church Coalition for Lesbian/Gay Concerns), summer 1989, 5.

62. In the UCC, a candidate for ordination is recommended by a local church to the Association-level Church and Ministry Committee, which grants "in-care

status" to a candidate during his or her seminary education and eventually approves or rejects the candidate for ordination.

63. In *Waves* (United Church Coalition for Lesbian/Gay Concerns), see Craig Hoffman, "Church Door Slams Shut in Penn Northeast," December 1989, 4–5; and "Personal News: Craig W. Hoffman," March 1993, 8.

64. See also Bill Johnson, "Leanne Tigert Comes Out in New Hampshire," *Waves*, summer 1989, 6; and Clare B. Fischer, "A Bonding of Choice: Values and Identity among Lesbian and Gay Religious Leaders," *Journal of Homosexuality* 18 (1989/90): 154.

65. Wolf, *Gay Priests*, 49, 51, 52, 54–55, 64; and Wagner, *Gay Catholic Priests*.

66. See, for example, "Responding to God's Call," *Open Hands*, summer 1986, 23.

67. See, for example, Julia G. Sauder, "Revelation to the Church: One Woman's Experience," *Dialogue* (Brethren/Mennonite Council for Gay and Lesbian Concerns), June 1993, 1–2; Bet Hannon, "Enough Is Enough," *More Light Update* (Presbyterians for Lesbian and Gay Concerns), February 1992, 15–16; Gloria B. Soliz, "Integrating Sexuality and Spirituality," *Open Hands*, spring 1991, 16–17; Melanie Morrison, "Claiming Our Freedom," *Waves* (United Church Coalition for Lesbian/Gay Concerns), September 1990; and "The Call and the Pain," *Open Hands*, summer 1989, 15–16.

68. "Responding to God's Call," 23.

69. Jeffrey G. Snyder, "The Cost of the Closet," *Open Hands*, summer 1986, 21–22.

70. See "Phyllis Athey," *Affirmation* (United Methodists for Lesbian, Gay and Bisexual Concerns), spring 1988, 18–19; and Patricia Broughton, "Standing Witness" (poem), *Open Hands*, summer 1989, 16.

71. "Newspaper Sensitively Covers Coming Out," *Waves* (United Church Coalition for Lesbian/Gay Concerns), March 1991, 7 (based on article from the *San Mateo County Times*, 11 October 1990).

72. Carney and Davies, "Yours in Sisterhood," in Davies and Haney, eds., *Redefining Sexual Ethics*, 78, 82.

73. "The Call and the Pain," 15–16.

74. Diana Vezmar-Bailey, "Ordination Set Aside," *More Light Update* (Presbyterians for Lesbian and Gay Concerns), April 1989, 1–2.

75. Mary Beth Murphy, "Bisexual Pastor Chose to Wed, Saved Ministry," *Milwaukee Sentinel*, 23 April 1993, 1A, 11A; Robert Horst, "Memo to Conference Staff regarding *Sentinel* article of Friday, April 23," 23 April 1993, Southeast Wisconsin Association, United Church of Christ, Milwaukee; and Margarita Suárez, "On a Journey toward Self-Naming," *Open Hands*, spring 1993, 15.

76. See, for example, "Entreat Me Not to Leave Thee," *Dialogue* (Brethren/Mennonite Council for Gay and Lesbian Concerns), November 1990, 4–5; Sauder, "Revelation to the Church," 1–2; Morrison, "Claiming Our Freedom"; Charles F. Whitemore, "Creating God's Economy — In 1995," *United Church News*, May 1995, 11; and Hannon, "Enough Is Enough," 15–16.

77. See "In Memoriam," *Affirmation* (United Methodists for Lesbian, Gay and Bisexual Concerns), fall 1992, 3; and Bruce Lambert, "The Rev. Paul Abels Dies at 54: Gay Pastor Led 'Peace' Church," *New York Times,* 14 March 1992, sec. 1, 12.

78. Soliz, "Integrating Sexuality and Spirituality," 16–17.

79. "Ralph McFadden Is a Chaplain and AIDS Staff Liaison with Hospice of Metro Denver (Colo.)" (sidebar), *Dialogue* (Brethren/Mennonite Council for Gay and Lesbian Concerns), June 1993, 7. In same issue, see also "John Linscheid and His Lover Attend Germantown Mennonite Church" (sidebar), 4.

80. Jim Bailey, "New Call Going 'Super' for Gay Couple," and "UCC Job Ended Long Search for Shull, Ilgenfritz," *Second Stone,* March/April 1995, 8–9; Kimberly Griffin, "Gay Pastoral Team in Seattle," *Open Hands,* winter 1995, 15; "Gay Couple Called," *United Church News,* July/August 1994, 11; and "Seattle Church Hopes to Hire Gay Couple as Joint Ministers," *New York Native,* 27 June 1994, 16.

81. See, for example, United Church of Christ, *Manual on Ministry: Perspectives and Procedures for Ecclesiastical Authorization of Ministry* (New York: Office for Church Life and Leadership, 1986), 58–59.

82. Tensho David Schneider, "Accidents and Calculations: The Emergence of Three AIDS Hospices," *Tricycle: The Buddhist Review* 1 (spring 1992): 78, 80, 83.

83. New York Conference, *New York Conference of the United Church of Christ Yearbook, Minutes and Directory, 1994–1995* (Syracuse: New York Conference, United Church of Christ, 1994), 79–89. My percentages are based on information provided under "Ministers in Full Standing in Associations of the New York Conference."

84. Fischer, "A Bonding of Choice," 171.

85. Wolf, *Gay Priests,* 50; and Wagner, *Gay Catholic Priests.*

86. Paul F. Bauer, "The Homosexual Subculture at Worship: A Participant Observation," *Pastoral Psychology* 25 (winter 1976): 118.

87. See, for example, "NGPA Welcomes New Ministers in Two Districts," *Apostolic Voice* (Churches of the National Gay Pentecostal Alliance), April/May 1993, 2.

88. Debra Nussbaum Cohen, "After Two Years, N.Y. Synagogue Hires Lesbian Rabbi," *Northern California Jewish Bulletin,* 3 April 1992, 9; and Mayer Rus, "Next Year in the Village," *Out,* October 1994, 86.

89. Schneider, "Accidents and Calculations," 78, 80, 83.

90. Katherine S. Mangan, "University Fires Homosexual Theater Director," *Chronicle of Higher Education,* 19 May 1995, A26. See also "Abilene Christian President Fires Play Director over His Sexuality," *Second Stone,* July/August 1995, 4.

91. "The Call and the Pain," 15.

92. Wolf, *Gay Priests,* 71.

93. Carney and Davies, "Yours in Sisterhood," in Davies and Haney, eds., *Redefining Sexual Ethics,* 78.

94. Wolf, *Gay Priests,* 54; and Wagner, *Gay Catholic Priests.*

95. None of the other studies presents its findings according to different sexual identities (lesbian, gay, bisexual). Wolf, *Gay Priests,* 31, 32, notes that twelve of his respondents identified as bisexual, but "the distribution of responses to the questions... by these twelve priests was not notably different from that of our homosexual respondents."

96. Average of four kinds of discrimination: not considered, not hired, fired, and not promoted.

97. Average of four kinds of discrimination: not considered, not hired, fired, and not promoted.

98. Average of four kinds of discrimination: not considered, not hired, fired, and not promoted.

99. Average of four kinds of discrimination: not considered, not hired, fired, and not promoted.

Chapter 6: Belief, Theology, Support, and Community

1. Wade Clark Roof and William McKinney, *American Mainline Religion: Its Changing Shape and Future* (New Brunswick, N.J.: Rutgers University Press, 1987), 173–74. Percentage for non-gay population is average of nonswitching Protestants, Catholics, and Jews who are "strong" members, from table 5.5, "Selected Characteristics of Switchers." I realize that the respondents in Roof and McKinney's study may include lesbian, bisexual, and gay members, but I choose to use the term "non-gay" in my discussion for the sake of establishing terms that will clarify comparison. Their study does not attempt to report data by sexual orientation of respondents.

Kent Franks et al., "Exploration of Death Anxiety as a Function of Religious Variables in Gay Men with and without AIDS," *Omega: Journal of Death and Dying* 22 (1990–91): 46–47. Percentage for gay population is combined responses of gay men with and without AIDS from table 1, "Chi-Square Analysis of AIDS and Non-AIDS Groups on the Religious Inventory."

2. James G. Wolf, *Gay Priests* (San Francisco: Harper and Row, 1989), 22; compared with the study conducted by the National Opinion Research Center, commissioned by the Ad Hoc Committee on Pastoral Research and Practices, National Conference of Catholic Bishops (NCCB), and analyzed by Andrew M. Greeley and R. Schoenerr, *The Catholic Priest in the United States: Sociological Investigations* (Washington, D.C.: United States Catholic Conference, 1972), and Eugene C. Kennedy and Victor J. Heckler, *The Catholic Priest in the United States: Psychological Investigations* (Washington, D.C.: United States Catholic Conference, 1972).

3. Alan P. Bell and Martin S. Weinberg, *Homosexualities: A Study of Diversity among Men and Women* (New York: Simon and Schuster, 1978), table 15.3, 151–53, 366.

4. Martin S. Weinberg and Colin J. Williams, *Male Homosexuals: Their Problems and Adaptations* (New York: Oxford University Press, 1974), 254–56.

5. Scott Thumma, "Negotiating a Religious Identity: The Case of the Gay Evangelical," *Sociological Analysis* 52 (1991): 333–47.

6. Paul F. Bauer, "The Homosexual Subculture at Worship: A Participant Observation Study," *Pastoral Psychology* 25 (1976): 115–27.

7. Henry Rabinowitz, "Talmud Class in a Gay Synagogue," *Judaism* 32 (1983): 433–43.

8. Karim Merchant, part of "Gay and Lesbian Voices," *Trikone: Gay and Lesbian South Asians,* July 1994, 8.

9. Thumma, "Negotiating a Religious Identity," 343–45.

10. Bauer, "Homosexual Subculture," 126.

11. Rabinowitz, "Talmud Class in a Gay Synagogue," 442.

12. See Gary David Comstock, *Gay Theology without Apology* (Cleveland: Pilgrim, 1993), 105–26.

13. See Roof and McKinney, *American Mainline Religion,* 52, 85–88, 226, 242–43.

14. Mearle L. Griffith and C. David Lundquist, *Survey of Delegates to the 1992 General Conference of the United Methodist Church* (Dayton: Office of Research, General Council on Ministries, United Methodist Church, 1992), 7.

15. See also Randy Miller, "On My Journey Now," *Open Hands,* spring 1991, 8–10.

16. See also Clare B. Fischer, "A Bonding of Choice: Values and Identity among Lesbian and Gay Religious Leaders," *Journal of Homosexuality* 18 (1989/90): 162–63.

17. In *Apostolic Voice* (National Gay Pentecostal Alliance), see Michelle M. Thomas, "A New Work in Vermont," December/January 1993, 5; and William H. Carey, "Until These Calamities Be Overpast: The Church in Time of Distress," August/September 1993, 4, 8–9.

18. Thumma, "Negotiating a Religious Identity," 340, 341, 344.

19. See, for example, Carey, "Until These Calamities Be Overpast," 4, 8–9.

20. Thumma, "Negotiating a Religious Identity," 343.

21. Paul Tillich, *Dynamics of Faith* (New York: Harper and Brothers, 1957; Harper Torchbook, 1958), 1–4.

22. Comstock, *Gay Theology without Apology,* 105.

23. Mearle L. Griffith and C. David Lundquist, *An Analysis of Major Issues Addressed by the 1988 General Conference and a Comparison with Beliefs and Attitudes of Local Church Members* (Dayton: Office of Research, General Conference of Ministries, United Methodist Church, 1990), 2, 6.

24. "Lesbian/Gay Religious Groups Denounce Coalition for Traditional Values Symposium," *Waves* (Unite Church Coalition for Lesbian/Gay Concerns), February 1990, 4.

25. Thumma, "Negotiating a Religious Identity," 339.

26. Michelle Thomas, "Confessions of a Born Again Dyke," *Apostolic Voice,* August/September 1993, 9–10.

27. Bauer, "Homosexual Subculture at Worship," 120.

28. Rabinowitz, "Talmud Class in a Gay Synagogue," 435, 441.

29. Paul Foster, "Why We Stay: Gay Men in the Roman Catholic Church" (Independent Research Project, Department of Sociology, University of Toronto, 1992), 20.

30. Comstock, *Gay Theology without Apology,* 105.

31. "Family" here refers to familial groups formed by gay people that may or may not include children (by birth to or adopted by gay people) and members of one's biological family of origin (parents, siblings, and so on). See issue titled *Rethinking Family Values,* especially Vince Benabese, Mike Underhill, and Nadia Underhill, "What Makes a Family?" *Open Hands,* spring 1993, 18–19; and Kath Weston, *Families We Choose: Lesbians, Gays, and Kinship* (New York: Columbia University Press, 1991).

32. Wolf, *Gay Priests,* 52–53, 71.

33. For accounts by people involved in campus ministry and chaplaincy, see *Campus Ministries with Sexual Minorities,* an issue of *Open Hands,* fall 1994; and *A Time for Understanding: Gay and Lesbian Concerns in Ministry,* a special issue of *Ailanthus: Journal of the National Association of College and University Chaplains,* February 1995.

34. Chad Heilig, "A Student Speaks," and Kim A. Smith, "A Pastor Speaks," *Open Hands,* fall 1994, 14–15.

35. Andrew Ulman, "MSF at IWU: Becoming Reconciling," *Open Hands,* fall 1994, 22.

36. Mary Council-Austin, "A Circle of Friends Standing in the Gap," *Open Hands,* fall 1994, 18.

37. Stephen G. Schneider, Norman L. Farberow, and Gabriel N. Kruks, "Suicidal Behavior in Adolescent and Young Adult Gay Men," *Suicide and Life-Threatening Behavior* 19 (winter 1989): 381–94. The authors define "suicidality" as "a reported history of either serious suicidal thoughts occasionally, serious consideration of a suicidal action occasionally, the formation of a suicidal plan, or a suicide attempt."

38. Odette Lockwood-Stewart, "A Report of Conversations with Students," *Open Hands,* fall 1994, 9. See also Katherine S. Mangan, "Conservative Students Challenge Support for Campus Gay Organizations," *Chronicle for Higher Education,* 27 January 1995, A38.

39. "Notebook: A Group of Rabbis at Yeshiva University Has Condemned Gay-Student Groups in an Open Letter to Yeshiva's President," *Chronicle of Higher Education,* 21 July 1995, A29.

40. Lockwood-Stewart, "Report of Conversations with Students," 9.

41. David Ward, "My First General Assembly," *More Light Update* (Presbyterians for Lesbian and Gay Concerns), September 1988, 8.

42. R. S. Umoja [pen name, UMC clergywoman], "My Cup Runneth Over," *Open Hands,* spring 1991, 17.

43. Anna Hurston [pseud.], "Suffering into Truth," in Ron Schow, Wayne Schow, and Marybeth Raynes, eds., *Peculiar People: Mormons and Same-Sex Orientation* (Salt Lake City: Signature Books, 1991), 21–22.

44. As discussed in chapter 1, these organizations are made up of gay and non-gay members of religious bodies but are not necessarily officially recognized by those bodies. For information, history, and data about various organizations, see "A Survey of Chapters," *More Light Update* (Presbyterians for Lesbian and Gay Concerns), November 1994, 12–14; "1972–1992: Twenty Years of Gay and Lesbian Jewish Community," *World Congress Digest* (World Congress of Gay and Lesbian Jewish Organizations), summer 1992, 1–5; Chris

Boisvert, "ABConcerned Celebrates 20 Years," *Voice of the Turtle* (American Baptists Concerned for Lesbians and Gay Men), winter 1992, 1, 5; *BMC: Celebrating Fifteen Years,* special issue of *Dialogue* (Brethren/Mennonite Council for Gay and Lesbian Concerns), March 1991; "Our History: Affirmation Time Line," *Affirmation* (United Methodists for Lesbian, Gay and Bisexual Concerns), summer 1989, 1, 3, 4–5.

45. Neil Miller, *In Search of Gay America: Women and Men in a Time of Change* (New York: Atlantic Monthly, 1989; Perennial Library, 1990), 232.

46. "President of World Congress Opens Dialogue with the Rainbow Coalition," *World Congress Digest* (World Congress of Gay and Lesbian Jewish Organizations), winter 1988, 1.

47. "A Closeted Minister," *More Light Update* (Presbyterians for Lesbian and Gay Concerns), February 1988, 1–2.

48. [Name withheld], "Conferences: Reports on 'Normal '89,' " *Dialogue* (Brethren/Mennonite Council for Gay and Lesbian Concerns), January 1990, 6.

49. Kevin Poole, "Open-minded Attitudes: A Family Value," *Open Hands,* spring 1993, 14. See also James B. Nelson, "Some Things You Have Taught a Straight, White Male during These 15 Years," address at UCCL/GC's Fifteenth Anniversary Dinner (Athens, Ohio: United Church Coalition for Lesbian/Gay Concerns, 1987).

50. Leonard Norman Primiano, " 'I Would Rather Be Fixated on the Lord': Women's Religion, Men's Power, and the 'Dignity' Problem," *New York Folklore* 19 (1993): 89–103.

51. See *Bisexuality: Perceptions and Realities,* issue of *Open Hands,* fall 1991.

52. See also Margarita Suárez, "Toward Self-Naming on a Journey," *Open Hands,* spring 1993, 15.

53. See, for example, Alan Hamilton, "Bisexual Exclusion" (letter), *UULGC World* (Unitarian Universalists for Lesbian and Gay Concerns), August 1991, 2; Bobbi Keppel, "The Welcoming Congregation Continental Training," *UULGC World* (Unitarian Universalists for Lesbian and Gay Concerns), January 1993, 7–8; Neil Fullagar, "Bi People in F.L.G.C.: One Friend's Perspective," *FLGC Newsletter* (Friends for Lesbian and Gay Concerns), spring 1992, 7; Rebecca Gorlin, "The Voice of a Wandering Jewish Bisexual," in Loraine Hutchins and Lani Kaahumanu, eds., *Bi Any Other Name: Bisexual People Speak Out* (Boston: Alyson, 1991), 252–53; and Tom Adams [pseud.], "My Bi-Story," *Open Hands,* fall 1991, 7.

54. Peggy Gaylord, "Claiming My Own Sexuality," *Open Hands,* fall 1991, 8–9. See also "Understanding for Bisexual Concerns" and "Speaking Out: Bi Any Other Name," *Affirmation* (United Methodists for Lesbian, Gay and Bisexual Concerns), summer 1991, 2–3; and "Spring Gathering, Washington, D.C.," *Affirmation* (United Methodists for Lesbian, Gay and Bisexual Concerns), spring 1993, 1–2.

55. See "Convo 93 Report, A New Name!" *Interweave World* (Unitarian Universalists for Lesbian, Gay and Bisexual Concerns), 15 April 1993, 1.

56. Denominations often identify and give "priority" to social issues that have been ignored or avoided and to which they plan to devote attention.

57. See also Margarita Suárez, "Reflections on Being Latina and Lesbian," *Open Hands,* spring 1987, 8–9.

58. For information on religion in the African-American community, see Barry A. Kosmin and Seymour P. Lachman, *One Nation under God: Religion in Contemporary American Society* (New York: Harmony, 1993), 130–37; and C. Eric Lincoln and Lawrence H. Mamiya, *The Black Church in the African American Experience* (Durham, N.C.: Duke University Press, 1990).

59. James T. Sears, *Growing Up Gay in the South: Race, Gender, and the Journey of the Spirit* (New York: Harrington Park, 1991), 67.

60. Michael C. Dickens, "An Analysis of Societal Racism and Homophobia and Their Effect upon Gay and Bisexual Men of African Descent" (M.A. thesis, Wesleyan University, 1994), 39–41. See also Craig G. Harris, "Cut Off from among Their People," in Joseph Beam, ed., *In the Life: A Black Gay Anthology* (Boston: Alyson, 1986), 63–67; Stefan Wade, "Cultural Expectations and Experience: African American," *Open Hands,* winter 1991, 8; and David W. Dunlap, "Leaders of Gay Blacks Emphasize Local Issues," *New York Times,* 20 February 1995, A13.

61. Renee McCoy, "Who Will Be There for Us?" *Open Hands,* spring 1987, 14–15. See also Renita Weems, "Just Friends," in *Christians and Homosexuality: Dancing Toward the Light,* special issue of *The Other Side,* 1994, 62–64.

62. McCoy, "Who Will Be There for Us?" 14–15. See also Roof and McKinney, *American Mainline Religion,* 90–91.

63. Dickens, "An Analysis of Societal Racism and Homophobia," 41–42.

64. "AIDS in the Black Community: An Interview with Harold Burris," *Open Hands,* summer 1988, 10–12.

65. See, for example, Albert R. Jonsen and Jeff Stryker, eds., *The Social Impact of AIDS in the United States* (Washington, D.C.: National Academy Press, 1993), 142–43; Angela Mitchell, "AIDS: We Are Not Immune," *Emerge,* November 1990, 30–44; H. L. Dalton, "AIDS in Blackface," *Daedalus* 118 (1989): 205–27; and National Black Consortium on Critical Health Needs, "Resolution on AIDS" (Washington, D.C.: National Urban Coalition, 1988).

See also news media coverage: Vincent Young, "Christian Soldiers in AIDS Fight; Black Churches in D.C. Nourish Body and Soul," *Washington Post,* 20 February 1993, D8; Judith Lynn Howard, "Network Preaches Compassion; Interfaith Reaches Out to Hispanics, Blacks," *Dallas Morning News,* 5 December 1992, 39A; Lucille Renwick, "A Different Front in the War on AIDS: Minority Activists, Facing Cultural and Religious Stigmas Tied to the Deadly Disease, Count on a Sense of Community in Fighting the Epidemic," *Los Angeles Times,* 4 October 1992, 21; Huntly Collins, "Black Churches Opening Arms to AIDS Sufferers," *Houston Chronicle,* 15 August 1992, 3; Adelle M. Banks, "Minister Speaks from Experience on AIDS," *Orlando Sentinel Tribune,* 12 July 1992, B1; Monica Copeland, "Black Clergy on the Spot as AIDS Fears Flourish," *Chicago Tribune,* 29 March 1992, C1; E. R. Shipp, "Reluctantly, Black Churches Confront AIDS," *New York Times,* 18 November 1991, A1; James Barron, "In Black Churches, Coming to Terms with AIDS," *New York Times,* 11 November 1991, B2; Jacqueline Trescott, "Silence of the Ministers: Will Black Churches Now Speak Out for Those with AIDS?" *Washington Post,* 9 November 1991, G1; "Faith in the Facts: Black Churches Courageously Break with AIDS Taboo," *Los Angeles Times,* 16 October 1991, B6; Mireya Navarro, "Three Black Church Groups to House AIDS Patients," *New York Times,* 13 October 1991, sec. 1, 1; Perry Land, "Black Church's AIDS Shelter, Oakland Congregation's 'Ark' Is Outside the Mainstream," *San Francisco Chronicle,* 27 August 1990, A8; Veronica T. Jennings, "Black Churches Allying against AIDS: Columbia Congregation Working with Md. on Help for Minorities," *Washington Post,* 3 July 1989, B1, B4; Sharon Epperson, "A Life Lost to AIDS Set the Challenge: Church, Fraternity Recall Late Leader with Resolve," *Boston Globe,* 12 June 1989, 17; Bruce Lambert, "Black Clergy Set to Preach about AIDS," *New York Times,* 10 June 1989, B29, B32; Alexander Reid, "Church, City Discuss Impact of AIDS on Blacks, Hispanics," *Boston Globe,* 21 May 1989, 32; Marlene Cimons, "Minorities Slow to React to High Rate of AIDS," *Los Angeles Times,* 5 December 1988, sec. 1, 1; Constanza Montana and Jean Latz Griffin, "Blacks Finding AIDS Crosses Color Lines," *Chicago Tribune,* 30 November 1987, C1; Lynne Duke, "AIDS Campaign Aimed at Blacks: D.C. Church Leaders, Metrobus Ads to Warn about Fatal Virus," *Washington Post,* 20 November 1987, C3; and Josh Getlin, "AIDS and Minorities: Fear, Ignorance Cited; Toll Is Especially Severe among Blacks, Latinos; Leaders Ask Funds for Information Programs," *Los Angeles Times,* 10 August 1987, sec. 1, 1.

66. Miller, *In Search of Gay America,* 249–50.

67. "AIDS in the Black Community: An Interview with Harold Burris," *Open Hands,* summer 1988, 12. See also George Chauncey, *Gay New York: Gender, Urban Culture, and the Making of the Gay Male World, 1890–1940* (New York: Basic Books, 1994), 254–56; Larry Icard, "Black Gay Men and Conflicting Social Identities: Sexual Orientation versus Racial Identity," *Journal of Social Work and Human Sexuality* 4 (1985–86): 87; Larry Bush, "An Interview with Andrew Young," *Blacklight* 4 (1983): 12–17; and "African-American Clergy Speak Out for Gay Rights," *Voice of the Turtle* (Newsletter of American Baptists Concerned for Lesbians and Gay Men), fall 1991, 7.

68. Shaffiq Essajee, "Guest Editorial," *Trikone: Gay and Lesbian South Asians,* April 1994, ii. See also in *Trikone:* Tinku Ishtiaq, part of "Gay and Muslim Voices," July 1994, 8; and Aziz Ahmed and Sharmin Islam, "Breaking the Silence: Reflections of Two Bangladeshis," September 1988, 1–5.

69. Eric H. F. Law, "A Spirituality of Creative Marginality," *Open Hands,* summer 1992, 10–11.

70. See also *Welcoming Churches: A Growing Ecumenical Movement,* issue of *Open Hands,* winter 1993.

71. Other events cited by UMC respondents were: denomination-wide AIDS conference (18 percent), national positions on social justice issues (15 percent), denomination-wide study of homosexuality (12 percent), activities of local church and pastor (12 percent), activities of Affirmation (9 percent), and local support of gay clergy (5 percent).

Other events cited by UCC respondents were: national positions on social justice issues (14 percent), acceptance of newly formed gay congregations

(12 percent), activities of United Church Coalition for Lesbian/Gay Concerns (10 percent), ordination of gay people (9 percent), activities of local church and pastor (8 percent), national positions on gay issues (7 percent), and denomination-wide worship/celebration service (5 percent).

72. A letter from a lesbian parishioner included as part of an article by the pastor of Peace Church of the Brethren in Portland, Oregon; see Sylvia Eagan, "Supportive Congregations Network: One Congregation's First Step," *Dialogue* (Brethren/Mennonite Council for Gay and Lesbian Concerns), October 1992, 3.

73. Pat Long, "Pullen Memorial Baptist Church: An Inside Look at a Journey of Affirmation," *Voice of the Turtle* (American Baptists Concerned), fall 1992, 5.

74. Ibid., 6.

75. See also Abigail Peterson-Finch, "A Conversation at School," *Open Hands,* winter 1991, 12, who as a fourteen-year-old wrote the following about her Reconciling Congregation, Dumbarton United Methodist Church, in Washington, D.C.: "I'm really proud of what my church has done, and it has taken a lot to get to where we are. I tell my friends about my church and its positions. A lot of kids don't know enough about homosexuals to *not* like them. I want my friends to understand. I wish they all had accepting churches and communities that educate kids about some of these fundamental questions of life."

Chapter 7: Evaluations, Feelings, Reasons, and Challenges

1. Thomas O'Brien, "A Survey of Gay/Lesbian Catholics concerning Attitudes toward Sexual Orientation and Religious Beliefs," *Journal of Homosexuality* 21 (1991): 29–44.

2. Ibid., 37, 41.

3. Partners Task Force for Gay and Lesbian Couples, *Partners' National Survey of Lesbian and Gay Couples,* special issue of *Partners: Newsletter for Gay and Lesbian Couples,* May/June 1990, 9–10.

4. Paul F. Bauer, "The Homosexual Subculture at Worship: A Participant Observation Study," *Pastoral Psychology* 25 (1976): 124; Henry Rabinowitz, "Talmud Class in a Gay Synagogue," *Judaism* 32 (1983): 442–43; and Scott Thumma, "Negotiating a Religious Identity: The Case of the Gay Evangelical," *Sociological Analysis* 52 (1991): 337–38, 345.

5. For a reprint of the letter, see Jeannine Gramick and Pat Furey, eds., *The Vatican and Homosexuality: Reactions to the "Letter to the Bishops of the Catholic Church on the Pastoral Care of Homosexual Persons* (New York: Crossroad, 1988), 1–10. The letter refers to homosexuality as a "moral disorder," claims that "the pro-homosexual movement within the Church" is "opposed to the truth about the human person," and forbids the sponsoring of any pastoral program that would "include organizations in which homosexual persons associate with each other without stating that homosexual activity is immoral." The letter also finds it "deplorable that homosexual persons have been and are the object of violent malice in speech or in action," but then claims that if homosexual activity is "condoned, or when civil legislation is introduced to protect behavior to which no one has any conceivable right, neither

the Church nor society at large should be surprised when other distorted notions and practices gain ground, and irrational and violent reactions increase."

6. O'Brien, "A Survey of Gay/Lesbian Catholics," 38, 41.

7. Lawrence A. Reh, "More Light Churches," *More Light Update* (Presbyterians for Lesbian and Gay Concerns), September 1989, 1–16.

8. Wayne Schow, "Homosexuality, Mormon Doctrine, and Christianity: A Father's Perspective," in Ron Schow, Wayne Schow, and Marybeth Raynes, eds., *Peculiar People: Mormons and Same-Sex Orientation* (Salt Lake City: Signature Books, 1991), 127–29.

9. Respondents were asked to "circle *any* of the following words which you feel describe how *you* feel about being in or associated with the UMC or UCC: hopeful, encouraged, committed, welcomed, challenged, loved, valued, affirmed, involved, uncertain, marginalized, empowered, nurtured, angry, loving, discouraged, ignored, sad, unwelcome, confused, uncommitted, certain, content, abused, hated, traumatized, harassed, (other) ________."

10. Christopher J. Alexander, "Suicidal Behavior in Gay and Lesbian Mormons," in Schow, Schow, and Raynes, eds., *Peculiar People,* 260.

11. Thumma, "Negotiating a Religious Identity," 339.

12. Dan Estes, "Emotions from the Midst of an Epidemic," *UULGC World* (Unitarian Universalists for Lesbian and Gay Concerns), January 1990, 4–5.

13. Kirsten Peachey, "Unwilling Alienation: A Mennonite Church Experience," *Dialogue* (Brethren/Mennonite Council for Gay and Lesbian Concerns), January 1990, 1, 3–4.

14. Deborah H. Carney and Susan E. Davies, "Yours in Sisterhood: A Lesbian and Bisexual Perspective on Ministry," in Susan E. Davies and Eleanor H. Haney, eds., *Redefining Sexual Ethics: A Sourcebook of Essays, Stories, and Poems* (Cleveland: Pilgrim Press, 1991), 82–83.

15. Susan Kramer, "Fanning the Vision," *More Light Update* (Presbyterians for Lesbian and Gay Concerns), 4–5.

16. Clare B. Fischer, "A Bonding of Choice: Values and Identity among Lesbian and Gay Religious Leaders," *Journal of Homosexuality* 18 (1989/90): 172.

17. James G. Wolf, *Gay Priests* (San Francisco: Harper and Row, 1989), 73.

18. Keith Kron, "Chair's Corner," *Interweave* (Unitarian Universalists for Lesbian, Gay and Bisexual Concerns), 15 April 1993, 2.

19. Chris Glaser, "Hope but Don't Get Your Hopes Up," *More Light Update* (Presbyterians for Lesbian and Gay Concerns), February 1994, 16.

20. Kron, "Chair's Corner," 2.

21. Neil Miller, *In Search of Gay America: Women and Men in a Time of Change* (New York: Atlantic Monthly, 1989; Perennial Library, 1990), 237.

22. The General Conference is the legislative body of the UMC and enacts all legislation governing all aspects of the denomination. This church law is printed as the Discipline or the Book of Discipline. The General Conference meets every four years and is comprised of approximately one thousand representatives from the United States and other countries. See "United Methodist Polity," *Open Hands,* summer 1986, 11.

23. "Going on a mission" is a rite of passage for young Mormons, one that they anticipate and prepare for with special care. See, for example, Anna

Hurston [pseud.], "Suffering into Truth," in Schow, Schow, and Raynes, eds., *Peculiar People,* 17–18.

24. Ron Schow and Marybeth Raynes, "Difficult Choices for Adolescents and Adults," in Schow, Schow, and Raynes, eds., *Peculiar People,* 197.

25. For chronology (from most recent to earliest) of votes on and discussions of resolutions, see in *Voice of the Turtle* (American Baptists Concerned): Chris Boisvert, "General Board Adopts Resolution Calling for Dialogue on Sexuality," summer 1993, 1; "Four Regions Submit Resolution to General Board Calling for Dialogue on Human Sexuality," winter 1993, 3; Chris Boisvert, "General Board Passes Anti-gay Resolution," fall 1992, 1–2; "Anti-gay Resolution before General Board," spring 1992, 3; Chris Boisvert, "General Board Votes No on Anti-gay Resolution," summer 1992, 1, 4; "General Board Considers Anti-gay Statement," winter 1992, 3; and Barbra MacNair, "Just the Facts Ma'am," summer 1991, 1, 5.

26. In Rick Mixon, "Rick's Report," *Voice of the Turtle* (American Baptists Concerned), see "New Life in Christ," summer 1991, 2; "Pride in Spirit," summer 1992, 2; "On Matters of the Heart," fall 1992, 2; "On Bearing Witness," winter 1993, 2; and "Reflections on San Jose, San Francisco and Geyersville," summer 1993, 2, 11.

27. "The Church at War," *Apostolic Voice* (National Gay Pentecostal Alliance), December/January 1993, 1–2.

28. Brother Carey, "Until These Calamities Be Overpast: The Church in a Time of Distress," *Apostolic Voice* (National Gay Pentecostal Alliance), August/September 1993, 4, 8–9.

29. Michelle Thomas, "Confessions of a Born Again Dyke," *Apostolic Voice* (National Gay Pentecostal Alliance), August/September 1993, 9–10 (reprinted from *Out in the Mountains,* April 1993).

30. See a description of this demonstration by Randy Miller in chapter 4 under "Advocacy: Demonstrations and Protests, at National Meetings."

31. Common Vision Planning Committee, *Report and Recommendations of the Common Vision Planning Committee to the Board of Trustees, Unitarian Universalist Association* (Boston: Unitarian Universalist Association, 1989), 9.

32. The terms used for the geographical structure of religious bodies vary; and one body's structural organization cannot be neatly imposed over another's. Most, however, have four levels that increase in size from the local congregation to regional and national organizations. For convenience and simplicity, I shall use the following common terms when referring to the structural levels of any religious body: local, district, province, national. Added to these four denominational levels as used in previous chapters I shall add here the UCC biennial meeting called the General Synod and the UMC quadrennial meeting called the General Conference.

33. I use the term "plurality" for "most often reported," that is, the rating (excellent, good, fair, poor) most often reported by respondents for each level (local, district, province, national meeting, national).

34. Common Vision Planning Committee, *Report and Recommendations,* 9. Also, in *UULGC World* (Unitarian Universalists for Lesbian and Gay Concerns),

see F. Jay Deacon, "A Mission for UULGBC," August 1991, 3; and "Scott Alexander Inspires the UULGC," May 1990, 1, 3.

35. Valerie Russell is currently the executive director of the UCC's national Office for Church in Society.

36. Ralph G. McFadden, "If We Would Just Turn Purple," *Brethren Life and Thought* 36 (winter 1991): 35–41.

37. "I Choose the Church," *Open Hands,* summer 1989, 8.

38. David Ward, "My First General Assembly," *More Light Update* (Presbyterians for Lesbian and Gay Concerns), September 1988, 9.

39. Beverly Brubaker, "Support and Advocacy," *Dialogue* (Brethren/Mennonite Council for Gay and Lesbian Concerns), March 1991, 5.

40. "American Zionist Youth Foundation's Bigotry," *World Congress Digest* (World Congress of Gay and Lesbian Jewish Organizations), fall 1993, 2.

41. Michael C. Dickens, "An Analysis of Societal Racism and Homophobia and Their Effect upon Gay and Bisexual Men of African Descent" (M.A. thesis, Wesleyan University, 1994), 15–16.

42. Carey, "Until These Calamities Be Overpast," 8.

43. Peachey, "Unwilling Alienation," 1, 3–4.

44. Bet Hannon, letter to PLGC Friends, in "Enough Is Enough: Two PLGC'ers Say Goodbye," *More Light Update* (Presbyterians for Lesbian and Gay Concerns), February 1992, 15–16.

45. Diane Vezmar-Bailey, "Ordination Set Aside," *More Light Update* (Presbyterians for Lesbian and Gay Concerns), April 1989, 1–2.

46. In *More Light Update* (Presbyterians for Lesbian and Gay Concerns), see Chris Glaser, "Hope but Don't Get Your Hopes Up," February 1994, 14; and "Why We Stay in the Church," May 1989, 13.

47. Wolf, *Gay Priests,* 28, 76; compared with the study conducted by the National Opinion Research Center, commissioned by the Ad Hoc Committee on Pastoral Research and Practices, National Conference of Catholic Bishops (NCCB), and analyzed by Andrew M. Greeley and R. Schoenerr, *The Catholic Priest in the United States: Sociological Investigations* (Washington, D.C.: United States Catholic Conference, 1972), and Eugene C. Kennedy and Victor J. Heckler, *The Catholic Priest in the United States: Psychological Investigations* (Washington, D.C.: United States Catholic Conference, 1972).

See also George DeStefano, "Gay under the Collar: The Hypocrisy of the Catholic Church," *Advocate,* 4 February 1986, 43–48.

48. Paul Foster, "Why We Stay: Gay Men in the Roman Catholic Church" (Independent Research Project, Department of Sociology, University of Toronto, 1992), 16–19.

49. These are the words of Gary Snyder, one of the original Beat poets, who draws on Buddhist ideas and Native American mythology to introduce his collection of poems and essays, *Turtle Island* (New York: New Directions, 1974). Snyder does not identify as gay; but since reading him in the early 1970s when I was first coming out as a gay man, I have relied on his work to develop my own theology and approach to social change.

50. Wlad Godzich, foreword to *The Resistance to Theory,* by Paul de Man, vol. 33 of *Theory and History of Literature,* ed. Wlad Godzich and Jochen Schulte-Sasse (Minneapolis: University of Minnesota Press, 1986), xiv–xv.

51. Gustav Niebuhr, "Baptist Group Votes to Repent Stand on Slaves," *New York Times,* 21 June 1995, A1, B7.

Appendix A

1. Numbers taken from Kenneth B. Bedell, ed., *Yearbook of American and Canadian Churches, 1994* (Nashville: Abingdon, 1994), 253–59; Barry A. Kosmin and Seymour P. Lachman, *One Nation under God: Religion in Contemporary American Society* (New York: Harmony, 1993), 16–17, 135, 151–53, 284–90; Martin B. Bradley et al., *Churches and Church Membership in the United State 1990: An Enumeration by Region, State and County Based on Data Reported for 133 Church Groupings* (Atlanta: Glenmary Research Center, 1992), xii–xiv, 1–3, 451, 453; and Barry A. Kosmin et al., *Highlights of the CJF 1990 National Jewish Population Survey* (New York: Council of Jewish Federations, 1991), 32. The term "adherents" refers to regular members with full membership status as well as to regular participants without membership status.

2. Numbers taken from Bedell, ed., *Yearbook of American and Canadian Churches, 1994,* 250–52. See also Kosmin and Lachman, *One Nation under God,* 289; and *First Look* (Toronto: Jewish Federation of Greater Toronto, 1991).

Appendix B

1. Resources for chronology include: Arlene Swidler, ed., *Homosexuality and World Religions* (Valley Forge, Pa.: Trinity Press International, 1993); Ron Schow, Wayne Schow, and Marybeth Raynes, *Peculiar People: Mormons and Same-Sex Orientation* (Salt Lake City: Signature Books, 1991); J. Gordon Melton, ed., *The Churches Speak on Homosexuality: Official Statements from Religious Bodies and Ecumenical Organizations* (Detroit: Gale Research, 1991), xviii; Richard Hasbany, ed., *Homosexuality and Religion* (New York: Haworth, 1990); Allan Berube, *Coming Out under Fire: The History of Gay Men and Women in World War II* (New York: Free Press, 1990); John D'Emilio, *Sexual Politics, Sexual Communities: The Making of a Homosexual Minority in the United States, 1940–1970* (Chicago: University of Chicago Press, 1983); Toby Marotta, *The Politics of Homosexuality* (Boston: Houghton Mifflin, 1981); Edward Batchelor Jr., *Homosexuality and Ethics* (New York: Pilgrim, 1980); James B. Nelson, *Embodiment: An Approach to Sexuality and Christian Theology* (Minneapolis: Augsburg, 1978); United Church of Christ, *Human Sexuality: A Preliminary Study* (New York: United Church Press, 1977); Ruth Simpson, *From the Closets to the Courts: The Lesbian Transition* (New York: Viking, 1976; Penguin, 1977); and Jonathan Katz, *Gay American History: Lesbians and Gay Men in the U.S.A., a Documentary* (New York: Thomas Y. Crowell, 1976; Harper Colophon, 1985).

Selected Bibliography

Allen, Paula Gunn. *The Sacred Hoop: Recovering the Feminine in American Indian Traditions.* Boston: Beacon, 1986.

"American Zionist Youth Foundation's Bigotry." *World Congress Digest* (World Congress of Gay and Lesbian Jewish Organizations), fall 1993, 2.

Bailey, Derrick Sherwin. *Homosexuality and the Western Christian Tradition.* London: Longmans, Green, 1955.

Balka, Christie, and Andy Rose, eds. *Twice Blessed: On Being Lesbian or Gay and Jewish.* Boston: Beacon, 1989.

Bauer, Paul F. "The Homosexual Subculture at Worship: A Participant Observation Study." *Pastoral Psychology* 25 (1976): 115–27.

Bell, Alan P., and Martin S. Weinberg. *Homosexualities: A Study of Diversity among Men and Women.* New York: Simon and Schuster, 1978.

Boisvert, Chris. "First Openly Lesbian ABC Minister Called," *Voice of the Turtle* (American Baptists Concerned), winter 1992, 1, 4.

———. "Gay Lutheran Pastor Defrocked." *Voice of the Turtle* (American Baptists Concerned), spring 1994, 1, 4.

Boswell, John. *Christianity, Social Tolerance, and Homosexuality: Gay People in Western Europe from the Beginning of the Christian Era to the Fourteenth Century.* Chicago: University of Chicago Press, 1980.

———. *Same-Sex Unions in Premodern Europe.* New York: Villard, 1994.

Brant, Beth, ed. "Introduction: A Gathering of Spirit." In *A Gathering of Spirit: A Collection by North American Indian Women,* 8–15. Ithaca, N.Y.: Firebrand, 1988.

Brenoff, Ann. "Jewish Paper in San Diego Tackles Difficult Subject; Reaction of Readers Has Been Mixed to Decision to Publish Announcement of Lesbian Couple's Commitment Ceremony." *Los Angeles Times,* 4 August 1992, E1.

Broughton, Patricia. "Standing Witness" (poem). *Open Hands,* summer 1989, p. 16.

Burris, Harold. "AIDS in the Black Community: An Interview with Harold Burris." *Open Hands,* summer 1988, 12.

Butler, Becky, ed. *Ceremonies of the Heart: Celebrating Lesbian Unions.* Seattle: Seal, 1990.

Carey, William H. "Until These Calamities Be Overpast: The Church in Time of Distress." *Apostolic Voice* (National Gay Pentecostal Alliance), August/September 1993, 4, 8–9.

Carney, Deborah H., and Susan E. Davies. "Yours in Sisterhood: A Lesbian and Bisexual Perspective on Ministry." In Susan E. Davies and Eleanor H.

Haney, eds., *Redefining Sexual Ethics: A Sourcebook of Essays, Stories, and Poems,* 75–83. Cleveland: Pilgrim, 1991.

Christians and Homosexuality: Dancing toward a New Light. Special issue of *The Other Side,* 1994.

Common Vision Planning Committee. *Report and Recommendations of the Common Vision Planning Committee to the Board of Trustees, Unitarian Universalist Association.* Boston: Unitarian Universalist Association, 1989.

Cook, Ann Thompson. *And God Loves Each One: A Resource for Dialogue about the Church and Homosexuality.* Washington, D.C.: Dumbarton United Methodist Church, 1988.

Curb, Rosemary, and Nancy Manahan, eds. *Lesbian Nuns: Breaking Silence.* Tallahassee: Naiad, 1985.

Dahl, Roy. "The Best of Times and the Worst of Times." *Dialogue* (Brethren/Mennonite Council for Gay and Lesbian Concerns), June 1993, 4–5.

Deacon, F. Jay. "Stonewall Plus 20: A Welcoming UUA." *UULGC World* (Unitarian Universalists for Lesbian and Gay Concerns), September 1989, 2–3.

D'Emilio, John. *Sexual Politics, Sexual Communities: The Making of a Homosexual Minority in the United States 1940–1970.* Chicago: University of Chicago Press, 1983.

Estes, Dan. "Emotions from the Midst of an Epidemic." *UULGC World* (Unitarian Universalists for Lesbian and Gay Concerns), January 1990, 4–5.

Dickens, Michael C. "An Analysis of Societal Racism and Homophobia and Their Effect upon Gay and Bisexual Men of African Descent." M.A. thesis, Wesleyan University, 1994.

Dossani, Shahid. "Gay by the Grace of Allah." *Trikone: Gay and Lesbian South Asians,* July 1994, 1, 7.

Evangelical Lutheran Church in America. *Human Sexuality and the Christian Faith: A Study for the Church's Reflection and Deliberation.* Minneapolis: Division for Church in Society ELCA, 1991.

Foster, Paul. "Why We Stay: Gay Men in the Roman Catholic Church." Independent research project, Department of Sociology, University of Toronto, 1992.

Fox-Shipley, L. Loreen. "Experiencing God's Love in a Painful Situation." *Dialogue* (Brethren/Mennonite Council for Lesbian and Gay Concerns), June 1993, 3.

Franks, Kent, et al. "Exploration of Death Anxiety as a Function of Religious Variables in Gay Men with and without AIDS." *Omega: Journal of Death and Dying* 22 (1990–91): 43–50.

Frost, Ruth. "Part of the Rainbow: A Lutheran Pastor Shares Her Views." *Voice of the Turtle* (American Baptists Concerned), fall 1990, 4.

Geis, Sally B., and Donald E. Messer, eds. *Caught in the Crossfire: Helping Christians Debate Homosexuality.* Nashville: Abingdon, 1994.

Gomez, Edward M. "If the Spirit Moves You." *Out,* October 1994, 84–85, 87, 89, 91, 93, 130.

Gordon, Kevin. *Homosexuality and Social Justice: Reissue of the Report of the Task Force on Gay/Lesbian Issues, San Francisco.* Revised edition.

San Francisco: Consultation on Homosexuality, Social Justice, and Roman Catholic Theology, 1986.

Gramick, Jeannine, and Pat Furey, eds. *The Vatican and Homosexuality: Reactions to the "Letter to the Bishops of the Catholic Church on the Pastoral Care of Homosexual Persons."* New York: Crossroad, 1988.

Greenberg, Jerrold. "A Study of Male Homosexuals (Predominantly College Students)." *Journal of the American College Health Association* 22 (1973): 56–60.

Grippo, Dan. "Why Lesbian and Gay Catholics Stay Catholic." *U.S. Catholic*, September 1990, 18–25.

Grisa, Greg. "Deliberately Diverse: The Sojourner Truth Congregation." *UULGC World* (Unitarian Universalists for Lesbian and Gay Concerns), January 1993, 4.

Gutiérrez, Ramón A. "Must We Deracinate Indians to Find Gay Roots?" *Out/Look*, winter 1989, 61–67.

Hall, Sid. "Same-Sex Unions: Perspectives from a Clergy Ally." *Open Hands*, spring 1993, 24.

Hannon, Bet, with Bruce Grimes, ed. "Iowa Yearly Meeting Forces Lesbian Pastor Out." *FLGC Newsletter* (Friends for Lesbian and Gay Concerns), winter 1991, 1, 3–5.

Harris, Curtis, and Leota Lone Dog (interview by Deborah Blincoe). "Two Spirited People: Understanding Who We Are as Creation." *New York Folklore* 19 (1993): 155–64.

Hart, Nett. "Radical Lesbian Spirituality." *Lesbian Ethics* 3 (spring 1988): 64–73.

Hasbany, Richard. "Scott Anderson's Story: A Tale of Homophobia, Betrayal, Anger, and Wholeness." *More Light Update* (Presbyterians for Lesbian and Gay Concerns), August 1990, 1–5.

———, ed. *Homosexuality and Religion*. New York: Haworth, 1990.

Heron, Alastair, ed. *Towards a Quaker View of Sex*. London: Friends Home Service Committee, 1963.

Heyward, Carter. *Touching Our Strength: The Erotic as Power and the Love of God*. San Francisco: Harper and Row, 1989.

"Homosexuals and Homosexuality: Psychiatrists, Religious Leaders and Laymen Compare Notes" (symposium). *Judaism* 32 (1983): 390–443.

Jay, Karla, and Allen Young. *The Gay Report: Lesbians and Gay Men Speak Out about Sexual Experiences and Lifestyles*. New York: Summit Books, 1979.

Jung, Patricia Beattie, and Ralph F. Smith. *Heterosexism: An Ethical Challenge*. Albany: State University of New York Press, 1993.

Kellstedt, Lyman A., et al. "Religious Traditions and Religious Commitments in the USA." Paper prepared for the Twenty-Second International Conference of the International Society for the Sociology of Religion, Budapest, 19–23 July 1993.

Kinsey, Alfred C., Wardell B. Pomeroy, and Clyde E. Martin. *Sexual Behavior in the Human Male*. Philadelphia: W. B. Saunders, 1948.

Kinsey, Alfred C., et al. *Sexual Behavior in the Human Female.* Philadelphia: W. B. Saunders, 1953.

Kosmin, Barry A., and Seymour P. Lachman. *One Nation under God: Religion in Contemporary American Society.* New York: Harmony, 1993.

Kramer, Susan. "Birthing." *More Light Update* (Presbyterians for Lesbian and Gay Concerns), September 1990, 3–4.

Laumann, Edward O. *The Social Organization of Sexuality: Sexual Practices in the United States.* Chicago: University of Chicago Press, 1994.

Law, Eric H. F. "A Spirituality of Creative Marginality." *Open Hands,* summer 1992, 10–11.

"Lesbian/Gay Religious Groups Denounce Coalition for Traditional Values Symposium." *Waves* (United Church Coalition for Lesbian/Gay Concerns), February 1990, 4.

Lockwood-Stewart, Odette. "A Report of Conversations with Students." *Open Hands,* fall 1994, 9.

Long, Pat. "Pullen Memorial Baptist Church: An Inside Look at a Journey of Affirmation." *Voice of the Turtle* (American Baptists Concerned for Lesbian, Gay and Bisexual People), fall 1992, 5–6.

McCoy, Renee. "Who Will Be There for Us?" *Open Hands,* spring 1987, 14–15.

McFadden, Ralph G. "If We Would Just Turn Purple." *Brethren Life and Thought* 36 (winter 1991): 35–41.

McNeill, John J. *The Church and the Homosexual.* Kansas City: Sheed Andrews and McMeel, 1976.

Melton, J. Gordon, ed. *The Churches Speak on Homosexuality: Official Statements from Religious Bodies and Ecumenical Organizations.* Detroit: Gale Research, 1991.

Miller, Neil. *In Search of Gay America: Women and Men in a Time of Change.* New York: Atlantic Monthly, 1989; Perennial Library, 1990.

Miller, Randy. "On My Journey Now." *Open Hands,* spring 1991, 8–10.

Murphy, Sheila. "Counseling Lesbian Women Religious." *Women and Therapy* 5 (winter 1986): 7–17.

Nadeau, Denise. "Lesbian Spirituality." *Resources for Feminist Research* 12 (1983): 37–39.

Nelson, James B. *Embodiment: An Approach to Sexuality and Christian Theology.* Minneapolis: Augsburg, 1978.

O'Brien, Thomas. "A Survey of Gay/Lesbian Catholics concerning Attitudes toward Sexual Orientation and Religious Beliefs." *Journal of Homosexuality* 21 (1991): 29–44.

Partners Task Force for Gay and Lesbian Couples. *Partners' National Survey of Lesbian and Gay Couples.* Special issue of *Partners: Newsletter for Gay and Lesbian Couples,* May/June 1990.

Peachey, Kirsten. "Unwilling Alienation: A Mennonite Church Experience." *Dialogue* (Brethren/Mennonite Council for Gay and Lesbian Concerns), January 1990, 1, 3–4.

Perry, Troy D. *The Lord Is My Shepherd and He Knows I'm Gay: The Autobiography of the Reverend Troy D. Perry.* New York: Bantam, 1972.

Perry, Troy D., and Thomas L. P. Swicegood. *Don't Be Afraid Anymore: The Story of Reverend Troy Perry and the Metropolitan Community Churches.* New York: St. Martin's, 1990.

Presbyterian Church (U.S.A.). *Presbyterians and Human Sexuality 1991.* Louisville: Office of the General Assembly PCUSA, 1991.

Primiano, Leonard Norman. "'I Would Rather Be Fixated on the Lord': Women's Religion, Men's Power, and the 'Dignity' Problem." *New York Folklore* 19 (1993): 89–103.

Purinton, Michael. "The Baltimore Demonstration." *More Light Update* (Presbyterians for Lesbian and Gay Concerns), May 1991, 11–13.

Pyle, George B. "A Man Marries a Man? Print It!" *New York Times,* 11 August 1993, A15.

Raphael, Lev. "Letter from Israel." *Lambda Book Report,* November/December 1994, 8–10.

Reh, Lawrence A. "More Light Churches." *More Light Update* (Presbyterians for Lesbian and Gay Concerns), September 1989, 1–16.

Remafedi, Gary, et al. "Demography of Sexual Orientation in Adolescents." *Pediatrics* 89 (1992): 714–21.

Robles, Jennifer Juárez. "Tribes and Tribulations: Despite Columbus Day Unity, Native American Gays and Lesbians Do Battle with Straights for Acceptance." *Advocate,* 17 November 1992, 40–43.

Roof, Wade Clark, and William McKinney. *American Mainline Religion: Its Changing Shape and Future.* New Brunswick, N.J.: Rutgers University Press, 1987.

Roscoe, Will. "The American Indian Berdache as Artist and Priest." *Southwestern American Indian Society* 12 (spring 1988): 127–50.

———, ed., and Gay American Indians, comp. *Living the Spirit: A Gay American Indian Anthology.* New York: St. Martin's, 1988.

Roy, Sandip. "An Indian Original: Gutsy and Provocative, Ashok Row Kavi Has Always Challenged the Status Quo." *Trikone: Gay and Lesbian South Asians,* October 1993, 5–7.

Sauder, Julia G. "Revelation to the Church: One Woman's Experience." *Dialogue* (Brethren/Mennonite Council for Gay and Lesbian Concerns), June 1993, 1–2.

Schneider, Stephen G., Norman L. Farberow, and Gabriel N. Kruks. "Suicidal Behavior in Adolescent and Young Adult Gay Men." *Suicide and Life-Threatening Behavior* 19 (winter 1989): 381–94.

Schneider, Tensho David. "Accidents and Calculations: The Emergence of Three AIDS Hospices." *Tricycle: The Buddhist Review* 1 (spring 1992): 78–83.

Schow, Ron, Wayne Schow, and Marybeth Raynes, eds. *Peculiar People: Mormons and Same-Sex Orientation.* Salt Lake City: Signature Books, 1991.

Sears, James T. *Growing Up Gay in the South: Race, Gender, and Journeys of the Spirit.* New York: Harrington Park, 1991.

Seubert, Xavier John. "The Sacramentality of Metaphors: Reflections on Homosexuality." *Cross Currents* 14 (spring 1991): 52–68.

Siker, Jeffrey S., ed. *Homosexuality in the Church: Both Sides of the Debate.* Louisville: Westminster/John Knox, 1994.

Siler, Mahan. "The Blessing of a Gay Union: Reflections of a Pastoral Journey." *Baptists Today,* 19 March 1992, 11.

Sipe, A. W. Richard. *A Secret World: Sexuality and the Search for Celibacy.* New York: Brunner/Mazel, 1990.

Smith, Michael J., ed. *Black Men/White Men: A Gay Anthology.* San Francisco: Gay Sunshine, 1983.

Smith, Richard L. *AIDS, Gays, and the American Catholic Church.* Cleveland: Pilgrim, 1994.

Snyder, Jeffrey G. "The Cost of the Closet." *Open Hands,* summer 1986, 21–22.

Spahr, Janie. "Rainbow's End: Creating a Safe Place." *Open Hands,* winter 1991, 6–7.

Steelman, Alissa Nelyn. "The Effect of the Organized Christian Church on Gay and Lesbian Spirituality." *Proceedings of Sixth National Conference on Undergraduate Research* 6 (1992): 615–20.

Suárez, Margarita. "Reflections on Being Latina and Lesbian," *Open Hands,* spring 1987, 8–9.

———. "Toward Self-Naming on a Journey." *Open Hands,* spring 1993, 15.

Sullivan, Andrew. "Virtually Normal." *South Atlantic Quarterly* 93 (summer 1993): 659–73.

Swidler, Arlene, ed. *Homosexuality and World Religions.* Valley Forge, Pa.: Trinity International, 1993.

Task Force on Same-Gender Covenants. *Task Force Report: Celebration of Same Gender Covenants.* Raleigh, N.C.: Pullen Memorial Baptist Church, 1993.

Thayer, James S. "The Berdache of the Northern Plains: A Socioreligious Perspective." *Journal of Anthropological Research* 36 (1980): 287–93.

Thomas, Michelle M. "Confessions of a Born Again Dyke." *Apostolic Voice* (National Gay Pentecostal Alliance), December/January 1993, 9, 10 (reprinted from *Out in the Mountains,* April 1993).

Thompson, Mark, ed., *Gay Spirit: Myth and Meaning.* New York: St. Martin's, 1987.

Thumma, Scott. "Negotiating a Religious Identity: The Case of the Gay Evangelical." *Sociological Analysis* 52 (1991): 333–47.

Tobias, Jan David. "A New Day: Ordination of Lesbian and Gay Persons." *Entree* (Campus Ministry Communications, Evangelical Lutheran Church in America), April–May 1990, 21–22.

Tyner, Tim. "Evangelism in the Gay/Lesbian Community: One Affirmation Group Story." *Affirmation* (United Methodist for Lesbian and Gay Concerns), winter 1988, pp. 7–8.

United Church of Christ. *Human Sexuality: A Preliminary Study.* New York: United Church Press, 1977.

United Methodist Church. *Report of the Committee to Study Homosexuality.* Dayton: General Council on Ministries, 1992 (from "Report on the Study of Homosexuality," *Daily Christian Advocate,* petition no. FM-10865-3000-A, 1992, 5 May 1992, 265–81.

Wagner, Richard. *Gay Catholic Priests: A Study of Cognitive and Affective Dissonance.* San Francisco: Specific Press, 1981.

Waltrip, Bob. "Elmer Gage: American Indian." *One Magazine,* March 1965, 6–10.

Weinberg, Martin S., and Colin J. Williams. *Male Homosexuals: Their Problems and Adaptations.* New York: Oxford University Press, 1974.

Weinberg, Martin S., Colin J. Williams, and Douglas W. Pryor. *Dual Attraction: Understanding Bisexuality.* New York: Oxford University Press, 1994.

Weltge, Ralph W., ed. *The Same-Sex: An Appraisal of Homosexuality.* Philadelphia: United Church Press, 1969.

Wheadon United Methodist Church Reconciling Congregation Task Force. "One Church's Journey toward Including Bisexuals." *Open Hands,* fall 1991, 16.

Williams, Robert. "Toward a Theology for Lesbian and Gay Marriage." *Anglican Theological Review* 71 (spring 1990): 134–74.

Williams, Walter L. *The Spirit and the Flesh: Sexual Diversity in American Indian Culture.* Boston: Beacon, 1988.

Wolf, James G. *Gay Priests.* San Francisco: Harper and Row, 1989.

The Wolfenden Report: Report of the Committee on Homosexual Offenses and Prostitution. Authorized American edition. New York: Stein and Day, 1963.

Wood, Robert W. *Christ and the Homosexual (Some Observations).* New York: Vantage, 1960.

Zanotti, Barbara, ed. *A Faith of One's Own: Explorations by Catholic Lesbians.* Trumansburg, N.Y.: Crossing Press, 1986.

Index